A 1000 DAYS ADVENTURE

Entrepreneur Journeys: The Crafting of Business

Manoj Nakra

INDIA · SINGAPORE · MALAYSIA

Notion Press

Old No. 38, New No. 6
McNichols Road, Chetpet
Chennai – 600 031

First Published by Notion Press 2018
Copyright © Manoj Nakra 2018
All Rights Reserved.

ISBN 978-1-948372-71-8

This book has been published with all efforts taken to make the material error-free after the consent of the author. However, the author and the publisher do not assume and hereby disclaim any liability to any party for any loss, damage, or disruption caused by errors or omissions, whether such errors or omissions result from negligence, accident, or any other cause.

The copyright and the rights of translation in any language are reserved. No part, paragraph, passage, text, photographs, artwork of this book should be reproduced, transmitted or utilized, in original language or by translation, in any form, or by any means, electronic, mechanical, photocopying, recording or by any information storage and retrieval system, except with prior written permission from the author except for brief passages quoted in book reviews or for the purpose of research.

Cover page image inspired by many sites – *https://edrempel.com/financial-planning-not-money-life/, https://www.aeroworkflow.com/planning-fallacy-wreaking-havoc-workflow-management/, https://hustleandgrind.co/and https://rosssimmonds.com/40-signs-takes-entrepreneur/*

Back page sketch inspired by many sites – *https://www.thefastlaneforum.com/community/threads/the-emotional-journey-of-creating-anything-great.71929/and https://www.quora.com/What-Things-entrepreneur-should-not-do-while-starting-up*

To the spirit of enterprise

The Power behind you is greater than the challenge ahead of you

Adapted from
Ralph Waldo Emerson

Contents

Preface	ix
Acknowledgments	1

❖❖❖

Food for Thought	4
Work on Your Company, Not in Your Company	
Ajesh Sivan/Teksalah	58
An Accidental Entrepreneur's Journey	
Akanksha Goel/Socialize	64
Starting a Low Margin Competitive Business in a Recession	
Albert Dias/Musafir	70
Complete Disregard for the Impossible	
Amer Qavi/SwipeZoom	76
Digitizing Knowledge Assets	
Mohamad Al Bagdadi and Rany Al Baghdadi/ TechKnowledge and Al Manhal	83
Hardnosed Stance on Value Drivers	
Binod Shankar and Mohit Malhotra/Genesis Institute	92
No Fear of the Unknown	
Michael Trueschler and Nicolas Bruylants/Citruss TV	99
The Social Attribute of Sports 105	
Davindar Rao/DUPLAYS	105
A Modern Twist to Cultural Inheritance	
Fathiya Ahmed Osman/Heritage for Henna	111
Starting a Business Is like Pushing a Wheel till the Wheel Picks up Momentum of Its Own	
Gilbert Ashram/INCON Infrastructure Contracting	116

Series of Experiments
Suhail Bin Ahmed/Happy Yummy — 122

A Mix of Boldness and Being Conservative
Ishwar Jodha/Triple Crown Shipping and Logistics — 127

A Good Way to Start a Business May Not Be the Best Way to Run the Business
Hydros Jassem/Fragrance Delivery Technology — 132

Business Is Not About Training but About How to Make It Happen
Jolly Thomas/Eduscope — 140

Differentiating a Trading Business
Kamran Torjani/Atlas Safety Products — 147

Gut Feeling Is Good but Finance Is Better
Kanwar Marwah/Curries and Grills — 151

Passion Is the Substance of an Entrepreneur
Stephane Jacques/Lemongrass — 161

Naiveté, Luck and Focus: Nothing in the Business Was Easy
Suzi Croft and Manar Al Jayouchi/Appetite and 1762 — 173

Architects of Information
Mark Hirst/Blue Beetle — 179

Getting the Right Bite
Mohamed Akbari/Naturalway — 184

Printing Success
Mohammad Al Hashimi/Emirates Trans Graphics — 189

We Shut Our Business. the Tough Choices of Entrepreneurship
Mohammad and Peyman Parham Al Awadi/Wild Peeta — 195

Time, Tenacity and Trust – Building Blocks of a Trading Company
Mohamed Sharif/Dimara International — 200

It Is Not like a Walk-in the Park
Murshed Mohamed Ahmed/Yebab — 204

It Is a Marathon, Not a Sprint
Omar Kassim/JadoPado.com — 209

Start the Business First and Then Make the Plan
Paul Joseph/AAA Middle East — 215

Developing a 'Fuzzy' Business like Consulting
Ramesh Mahalingam/Ideal Management Consultants — 223

Entrepreneurial Intelligence: Knowing When You Need a Team
Saif Abdullah and Omran Yousef/HiPhone Telecom — 227

I Knew Nothing About the Business. I Focused on Costs and Learnt Everything
Salem Abdulla Majia Al Muhairi/Abu Dhabi Pallet — 233

Entrepreneurship Is the Crafting of the Business, Not the Execution of a Plan
Sana Rifai/Tintbox — 237

I Love Startups
Shirin Abulrazak/Sisters Beauty Lounge — 247

Starting a Business Is like Swimming Against the Tide
Shobha Moni and R. S. Moni/Triad Software Services — 255

Third Eye of Retail
Zayan Ghandour/S*uce — 261

Business Becomes a Business by Selling
Govinda Siddartha/Audioviz — 266

Be Prepared to Rough It Out
Toufic Kreidieh and Yasser Beydoun/Brands For Less — 274

Need to Be Tense All the Time
Mohamed Nasser/WMS Metal Industries — 281

Belief Was in Me and the Bet Was on Me
Khalid Al Shami/Al Shami Sugars — 289

Discounting Is a Downward Spiral of a Business
Ibrahim bin Shaheen/DGT — 296

Building a Business On-The-Job
Meghna Kothari/McCollins — 303

Be Paranoid
Paul Oliver/Absolute Adventure — 313

Middle of the Whirlpool
Mini Joshi/Good Platters — 327

Surprise Customers
Boy and Mike Adnani/Costra — 336

Summary of the Book	343
Appendix 1	
How Experienced Entrepreneurs Create	347
Appendix 2	
How Artists Work	349
Appendix 3	
Mindset and Mental Models	351
About the Author	373
References	375

Preface

This book is a collection of startup journeys of entrepreneurs in their own words. The interviews portray how entrepreneurs create businesses. Social representation of entrepreneurship is simple. Successful entrepreneurs are visionaries, adept at identifying opportunity, planning, implementing and realizing the opportunity. The reality of business creation is very different. Creation of business is a capability that entrepreneurs learn on the job.

So how do entrepreneurs create businesses?

Soon after an entrepreneur starts his business, he realizes two things: his ideas about how the new business will work were actually assumptions, and that he needs to validate all his business assumptions by testing them with real customers before a business can be established. He breaks down the creation of business into small action steps. Each action step is a test to confirm what consumers will buy, price at which sales will occur, prices at which suppliers will deliver, costs of producing the units and so on. He takes each small step, keeping the picture of the new business in his mind. He fine-tunes and reworks his ideas listening to consumers, suppliers and other stakeholders. This adaptation continues until consumers accept what he has to offer at a justifiable price and cost. Entrepreneurs think about both the big picture and the fine details. Their mind constantly goes back and forth, one moment concerned with the working details, the next moment stepping back and assessing the consequences in the context of the business. The way entrepreneurs work is similar to how film directors create movies.[1] When we watch a movie, we watch it as a developing story. When a director makes a movie, he films the story in small clips. The clips are not filmed in the storytelling sequence. They are edited and arranged to narrate the story. When a director is filming a segment, he visualizes and shapes the scene in the context of the story in his mind. A viewer of the film sees a coherent narrative. He doesn't imagine the story the way it was filmed.

A startup is not a business. It is a business under construction. The interviews distinguish the startup phase, when a business is being built, from an operating phase, when a business begins to work and grows. The interviews portray how entrepreneurs think and take decisions, what they choose to do in the startup phase. The interviews reveal their uncertainty and determination to create their businesses. 'Crafting' is an apt descriptor of the way entrepreneurs create businesses. The following table compares the work of artists and entrepreneurs in multiple dimensions.

Artists and Entrepreneurs: Are they different?

Feature/ Characteristic	Artist	Entrepreneur
Involvement	Personally invested in the work	Is personally engaged in each aspect of the creation of the business. Entrepreneur is the pivot.
How	His hands touch the material. Artist knows when the work is complete.	Entrepreneur is the touchstone to assess progress.
Input	Artistic vision, skill and experience	Entrepreneurial drive, skills and experience
Belief	Understanding of buyers and past work	Intuition of an opportunity
Uncertainty	High	Very high
Raw Material	Art raw material – clay, paint, stone, etc.	People and capital
Nature of task	Creative	Creative
Creative vision	Balances art and commercial value	Commercial
Execution	Imagines, works, looks, thinks and reworks	Formulates, implements, learns and reworks

An entrepreneur, like a craftsman or artist, is personally invested in his creation. Business creation is a creative endeavor. Nothing exists when it starts. An organization doesn't exist. Suppliers, employees and stakeholders hesitate to engage. There are no business capabilities. His raw materials are his skills, vision and commitment. Business becomes his clay or paint, malleable in his hands. He creates new business by his hands-on engagement. He focuses on execution. He doesn't overanalyze. He has to do and learn many things. Without personally understanding and mastering the details, nothing will happen. When a business begins formulating, implementation and learning merge into one process. Entrepreneurs reveal critical thinking skills; they acquire practical knowledge by asking questions, creating hypothesis, testing and reflecting on outcomes. Entrepreneurs are experimenters. Every task requires multiple iterations. The eleven bulls (Figure 1) painted by Picasso are a metaphorical representation of how entrepreneurs test and rework their offering till it resonates with customers.

Figure 1. Eleven bulls painted by Pablo Picasso.[2]

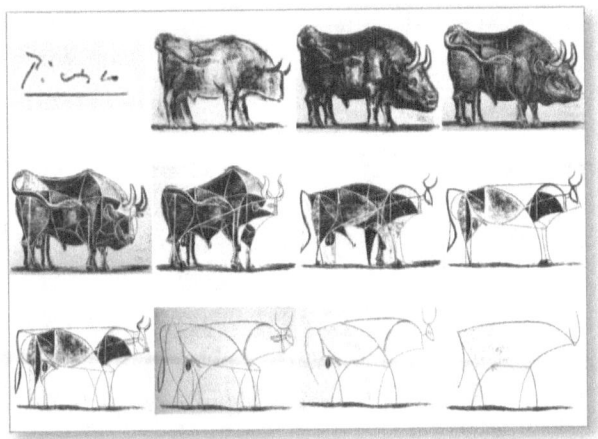

My musings on what entrepreneurs do when creating new businesses are echoed in entrepreneurship literature.[3]

I have labeled an entrepreneur's thinking and actions as the 'craftsmanship' of new business creation.

I am not a painter or a craftsman. I cannot draw upon my own experience to identify similarities between entrepreneurship and art. However, the descriptions of how entrepreneurs create their businesses, as revealed to me in the interviews, are similar to the descriptions of how artists create their work. I underscore that the similarities are in how entrepreneurs and artists work, the emotions they experience, the fact that the end result of their effort may be different from what was envisaged and the attitudinal drivers of the two endeavors.[4]

Why another book on entrepreneurship?

Magazines and articles often portray the eventual wealth and success of entrepreneurs. This image and social benchmarks of successful entrepreneurs are imagined to be in their trappings. This depiction often evokes a feeling in startup entrepreneurs. They assume all entrepreneurs become wealthy and imagine their lifestyle too will be similar. Exceptional wealth and glitzy lifestyles are exceptions. All entrepreneurs experience the exhilaration of intense and engaging work. The entrepreneurial experience is priceless. However, the journey is tense.

Successful entrepreneurs very often epitomize failure as an ingredient of business creation. Failures are imagined to be badges of honor. The startup journey is more complex. Imagine the early days of a startup. Success is still down the line. An entrepreneur experiences setback when an idea doesn't work. He needs to keep his motivation high. He musters all his strength to get up and keep going. Perseverance needs courage and conviction amidst uncertainty, confusion and often desperation. Entrepreneurs are always grappling with dichotomous ideas. Should they trust the path they are on, focusing their energy on 'how' to do what they are doing, better? Or should they question and change their path, deciding where to go and what to do?

These three aspects – discovery as a way, failures and eventual success – conceal the tumultuous psychological undercurrents that entrepreneurs experience and manage every day, for years, before an idea becomes a business. There is a difference in how these moments are experienced by entrepreneurs as they occur and read by others ex post facto.

The book attempts to capture the thinking and behavior of a pre-success entrepreneur. A pre-success entrepreneur has to have self-confidence in a business that doesn't exist. He has to believe he can do it without having done it before. He has to sustain the belief over time, whatever be the challenges. And evoke the same belief in customers, suppliers and other stakeholders.

I intuit that the entrepreneurial process revealed in the interviews may have universal application as a way of entrepreneurship. Is it that entrepreneurship is not about 'what' successful entrepreneurs do or 'who' they are but about 'how' they do it?

I believe:

1. Entrepreneurs are not totally unlike you and me – an average Joe.
2. Everyone has latent potential to be an entrepreneur.
3. Ideas and opportunities emerge from their way of thinking and doing.
4. Skills are developed and knowledge is gained in the process of business creation. There is no graduation or accreditation in entrepreneurship.
5. Preparing a robust business plan is not entrepreneurship.
6. The way entrepreneurs work and think appear to be a significant variable in the creation of a new business. Methods of working and thinking are free resources accessible to everyone.
7. Entrepreneurs reveal abilities like managing self-doubt, managing ambiguity, doggedness and self-confidence.

The roots of the book lie in my work with entrepreneurs. I joined Mohamed Bin Rashid Establishment for Leadership Development (MBRE), Government of Dubai's entrepreneurship development organization, in 2005. The book collates knowledge I have acquired in incubating, funding and enabling businesses over the years. Words of entrepreneurs carry credibility. I have captured the knowledge in their words. I interviewed forty-two entrepreneurs in their startup years, when the experience of the startup was still raw and palpable. The entrepreneurs created new businesses in economic sectors that mimic the UAE economy (e-commerce, Home TV shopping, creation of social communities, high tech manufacture, IT portals, IT infrastructure, IT software, manufacturing, training, tourism, trading and F&B). Three entrepreneurs were creating their second business. One entrepreneur had shut down his business. Each interview was for about an hour. The entrepreneurs approved the transcript. Gulf News, a newspaper in Dubai, published short versions of a few interviews in 2013.[5] Most businesses have since evolved and grown. A few businesses have become household names in the region. Some have raised external equity capital. Some have been acquired. A few have shut down. The following characteristics are observed across the interviews:[6]

1. Most startups started as individuals seeking 'psychological' independence. Self-employment was not a principal goal.
2. Most entrepreneurs started their businesses while being employed.
3. Entrepreneurial intent was to create new products and services. They attempted replication of an idea or experience encountered during employment.
4. There was not much research or writing of business plans.
5. Entrepreneurial initiative was a driver of business.
6. Entrepreneurs were enthusiastic founders who initially do all functions of the business.
7. They searched for customers. They had to persuade customers to 'risk' taking a chance with both a new business and an entrepreneur.
8. Entrepreneurs met customers and did a lot of face-to-face selling.
9. A key role of an entrepreneur during startup is to skew customer preferences.
10. In interactions with customers, entrepreneurs discovered what customers wanted, what was missing in existing offerings and how they should sell. They learnt to differentiate their products through their personal engagement with customers.
11. They learnt to cope with rejection.

12. The focus area of initial opportunity of new businesses was often a small market niche of a large industry, which big players were ignoring.
13. There were many unknowns when businesses started. They manage and resolve doubts in bite-sized customer facing actions/experiments.
14. Entrepreneurial learning was endemic and appears essential to creation of new businesses.
15. Stumbles and detours characterize the evolution of business. Entrepreneurs see opportunity in surprises during execution. Startups often are a result of opportunistic adaptation in small market segments to unexpected events.
16. Entrepreneurs adapted, did things they had not envisaged, in response to unexpected opportunities and problems to keep the cash flow going.
17. Most entrepreneurs start with a belief of giving higher value at a lower price and quickly realize that discounts don't work.
18. They work with accessible employees whose skills are average but who are motivated to deliver exceptional performance for a fledgling enterprise through long hours of hard work.

I am often asked about my learning from the undertaking.

- Entrepreneurship is about how business is created.
- Business startup is a 1000 days game.
- Endeavor if you can manage 1000 days of being worse off than in your current job/situation.
- New business creation is an outcome of how entrepreneurs think, decide and act. It is not about what they do and who they are.
- The way of entrepreneurship is based on personal mastery.
- Entrepreneurship is not the same as opportunity identification. Opportunities arise in how entrepreneurs work. Entrepreneurs are skillful in how they find, recognize and create opportunities.
- Business ideas need rigorous testing.
- The end business is often different from the one originally anticipated. Creation of new businesses often appears to be almost serendipitous. Innovation comes from exploration, luck and accidents. But a person has to be on a journey of exploration for a lucky accident to happen.
- Return on time invested (ROTI) is more important than return on capital invested (ROCI). New businesses take more time and capital from that estimated using Excel.

- Managing stress and emotions of hope as well as fear is a part of an entrepreneurial identity.
- Entrepreneurial ability to define problems, bias for action, cognitive ability, critical thinking, intellectual agility and plasticity are influencers of new business creation.
- Many entrepreneurs work on their business while employed and then parachute out. Riding two horses is both good and bad. I believe that spending a few hours a day to create a new business doesn't work. Knowing when to commit full time to the entrepreneurial effort is key.

Manoj Nakra

Acknowledgments

I thank all entrepreneurs (list hereunder) who shared their startup experiences with me. This book emerged because of them. A few entrepreneurs did not consent to publish their interview. I also thank entrepreneurs who gave me the opportunity to serve them over eight years when I was a part of the Dubai SME team. I learnt from them. The granular engagement with them, as they created their businesses, enabled me to crystallize my ideas of how businesses are crafted.

I am especially grateful to my erstwhile colleagues (listed below) of MBRE. We worked together to make entrepreneurship happen. We learnt from each other.

Abdul Baset Al Janahi (CEO), Akil Kazim, Ibtihal Naji, Lena Kayed, Vinod Kumar, Abdelaziz Al Mazem, Yousef Sharaf, Affan Kouri, Dalal Jasem, Khadija Ali, Saer Imad, Dalia Alwan, Nisrin Safar, Rany Eid, Wafa Al Feeli, Firas Al Mudallal, Ahmad Ibrahim, Sahar Ismaeeli, Hind Al Kindi, Sanjay Koul, Yousef Lootah, Essam Omran Saleh, Rania Sheir, Rafat Wahbeh, Budoor Wahidi, Natasha Husain, Bader Al Awadi, Sharifa Miran, Thuraya Mohammed, Ahmed Al Hashemi, Osama Al Muharam, and Alexandar Williams.

I am immensely grateful to Prof. Bo Carlsson, Weatherhead School of Management, Case Western Reserve University, who read an initial draft of my ruminations and who made invaluable suggestions.

Manoj Nakra

Entrepreneurs featured in the book

S No	Name	Business	Industry
1	Ramesh Mahalingam	Management consulting	Consulting
2	Gilbert Ashram	Contracting	Contracting
3	Mohamed Sharif	Manufacture and supply of guest amenities and supplies to hotels and airlines	Distribution
4	Ibrahim bin Shaheen	Distributing foodstuff and grocery products	Distribution
5	Omar Kassim	e-commerce portal for electronics and IT products	e-commerce
6	Mini Joshi	Commercial catering company	F&B
7	Ibrahim Mohammed Abdullah and Mohamed Akbari	Manufacturing cereal, energy and nutrition bars	Food manufacture
8	Suhail Bin Ahmed	Food and beverage	Food retail

(Cont.)

S No	Name	Business	Industry
9	Kanwar Marwah	Sandwich franchise and Indian food restaurant	Food retail
10	Stephane Jacques and Pornthep Booncham	Thai restaurant chain	Food retail
11	Suzi Croft and Manar Al Jayouchi	Packaged sandwiches, salads and a gourmet deli	Food retail
12	Mohammad and Peyman Parham Al Awadi	Gourmet shawarma café	Food retail
13	Hydros Jassem	Manufacture of fuel cell based fragrance dispensers	Hi-tech Manufacturing
14	Kamran Torjani	Trading safety equipment and manufacturing chemicals	Industrial distribution
15	Mohammad Al Hashimi	Distributor of printing machinery and consumables	Industrial distribution
16	Govinda Siddartha	IT consulting and solutions	IT
17	Ajesh Sivan	Installation of IT networks and services	IT
18	Mark Hirst	Web Design and digital marketing	IT
19	Amer Qavi	Online payment processor and logistics company integrator for cross-border e-commerce	IT platform
20	Mohamad and Rany Baghdadi	Creation and distribution of digital databases	IT platform
21	Murshed Mohamed Ahmed and Mareyah Mohamed Ahmed	Regions biggest online wedding directory	IT platform
22	Shobha Moni and R. S. Moni	Software solutions and services	IT services
23	Ishwar Jodha	Freight forwarding	Logistics
24	Mohamed Nasser	Fabrication and installation of steel structures	Manufacture
25	Salem Abdulla Majia Al Muhairi	Manufacture of wooden pallets	Manufacture
26	Boy and Mike Adnani	Retail fixture manufacturing	Manufacture
27	Sana Rifai	Boutique design studio	Media services
28	Khalid Al Shami	Packaged sugar	Repacking and distribution
29	Saif Abdullah and Omran Yousef	Retailing telecom products and accessories	Retail
30	Zayan Ghandour	Fashion retail	Retail
31	Toufic Kreidieh and Yasser Beydoun	Outlet retail	Retail
32	Paul Joseph	Roadside assistance and vehicle logistics	Services
33	Fathiya Ahmed Osman	Henna services	Services

S No	Name	Business	Industry
34	Shirin Abulrazak	Grooming business for ladies	Services
35	Davindar Rao	Creating communities around sports	Social community
36	Akanksha Goel	Full-service digital media	Social media
37	Meghna Kothari	Digital media company	Social media
38	Paul Oliver	Adventure tourism	Tourism
39	Binod Shankar and Mohit Malhotra	Specialized CFA training institute	Training
40	Jolly Thomas	Specialized training	Training
41	Sheikh Mohammed Al Thani, Albert Dias, and Sachin Gadoya	Online travel services portal	Travel portal
42	Michael Trueschler and Nicolas Bruylants	TV Home Shopping Network	TV shopping

Food for Thought

My ideas about how businesses nucleate[7] reflect insights I sensed enabling[8] entrepreneurs developing their startups over eight years as a profession. The ideas developed when I interviewed entrepreneurs for the book. I have started two businesses. One exists and the other was shut down after three years. I continue to serve on the Advisory Boards of a few startups. My personal experiences are embedded in this work.

My first startup business was in a corporate setting[9]. My thoughts about how to start a business were conditioned by my education and work experience. I had worked as a design engineer. I designed and detailed everything on drawings. Anyone trained to read engineering drawings could implement the designs on the ground.

Creation of new businesses also followed a linear path. I started with negotiated and approved goals. Followed that with meticulous planning, access to the best resources money could get as well as the fastest, cheapest and most efficient pathway to the goal. Raising and allocating capital was not pertinent. Cost or time overruns were managed through discussion. The idea is visualized in Figure 1a[10].

To me, Entrepreneurship was:

- Introducing and improving products and services.
- Having a problem to solve.
- Responding to what customers want and deciphering this through research.
- Creating a robust business plan akin to an engineering drawing.
- Projecting/inferring the future by analyzing the past data.
- Selling more to customers and winning new customers.
- Planning well and implementing the plan.
- Success was based on the quality of planning and execution.
- Uncertainty and ambiguity were low.
- Knowledge needed could be acquired.

I experienced a different reality while creating a business and supporting entrepreneurs. I discovered that entrepreneurship entailed:

- Not creating a detailed engineering drawing to execute.
- Not projecting the future as a projection of the past.
- Being flexible because goals and plans change.

- Being aware that resources were scarce and not easily accessible.
- Customer behaviors are more important than their opinions because real feedback is available when customers buy.
- Building products and services engaging with customers.
- Quickly sensing knowledge gaps or unknowns.
- Acquiring business knowledge during implementation.
- Continually learning through experiments.
- Not being downcast when I lack knowledge and when you realize you need more knowledge.
- Believing in the capacity of human ingenuity to discover solutions.
- It always works out, not necessarily the way it was planned.

Figure 1a. The image depicts an ideal linear step-by-step business creation

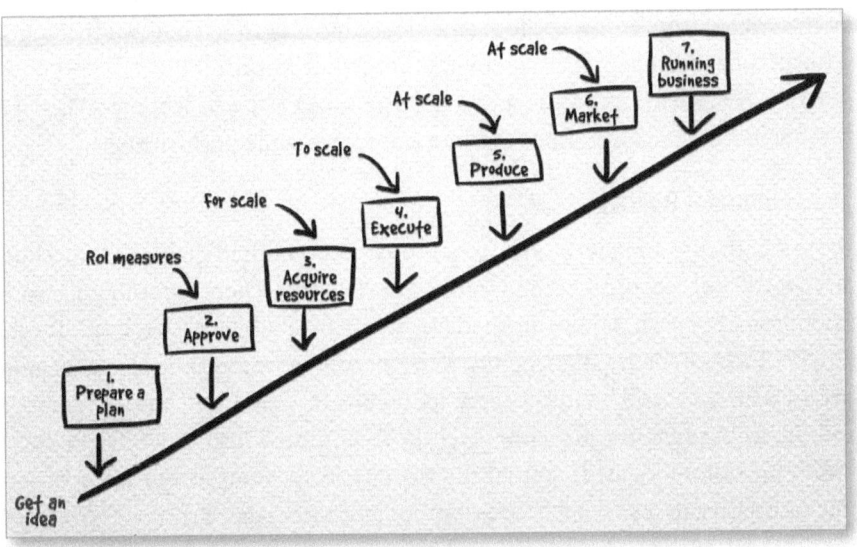

Figure 1a (numbers in parenthesis identify the step of the journey)

Ideal undeviating journey of converting business ideas into running businesses. The journey starts with an idea (left bottom) that is made into a plan(1). After its approval (2) the entrepreneur acquires resources (3), implements the business (4), produces (5) and markets the product (6). Acquisition of resources (raising of capital, equipment and people) and execution of the business happens at the planned scale. No uncertainty in the business. No aspect of the business requires to be tested or proven.

The figure depicts my corporate mindset of smooth trouble free execution from idea to business with best possible resources.

- My time perspective of thinking was in years based on 5-year plan
- All challenges of execution are managed by access to resources
- All unknown costs before business start to work are pre-operative expenses which is an accounting issue

Entrepreneurship in Corporate Settings

I use my own example to contrast pure entrepreneurship with new business creation in a corporate setting.

In a corporate setting, I was executing a well-conceived plan with access to resources. My ego increased the belief that the plan was right. I was also less sensitive to disconfirming signals that things were not progressing according to plan during execution. Deviations from forecast had to be extreme to trigger a response from me. It took a while to realize that a logical or well-reasoned plan can be inexecutable. I call my unwillingness to be flexible as "intellectual path dependence."

I realize now that execution of new business in a corporate environment is akin to writing a musical piece in two parts. First, write the piece without playing a note. This is similar to preparing a business and project plan. Second, play live music from notes without practice. This is akin to rigidly adhering to the business and project plan, believing that it will work.

An entrepreneur, in contrast, creates the musical piece while playing. He writes, experiments and refines the musical script while performing.

Entrepreneurial Reality

Entrepreneurship journeys are circuitous and unpredictable. Sometimes plans work and on other days, things don't work. There is ambiguity and desperation. Survival is the immediate goal. Profitability isn't even in the dialogue. Entrepreneurs manage the journey of new venture creation through a set of attitudes and commitment to behavior that I call entrepreneurial mindset. Entrepreneurs are concurrently determined and agile. They focus intently on testing ideas. If something doesn't work, they search for a variant or an alternative to test. This frame of mind and associated drive energizes new business creation. The journey of new business creation is depicted in Figure 1b.

Entrepreneurs depict following traits:

- Uncomfortable with status quo.
- An inexhaustible need to learn.
- Demonstrate an active curiosity (as different from theoretical curiosity) that manifests in engaged experimentation.
- Perseverance.
- Intellectual agility to reframe and recalibrate ideas.
- Rework repeatedly till outcomes are achieved.
- Desire to measure their work.

Figure 1b. The image depicts what really happens

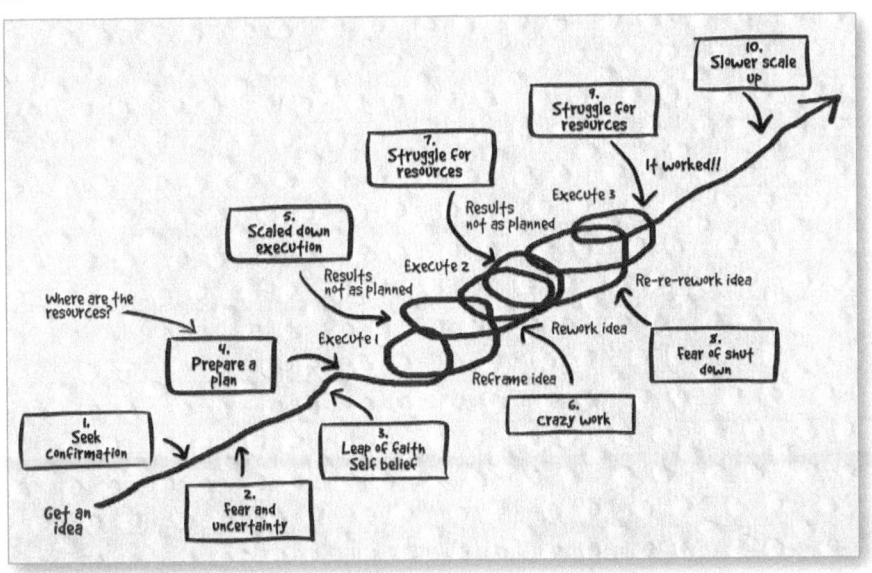

Figure 1b (numbers in parenthesis identify the step of the journey)

A circuitous journey of converting a business idea into running businesses. The journey starts with an idea (left bottom). The entrepreneur seeks confirmation (1) since he is uncertain (2) about his idea and scared about what may happen if the business fails. He takes a leap of faith based on self-belief (3) and prepares a plan (4) not yet knowing where he will get the resources to realize his dream. He implements a scaled down version of the idea (5) working like crazy (6). Results may not be as planned. He reworks his idea based on his learnings and implements again. Resources are scarce (7). He again reworks the idea if the trial again doesn't work. He keeps tweaking his idea and reworking. Fear of shut down is always around (8). He continues to struggle for resources (9) because cost over runs happen in multiple iterations of execution. Once a trial is successful, he scales the business (10).

Acquisition of resources (raising of capital, equipment and people) and initial execution of the business happens at a modest scale. An entrepreneur doesn't bet all his resources on the idea alone. Entrepreneurs have uncertainties about their businesses and test their ideas with customers before investing to scale-up.

This figure depicts the reality of small business startup with access to insufficient resources.

- An entrepreneur's time perspective is managing a day-at-a-time based on a dream
- Challenges of execution are managed by ingenuity
- All unknown costs are a cash drain which accounting can't fix

Crafting of New Business

An entrepreneur drives new business creation. He carries the vision of the business in his mind. He engages with stakeholders – employees, suppliers, financiers and customers. He identifies what to do, what steps to take and when. He evaluates the outcomes of the actions. His analysis guides him in his subsequent decisions and actions. This cycle of decision making and evaluation by the entrepreneur continues till the idea becomes a business. The process of new business creation can be visualized as a decision-making process driven by the entrepreneur.

The skills and disposition of the entrepreneur effect and power the decisions as well as actions of business creation. The interviews reveal that entrepreneurs acquire new knowledge, skills and abilities as they create businesses. A new business is an action-learning laboratory of an entrepreneur.

The creation of business occurs at three conceptual levels – what entrepreneurs do, how they think, their mindset and disposition. I call this the 'iceberg' of new business crafting (Figure 2). Iceberg is an appropriate metaphor because most of it is hidden below the surface of water. Only what entrepreneurs do, their actions, are visible to others.

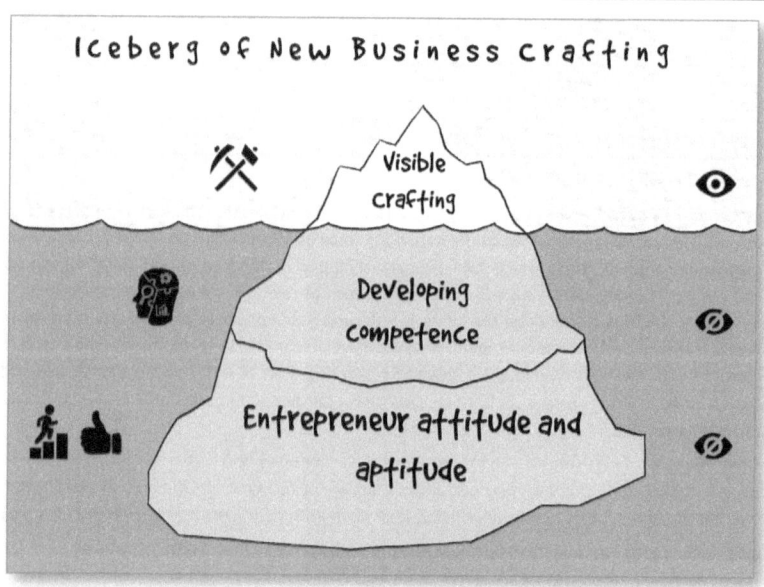

Figure 2. Iceberg of new business crafting

1. What an entrepreneur does can be observed and experienced by consumers, suppliers, stakeholders and even those not involved with the business. I label the actions, the visible portion of the iceberg, as "Visible Crafting." I use the word crafting because this is where decisions and actions of the entrepreneur, tools with which he creates his business, manifest.

2. "Developing Competence" is the first invisible layer. Before entrepreneurs act, they think, interpret and decide what they have to do. The cycle of think-act-do-interpret is a cycle that repeats as entrepreneurs create a business. Interviews suggest that the

entrepreneurs develop new competencies through experiential learning in the repeated cycles of think-act-do-interpret.
3. The last invisible layer is labeled "Entrepreneur Attitudes and Aptitudes." The entrepreneur is the nucleus of new business. His personality, motivations, cognitive ability and critical thinking skills are the mechanisms that power business creation.

Visible Crafting – what entrepreneurs seem to be doing when they create businesses – from mental models[11] to business model innovation.

The interviews reveal four stages of business creation. I tag them as – problem-solution fit, product-market fit, verification of the business model and scaling the business with metrics. The stages are symbolically depicted in the graph (Figure 3). The vertical axis is business scale. Growth of a business is plotted against time.

Figure 3. Four stages of business creation

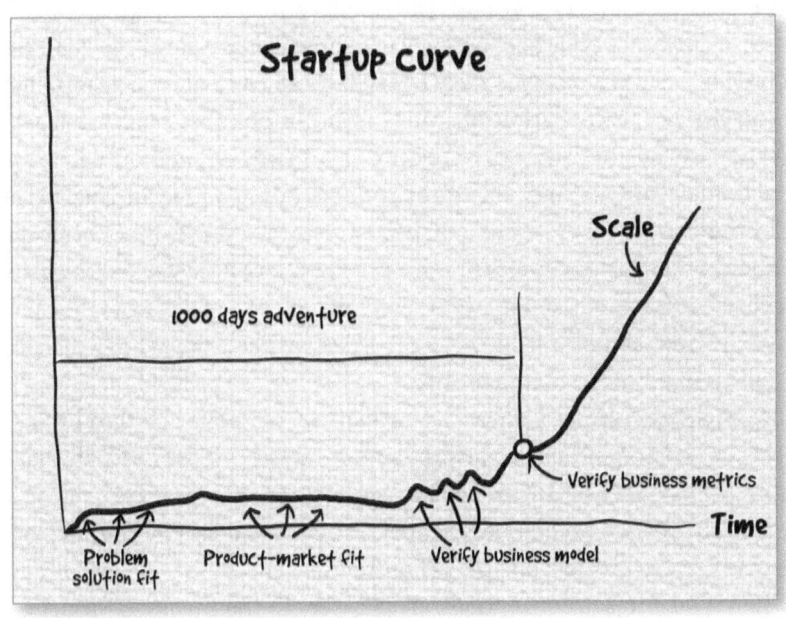

A startup takes three years, if not more, to become a business. Entrepreneurship is a 1000 day extreme adventure akin to an extreme sport – intense, risky and thrilling.

The interviews suggest that a business idea becomes a business in four stages. An entrepreneur starts his business by engaging with customers and presenting his solution to their need/problem. Customers often require the solution to be reworked and/or the problem to be redefined. The entrepreneur iteratively establishes the problem-solution fit by redefining and refining the problem definition and his solution. The product is rudimentary. The scale of the business small.

The entrepreneur improves and upgrades the product to assess the traction of his solution with a larger segment of customers. This is also an iterative process. This stage of business development is labeled as product-market fit. The scale of the business remains small. The market potential is defined.

The entrepreneur invests in increasing the production of the product and invests in reaching potential consumers. The scaling of capacity and market size enables price and cost structure to be established i.e. business model is validated.

The entrepreneur scales the business keeping a close tab on business metrics i.e. he verifies business metrics and scales the business.

Entrepreneurs begin with hunches and assumptions about the business they intend to create. They define, often intuitively, a market/consumer need. They feel they understand their potential consumers, the price they will be able to charge and the price consumers will pay. They believe they will make money at that estimate of price and cost. I deliberately use three words – intuit, feel and believe. Entrepreneurs intuit a business idea, feel that it can work and begin to believe it.

I categorize the collection of initial assumptions that entrepreneurs have about the new business they are creating as a mental model of their business. Mental model [12] or paradigm is a way of understanding the world. Mental models used in the context of entrepreneurship encompass beliefs that entrepreneurs have about what drives success in their business and industry; what customers to serve, what those customers want, what product to make, how they will buy and use it, how to price it, how to organize production, which distribution channels to use, how to compete, etc.

The Business Model Canvas [13] is a startup template for developing new business or documenting existing business models. It is a visual chart that describes a product's or a firm's value proposition, infrastructure, customers, revenues and costs. The Business Model Canvas identifies questions that need to be answered to create a business (Figure 4).

When a business is conceptualized, answers to the Business Model Canvas questions are assumptions.

A mental model of beliefs about the business is the start line from where an entrepreneur begins creating a new business. His beliefs are theories about why he believes the business will work. For startup, the theories about the proposed business model questions are a collection of hypotheses to be validated. Theories are validated or modified and established during startup implementation.

Figure 4. Mental model of a business are assumptions that are validated during implementation
(Apologies for a transverse figure)

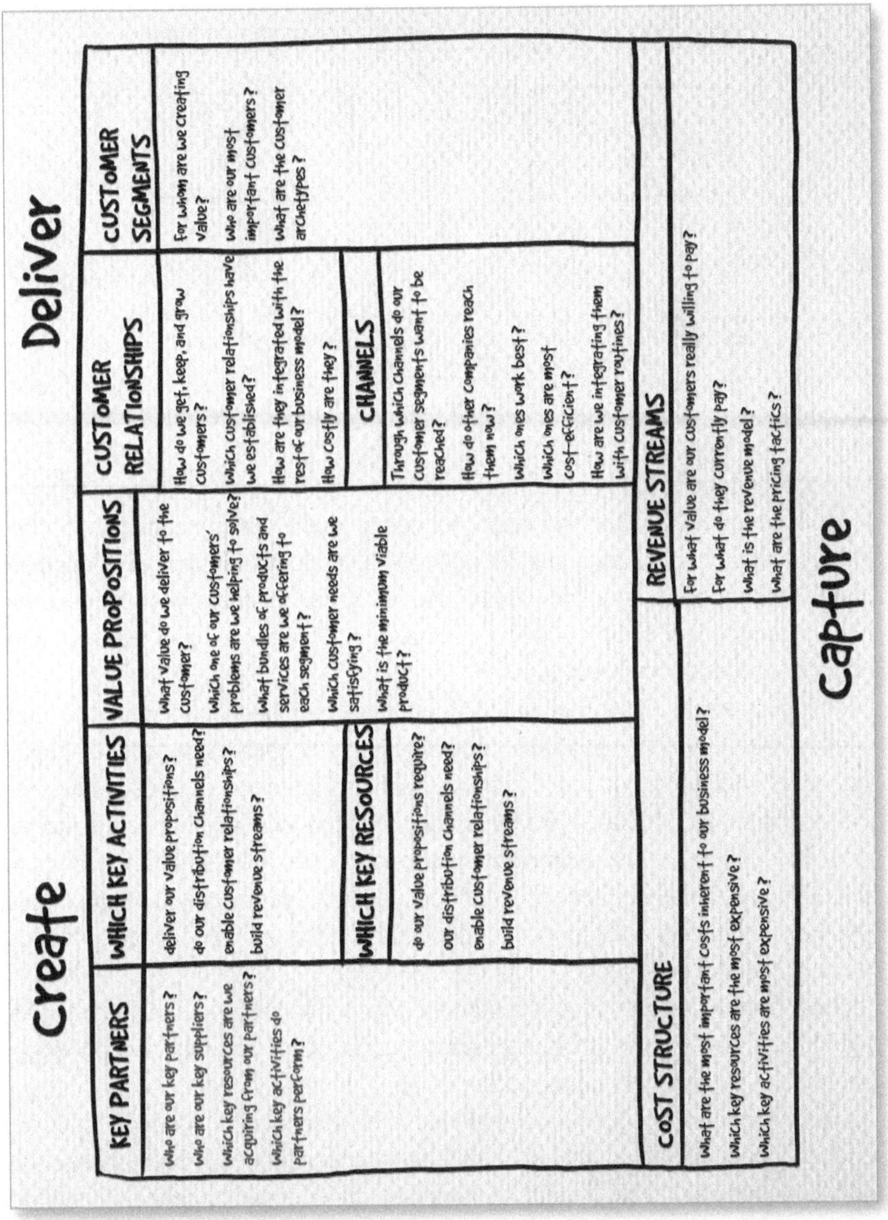

Create

KEY PARTNERS
- Who are our key partners?
- Who are our key suppliers?
- Which key resources are we acquiring from our partners?
- Which key activities do partners perform?

WHICH KEY ACTIVITIES
- deliver our value propositions?
- do our distribution channels need?
- enable customer relationships?
- build revenue streams?

WHICH KEY RESOURCES
- do our value propositions require?
- our distribution channels need?
- enable customer relationships?
- build revenue streams?

Deliver

VALUE PROPOSITIONS
- What value do we deliver to the customer?
- Which one of our customers' problems are we helping to solve?
- What bundles of products and services are we offering to each segment?
- Which customer needs are we satisfying?
- What is the minimum viable product?

CUSTOMER RELATIONSHIPS
- How do we get, keep, and grow customers?
- Which customer relationships have we established?
- How are they integrated with the rest of our business model?
- How costly are they?

CHANNELS
- Through which channels do our customer segments want to be reached?
- How do other companies reach them now?
- Which ones work best?
- Which ones are most cost-efficient?
- How are we integrating them with customer routines?

CUSTOMER SEGMENTS
- For whom are we creating value?
- Who are our most important customers?
- What are the customer archetypes?

Capture

COST STRUCTURE
- What are the most important costs inherent to our business model?
- Which key resources are the most expensive?
- Which key activities are most expensive?

REVENUE STREAMS
- For what value are our customers really willing to pay?
- For what do they currently pay?
- What is the revenue model?
- What are the pricing tactics?

The figure is adapted from the Business Model Canvas.[14] It lists the nine building blocks of the business model with the questions that need to be answered to create a business. When a business is conceptualized answers to the questions are assumptions. Assumptions are unproven when implementation begins. They are theories, hypotheses that need practical validation. I label the Business Model Canvas at this stage as a mental model of the business.

When a business is conceptualized, a business model is a mental model (Figure 5).

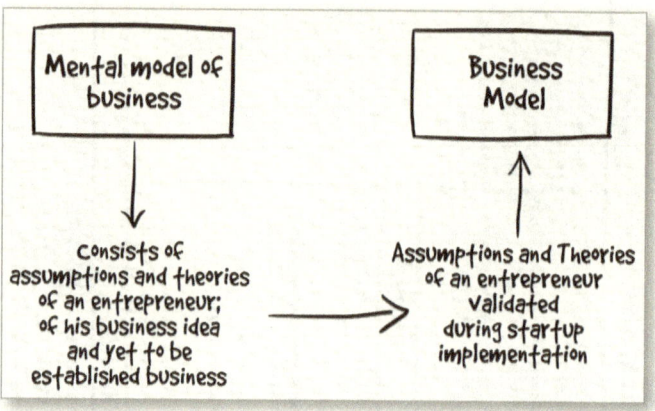

Figure 5. Mental model become business model during startup implementation

Entrepreneurs realize the need to verify their assumptions when they present their product and engage with customers. Validation of a business model is done by testing the mental model of the business with transacting customers who pay to buy and use the product. Businesses also transact with suppliers and other stakeholders.

Business startup involves the validation of the assumptions of the nine building blocks of the business model (Figure 6). An entrepreneur meets customers with prototypes/products to confirm the problem being addressed and his proposed solutions (Step 1 and 2). He then validates the go-to-market path (Step 3), the required distribution infrastructure (Step 4) and the revenue model (Step 5). The emphasis then shifts to how the product will be produced, how raw materials will be sourced and the cost of producing products (Steps 6, 7, 8 and 9).

How does a business model juxtapose with a mental model of the business in practice? The iPhone story represents a connection between mental model innovation and business model innovation.

Steve Jobs and Apple had no experience in designing telecommunications products. In 2005, Apple experimented by collaborating with Motorola on the Moto Rokr phone.[16] The idea of a single device – the convergence of an iPod, phone, camera and a touch screen [17] – was conceptualized by Apple in the form of a tablet, but Jobs directed the focus towards the iPhone.

Figure 6. Beliefs as unanswered questions [15] when implementation begins

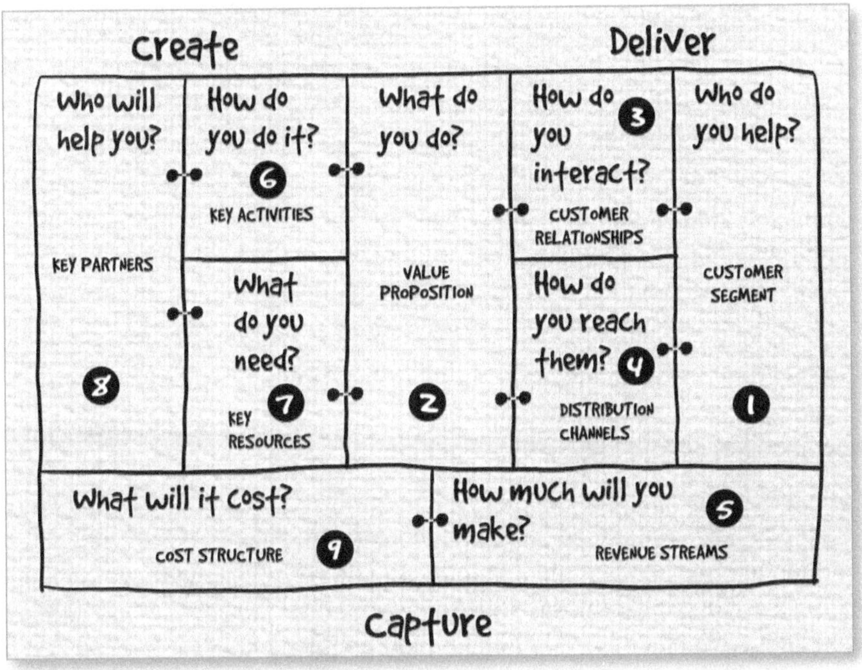

```
              create                                    Deliver
  ┌─────────┬──────────┬──────────┬──────────┬──────────┐
  │ Who will│ How do   │ What do  │ How do   │ Who do   │
  │ help you?│ you do it?│ you do?  │ you      │ you help?│
  │         │    ⑥     │          │ interact? ③│         │
  │         │KEY ACTIVITIES│       │ CUSTOMER  │         │
  │         │          │          │ RELATIONSHIPS│      │
  │ KEY     ├──────────┤  VALUE   ├──────────┤ CUSTOMER │
  │ PARTNERS│ What     │PROPOSITION│ How do  │ SEGMENT  │
  │         │ do you   │          │ you reach│          │
  │         │ need?    │          │ them? ④ │          │
  │    ⑧    │   ⑦      │   ②      │ DISTRIBUTION│  ①   │
  │         │ KEY RESOURCES│      │ CHANNELS │          │
  ├─────────┴──────────┼──────────┴──────────┴──────────┤
  │ What will it cost? │ How much will you make?  ⑤    │
  │ COST STRUCTURE ⑨  │ REVENUE STREAMS                │
  └────────────────────┴────────────────────────────────┘
              capture
```

Business startup consists of 'validation of assumptions' of the nine building blocks of the business model. An entrepreneur meets customers with a prototype to confirm the problem being addressed by verifying their needs and pain points and his proposed solutions (Step 1 and 2). He then validates the go-to-Market path and defines the required distribution infrastructure (Steps 3 and 4). Finally, validation of the revenue model occurs over multiple iterations as the assumptions are firmed up (Step 5). This followed by establishing the cost of producing the product (Steps 6, 7, 8 and 9).

When the iPhone was announced in January 2007, Steve Ballmer of Microsoft said the following:

"500 dollars? Fully subsidized? With a plan? I said that is the most expensive phone in the world. And it doesn't appeal to business customers because it doesn't have a keyboard. Which makes it not a very good email machine... Let's take phones first. Right now, we're selling millions and millions and millions of phones a year. Apple is selling zero phones a year. In six months, they'll have the most expensive phone by far ever in the marketplace." [18]

Within five years, iPhone became the most successful smartphone and greatest profit maker for Apple, capturing close to 90% of industry profits.[19] The mental model innovation that powered the design and popularity of the iPhone resulted in significant changes in business models of telephone carriers. The two pricing models – from phone manufacturers to the telephone carriers and from the phone carriers to customers – changed. Apple sold the phone to selected telephone carriers on volume commitments. Customers purchased the most expensive phone on affordable monthly fees. The monthly charge had three components built in: one for use of telephony and data and the other two for repayment of principal as well as finance charges for the purchase of the phone, respectively.

Mental models and business models have a symbiotic relationship. In new business creation, mental models influence business model innovation and vice versa. Entrepreneurship consists of a mental model innovation that manifests in a business model innovation. Creation of new business is based on business model innovation which in turn changes the mental models of the industry incumbents towards how their industries and businesses operate.

Mental models lead to business model innovation – How does it happen?

Entrepreneurs co-opt customers to create new businesses. The validation of all business ideas and assumptions happens in multiple iterations of engagement with customers.

A new business is an organization of few people, its processes are rudimentary and it has limited resources. The entrepreneur first attempts to establish his value proposition. He does this by creating a product and engaging with customers. He tries to sell and keeps a watchful eye on the interaction and exchange that take place with customers. His engagements with customers are deliberate interactions in which he personally participates. He attempts to understand whether his customers understand the offering the way he intends, if customers discern a difference amongst various competing offers and how they choose what to buy. He learns to motivate customer choice towards his offering. Once a unique value proposition is validated by customers, the focus of the entrepreneur shifts towards identifying value-creating processes of his business, what he has to create, manage and sustain to found a business.

Customers also like to engage with entrepreneurs to give feedback. They offer their knowledge, either because they know the entrepreneur or are selfishly motivated, cognizant that they may get better value when they buy his products. Entrepreneurs engage with customers they know when they are starting out and their interactions are overt. They are aware that to truly succeed they will have to test and get their products accepted by a wider set of customers.

The nature of entrepreneur engagement with customers in the startup phase is recursive. If the initial product offering doesn't work he modifies his business goals, refines the offering and retests the product iteration with customers. This cycle of presentation, feedback, redefining goals, product modification and retesting continues till product iteration gains traction. The engagement with customers is a dynamic interaction process where the entrepreneur redefines the business problem and/or changes the product and/or modifies customer perceptions to accept the product. This framework (Figure 7) depicts the recursive nature of new business creation. The arrows in the middle represent engagement between entrepreneur and customer. These arrows point in both directions highlighting the interactive nature of entrepreneur customer encounters. An entrepreneur takes action and customers respond. A feedback is implicit in how customers choose, buy and use the product. The customer gives feedback, entrepreneur learning occurs and knowledge becomes available for the entrepreneur to modify the product offering.

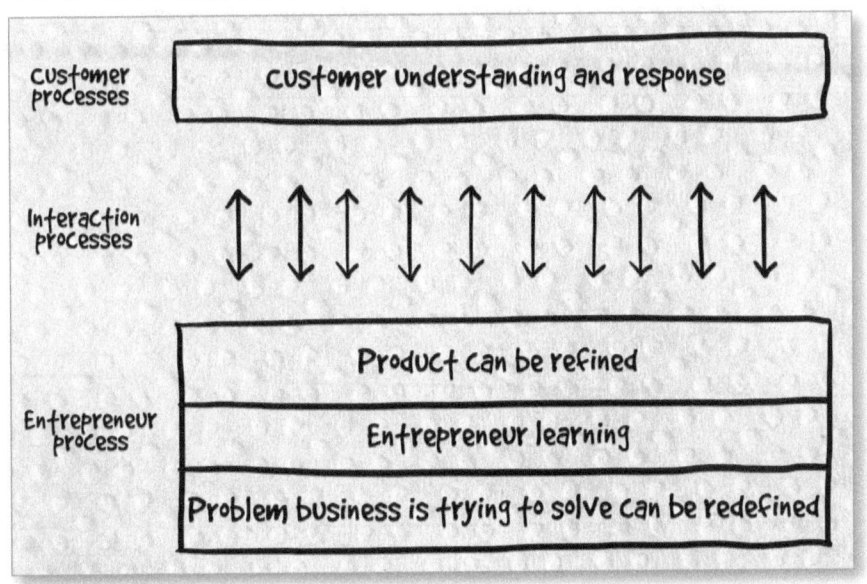

Figure 7. A depiction of the recursive interaction of entrepreneurs and their customers

Entrepreneur learns and can redefine the business problem and/or change the product and/or modify customer perceptions to accept the product.

FLIP OVER

I elaborate the four phases of business creation, the startup curve (Figure 3).

Problem-Solution Fit

At a philosophical level, a new business serves a consumer need. Every consumer need is a problem that has not been identified and addressed or a product functionality gap of an existing product that needs a solution (Figure 8a). The entrepreneur solves the problem by creating a product that solves the consumer problem, that is, delivers a solution as a value proposition (Figure 8b). A value proposition is embedded in the product and is delivered through product performance, (Figure 8c) that is, product performance is the solution to the customer problem (Figure 8d).

Figure 8. New business is a customer problem that is solved by a new product

Figure 8a. Every consumer need is a consumer problem that requires a solution. The need defines the problem that leads to discovery of a solution.

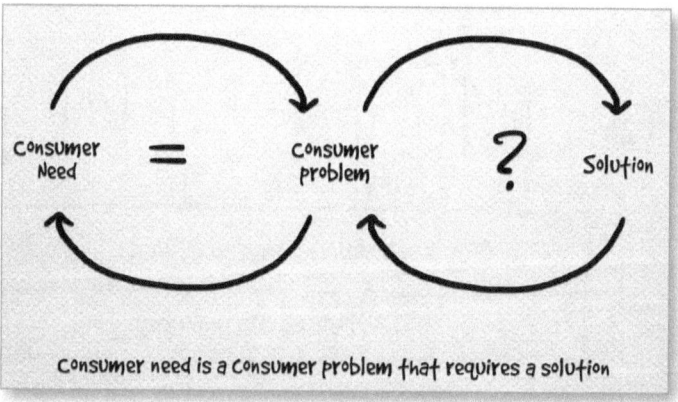

Figure 8b. A business creates a product to solve a consumer problem. The solution to the problem is the value proposition of the business.

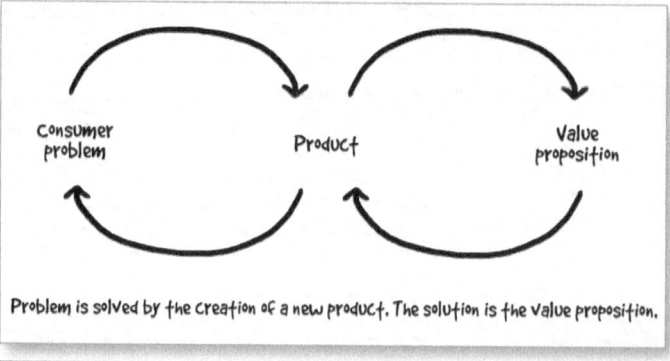

Figure 8c. The value proposition is a result of the product solving the customer problem or the product performance.

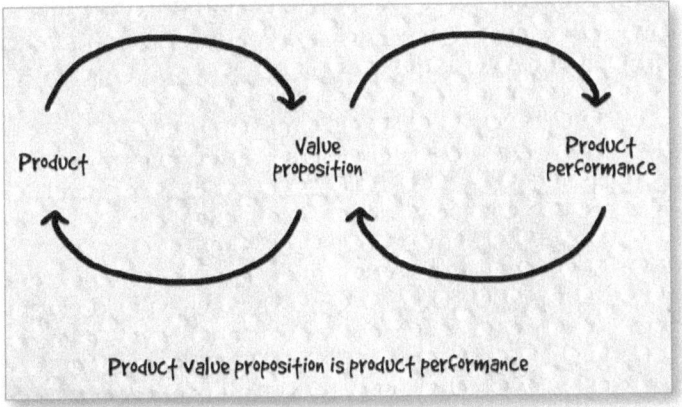

Figure 8d. The solution to the consumer problem is embedded in product performance.

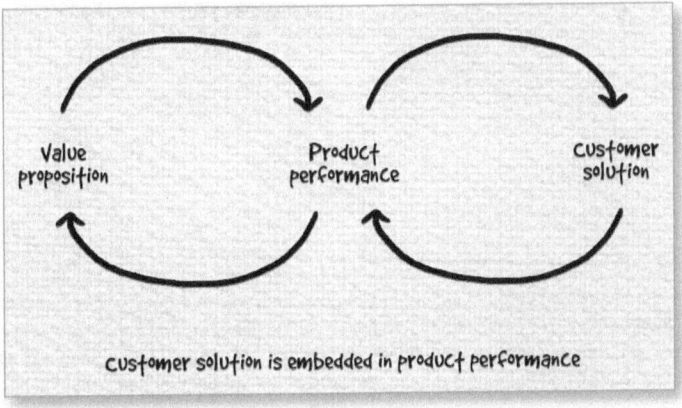

The initial startup task of an entrepreneur is to demonstrate to customers that his product is a solution to their needs, i.e., validate his definition of the business problem and his proposed solution (Figure 9 overleaf). As entrepreneurs take the first steps to create their businesses they realize:

1. Business outcomes are different from assumptions.
2. Customers take time to understand and switch from competition.
3. They have to win the trust of customers before any transactions happen.
4. Unpredictable incidents happen and unanticipated ideas emerge.
5. Initial transactions occur one customer at a time.

An entrepreneur refines and redefines the business problem as well as reworks his initial solution based on customer ability to differentiate his offering from competition and their willingness to buy. He works recursively engaged with customers. All business assumptions the entrepreneur started with about his new business can change; he can choose new business goals, develop new and different products and target different customers.

Figure 9. Problem-solution fit

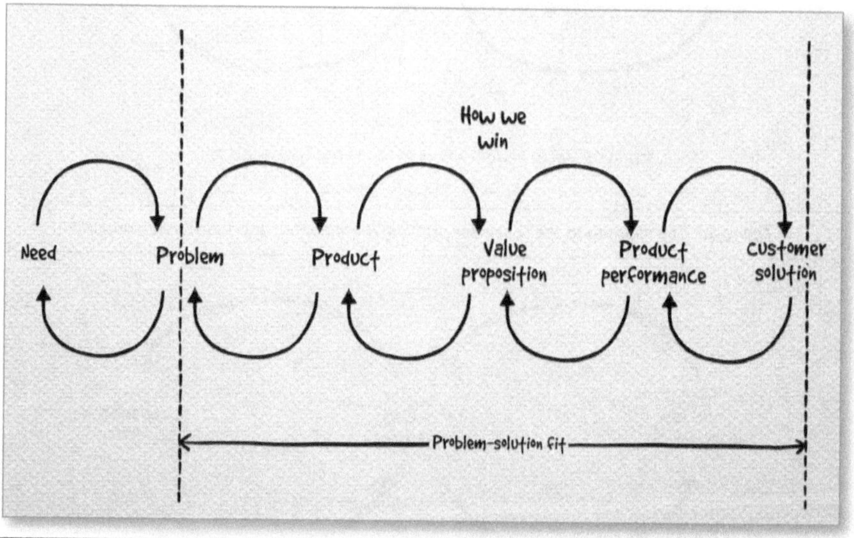

An entrepreneur validates his definition of the customer problem and his proposed solution. He engages with few customers. He refines and redefines his articulation of the business problem and/or reworks his product solution based on customer ability to differentiate his offering from competition and their willingness to buy. The circular nature of arrows suggests that he works recursively engaged with customers.

Product-market fit

Entrepreneur presents the developed product to a larger cohort of target customers. He creates and refines a communications strategy and establishes a distribution platform to reach the wider target market. This is the go-to-market strategy (Figure 10a). He simultaneously works on business activities to produce the product and its value proposition (Figure 10b). The entrepreneur has, until now, spent minimal capital and resources in product creation, customer understanding and acceptance of products and distribution. He is testing what works and what doesn't. I label the second phase as product-market fit.

Figure 10a. Product-market fit - the go-to-market strategy

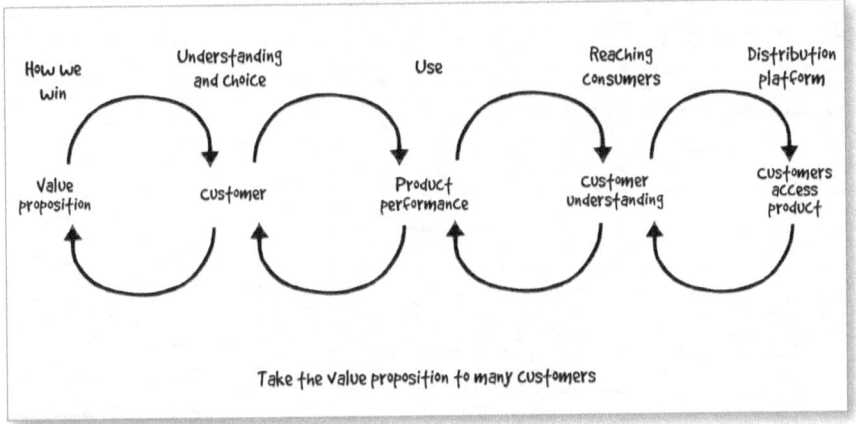

The entrepreneur takes the value proposition to the target market. The entrepreneur works to create communication that works and establish a distribution platform to reach the target market. He continues to work recursively engaged with customers.

Figure 10b. Product-market fit – business activities

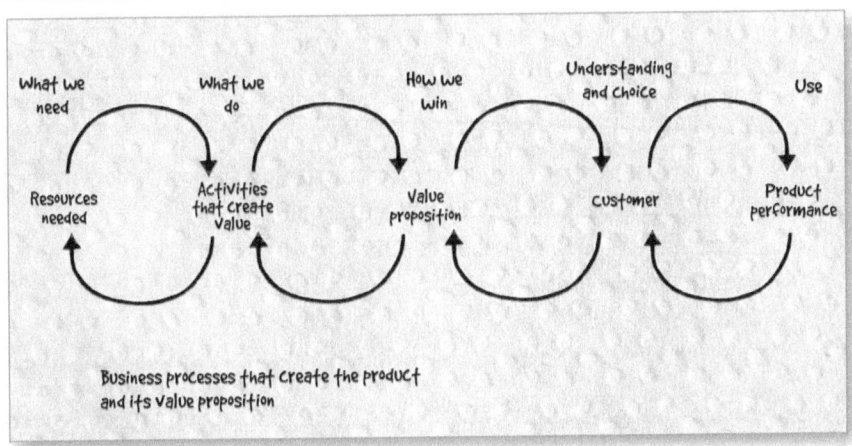

Once customer traction begins the entrepreneur focuses on identifying the business activities that create the product and the value proposition.

Validation of Business Model

A workable business is implicit in the business transactions if the price realization is greater than the costs of producing and delivering products. The entrepreneur verifies the cost structure to create and deliver products to establish business viability (Figure 11).

Figure 11. Validation of business model

Who we need	What we need	What we do	How we win	Understanding and choice	Use
Partnerships	Resources needed	Activities that create value	Value proposition	Customer	Product performance
Who we work with to create value	Business processes and resources that create the product and its value proposition				

←—————— Cost ——————→ ←—— Price ——→

Business model metrics

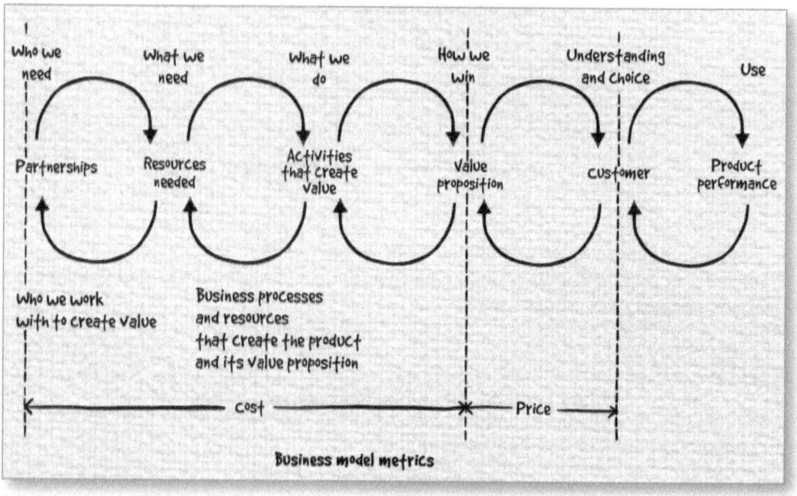

The entrepreneur uses the go-to-market strategy to establish price customers will pay and business activities to establish the cost structure to create and deliver products. A business model is the way in which a company generates revenue and makes a profit from company operations.

When the business model is validated, the entrepreneur knows:
1. Customers who will buy the product.
2. What they 'may' pay.
3. What it 'may' cost to reach and convert them.
4. What it 'may' cost to make the product.

I emphasize the word 'may.' The assumptions have been validated using initial products engaged with some key customers in an experimental way. The business is not yet operating at scale. The business model established has the following limitations:

1. Product is a trial product. It may not have full features.
2. Business interpretations may be based on customers buying and using prototypes and giving opinions.
3. Entrepreneurs have engaged with customers for the market test.[20] In direct engagement with entrepreneurs, customers are prone to give biased feedback.

4. Natural customer traction is to be established. Sustainability of a new business needs a wider customer base where each customer will need to independently understand, choose and buy the product.

Business Drivers

Validation of business model assumptions is the beginning of new business creation. It is a beginning because the entrepreneur has estimated the cost structure to produce and deliver the product and the price customers are prepared to pay. He has to now build an operating business.

An entrepreneur knows 'what to do' and 'how to do' different business activities to produce and sell. To achieve higher sales and profits, he needs to sell more units, increase or decrease price and control costs. He has to identify ways and means to achieve control and influence over unit sales, prices and costs. I exemplify below:

Figure 12a represents the business activities starting from resource (1), business activities (2) that produce the offering (3) with a value proposition (4) that reaches a customer (5) and commands a price (6). Profit (7) is a result of revenue less cost (8).

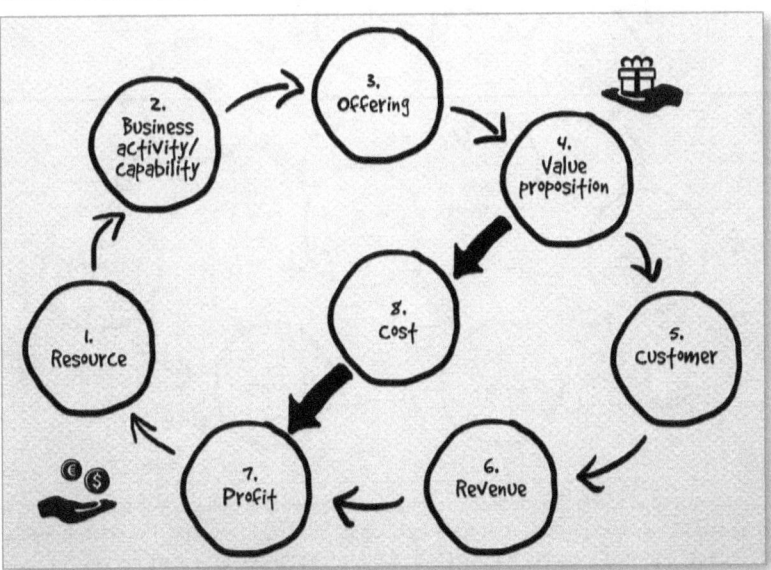

Figure 12a. Business activity

The circle of activities starting from resource (1), business activities (2) that produce (3) the offering with a value proposition (4) that reaches a customer (5) and commands a price (6). Profit (7) is a result of revenue less cost (8).

The entrepreneur knows this as he validates the business model. As the business starts to operate, the entrepreneur takes a decision to increase investment in resources and productive business activities. Figure 12b depicts the impact of this decision – investment in resources (1) and improving business activities (2) (indicated with a plus sign) lead to an improvement of the offering (3) and its value proposition to customers (4). This results in an increase in revenue (6), as customers pay more for improved value and new customers are attracted by the better value proposition. The profit (7) is higher if increase of revenue is greater than the increased cost (8) of improving the value proposition.

To convert this experience to knowledge, he adjusts investment and monitors business outcomes. Through increments and/or decrements, the entrepreneur acquires working knowledge of the impact of investment on business results. This understanding, the contributory influence of investment as a managerial instrument to influence business results, is the leverage the entrepreneur acquires to achieve business outcomes.

Figure 12b. Business drivers

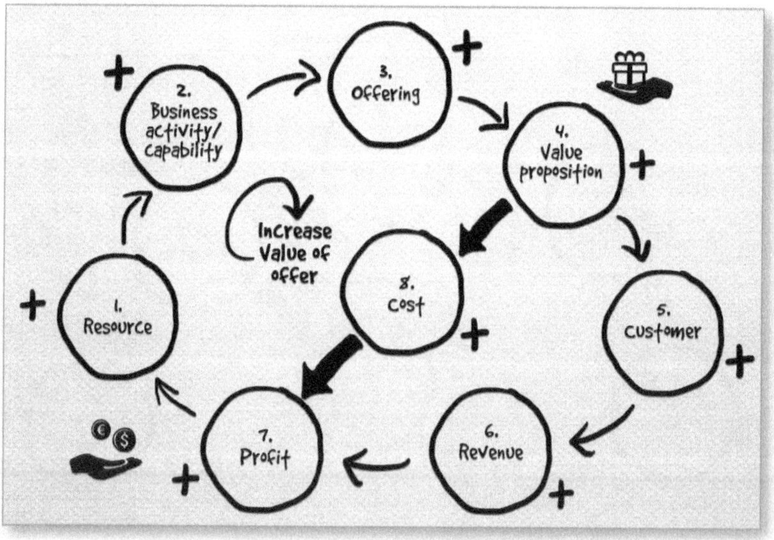

Investment in resources and improving business activities (indicated with a plus sign) leads to an improvement in offering and its value proposition. This translates into an increase in revenue. The profit is higher if the revenue increase is greater than the cost of increasing the value proposition by investments.

A business model shows interconnections between different building blocks of the business. In a running business all components of the business model – customer relationships, distribution platforms, business activities, partnerships and resources as well as target customers – work together to create value. Entrepreneurs deliberately work to acquire influence and control of each component of the business model. They take decisions to incrementally increase and/or decrease inputs that they manage and control, relating to each competent of the business model and monitor outcomes. In an experimental way, they acquire working knowledge of business drivers and learn to manage inputs to drive business outcomes to influence business performance. Each business driver has connected input and output metrics (Figure 13). Inputs are lead measures of the business decision. As the name suggests, lead measure quantifies the managerial decisions and actions an entrepreneur takes to achieve a targeted outcome (Figure 13a).

Fig 13. Leverage over business drivers [21]

Figure 13a Business drivers connect 'business decisions' to 'what we wish to achieve.' Inputs are 'lead' measures of the business decision – what we do. Output is a 'lag' measure – what we wish to achieve.

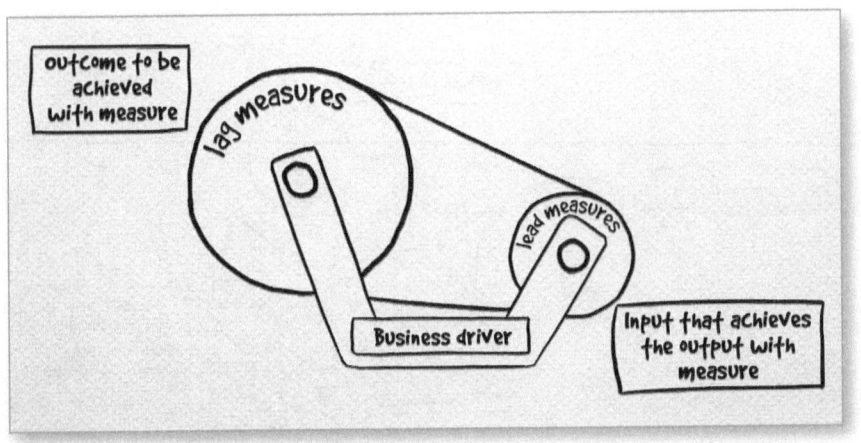

FLIP OVER

Figure 13b. Entrepreneur takes a business decision and assesses outcome. Gap of lead and lag measures (scoreboard) identifies distance from business goal.

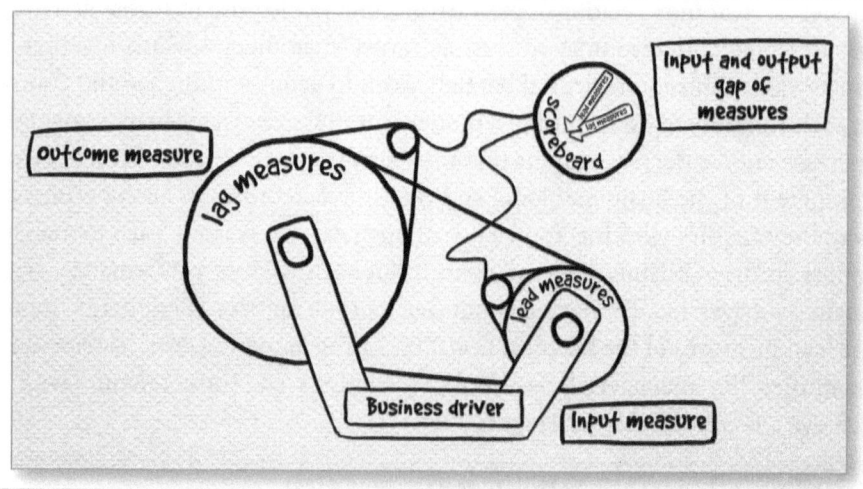

Figure 13c. Entrepreneur drives the input (changes lead measure) which in turn influences the outcome. Entrepreneur acquires working knowledge by understanding how he influences and controls business outcomes.

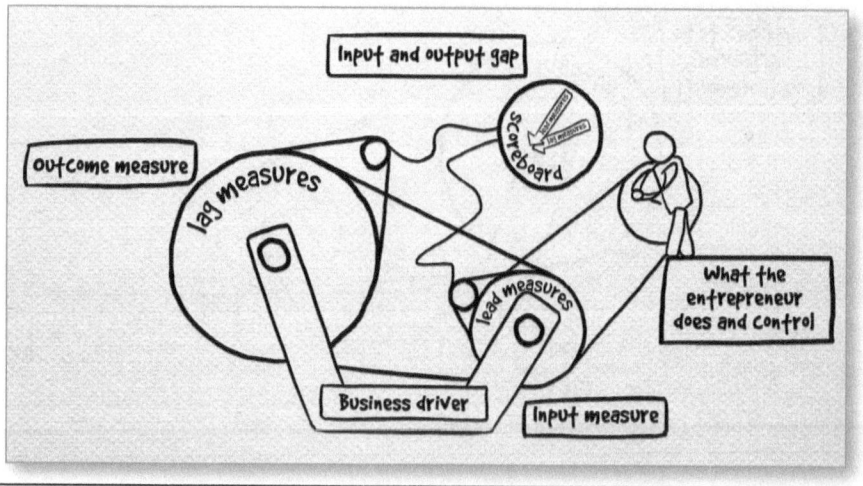

The outcome is measured with a lag measure (Figure 13a). The gap of lead and lag measures, depicted as a scoreboard, measures how far the lag measure is from the targeted business goal (Figure 13b). Entrepreneur acquires working knowledge by understanding what he can do to drive, i.e., influence and control business outcomes Figure 13c). Business driver is a term used to describe resources and capabilities that entrepreneurs use to steer business performance.

At this stage of new business creation, an entrepreneur knows 'what to do,' 'how to do' and 'how much to do.'

Establish business metrics – change perspective from working 'in' the business to working 'on' the business

After entrepreneurs acquire capabilities to manage business performance, they work on scaling the business.

I use the metaphor of a symphony to explain the idea. A conductor of an orchestra, leading an orchestra of different musical instruments, conveys his interpretation of a musical score to members of his ensemble. Conductors create music. Musicians become conductors when they have knowledge and skill to play a musical instrument, knowledge of music and all instruments used in an orchestral performance as well as an ability to interpret music in their own unique way.

Figure 14 graphically represents how the business model components integrate. Each mechanism in the cog schematic represents a business model component.

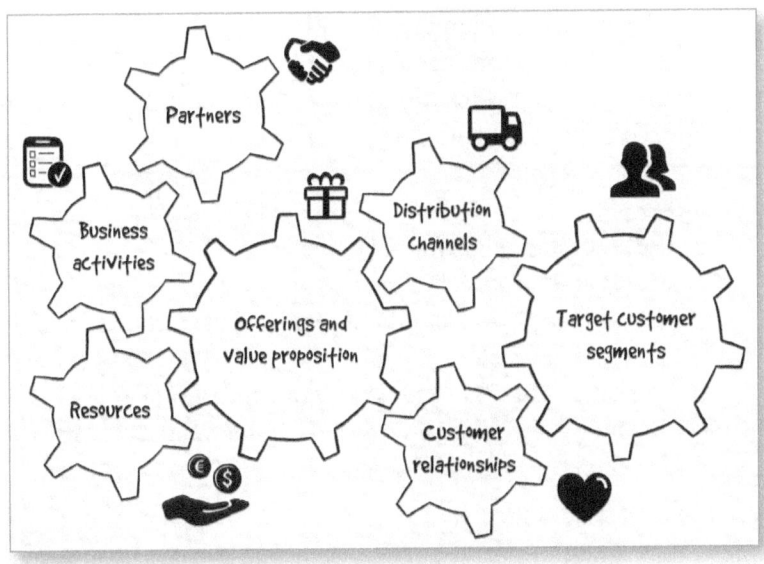

Figure 14. How building blocks of the business model integrate

An entrepreneur has been working 'in' the business, acquiring working knowledge of each component of the business model. When an entrepreneur is acquiring control over business drivers, he is conceptually working to understand the functioning of each cog of his business, akin to a musician acquiring mastery to play an instrument. The new business is at a phase where all components of the business model are functioning and delivering value to customers. The entrepreneur now works 'on' the business. This is akin to a player of a musical instrument graduating to become a music conductor. The entrepreneur acquires capability to drive the business by influencing all the operating mechanisms working together.

Establishing and managing business metrics is a way of acquiring control over the business. Business metrics reveal the health of the business. They enable the entrepreneur to manage the business as it grows.

Business metrics of a startup are different from that of a mature business. The entrepreneur focus is on growing the business by acquiring customers. The growth trajectory is measured by the pace of customer acquisition. Indicative metrics are:

1. Addressable market opportunity-potential customers in the geographic vicinity of the startup.
2. Measure quality of the customer acquisition process.
   a. Number of new customers targeted
   b. Numbers of customers engaged
   c. Acquisition rate of new customer
   d. Average value of a customer
   e. Customer retention or loyalty (or churn)
   f. Cost of new customer acquisition
3. Measures of business health. The customer acquisition measures are evaluated juxtaposed with measures of business financial health. This ensures that business is growing without compromising business health.
   a. Revenue and quality of revenue
   b. Gross and net cash burn rates
   c. Gross margin and trends to manage price, volume and average revenue per customer
   d. Variable costs and productivity of expenditure
   e. Economies of scale and overhead costs trends with growth
   f. Inventory velocity and stock turn

Stages of Business Growth

My thoughts regarding phases of new business creation reflect in the work of Steve Blank.[22] Blank[23] (2013) identifies the following phases of new business creation:

1. Identification of business model hypotheses to test and validate customer needs.
2. Creation of a minimum viable product to test the proposed solution on customers.

3. Validation of customer interest based on feedback, early orders or usage.
4. Modification of initial hypotheses to validate again or the startup pivots based on customer feedback.
5. Product is then refined to sell.
6. The business scales as marketing and sales are activated to reach customers.

This is presented in Figure 15.[24] Customer discovery, the first step, correlates with problem-solution fit. Customer validation, the second step, is labeled by me as product-market fit. Customer creation, the third step, is about reaching out to a larger pool of customers and understanding the drivers of business, i.e., firming up the business model using metrics. Company building, the fourth step, is about scaling up the business.

Figure 15. Scaffolding of ideas

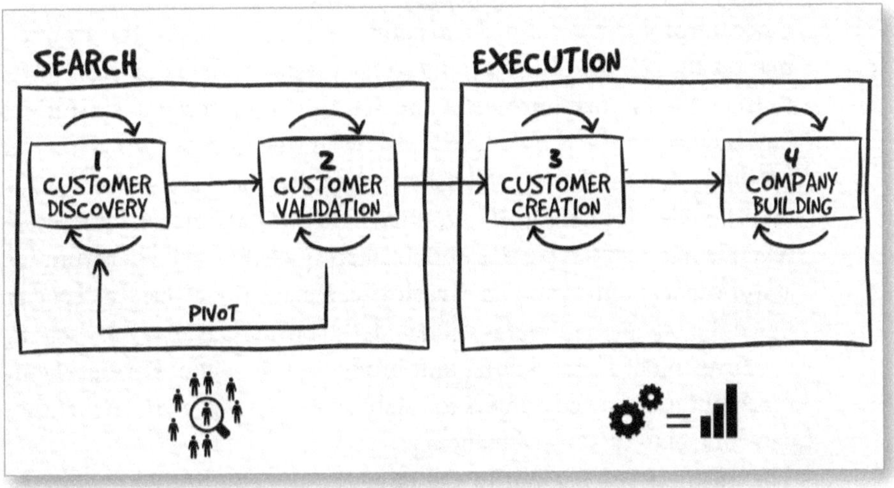

SEARCH — EXECUTION

1 CUSTOMER DISCOVERY → 2 CUSTOMER VALIDATION → 3 CUSTOMER CREATION → 4 COMPANY BUILDING

PIVOT

In customer development, startup searches for a business model that works. If customer feedback reveals that its business hypotheses are wrong, it either revises them or "pivots" to new hypotheses. Once a model is proven, the startup starts executing, building a formal organization. Each stage of customer development is iterative

Blank[25] (2013) model is a reliable and effective way of creating a new business. The process of business creation depicted in the interviews is identical to the model proposed by Blank (2013).[26] The interviews suggest an earlier starting point. Entrepreneurs start with hunches or beliefs about the business they intend to create. They start the business based on their beliefs. When they realize that things are not working according to plan, they reflect, learn and change their way of working. After they adapt, the entrepreneurs create businesses following the method suggested by Blank (2013).[27] Steve Blank has developed the method of helping entrepreneurs create new businesses based on his experience. The model elaborated here is revealed by entrepreneurs creating businesses. The correspondence reinforces the power of Steve Blank's approach.

I summarize the visible portion of the iceberg- what entrepreneurs do to create businesses:

1. Entrepreneurs start with a mental model of the business, an idea of what they want to make and beliefs about why customers will buy and at what price. They engage with customers, experience unpredicted outcomes and recognize the need to go back to the drawing board to tweak and/or change their original ideas.
2. Entrepreneurs realize that their business assumptions need validation. They test their business hunches in small tests. They do this in stages.
3. Entrepreneurs first confirm the problem-solution fit, i.e., the validity of the problem they intended to solve with the product as a solution.
4. Once the problem is defined and confirmed, they establish the product-market fit, i.e., detail the product that meets the need of customers. Entrepreneurs create products and sell to real customers. Customers buy and use products. Sale levels are low. Entrepreneurs work to deliver products. Entrepreneur establishes price customers are willing to pay and the cost of making the product. The business model structure – revenue less cost – is partially established since the business is running at low capacity; investments have not been made to produce at capacity.
5. Once the business model is validated, the business is ready for scaling up. Investment in marketing and production is made. Entrepreneurs reach out to many customers to establish business drivers – what they can control to drive the business.
6. The business reaches out to the target customers. Entrepreneurs use business metrics to check the health of the business as it grows.

Figure 16 depicts what transpires in the five stages of business creation. The entrepreneur starts with a mental model of the business. He refines and defines the business problem and the proposed solution. After the hypotheses underlying the business is established, he determines the working (causal) model of business. He then scales the business, keeping an eye on business growth and health metrics.

Figure 16. Activities at each stage of business growth

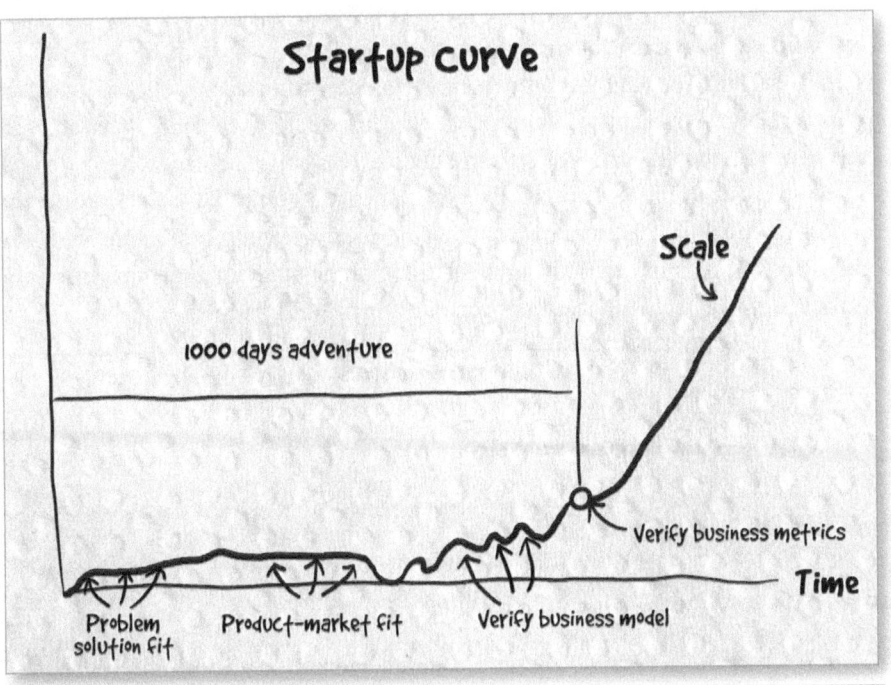

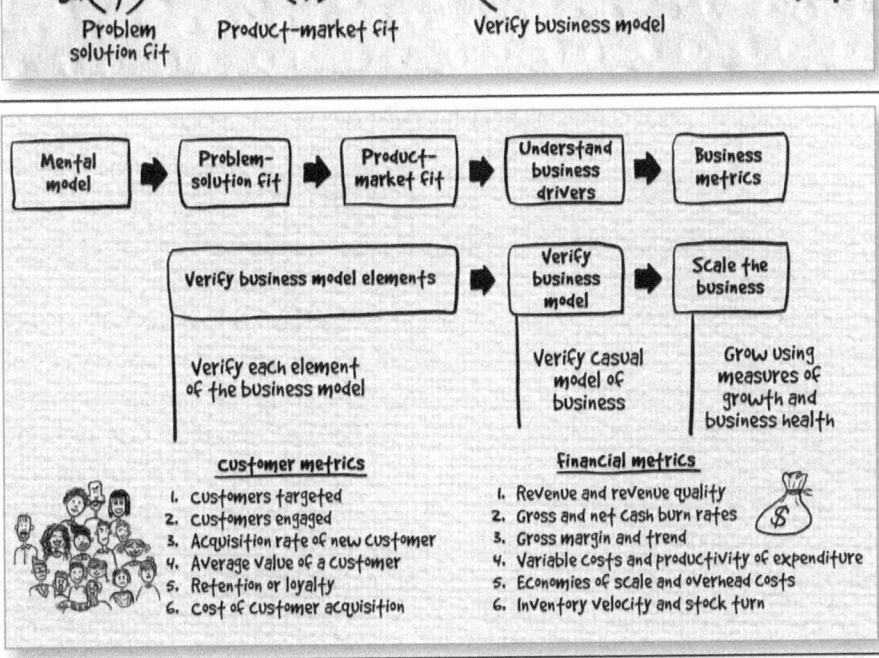

Emerging Competence

Creation of a new business is akin to the construction of a new mental model and business model. Entrepreneurs first attempt to validate their mental models when they begin implementing their business idea. Mental models, like theories in use, are like input-output beliefs that entrepreneurs have about what may be an outcome when an action is taken (Figure 17). Say an entrepreneur desires to start a contracting business. His experience suggests that he will enter the market by bidding 5% lower than what he used to when employed and win one out of ten bids made. This is an assumption or mental model on which the entrepreneur plans his investments in equipment and people.

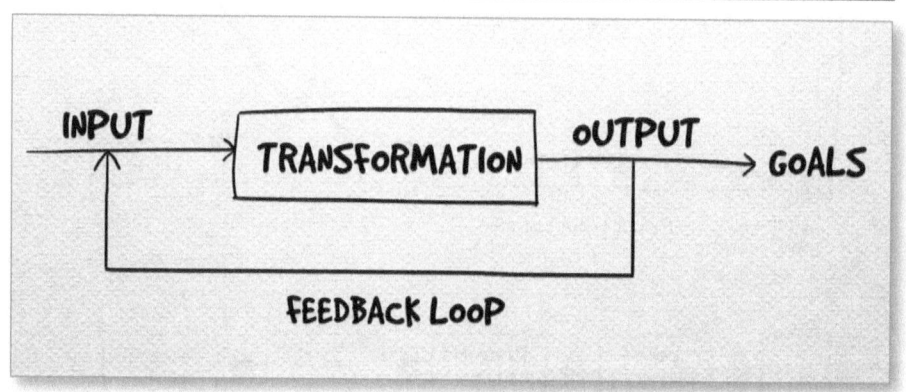

Figure 17. Systems thinking

Entrepreneurs create the business in incremental steps. They disaggregate their mental models into its components. Each component is tested to validate its functionality (what can be achieved) and utility (how is it useful). Then they integrate the validated components to build the business. The reconstructed whole is a business model. The business model functions to produce outcomes. Continuing the contract business example, the entrepreneur first tests his customer acquisition assumptions, i.e., 5% lower price and 10% win rate, by investing in the bare minimum assets to demonstrate that he has the ability to deliver on his promise. He creates the organization after he wins a bid and progresses to establishing his project delivery and cost infrastructure.

The word learning is pervasive in the entrepreneur interviews. The entrepreneur crafting a business can be likened to a person engaged in creating new knowledge. The entrepreneur is the protagonist for learning to occur. In the startup period, his knowledge is the same as business knowledge. The creation of new business is a function of how quickly he learns and is willing to evaluate and adapt his beliefs based on new information. I refer to this as the plasticity of the mind of the entrepreneur. Entrepreneur learning can be visualized as the changing of mental models of the entrepreneur.[28]

I portray here how this is reflected in the interviews. The ideas are intuitive and need to be validated empirically. Figure 18 is a linear visualization of the steps of business creation. The flow from the problem (left) to purpose (right) mimics the steps of the business model. Definition of a problem and its solution are the *raison d'etre* of the new business. The implementation plan of the solution is strategy, i.e., how the outcome will be achieved. The implementation of actions results in a business outcome. The outcome results in the purpose of the business being achieved.

If there is a gap in outcome and purpose, the entrepreneur can rework any or all constituents of the chain – he can redefine the problem and/or the solution, he can develop a new strategy, or he can do new things (actions) to achieve the business purpose. Entrepreneurs exhibit three cognitive responses to minimize the gap.

Figure 18. Steps of business creation

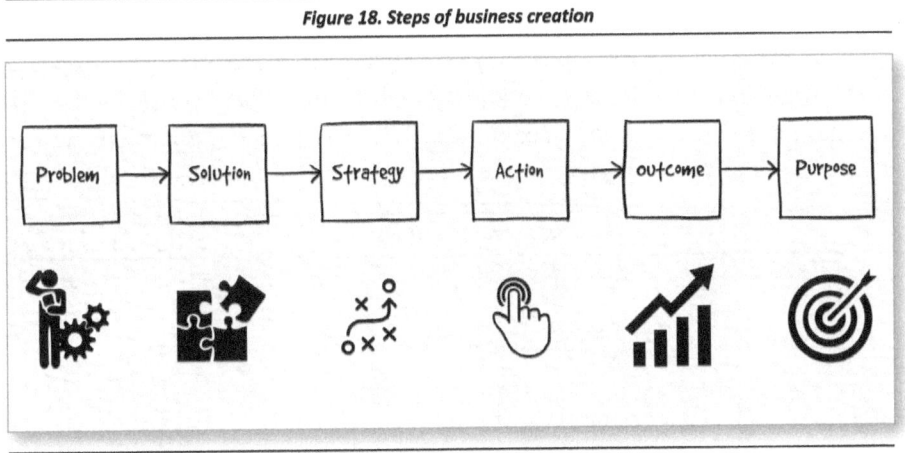

FLIP OVER

The entrepreneur takes an action to create a business and senses a gap between what is achieved and what he expected. He responds to the gap of output by reviewing the assumptions that formed the basis of his actions. He decides that no change is necessary and works to do what he did better. His focus improves the way he works (Figure 19).

Figure 19. Doing things better

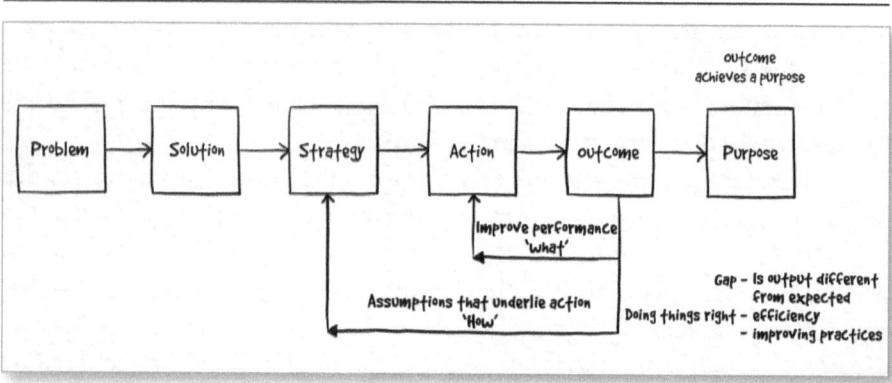

The entrepreneur responds to a gap in the achievement of purpose. He searches for an alternative strategy and action to achieve the purpose (Figure 19). He may have to acquire new capabilities. To do things better, the entrepreneur may go back to the drawing board and rework the solution (Figure 20).

Figure 20. Doing right things

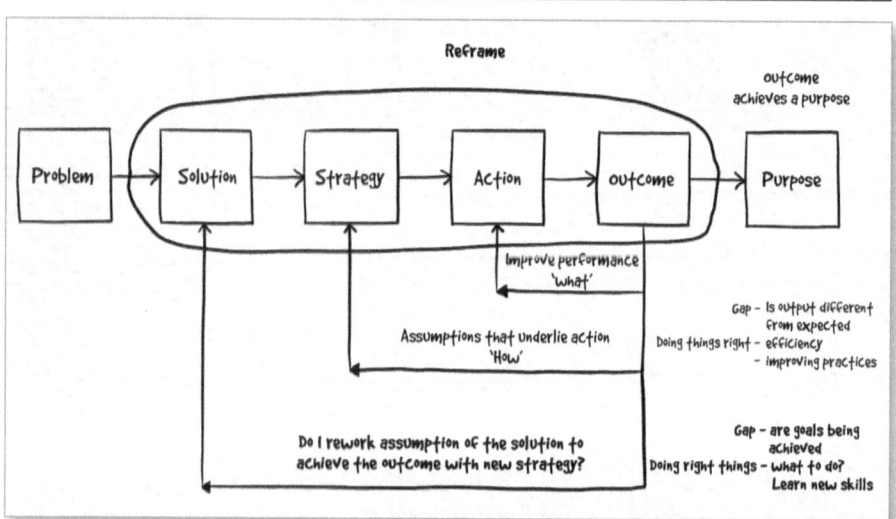

Entrepreneurs can also change the definition and assumptions about the business, i.e., he can 'reframe' the way he was 'looking' at the problem and opportunity. Figure 21 exemplifies reframing.

Figure 21. Reframe the problem and opportunity – three frames, three views and three images looking at the same vista

What we perceive and how we interpret it depend on the frame through which we view the world around us.
Individuals do not respond to objective experiences but to their mental representations of experience. In constructing their mental representations, people use interpretive frames provided by mental models. People may have access to multiple and conflicting mental models. Context can activate a particular mental model. Using a different mental model can change the individual's mental representation of the world around him.

The entrepreneur responds to a gap by revisiting the assumptions underlying the business model (Figure 22 as encircled).

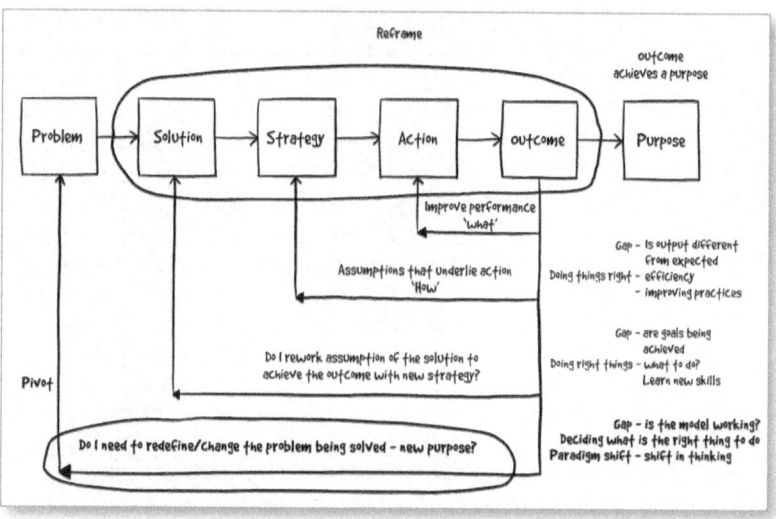

Figure 22. Pivot with new business model

This changing of beliefs and ideas is referred to as entrepreneurial pivot. An entrepreneur pivots the way he was looking at the problem and opportunity. He changes the business model by redefining the problem, goals and whatever else is necessary. An entrepreneur can pivot to the extent of redefining the business (Figure. 23).

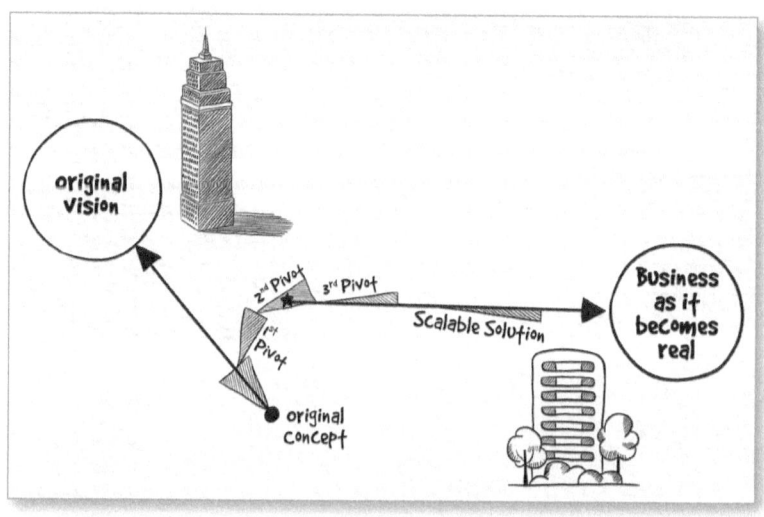

Figure 23. Pivot of an entrepreneur

Creation of new business requires the intense personal engagement of an entrepreneur. He is the touchstone to assess implementation. He is continuously engaged in making sense of evolving situations to take decisions. He interprets connections between diverse fragments of information, assesses what they mean for his business, anticipates trajectory of the business based on his decision options and takes decisions. He evaluates and benchmarks outcomes against his business assumptions. He then decides what is to be reworked.

Entrepreneurs demonstrate a 'situational alertness' to what is transpiring, 'situational awareness' of emergent issues as they relate to business creation and 'situational intelligence' to reframe ideas and decision making. The entrepreneur is immersed in his business. He is mindful at all times about what is transpiring in every aspect of his business. His decision making considers thinking about the past and the future. He creates his new business in the moment.

Boyd's OODA [29] loop is an apt descriptor of what happens in the mind of the entrepreneur as he creates his business. Boyd [30] developed the OODA to depict how fighter pilots comprehend, shape and adapt to an unfolding reality which is changing and unpredictable. Fighter pilots take decisions immersed in combat. They are required to be alert and aware. They make split-second decisions. Each decision is a matter of life and death. The OODA loop refers to the decision cycle of observe, orient, decide and act (Figure 24 Simplified OODA loop). OODA loop can be visualized as a learning system.[31]

Figure 24. Simplified OODA loop

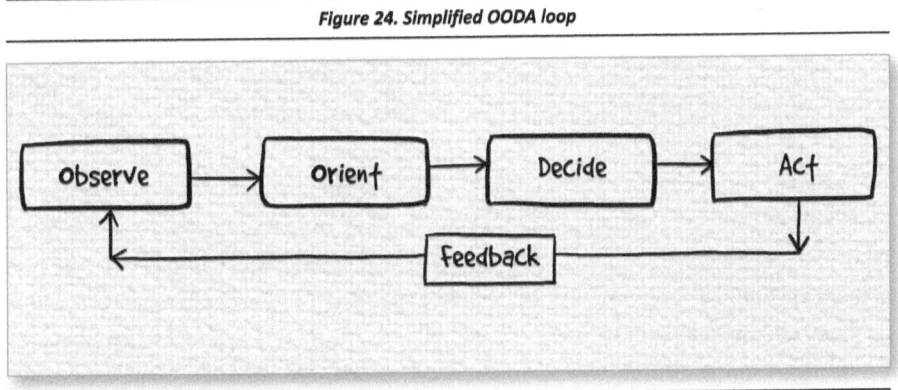

FLIP OVER

The underlying process of the OODA loop depicts how an entrepreneur learns as he builds his business. I use the detailed OODA loop diagram to depict how learning occurs. The diagram (Figure 25) is a partial OODA loop with adapted labels.

Figure 25. Partial OODA loop

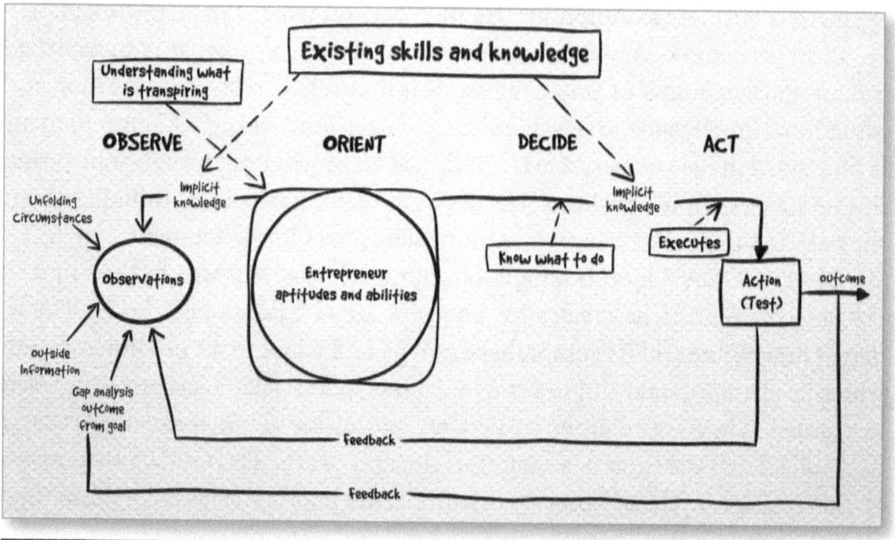

The first O of the OODA – Observe (and Observations) on the left of the diagram – is how the entrepreneur observes the unfolding business situation. It is depicted as the intermingling of three different influences – the unfolding circumstances, new outside information and gap analysis of the outcome of previous actions.

The second O of OODA – Orient – is how the entrepreneur is positioned to see and interpret what is happening. In the orient box, there is filtering of information based on the entrepreneur's antecedents – what he brings as a person, his abilities and his previous experiences. Orientation is the pivot around which the OODA loop occurs. Orientation is a pre-existing mindset the entrepreneur brings to the business. It is a filter through which he sees, reads and interprets situations based on his experience and background. The implicit knowledge link represents what the entrepreneur does using his existing skills and knowledge. In the figure this is depicted as actions he takes using his existing repertoire of skills and knowledge. He is able to understand what is happening. If something changes, he interprets it and knows what to do. The following diagram (Figure 26) is the full OODA loop with adapted labels:

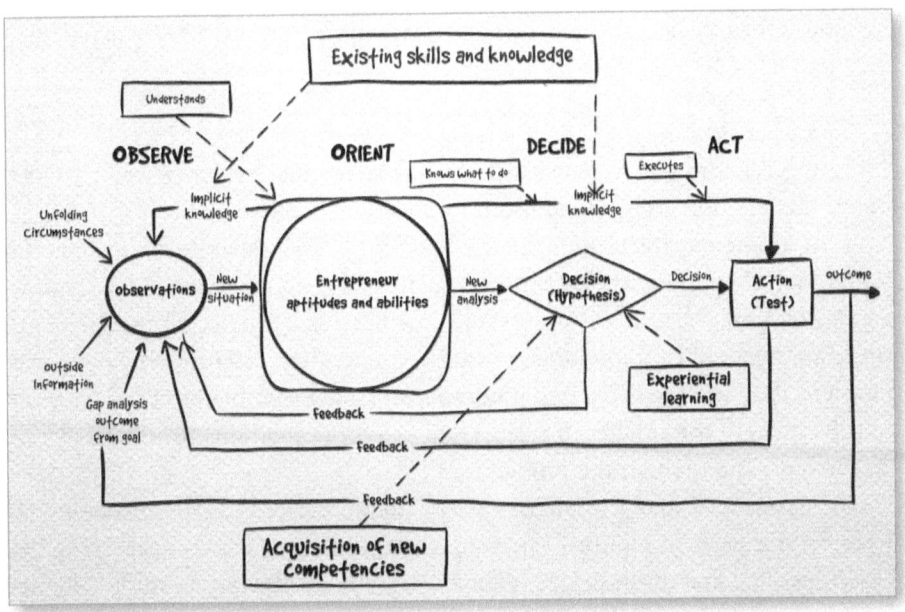

Figure 26. Full OODA loop

The second horizontal link (Figure 26) has a decision hypothesis node. It is the path by which the entrepreneur acquires new capabilities through experiential learning. Starting from the observe node, this link is activated when the entrepreneur senses that he cannot make sense of an emerging situation using his existing knowledge. He then orients himself to search for new patterns in the observations and information. He analyzes, creates a new hypothesis and decides the action to take. The action that follows is a test of effectiveness of his decision. By repeated looping – the cycle of observation, analyses and synthesis, hypothesis and test – he acquires new skills and knowledge. In the figure the decision node is labeled as the point where acquisition of new competencies occurs. To learn and adapt requires an entrepreneur to reposition himself to see new things. Boyd used the following example to vividly exemplify this idea:

"Imagine that you are on a ski slope with other skiers…that you are in Florida riding in an outboard motorboat, maybe even towing water-skiers. Imagine that you are riding a bicycle on a nice spring day. Imagine that you are a parent taking your son to a department store and that you notice he is fascinated by the toy tractors or tanks with rubber caterpillar treads.

Now imagine that you pull the skis off but you are still on the ski slope. Imagine also that you remove the outboard motor from the motorboat, and you are no longer in Florida. And from the bicycle you remove the handle-bar and discard the rest of the bike. Finally, you take off the rubber treads from the toy tractor or tanks. This leaves only the following separate pieces: skis, outboard motor, handlebars and rubber treads."

Boyd then challenged his audience to imagine what emerges when you put these particular parts together.

Did you figure it out?

It's a snowmobile.[32]

Entrepreneurs create new businesses in a gradual evolving way through iterative execution and re-execution.

Entrepreneurs are unique in the way they first separate or isolate the individual elements that constitute the business model for understanding and validation. They then understand business as a whole, all the elements working together. Entrepreneurs are akin to scientists. Scientists break up any problem they wish to solve into a number of smaller problems. Then they try to solve each of the smaller problems and use these solutions to see if they can understand and manage the problem.

Picasso's creation of the Guernica[33] is a metaphor for the way entrepreneurs work. The images in Figure 27 present stages of Pablo Picasso developing the Guernica. The first three images (Figure 27a), titled composition studies, depict how Picasso took a section of the painting and sketched his ideas. The next two paintings (Figure 27b) are a composition study of the complete painting. The next four images (Figure 27c) show the emergence of the details in the painting. As Picasso worked on finishing the painting, he continued to make radical changes.

SEE NEXT PAGE

Figure 27. Stages of Pablo Picasso developing the Guernica

Figure 27a. Composition Studies

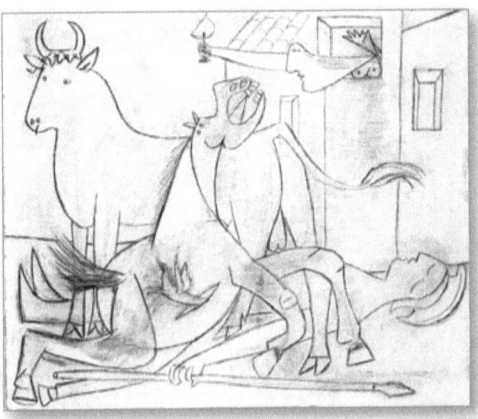

Figure 27b. Composition studies of the complete painting

Figure 27c. Emergence of complete painting

Figure 27c. Emergence of complete painting (Contd.)

2

3

4

Summary

The graphic (Figure 28) depicts series of OODA loops through which the business is implemented. The process is emergent. Entrepreneurs develop the product/service, engage with customers, gauge their responses, reflect, rework and re-execute. In the figure, the cycle is depicted as what an entrepreneur does: he defines, tests, reviews, reworks and retests. The OODA loop is how he learns in each loop: he observes, orients, decides and acts. Thus multiple OODA cycles occur until entrepreneurs achieve responses they deem appropriate. They then repeat the process for the next stage evolution of the business.

Figure 28. Iterative execution and re-execution

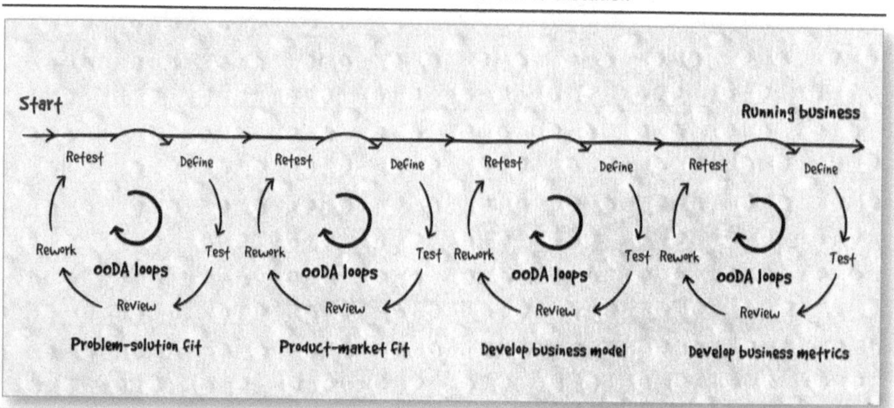

Entrepreneur Aptitude and Attitude

An entrepreneur starting business has two concurrent emotions – self-belief and fear.

Entrepreneurs start based on a belief about the future. They are confident that they will reach the goal – finding a way around every situation they confront, known or unknown. For them there is no such thing as a dead end on their entrepreneurial journey. Flow of water is an apt metaphor for entrepreneurial behavior. Water doesn't plan its journey from the hills to the ocean. It starts moving and finds a way to get to the ocean. Water doesn't stop at a barrier. It forces its way through or finds a way around it. Water changes course a lot.

Fear is evoked by the unknown. I enumerate a few below:

- There are business skills to learn. The entrepreneur may have never priced products. He has to learn to sell, never having sold anything. He has to discover the art of chasing customers to collect money, manage cash flows and so on.
- He may be anxious about recruiting key skillsets. Will he be able to afford them? Can he not learn and do the job?
- He has to compete with existing large companies (anything larger than a startup is large) and get into the choice set of customers.
- He could also be uncertain about the time it will take to create a business, whether the business will form as envisaged or need to change a great deal. He may be aware that he will confront unforeseen and potentially uncontrollable situations.
- Above all, he could be anxious about running out of money.

Entrepreneurs are not frozen by uncertainty. They focus on what they know. They simplify complexity by centering on a few things that need to be done, not letting many unresolved issues overwhelm them. Entrepreneurs progress their way into the future, adapting as they proceed. Their willingness to act relies more on intuition and judgment and less on rigorous analysis. They value real-world experimentation over analytic certainty. Uncertainty makes them work hard. They want to learn everything they don't know by doing it. They lean towards choosing low-cost and low-risk actions, not wanting to exhaust capital in sunk costs and time. They have doggedness and self-belief that they will build the organization around the business idea. Entrepreneurs engage in building an organization as they are creating a business. They are perpetually engaged with outsiders convincing them that they can do it, they will survive and it is not a risk working with them.

The dichotomous emotions that move back and forth between self-belief and fear before embarking on the entrepreneurial journey become extreme, euphoria and terror, as the business creation begins.[34] The entrepreneur learns to manage this intense vacillation. For every moment of joy and hope – when the first product is created, the first customer buys and entrepreneur receives revenue – to the survival uncertainty – when the business is running out of money, customers renege on their purchase intent or employees leave – entrepreneurs reflect on why they got into entrepreneurship. Their thoughts – which dwell on issues like their ability to meet payroll, reasons the business is not working, where they went wrong or even doubting their fitness to be an entrepreneur – are momentary. Entrepreneurs demonstrate the behavior to struggle, focus and slog to discover the goal. I use two images to depict the extreme contrasting emotions (Figure 29). These extreme and contradictory emotions recur during the business creation phase.

Figure 29. Extreme dichotomous emotions of the entrepreneurial journey

Fear	Euphoria

Entrepreneurs differ in how they think and feel when confronted with challenging and unknown situations. They either believe in themselves or doubt their ability to overcome the challenge. The confidence scale depicted horizontally, ranges from self-belief to self-doubt (Figure 30). Their feelings, as they confront challenges, span from being composed to being scared (Figure 30). In the figure I name the left lower grid as self-control; where an entrepreneur is self-confident and composed. I name the left-right grid as anxious; where he feels composed even though he has a self-doubt. I name the left upper grids as apprehension; where an entrepreneur has self-belief yet feels scared. I name the right upper grid as distress; where the entrepreneur has self-doubt and is scared. The spiral depicts that entrepreneurs go through myriad contradictory emotive states as they confront different unknown and complex situations when creating a new businesses. Entrepreneurs learn to manage extreme emotive states.

The interviews reflect this and the underlying aptitude as well as attitude.

Figure 30. The cyclical nature of contrarian emotions

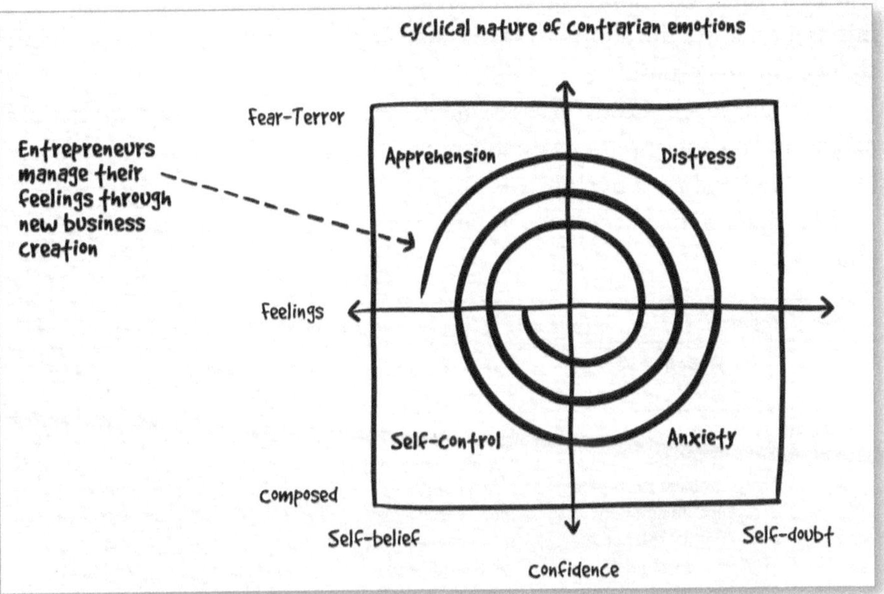

cyclical nature of contrarian emotions

Entrepreneurs manage their feelings through new business creation

Fear-Terror — Apprehension — Distress
Feelings
Self-control — Anxiety
Composed
Self-belief — Self-doubt
Confidence

Entrepreneurial Mindset

The way entrepreneurs see, think, act and learn is atypical. The way they recognize, find and make opportunities come to life is their unique difference. I emphasize 'make' because opportunities are discovered and created by entrepreneurs in the way they work. I label the way entrepreneurs approach and execute their work as the entrepreneurial mindset. This is very different from the way the term entrepreneurial mindset has been used. Financial Times[35] defines entrepreneurial mindset in a tautological way – it is a specific state of mind which orients human conduct towards entrepreneurial activities and outcomes. The use of the word 'orient' suggests a directional or positional view, a way of looking. McGrath and MacMillan[36] (2000) define entrepreneurial mindset as a way of looking (frame of mind) and thinking that enables identifying uncertain, yet high potential business opportunities and then exploiting the opportunities. They qualify high potential with high uncertainty and therefore unknowingness, implicitly attributing a novelty to a way of seeing. The emphasis is again on a way of seeing. The seeing of an opportunity is delinked from its realization. Once an opportunity is identified its realization becomes a project. McGrath and MacMillan[37] (2000) apply entrepreneurial ideas in corporate settings. Entrepreneurial mindset is characterized as an orientation of the mind towards opportunities, innovation and new value creation. The attitudinal characteristic of an entrepreneurial mindset includes the ability to take calculated risks and accept the realities of change and uncertainty.

This approach needs reassessment. There is a difference in the way managers and entrepreneurs establish new businesses. The way entrepreneurs identify and realize opportunity is unique.

Managers and entrepreneurs differ in how they create new businesses (Table 1).

Table 1. Comparison of how entrepreneurs seem to be working and how managers do new businesses

	What they do	How they work	Nature of questions they confront	What they achieve
Entrepreneurs	Define a problem and search for a solution – problem exists when implementation begins, solution is discovered during execution	When entrepreneurs start – rudimentary, intuition, analyze by doing (engaging with customers, suppliers, stakeholders, etc.) and adapt	Can I build it? Can I deliver it? Does anyone want it? What will they pay for it? What is the cost? Can I get enough customers?	Discover the business model through trial and error, then investment and scale-up.
Managers	Implement a solution to a problem – solution exists before implementation	When executives start – lots of detail, research, analysis, and decision trade-offs	I can build it. I can deliver it. I know what to price. I know the cost. I have a target number of customers.	Business model is known, investment follows business model assumptions, and then search begins for customers.

They differ in what they do and how they do it. In essence entrepreneurs 'implement and discover' and managers 'identify and implement.' Entrepreneurs also see opportunity. This is implicit in what they do. They are adept at framing opportunity. The 'seeing' is not deterministic as an endpoint; it is directional towards a fuzzy goal. The entrepreneurial skill is in how a business is realized and opportunity exploited. Figure 30 depicts the generic difference between managers and entrepreneurs implementing new businesses. Entrepreneurs and managers differ in how they think (cognitive – horizontal axis – Figure 31) and behave (behavioral – vertical axis – Figure 31). Entrepreneurial thinking is a mix of imagination and analysis; hence the scale of the cognitive dimension is from imagination to analysis. Entrepreneurial behavior extends from developing new products, taking them to market to scaling a growing company, i.e., exploration to managing operations. I name the two lower grids, where an entrepreneur imagines and explores as crafting and where he analyzes what he creates and does as discover/identify. I name the two upper grids, where an entrepreneur imagines and operates as skill acquisition through experiential learning and where he operates and analyzes as managing. The triangle of arrows represents how entrepreneurs work. They craft a product and take it to customers (operate) and then analyze outcomes. The vertical arrow represents how managers work. They identify an opportunity and manage its implementation.

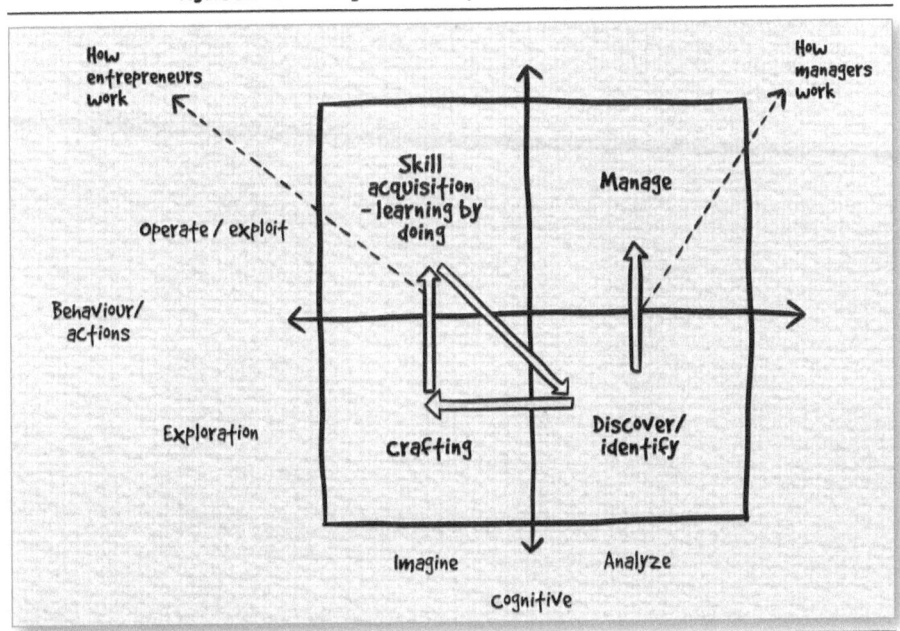

Figure 31. How managers and entrepreneurs implement businesses

Formica[38] (2015) explains this vividly. He differentiates path creators and pathfinders. Managers are pathfinders who search for a path on a map. A pathfinder is a problem solver. He uses existing knowledge to solve problems that are given as defined. Entrepreneurs are path creators; they create a new path to go where no one has traveled. Path creators, when confronted with a challenging situation, strive to acquire knowledge and redefine problems to create new ways to reach the goal. Figure 32 is a reproduction of an image from Formica[39] (2015) that portrays the difference. Pathfinders work with explicit knowledge – use rules, procedures, concepts and principles to develop strategies. Path creators use their intention, imagination and open-mindedness to perceive, intuit and develop novel insights.

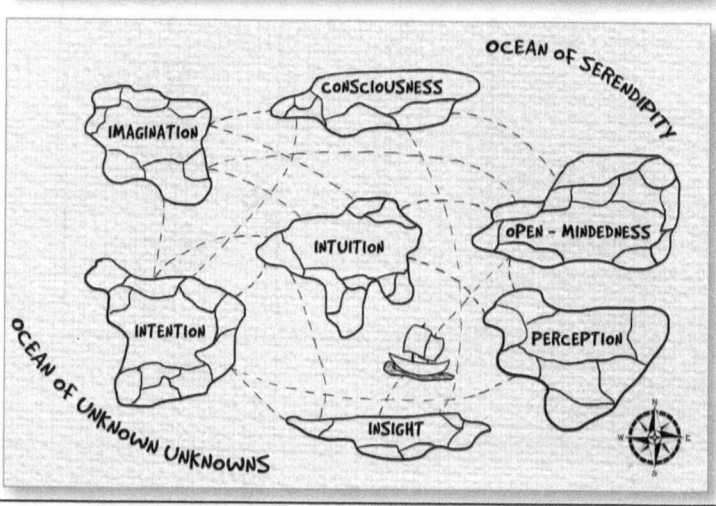

Figure 32. Top image Pathfinder bottom image Path-Creator

Sarasvathy[40] (2001) vividly contrasts entrepreneurs from managers. Sarasvathy[41] (2001) identifies two types of entrepreneurial thinking, labeled as causation and effectuation. She uses cooking of a meal to exemplify the difference between effectual reasoning and causation. Causation is exemplified when I choose an item in a menu and the chef prepares the dish by using the right ingredients and the defined recipe, i.e., the end goal, the dish, determines the way which is cooking with right ingredients. Effectual reasoning is exemplified if I tell the chef to make whatever he wants with whatever ingredients are available. The chef has an open-ended goal and has the opportunity to cook whatever he believes is possible with available ingredients. Transposing the example to entrepreneurship, with causal reasoning, entrepreneurs determine the goals to achieve and then acquire resources required. In effectuation, entrepreneurs use the resources available and choose a goal amongst the goals that they can possibly achieve.

> Causation processes take a particular effect (*outcome*) as given (*defined*) and focus on selecting...(a) means to create (*achieve*) that effect. Effectuation processes take a set of means (*resources*) as given and focus on selecting between possible effects that can be created (*achieved*) with the set of means.[42]

Managers exemplify causal thinking. Entrepreneurs, starting with lean resources, are effectual thinkers. The following two images (Figure 33) adapted from the Sarasvathy[43] (2001) contrast managerial and entrepreneurial way of thinking. Managerial thinking (left image) pivots around the defined goal. Their choice-making is about selecting a means – what should be done and how – that is efficient and effective. Sarasvathy[44] (2001) theorizes that entrepreneurs face the challenge of choosing from a variety of goals and means. They may begin focused on an end E1 (right image). After a few steps down this path, they learn and pivot. They decide to switch focus to end goal E2, by taking a detour as shown. They start with their skills, experience and networks as resources which are their set of means. They have to select the goal they wish to target. They select an efficient and effective way or means by doing and assessing outcomes. Entrepreneurs experiment to test ideas as well as assumptions and adapt. They tweak their ideas and/or target customers and adopt new ways of working to make the business work. Entrepreneurs don't start with brilliant ideas, they discover them.

Figure 33. Managerial and entrepreneurial thinking

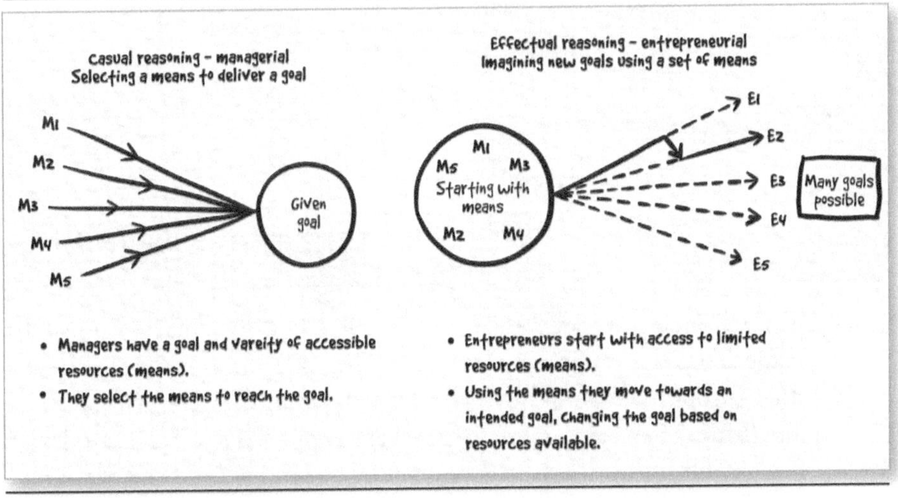

Casual reasoning – managerial
Selecting a means to deliver a goal

M1, M2, M3, M4, M5 → Given goal

Effectual reasoning – entrepreneurial
Imagining new goals using a set of means

M1, M2, M3, M4, M5 Starting with means → E1, E2, E3, E4, E5 Many goals possible

- Managers have a goal and variety of accessible resources (means).
- They select the means to reach the goal.

- Entrepreneurs start with access to limited resources (means).
- Using the means they move towards an intended goal, changing the goal based on resources available.

Mindset Powers Creation of New Business

Entrepreneurial mindset is the engine that powers creation of new businesses. The engine can be defined by attitudinal, emotional and behavioral characteristics. The entrepreneur is the organization when business creation starts. The knowledge of the entrepreneur is organizational knowledge. Business creation happens through decision making, actions and experiential learning of the entrepreneur. Entrepreneurs are flexible and agile learners. They confront situations where they need to adapt their original idea. They manage an emotional roller coaster of diverse emotions on the entrepreneurial journey. They change their frames of reference. The pace at which entrepreneurs learn and business creation happens is influenced by their motivations, attitudes, cognitive abilities and critical thinking skills. I have collated attitudinal and behavioral attributes observed in the interviews (Figure. 34). They are identified hereunder:

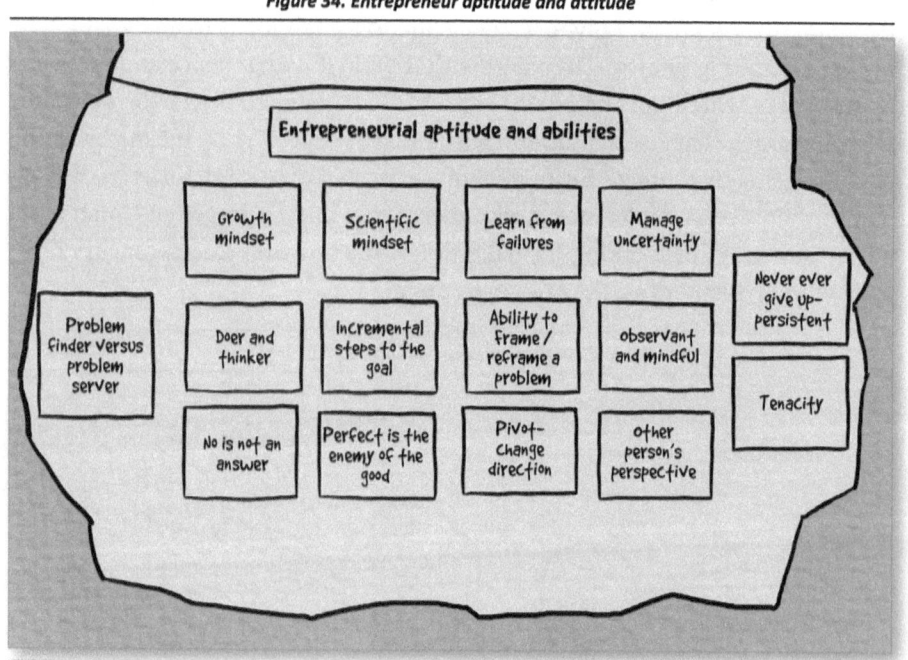

Figure 34. Entrepreneur aptitude and attitude

1. Entrepreneurs are self-aware individuals. They are conscious of skills/experience they have and don't have. They have tremendous self-belief that through effort, hard work and dedication they can learn and do anything. They have a growth mindset as opposed to a fixed mindset.[45]

2. Entrepreneurs are thinkers and doers, thinkers who enjoy executing. The willingness to learn by doing enables them to think at 30,000 ft. and descend into the weeds to implement their idea. Entrepreneurs are reflective doers.
3. Entrepreneurs accept a decline from a customer or stakeholder as a response. Decline is a better answer than no answer. A decline pegs them from where to restart in order to discover ways to get to acceptance.
4. Entrepreneurs demonstrate a scientific approach to business creation. Scientists test hypotheses through experiments. Entrepreneurs decompose business problems into small executable experiments to test and answer questions. They adopt an iterative and incremental approach to acquiring knowledge to build the business. They are rigorous, highly analytical, perceptive as well as pragmatic and search for what works.
5. Failure in business creation is an unanswered question. If things don't happen as planned, experiments fail; it is time for review, recalibrate and rework.
6. Entrepreneurs quickly meet customers with offers and proposals. They don't wait till they have created a perfect product. They are keen to get feedback and rework their offer, if required. Perfect is the enemy of good.
7. Entrepreneurs frequently question the path and direction they are taking for creating their business. Upon reflection they may reframe (redefine) their problem, pivot and head down a different path.
8. Uncertainty is implicit in new business creation. Entrepreneurs don't need to embrace uncertainty. It is their life. They manage it.
9. Entrepreneurs are hands-on in the creation of their business. They are in the middle of the action, mindful of what is happening and are unemotional observers of progress (and business measures) at the same time. Akin to surgeons, watchful, absorbed and objective.
10. Entrepreneurs are determined and motivated to achieve the goal of establishing a business. They relentlessly persevere to progress. Concurrently, entrepreneurs demonstrate a nimbleness to change direction if business assumptions are invalidated.
11. Entrepreneurs demonstrate a doggedness to progress. Nothing gets them down.
12. Entrepreneurs are adept at looking at their work from another person's perspective, i.e., perspective-taking. This facilitates negotiations as

they craft their offering, presentations and proposals to win the trust of stakeholders in the startup phase.

I present the following distinctive observations regarding the entrepreneurial mindset:

- Entrepreneurs demonstrate drive which is different from passion. Passion is a Ferrari in a garage, which is of no use.
- Entrepreneurs demonstrate a very high level of commitment to behavior. They are committed to what they want to achieve and what they have to do to get there.
- They have many questions and unknown factors related to their business.
- Building a business starts with entrepreneurs being confident about what they know. They also identify knowledge they need to acquire, i.e., what they don't know. They really don't know how much they need to know. As they start to implement the businesses, entrepreneurs realize the extent of their knowledge gaps. Customers and partners show them how much more there is to learn.
- They spend less time thinking about how to seek the right answer. They quickly find/intuit solutions that are roughly right and act, rather than being analytically correct before implementation and therefore slower. They discover the answers to their doubts and unknowns by doing.
- They prefer to act. They relentlessly pursue execution.
- They focus on continuous improvement and adaptation, till the business starts to take shape.
- They do and learn. The emphasis is on continuous learning.
- They emphasize results, not processes. They know it is better to right a wrong than to do nothing.

Summary

If one listens to entrepreneurs with established businesses talk, it may appear that they create businesses based on who they are, what they know, whom they know and what resources they can access.[46] These ideas emerged from research that engaged with 'expert' entrepreneurs.[47]

Is this thinking transportable to rookie entrepreneurs?

Rookie entrepreneurs start their entrepreneurial journey and decision making with the means at their disposal and a goal. They select their first customer based on whom they know and try to sell to him/her based on what they can deliver based on what they know. They can start the business with what they have. When they start the business, they rarely think in terms of potential returns from it. They also may not know how much they need to invest to create a running business. Their business plan, based on their assumptions, is invalidated in the first contact with customers. The goal which appeared within reach recedes into the distance and becomes fuzzy.

What happens after that?

Entrepreneurs adapt. They break down their business creation journey into smaller business activities. They engage with consumers, validate their business assumptions and establish the business. When deciding what to do, they think of what they need to do (action) and achieve (goal). Once they estimate what it costs, they gauge the plausibility of goal achievement. They then assess whether they can afford it. After which the risk of the activity failing or affordable loss[48] comes into play. Affordable loss is not a way of deciding what to do but a way of assessing the riskiness of the choice vis-à-vis resources being allocated. Roger Federer[49] once said, "You play the ball, you don't play the opponent." Focusing on affordable loss to decide what to do is akin to focusing on the opponent and not the ball. Affordable loss or downside risk of becoming an entrepreneur is what entrepreneurs think about when they decide to become entrepreneurs, at the moment of the plunge. Not when they decide what to do and how to do it. Entrepreneurs are adept at minimizing the scale of what they decide to do with the resources available.

From a macroscopic perspective new business creation can be visualized as a network of relationships created, anchored and used by the entrepreneur who builds his business by acquiring expertise, building and exploiting networks, as well as accessing financial resources. This is akin to using social, intellectual and financial capital to create a business. At a granular microscopic level entrepreneurs appear to be building their businesses progressively, learning by doing using the scientific method.

I believe that an entrepreneur is not heroic person, a visionary who is able to see farther into the future than the average person, of rarer genetic makeup, a predisposition to take higher risk, who works out a profitable opportunity better than others, bringing together financial resources, key people and capabilities that create a large and sustainable competitive advantage. I don't discount the role of who you are, what you know and who you know. I have sensed that entrepreneurs create businesses based on what they do, how they do it and how they learn by doing (Figure 35).

Figure 35. Complementary approaches to entrepreneurship.

Network of relationships | **Active progressive execution**

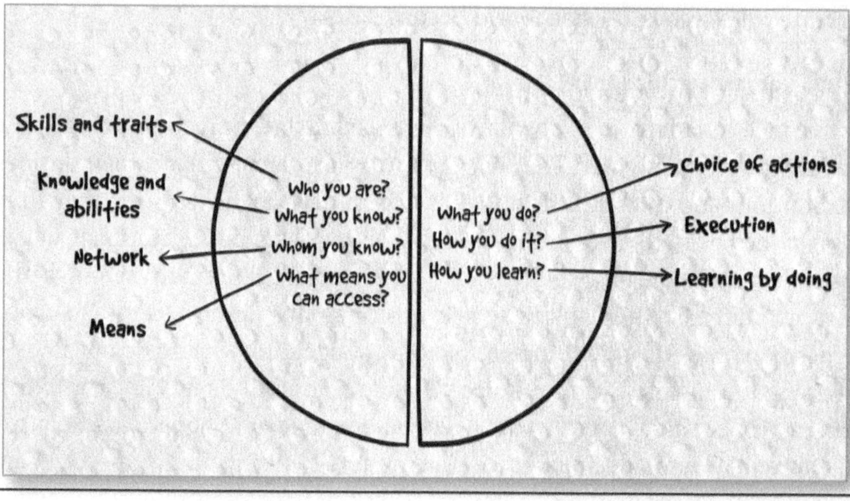

- Skills and traits
- Knowledge and abilities
- Network
- Means

- Who you are?
- What you know?
- Whom you know?
- What means you can access?

- What you do?
- How you do it?
- How you learn?

- Choice of actions
- Execution
- Learning by doing

SEE NEXT PAGE

An entrepreneur is an artist and a craftsman of new business. Entrepreneur is the chief protagonist. Entrepreneurs demonstrate situational alertness, awareness and intelligence. I present business creation as a learning journey of the entrepreneur. The business creation journey has four phases. Each phase has unique goals. The entrepreneur does different things to reach the goals. Business creation happens through recursive execution. Every action taken by the entrepreneur is a learning cycle, akin to scientific learning; he creates business hypotheses and validates them through execution.

Entrepreneurial mindset is a driver of business creation. I identify the attitudinal, behavioral and cognitive features that have manifested in the interviews.

I have visualized business creation as a three-tier model (Figure 36). Drawing upon my work with entrepreneurs and this reflective work, I now believe that entrepreneurial method is unique. It should be based on practice, moving away from emphasis on business plans and planning. Entrepreneurial methods can be learnt by everyone through practice. The caveat is that the insights shared are intuitive and are yet to be empirically verified.

FLIP OVER

Figure 36a. Iceberg of business crafting

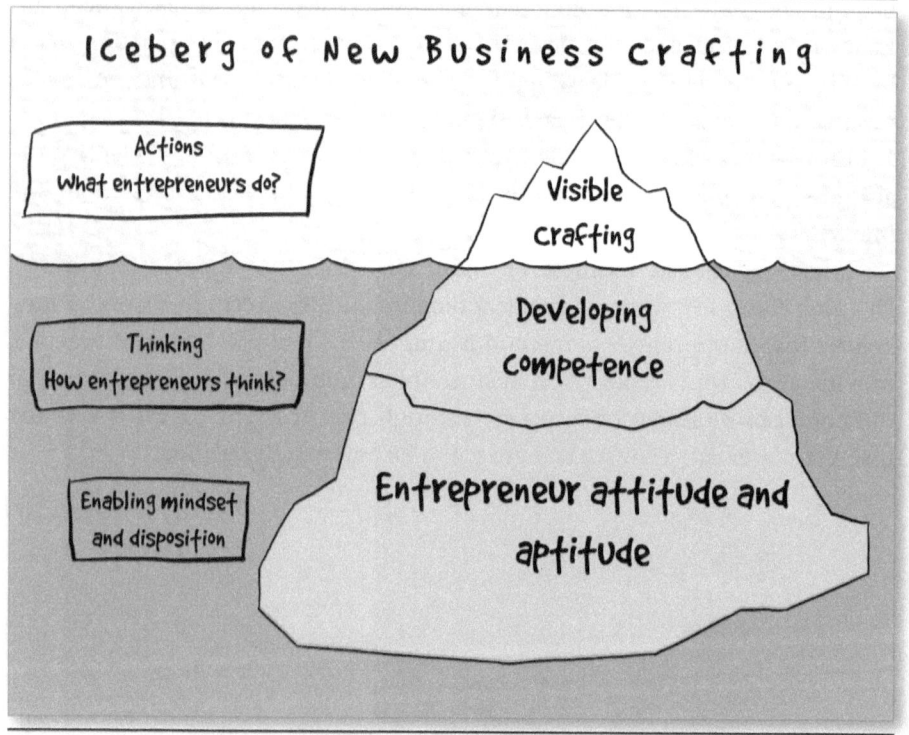

Figure 36b. Three-tiers of business crafting

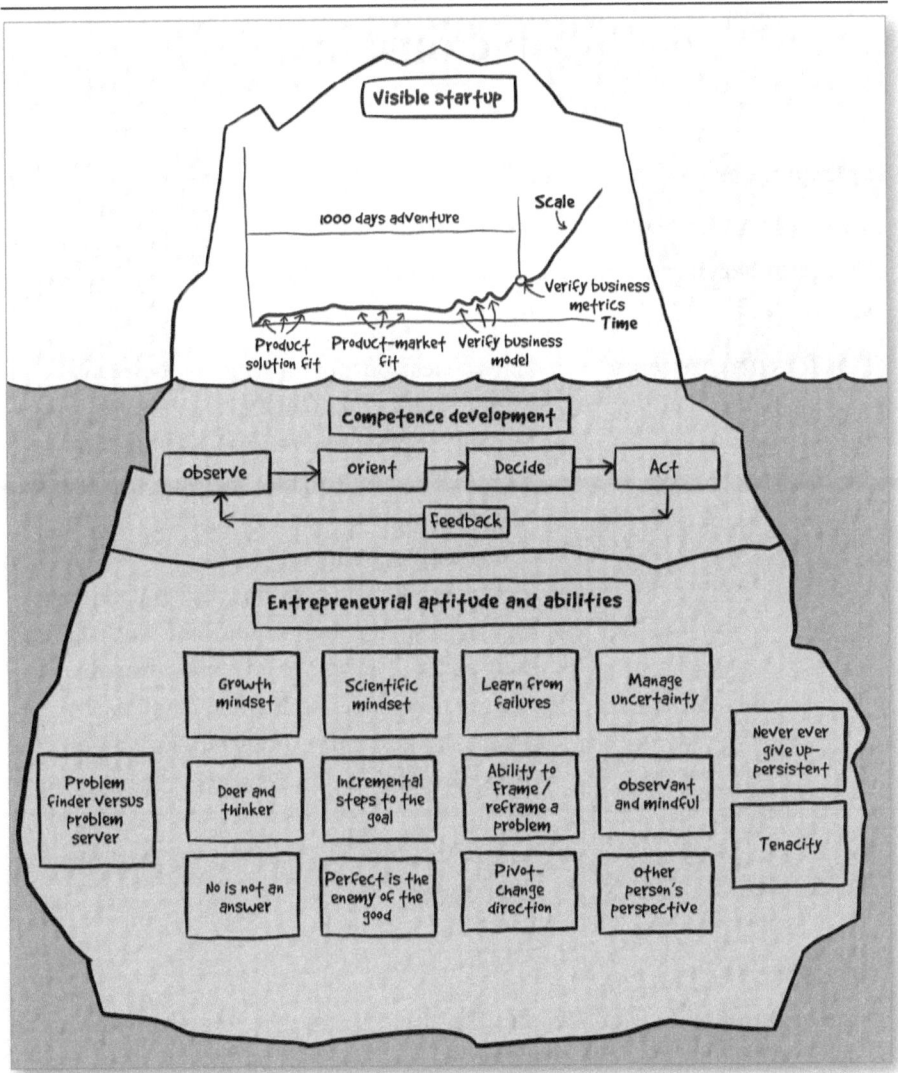

***

Work on Your Company, Not in Your Company

Entrepreneur	Ajesh Sivan
Company and website	Teksalah[1]/www.teksalah.com
Company services	IT infrastructure solutions
Year started	2007
Tips for entrepreneurs	• Have a clear purpose – why do you really want to start a company?
	• The initial years will require 100% focus 24 × 7/365 with irregular working hours and without holidays. Can you manage such a demanding schedule?
	• Be prepared for lots of unforeseen challenges.
	• Be driven to grow. You should be working 'on' your company and not 'in' your company.
	• Partnership agreements must detail each partner's roles and responsibilities, values, decision-making process and even an exit plan.
	• Use professional HR advice as soon as you can afford it.

Why 'Teksalah'?

In the beginning, it was a simple wish and a belief that something big could be achieved. The belief was based on the understanding that business and IT managers needed a technology partner with the combination of know-how and good service. We have now become a platform for growth of 'techno-passionate' team members. These individuals are positively transforming themselves and our customers. The vision now is to create a technology organization, built on goodness and contribute to the success of all.

---

1 Teksalah is a hybrid name, a combination 'Tek' for technology and 'salah' for advise in Urdu.

What do you do for an SME?

Today, information technology has become the backbone of every business – small, medium or large. All CRM, ERP, Email and Voice applications need a platform to run. It is very important that this platform is secure, always available and performing. The platform needs to be enterprise class and at the same time affordable for SMEs.

Teksalah provides innovative infrastructure solutions to the SMEs in the UAE, at the same level of quality as is provided to larger enterprises. We do this at a price point that is affordable to the SMEs. We have also expanded our SME portfolio by adding an SME ERP solution and managed desktop services.

When do customers start thinking of a hardware platform?

IT spending for businesses is mostly on the business applications that are visible. IT infrastructure is invisible. Most of the time, customers make mistakes before identifying the criticality of IT infrastructure. Software solutions partners also hesitate to highlight optimum infrastructure needs when selling their solutions; investment in infrastructure adds a cost to the evaluation. We are usually approached when things stop working. The ideal way for customers is to work with a specialized infrastructure partner in the early stages of planning, so that a solid foundation is built early.

How is Teksalah different?

In every project we do, we de-risk the customer by taking ownership of the entire engagement lifecycle. This is very important because in an information technology initiative there are multiple potential points of failure.

Our technically enabled sales team provides consultation, design engineers bring out the optimum design, project teams integrate and SLA teams provide ongoing support. We have adopted a global delivery model with most of our operational activities happening in our back office in India. This helps us offer our solutions cost-effectively. These factors have helped us maintain a near impossible 98% success rate for all projects executed.

How did you become an entrepreneur?

It was more of destiny than anything else. I was working at the time and during weekends, would attend courses to expand my learning.

We had a family friend who had spent over 35 years in Dubai. He offered AED 100,000 and urged me to start something of my own. Having seen my keen interest in technology, he would say there was some latent potential but I wouldn't take him seriously.

It so happened that the trainer of my weekend class, in a casual conversation, mentioned his plans of starting an IT business. The business did not take off as his investor backed out. I told him about the family friend. The capital came in and we became equal (50%) partners in the formation of the company. This was my first entrepreneurial experience.

Did you know how to price projects? You had no experience.

Our focus, when we started, was on technology training, leveraging the skills of my partner. Our investment was minimal. We rented the infrastructure and equipment. Our fixed cost was low. We offered training cost-effectively.

Training gave us the opportunity to interact with IT engineers and managers who were involved in IT decisions. They came, learnt about technology and started engaging us in their projects. From these interactions we learnt how the market was being priced for IT projects and services. This enabled us to learn and slowly develop our pricing strategies.

How did Teksalah come into being?

In the year 2007, my partner and I made a mutual decision to close the company and go our separate ways. The feeling that we had individually grown enough to create our own success drove the decision.

In May 2007, Teksalah was born and here we are today, serving more than 400 customers in the UAE and other ME countries.

Any lessons on how to partner?

Partnerships should be based on mutual trust, common vision and values. If your values are different and you think it will work out somehow, know that it never will. Things will get more complicated as you grow bigger. Just like any other partnership, a business partnership also requires high levels of compatibility, mutual respect and trust.

It is also important that you agree and detail (in writing) the terms of your partnership including each partner's roles and responsibilities, values, decision-making process, conflict resolution plan, profit sharing and even the exit plan.

How easy was it to restart?

I had four teammates when I restarted. They were enthusiastic, selfless and eager to learn. That became our foundation and strength. I had acquired knowledge about multiple domains and had built relationships with our clients. We had built credibility in the market, so there was extended support from our Vendors and Suppliers. They helped us a lot in the transition. All these factors worked positively to help us kick-start Teksalah.

What challenges did you face after you restarted?

The challenge came in the form of cash liquidity. We had to set up a new office, arrange salaries for the team and hire additional staff. We also needed cash to support projects which were executed on credit. But having made the decision to start, we set out as one team with AED 100K cash-in-hand and a personal loan of AED 200K.

Another challenge we faced was regaining customer confidence. Many customers were hesitant. They wanted to reconsider working with us. I introduced my team, the team we had built, and explained to them why we believed we could serve them. There were maintenance agreements with companies for which advances had already been paid to the previous company. We promised to honor the contracts by continuing the services for the duration of the contract, without seeking additional payment.

Over a period of time our quality of service rebuilt their confidence.

How has your HR experience been, considering Teksalah is a service business?

It has been a mixed one. I am directly involved in almost all recruitments. I have always gone by my gut feeling to determine a 'good' person. We look for values and commitment more than anything else. The excellent team today is a result of the value-based hiring decisions we made.

We also made many mistakes as we learnt that all good people are not necessarily good performers and also that good performers elsewhere may be unable to recreate their success with you. Another mistake was that we never tried to fit the person and their skills to the required job description. We also did not define our expectations from the employees. We also did not have enough measures of performance in place to warn us of a wrong recruit. We believed that people would create their own success given the opportunities.

I would advise any startup to engage a reputed HR team as soon as finances permit. HR is a specialized activity and with multiple activities that a startup demands, you may easily forget to focus on it and this could be very costly.

Is the IT network business a competitive market? Is it commoditized?

Surprisingly, no! Even though there are many IT companies, customers have a wide range of choice and hardware margins are thin. I feel that the IT network business is far from being commoditized because system integration service forms an unavoidable part, is complex and needs specialization. It is in this segment that you can prove your mettle and differentiate yourself from the rest of the players. Right skill and right service are still scarce. Clients value know-how and quality service.

How do you acquire customers?

Three ways. Our vendors, i.e., suppliers of products we integrate to offer solutions, work with us to create opportunities. When customers come to them searching for solutions, they often point them in our direction. Positive customer experience is priceless. Customer recommendation is the second way. The traditional way of a sales team prospecting for customers is the third.

Milestones of growth?

The growth of Teksalah has been organic. We are very conservative. Our focus has been on delivering quality service to all our customers, at all times. This has seen our turnover grow from AED 4 Million in our first year to AED 18 million now.

We have achieved premier partner status with all the vendors we represent. We are the first Platinum-certified partner in the Middle East for Riverbed. We have specialized partnerships with Cisco, Citrix, NetApp, Trend Micro and so on.

Creating the back office in India to manage accounts and order processing is another milestone.

And being a service business moving to a new larger office in the Business Village, adding high fixed costs believing in growth, was a big decision. It has given our team an inspiring and happy working environment.

What makes you an entrepreneur? Or you have been lucky – right place, right time?

I feel I have many more lessons to learn and need to still grow as an entrepreneur. I have been wonderfully lucky in the way the initial capital came, to be gifted with a wonderful team and to be associated with the growth initiatives in UAE. I was indeed at the right place at the right time. As I look back I also see that we have responded positively to opportunities that came our way by putting in absolute commitment, continuous efforts and a focused vision. All that we have achieved, I believe, has been a natural outcome.

Your strategy of change?

We are a knowledge centric organization and our biggest assets are our people. In an industry where attrition rates are high, I think the reason why the core team still finds Teksalah their home is because we could grow the organization at a fast pace and provide our team enough challenges as well as opportunities to grow within the company. After six successful years I feel it is time to accelerate our growth and replicate our success multifold. I am currently in the process of furthering the skills of the next line of leaders who will take Teksalah to greater heights. I am also securing investors who would be able to take Teksalah's presence and growth across the Middle East.

What worries you about the business?

The primary concern I have always had, ever since the economic downturn, is payment collection and management of cash flows. Even during the hard times, Teksalah never had to delay a single supplier payment and has always paid salaries on time. Being able to continue doing so is very dear to me.

An Accidental Entrepreneur's Journey

Entrepreneur	Akanksha Goel
Company and website	Socialize/www.socializeagency.com
Company Services	A creative agency specializing in digital communications companies
Year started	2010
Tips for entrepreneurs	• Listen to what your customers want. • Focus and refine your value proposition. • Don't be sidelined by social media. It is a part of the marketing mix. • Social media is cost-effective for startups. Once business picks up, balance marketing expenditure across channels.

If I was a company requesting your services, tell me what you do and what I will pay you for.

Socialize is a boutique digital media agency and training house. We teach and help businesses harness the power of online platforms/tools to drive innovation in their marketing communications.

Typically, you would pay us to:

- Create content about your brand/products and seed that via online communities to reach potential customers and drive sales.
- Manage your brand's presence on social networks and build digital ecosystems that will help you have a dialogue with your consumers and create brand preference.
- Develop games, websites and applications that allow you to engage consumers and build a database.

In some cases, you may also pay us to train/consult you on best digital media practices, so that you can manage the execution of the strategy in-house.

How do you assess effectiveness of digital campaigns?

It depends on why we designed and executed a campaign. The key performance indicators for every campaign are different. For companies that are looking to drive brand awareness, we measure success with the impressions that a campaign received. In cases where retail brands want to drive sales, we measure the conversion between online marketing and offline footfall (using e-coupons/vouchers). Or sometimes when clients want to build databases and engage consumers, we use innovating applications/games and measure the hits and participation it received. The beauty of digital media is that it is very measurable and versatile.

Where did the idea of the business emerge from?

I sort of tumbled into it.

I studied marketing communications in Singapore. I worked with one of my professors on a paper on how Web 2.0 was redefining culture across Asia and how consumers in different countries use the web differently. This was in 2006 and there were very few people talking about the nuances of Web 2.0. Being one of the early adopters, I had an opportunity to present my paper at Stanford and thanks to my professor Michael Netzley, I was interviewed on a podcast by Mitch Joel, who was one of the pioneers in our industry. This helped me get a job in Singapore as editor of STUFF magazine and eventually in 2008 get offered a position in Dubai to lead the marketing team for a CRM/Loyalty company. With the financial crisis just having hit the region, we first had a 10% salary cut followed by a 30% cut. At 30% my ego started to hurt. I was worth more.

Meanwhile, I was also being invited to speak about digital media by Murdoch University, Knowledge Village and other local organizations. I was surprised to see 250 people register for one of the events.

When things started to get rough at work, I thought, 'Clearly there is a demand for social media. I am doing talks and trainings. There is a gap in the market for digital media education, why not monetize this rather than just moonlighting'. I got a call about the 30% cut on 7th Jan 2010, a Thursday evening. I stayed awake till 4 am the next morning, came up with the brand name 'Socialize' and identified what it would do. We would train companies on harnessing the power of social media. My master plan was to have Socialize as a sub-brand within my employer's company. A nice way to make my employer more money and in return hopefully, nullify the company-wide salary cuts. By 9th Jan, Saturday, I had designed a logo using basic powerpoint, created a website using wix.com and had a business plan, thanks to my business school education. On Sunday I told my CEO, 'I have a solution to our financial problems.' Then I reached out to our press contacts about the new division. Within the month, we were on the first page of Gulf Marketing Review as 'Social Media Training

Unit launches in Dubai.' The day the article ran we got a call from Swarovski and DIFC to come and talk about social media. Within 3-4 months, this new adventure called 'Socialize' was making more money than the entire division. However, the cash cycle of the service industry became an issue. In the service industry clients pay after 60 or 90 days. We had to invest and had an outflow of money before the revenue came in. And my company failed to pay me my salary. That was when epiphany hit me. Socialize was my brainchild. It was time to move on from living paycheck to paycheck and start living adventure to adventure. I decided to resign and start Socialize again. I had started the brand as a part of the company, so I thought the company owned the name. They were magnanimous and said, 'You can keep the name, it is your brand.'

From digital media training to a digital media agency, how did that happen?

After I started doing trainings, companies started asking us to go beyond consulting and execute the strategy. Initially we stayed clear of this, as I believed that every brand must invest in owning and managing their brand voice online. However, our hesitation flew out of the window when we were asked to execute a campaign for one of my favorite consumer technology brands, by their advertising agency. The campaign targeting youth via social media, was a success. This changed everything. Within a month we signed on two other international consumer tech brands to manage their digital media communities and campaigns. This is how our journey began.

How did pricing develop for something with no benchmarks?

Like how the best inventions happen: trial and error. It wasn't based on structured man-hour calculations or the various models they teach you about in business school. I learnt pricing when I had to price our training courses. I researched, speaking to people to find out the correct price for training. We won contracts at the price we pitched and our prices for trainings have not changed since. I followed the same discovery process for pricing agency work. There were no benchmarks, as we were the first dedicated social media agency in the region. The price I estimated through networking was completely out of sync from what the market was willing to pay. Customer reactions told me that pricing needed correction. I reduced prices till customers were comfortable buying our services.

Our pricing is the PR agency model; a retainer where clients pay us for a menu of services. Additional services, like digital production, media buying and blogger programs are paid for separately.

How much did you invest in Socialize?

I had managed to save up about 60,000 Dirhams when I resigned. I put every penny into a free zone trade license, online software to manage finance, business cards, a hot spot courtesy the Free zone and worked from home. Now that we have a team of over thirty-five people, with a real office, I can admit that the first two people I hired (in 2010) worked out of my extra bedroom. This was a perfect setup, till the building security started asking too many questions! We then sublet, shared an office with another company by bartering our digital media expertise for office space.

Your business was incubated in a job. When did you feel it could become a larger business?

When I got a phone call from DIFC I felt, 'Maybe I have done something right.' And then when we got our first check, which was more than I made in a month, I felt this could be something.

You didn't plan your business. How has it picked up momentum?

I fell into business, despite myself and not as an active initiative. The growth that Socialize has had follows a similar path. We don't actively seek out business; we discover 'it' along the way with the new opportunities that present themselves, every day.

I like to experiment. Everything I have really done in my life I start by trying. I do a lot of research and try to put ideas together, always thinking of a solution. To others I may appear mercurial because I am flitting from idea to idea. Maybe it is this constant churning that has helped Socialize grow.

Also, we entered the market at the right time. First-mover advantage. We grew our service offering organically. When enough clients asked for a service, we hired people who could provide that. We never took on additional fixed costs, before signing on new business. This allowed us to have a healthy cash flow. For example, when clients wanted to invest in digital production and Facebook applications, we in-sourced a development team. Decisions and agency offering emerged as a result of our clients' needs. Till date, we are completely self-funded and have a conservative approach to business expansion. Serving our existing clients' needs is more important to us than growth and expansion. In return, this approach has given us a nation-wide reputation for good work and allowed me to have the bandwidth to still personally be involved in all of our clients' digital media strategy recommendation and executions.

How is Socialize organized?

We are very un-ad agency like. We have always had a very horizontal structure, with few departments and fewer hierarchies. However, as we grow, I have to rethink this. In the past our client servicing team could also double up as planning, creative and business development! However, now with shifting technology and a fast-growing industry, we have to add specializations and silos. It's not ideal, but as we grow the challenge is to provide big agency competencies, while maintaining our boutique agency flexibility.

Self-reflect, what drives you? You became an accidental entrepreneur.

I think a part of it is my upbringing. I was brought up in a very competitive environment. I once scored 99% in a math paper and my grandmother asked me, 'What happened to the 1%?' I don't come from a wealthy family. I have seen my parents have financial troubles. This pushed me to work hard and make it on my own. I had to. My passion and ambition drive me. Thankfully, ambition is never fully realized, because the day you stop dreaming and stop planning is the day you stop living and start surviving.

Also, I am a perfectionist, so I can drive myself mad and other people too. Anyone at Socialize will tell you that. At the same time, I think that's one of the reasons we are successful. It takes a funny kind of obsession, an insatiable hunger, to be the best.

What is your management style?

I know entrepreneurs who chase numbers and their '3 year plans'. I don't. Maybe it's because I don't know better – but for now Socialize is the reason I love going to work every morning. It is more than a business. So, I think my management style reflects that. It is hands-on, decentralized and participatory. I spend time hiring the right people and then empowering them to do the best for our clients. The team decides how we bill our clients, based on the value we add and effort, not a goal that we need to chase for our balance sheet.

Staffing, is it easy?

Not at all. In a service industry, your best assets go down the elevator every evening. Not only is finding the right talent, in a new industry, challenging – but it is equally challenging to keep them loyal. The strawberry generation as the Chinese call them, are rarely loyal to their jobs and would move to a new position for even small salary increments.

It is a very competitive industry and everyone is vying for the same pool of talent, since there are very few media practitioners regionally that understand digital marketing. We use our social media channels to get the word out about new opportunities – but investing in a good recruitment agency has served us well.

How did you manage the cultural understanding of the Arab world?

With more than fifteen nationalities at the agency, it sometimes feels like a cultural melting pot.

I am sensitive to the fact that I am an Indian expat in an Arab environment. It is important that our clients work with an agency whose leadership understands its core target audience. Thus, we have hired a competent team that comes from different parts of the region and compensates for any lack of cultural understanding I may have. Over the last five years, my friends, my team and our clients have helped me gain a deeper perspective of this unique region and culture.

How many companies work with you?

While the number keeps changing, we have typically had approximately 43- 45 brands annually on retainer.

Starting a Low Margin Competitive Business in a Recession

Entrepreneurs	Sheikh Mohammed Al Thani, Albert Dias and Sachin Gadoya
Company and website	Musafir/www.musafir.com
Company services	A premium experience travel website
Year started	2007
Tips for entrepreneurs	• Things rarely work according to plan. • Get ready for higher costs and lower revenues. • Plan for the unknown.

Interview with Albert Dias

How did it begin?

It began over a discussion at Starbucks; three classmates from American University of Sharjah meeting after a period, searching for ways to make a difference. Post University Sheikh Mohammed bin Abdullah Al Thani and Sachin Gadoya had started a travel company and I had gone into advertising. The opportunity was simple – bring the ease of an Expedia and Travelocity to the region. Musafir is an online travel company, different from an 'agency'. We offer travel services both the 'traditional' way- through offices and online.

If I need a ticket, how are you different?

A customer with simple travel needs, getting from point A to B, doesn't require a significant amount of handholding. He wants to be able to choose amongst different options. An online travel site reveals these options. We believe that options and prices are key purchase criteria.

Musafir is a local outfit with brick and mortar presence. A customer can connect with us on phone or visit us.

Help me understand the value that Musafir adds.

Musafir online is still predominantly a business travel company. About 80% of our business today comes from corporate customers where our service is a differentiator. We take care of all the peripheral needs of the clients relating to travel that make the journey comfortable and hassle-free – seats, meals, ground transportation and lodging.

With our large customers we are able to negotiate better deals with the airlines and hotels to pass on discounts to customers. Our pre-purchase price is a differentiator.

Once a customer has chosen an Online Travel Agency (OTA) the purchase process and experience is similar amongst the OTAs.

A company makes a choice to work with Musafir. How does it work?

We build our business by building relationships with companies. We have a team that goes and introduces our value proposition – online services complemented with a human touch, an accessible person who can visit the office if needed as well as a brick and mortar presence. Companies always work on competitive terms. Once they choose us, we empower them to use the website using a login. We offer a self-service and a serviced proposition.

If a customer is hands-on, he can do his travel bookings personally. Or he can call, speak to a designated travel coordinator and do bookings. With a CRM underlying Musafir, all the client needs – seat requests, frequent flier numbers, timing preferences, meal needs – are visible to the travel coordinator, making the engagement efficient.

Musafir offers customers an opportunity to reserve their initial travel choice without buying a ticket- what I call a post-decision pre-purchase option. This is advantageous because a consumer may not be sure about the travel date but doesn't want to lose out on a good flight option.

Does Musafir integrate with Client Company IT systems, HR processes and accounts giving them an in-house travel portal?

We believe that the integration model is applicable to large companies. Smaller companies need cost-effective solutions. We are an independent web-based service. We do not integrate into the back-end HR processes and accounting systems. The client can establish these processes on Musafir.com.

How does Musafir actually work?

We primarily work with Amadeus, a Global Distribution System (GDS) behind Musafir, to facilitate flight purchases. Once a customer provides details, the system 'talks' to consolidators and airlines to find the best options, agglomerates and displays them. To this extent we are similar to every other travel site.

We have added options on top of the standard options that GDS churns out. If a customer chooses to find flights ex-Dubai, we also show flights ex-Sharjah, presenting a value proposition. The system is engineered for intuitive intelligence, stepping in and understanding customer needs.

Does Musafir offer home-to-home service – identify all the services needed on the journey?

If a customer sitting in his room says, 'I want to fly to XYZ in the next 5 hours or 5 days,' we can take care of transfer to airport, arrange visas where possible, upon arrival at the destination take care of transfer from the airport to hotel and make arrangements for the stay. And on the return trip, bring you home.

The present Musafir site offers flight and hotel booking services. Corporate customers can choose an option to contact us for additional services. We do the same offline.

How did you become an entrepreneur?

I will say frustration and it is the truth. I had an opportunity to become an entrepreneur the day I graduated. I spent 4 years in advertising, learning how the world works. It brought with it a certain degree of frustration. I was working 60–70 hours a week and wondered why I couldn't do it for something I was passionate about.

Capital?

Sheikh Mohammed and Sachin are lead investors. I am the minority. They are providing patient capital, focusing on innovation and new offerings.

You had an advantage. They had an existing travel agency. You didn't have to go searching for and negotiating with suppliers. You just had to build a platform.

True. But this accelerated execution milestones. We had to get ourselves off the ground with a beta product in six months. This took nine. We issued our first ticket on Dec 17th, 2008.

We had set a goal of becoming profitable within 18 months. We quickly learnt the costs of running the business were twice of what we planned and the profit, almost half of what we expected. Entrepreneurs underestimate costs and overestimate profits. We became profitable in 2011, after three years.

Did Sheikh Mohammed and Sachin take a bet on you? You had the brainpower, without capital. They had a running business.

Sheikh Mohammed and Sachin had a vested interest in the success of Musafir. They wanted to do the OTA business. They took a leap of faith investing in Musafir. I was making a financial commitment and taking a personal risk even though the model had worked elsewhere.

It was never really a question of whether your risk is greater than mine. We genuinely believed that the service was a worthwhile offering. The question of whether we will succeed or fail never crossed our mind. More of how we will succeed.

I labor this point because expanding product offering in an existing company is not blue blood entrepreneurship. I see you as an entrepreneur and your partners as investors.

I led Musafir in giving the product life, with my partners. While I may be more hands-on, they took a very active role in giving me an understanding of the travel industry, which I did not have. Sheikh Mohammed was very involved, given his role with Air Arabia. They know how the industry works from the inside.

Where did you develop the IT platform?

This is a differentiator of Musafir. We fixed an early question – do we put in 'X' amount of money and buy a platform off-the-shelf or do we invest '10X' and craft it in-house? This was not an easy decision because of the risks. One needed to look at it objectively, from the investors' and company's perspective. And we chose early on to go with the 10X option, craft a product right here in the UAE because it would give us IP in terms of a platform to build a company on and an opportunity to have a product that we could retail.

You used the word craft. Why?

We crafted the user experience. When we started we asked ourselves questions at each step of the customer journey, 'Is this the way a customer chooses or does that?' Take the example of showing prices with the schedules of alternative ticketing options. Our competitors used to show prices after the flight choice was made. This was not the way companies worked. They balanced costs with comfortable schedules. Subtle differences were engineered at numerous points.

Any challenges?

When we started in December 2008, we targeted the online consumer segment. The travel industry, for years, had operated on a commission driven model, but then the zero commission model happened in UAE in 2008. Customers were hesitant to pay for services they had taken for granted earlier or for what they could do themselves online. Our income stream just dried up. Plus, in September 2008 global recession hit the travel business hard. Suddenly the returns in the online consumer travel market were negative on transactions. We pulled back from online consumer travel in 2009 and shifted our attention to the corporate business, but resumed the former again in 2013.

You changed the business model?

2009 was not an easy year; very unsettling when the basis of the business changes. In August 2009 we questioned ourselves. We doubted ourselves. We wondered what happened to the confidence that the business would work. This was when the association with Universal Travels & Tourism (brick and mortar agency of the other two cofounders) and expertise of Sheikh Mohammed and Sachin came in handy. They guided the switch towards a corporate business model. They had intuited the model for three years. The recession accelerated the implementation.

Did you run out of money?

There were times when we were cash-strapped. It was a tough learning experience. I had to demonstrate the profitability and valuation of the business. I read an article from India where entrepreneurs were raising money of businesses with negative income, based on multiples of the number of customers. We need to demonstrate real income.

What was your customer acquisition strategy for the business?

We expected our retail presence to be the driver. We believed that the customers would come to us, a lot of them through the corporate customer base. With Musafir there was a lot of learning. I had been on the product side of business, never on the acquisition side. Acquiring customers was learning experience and quite an expensive one at that. We learnt very quickly that the cost of customer acquisition was high. We had taken it for granted but that is why the real cost of the business was a surprise.

And the expansion into India?

Our expansion into India wasn't originally intended. Our dream was to become the MENA region's leading travel portal. In 2010 my co-founder Sachin had an opportunity to be a ticketing sponsor for the Rajasthan Royals cricket team. It didn't quite add up. We are a travel company and we got into ticketing of cricket in India. We just decided to do it. It required a little technological effort. We said that if anything, we will learn how to do business in India. The sponsorship created a buzz. The experience taught us the sheer scale of the mid-income mass consumer. From that point on, through 2010, we slept on the idea. We were uncertain about going in. From the outside, the Indian travel market looked very competitive and saturated. We set a return rate that was slightly less optimistic and established it in 2010.

What is the source of revenue?

In our corporate model we earn 60% from service fees, 30% from airline incentives and the remainder from partners/distributors. Hotels currently make up only a small fraction of total gross sales. The revenue is driven by customers and this defines where our loyalties should lie; servicing customer needs and not airlines' demands.

What worries you about your business today?

Price pressure. This is the number one worry for anyone in the OTA industry. Customers walk away if we are unable to match market prices. Service is still not valued.

Do you see India defusing your attention on the business?

Yes. It is not easy setting up a new market. In UAE we, the cofounders, have always been here on the ground. None of us are in India. My attention was torn between both markets earlier this year, but we've become more focused with the growth of our teams.

How have you changed as a person?

I would like to believe that I am who I was when I started. From a business point of view, I have grown more cynical. I have learnt that optimism is good to have but is difficult to achieve and sustain. The entrepreneurial journey is tough. It requires a lot of hard work to get to the goal. Sometimes when you discuss goals other people's eyes seem to be asking, 'Are you dreaming?'

Complete Disregard for the Impossible

Entrepreneur	Amer Qavi[2]
Company and website	SwipeZoom/www.swipezoom.com
Company services	SwipeZoom is an online payment processor and a logistics company for cross-border e-commerce across the world. SwipeZoom manages store-to-door logistics in 238 countries, payment processing in 120 currencies, 14 payment methods, duties and taxes in 76 countries and customs brokerage in every border crossing.
Year established	2011
Tips for entrepreneurs	• Solve problems. • Even if it is a chance in a billion, it is still a chance. • Don't get attached to an idea. Businesses are crafted. • Everyone has ideas. Entrepreneurs fearlessly execute. • Be open and observe; opportunities are everywhere. • Structure a business, assign responsibilities, allow people to make mistakes.

Where was entrepreneurship in you?

After returning to Dubai in 1991, I joined a regional trading company. Got tired and left in 1995 to start my medical distribution business. That was all I knew. It was easy and some principals followed me.

I thought business was simple – buying from A, selling to B and making a margin. But everything gave me a jolt. I had to teach myself about accounts, balance sheets and P&L accounts – the granular stuff. I learnt that the

---

2 SwipeZoom is his third business.

foundation of business is people-to-people relationships. Today I would rather have few suppliers and customers, each with a deeper business relationship.

I had to teach myself all of this. I learnt, searching for solutions when problems cropped up.

The business grew till 1999 when I needed bank facilities. My banker wanted a balance sheet. I appointed an auditor who did the accounts using the bits of paper I had accumulated. He commented upon completion, 'You seem to have done well. I think you can sell a part of your company.' Two weeks later he got me an offer. I sold half the company. This took place in 2000. In 2002 the relationship with the investor came to an abrupt, messy end. My investors were from a different industry and couldn't figure out my business. I was running the show. They took over the company because they had the option to capitalize every cash infusion into the company. After the split I had nothing but the fillings in my teeth.

Your decision to sell a trading company was odd.

I wanted to feel and believe that I was doing well.

I was also in an industry that had few buyers and many sellers, plagued with rampant price discounting and problem of delayed payments. A distributor in this region ends up becoming the buyer's bank. I was not mentally prepared to take a risk on receivables.

Then?

I started again in the same field, avoiding all the mistakes.

Example?

I learnt not to get emotionally intense about my business. As an owner you think you can always do everything better, with a greater attention to detail. You end up micromanaging, controlling everything.

I was able to refine and perfect my pitch to various stakeholders at different points of the company's lifecycle; whether it was with customers, suppliers or banks. I knew what they wanted, why they wanted it and what they would like to hear and see.

Learning about investors?

I'm thankful to the investors for giving me a tough time. If they hadn't, I would have become complacent. I scaled the new business in just 8 months, instead of the 7 years it had taken me earlier.

Why a new business?

I streamlined the new business in 2006 and felt that I had the bandwidth to do something new. I partnered with a friend to start a food business, of which I had zero experience. I thought it was a common sense thing.

We opened doors in 2007. What started as a fast food concept grew into something that we could have never imagined. We now supply ready-to-eat meals under two different labels. We have about 180 different items that are sold every day across all major supermarkets. The business continues to grow without my involvement.

Why SwipeZoom?

I started SwipeZoom sensing an opportunity, without a business idea. I envied entrepreneurs who say they love what they do. I hadn't found that niche. I wanted to do something really interesting. Doing something that I hadn't done before was not a deterrent. I realized that every industry needs a new pair of eyes to innovate. I also experienced ideas changing during implementation. The key was to start, learn and develop.

For your first business you had domain expertise and networks with customers and suppliers. What was the business model – trading or indenting? Did you have adequate capital?

I managed to pre-sell something just when I was at the cusp of starting the new business. I started the business with £1850. Cash was advanced to me by a customer who came for a medical exhibition. He visited a booth, saw something he liked and wanted. I promised to get it for him. I visited the manufacturer, managed to convince him for the agency and to sell me the display piece. I purchased it for £1400 with 30 days credit and resold it for £1850. I deposited the cash received, issued two checks, one with a 10-day window and then worked hard to sell to generate cash.

Stress helps the brain focus. I ran after doctors, hospitals and private clinics. For survival, I couldn't wait for government tenders. I concentrated on the private sector. I sat with many decision makers, learning to read body language, interpreting whether I was going to make the sale or not.

What else?

I made assumptions and mistakes and learnt. I was young and caught up in window dressing. I thought it was very important to have an office in a great location, even though we didn't have customers visiting us.

How did you select the products to distribute?

I had been pigeonholed by my previous employer as a product specialist. I was going into operation theaters with doctors, teaching them how to use equipment. I specialized in surgical equipment for ophthalmology. When I started my own company, I was a product specialist on lasers; products that had not yet entered the mainstream. This was my opportunity. I pushed the envelope in whatever I did, focusing on newer technologies and their adoption.

Why would a supplier deal with you?

Every salesperson wants bigger numbers every year. People want to know if you can pay them, sometimes in advance, pick up the product and give them bigger numbers than they're getting right now.

How do you manage the trading business with a team?

I separated purchasing and sales. The salesperson is unaware of the product cost and supplier terms. He should focus on customers and not be in a position to put 'internal' pressure on price to achieve sales numbers. Similarly, the buyer should not be aware of the final selling price. This is my modus operandi.

The entry barrier to get into trading is low. I was paranoid about this. I couldn't control external competition but I didn't want to create new competition from within- employees starting businesses. I also have to develop personal relationships with suppliers and customers. If one of my employees were to connect with them, they should revert.

What was the difference in Biryani Express?

We launched Biryani Express when the rental costs of outlets were sky-high and traffic congestion was endemic. We were going to take the food to the people. We planned a hub-and-spoke distribution model for Biryani. A central kitchen would pre-cook Biryani. And vans, modified internally with a chiller and microwaves, would deliver fresh hot Biryani. Each van was planned as a profit-center to service a neighborhood. A central kitchen would support many vans in the city, each van creating brand visibility. A call center would handle orders transferring instructions to vans, proximate to the customer, for delivery.

What happened?

We were selling Biryani in its myriad variations. No customer eats Biryani three times a day. The menu needed variety.

You created an innovative model, but this required a certain degree of investment. How were you sure it would pay back?

I have never been one for fancy business models and analysis. I rely a lot on gut judgment. I left all the number crunching to my partner. We were looking at a 3–4 year payback. We knew we would need to venture into other products. What I didn't know was what those products would be.

In every single business I have started I have never stuck to the original idea. It just morphs and multiplies. Majority of our business is now B2B.

How did the food business morph over time from B2C to B2B?

A customer visited our kitchen and said, 'You have all this empty space and all you are doing is Biryani. Could you supply us with additional products?' Today we make 180 items – snacks, gourmet sandwiches, salads and open food sold at deli counters. Biryani is branded as Biryani Express. Everything else is sold under The Daily Gourmet label.

What is SwipeZoom?

SwipeZoom is solving a simple problem. If a customer in Dubai orders a shirt from a US retailer he often gets a message that his card is unacceptable or they don't ship to Dubai. SwipeZoom solves the problem of a retailer who wants to sell internationally but wants to do nothing beyond the transaction. SwipeZoom does everything else. We enable retailers around the world to sell and ship products internationally by eliminating all obstacles in payments, logistics and customs, via a single relationship.

You make money doing the physical work or IT work?

SwipeZoom has a transactional business model. We make money only when the transaction happens. We are a payment service provider that also does logistics. This requires networking with organizations across the world to make things happen in a cost-effective and efficient way. We have created a solution that has over 5300 customs and shipping related documents that exist on the planet. For example, there are 169 types of invoices in the world today. We ensure that the automated paperwork for every transaction is correct in terms of content, format and language. We are integrated with logistics companies and have 62 brokerage relationships around the world. This enables us to give the end customer a guaranteed landed cost calculation and the capability to prepay that at the time of the transaction. SwipeZoom ensures exchange rate transparency so the customer gets an exact price at checkout in his or her local currency with no hidden transaction costs.

Team building in a new domain?

The key has been to recruit a team to implement an idea. I had a very simplistic view of the solution when I started. I found out quickly that I needed people with skills in each sub-sector of IT; software architecture, developers, quality assurance, networking and hardware. Other skillsets I hired included trade compliance, risk management and treasury management. I found my whole team on social media. I was careful. I wanted experienced people. I didn't want people to come and learn with me. My learning was good enough!

Are you now focusing on return on this investment?

Consciously, no. Subconsciously, maybe. I am crafting a business model. This is not what I expected to do two years ago when I started thinking about this. I was thinking about just logistics. Then I discovered issues with payments and currency fluctuations. Then it was online payment fraud. Bits kept getting added.

I can't assume the role of an investor as yet and test every decision with ROI criteria. Nothing will get done. I suspect that will happen when revenues start to flow.

How did you convince Visa, MasterCard and others to work with you?

I had to fill out a lot of forms! But when it comes to decision making, subjectivity creeps in. My business model didn't exist, so nobody knew how to handle me. They asked me about the numbers of merchants I handled. I said none. Many heated chicken and egg situation conversations ensued. It took 9 months before I finally won the arguments.

Will I see SwipeZoom when I go to an online retailer?

You will see 'Powered by SwipeZoom' at the bottom of the page. And we will be in the 'Terms & Conditions' of the sale. We will have visibility on the boxes that reach customers too. We do want the customer to know about us.

How are you going to convince retailers to buy the idea?

International or cross-border e-commerce is the Big Enchilada at the moment. A lot of online retailers have reached a saturation point in their domestic or regional markets and the most obvious source of growth is now going to come from international sales. Over 90% of online retailers don't sell and ship their product overseas. Enter SwipeZoom: a risk-free and cost-effective way to tap into the rest of the 7 billion people on this planet, without disruption to a retailer's e-commerce platform. SwipeZoom's compelling value prop of curing multiple pains, together with a 'nothing to lose' model, is convincing retailers all over Europe, even as we speak.

How are you different from others?

I always start a business with a simple premise that I know nothing. This enables me to become hungry and receptive to new knowledge. Knowing new things helps me think outside the box. I can often see things that domain specialists may not.

Entrepreneurs need to understand the key issues/underlying drivers. I am not a programmer but I can tell when someone is bullshitting.

I am reflective and observant. Observation is what leads to opportunity, also known as 'luck'. Opportunity never knocks.

Entrepreneurs get involved in everything. This isn't micromanagement. It's trying to understand what causes the business to work.

I have a complete disregard for the impossible. Challenge excites me. If something is labeled 'impossible', it's probably because no one has tried it. In my entrepreneurial career I have had to kiss a lot of frogs on the way to finding a prince, but that is what kept me going.

Digitizing Knowledge Assets

Entrepreneurs	Mohamad Al Bagdadi (M) and Rany Al Baghdadi (R)
Company and website	TechKnowledge (www.techknowledge.me) and Al Manhal (www.almanhal.com)
Company services	TechKnowledge partners with leading publishers and research institutes to provide academic, medical, corporate, government, and schools libraries across the Middle East with electronic resources. Al Manhal is the world's first Arabic full-text database provider.
Year started	TechKnowledge in 2004 and Al Manhal in 2010
Tips for entrepreneurs	• Passion for what you are doing. Passion evokes determination. • Be prepared to work much harder than you have ever imagined. • Decide what not to do and differentiate it from what you have to do. You can't do everything. • Budget. Budget. Budget.

What does TechKnowledge do?

M: Our business is similar to an importer and distributor of books and journals. We distribute the resources digitally. As a solution provider we create electronic libraries by collecting electronic material and provide customized information as well as resources for end users. Our customers are schools, universities, hospitals, oil and gas companies, engineering firms, research centers and government organizations.

We help doctors stay updated with latest research, procedures and drug information. We help engineers with current engineering codes and standards. We provide researchers in oil and gas companies with access to the latest chemical and patent databases. When researchers work in universities, we give them access to the latest research. When teachers teach children how to do their homework online, we provide the authoritative materials.

Your value proposition?

M: Our objective is to ensure that knowledge-intensive organizations are able to build the largest libraries of content with their budgets and provide access to their students, researchers and practitioners seamlessly.

How did the idea arise?

M: Before Rany and I founded Techknowledge in 2004, I co-founded ebrary, the world's first academic ebook technology platform company, in Silicon Valley in 1998. We reinvented the business model of annual subscription to a database of ebook content. I was responsible for all sales outside the US through a network of distributors. I discovered that the usage of all the products in the Middle East was the lowest compared to the rest of the world. We took it upon ourselves to establish a reliable, transparent and efficient electronic information service provider, who, realizing the long-term potential would invest in providing a needs-based consultancy service.

I understand distribution of tangible products. But clarify this for electronic products.

M: This question informs the strategy of electronic database creation and pricing. If a researcher is looking for a research paper, he can visit a website and buy the research paper. This is like iTunes where I download songs one at a time. This is an expensive proposition. Therefore, publishers bundle their offerings and sell access to multiple databases to an institution for all its users. This increases the total amount of money the institutions spend with the publisher (thus increasing the publishers income) while minimizing the price for document in the database. This in turn minimizes the cost for each user to access and use the information. In addition, the databases are regularly updated. There is no threat of obsolescence which is the need to acquire books and publications each time a new edition comes out.

Have you made a cost center into revenue?

M: For a university, a library is an investment. We ensure they get the maximum bang for the buck. We are able to track usage and assess the utility of expenditure. This would not have been possible in the old print distribution model that was cost plus.

Are you compensated by publishers?

M: Yes. Customers see the same price when buying directly from publishers or from us. Our customers spend less by working with us since we consult and advise our customers to invest in only the resources that are needed and further negotiate on their behalf for the lowest possible prices.

Competition in the market?

M: There used to be many. A shakeout has happened. Our strategy of transparency has impacted prices; forced them downwards. Distributors are not basing their prices on cost-plus models targeting high profits. And distributors are forced to provide quality service in order to retain their customers and publishers.

Do you create products for customers by aggregating databases?

M: We assess the information needs of the institution, identify the available budget and advise on the most valuable combination of resources that provide maximum access for the available budget. We then take a step further by becoming a provider with our own customized elibrary portals that maximize discovery and usage of the purchased resources. We then invest heavily in ensuring we have the right people to train our customers utilize and benefit from the resources they invest in. TechKnowledge doesn't employ salespersons. We have specialists, people with domain knowledge – librarians, doctors, pharmacists, teachers, and engineers – who have experienced knowledge needs of their sectors.

How did you decide to become an entrepreneur?

M: An idea was always in my head; what can I bring from the West to the East. I thought about everything from fast food franchises to donuts to trading steel. In graduate school I wrote a business plan for entering the environmental management industry, moved to Beirut and set up an office in 1997. I was selling solar lighting and industrial laundry wastewater recycling treatment solutions that saved energy and consumption of fresh water. I ran the business for two years until I ran out of money. I was 27, returned to the US, met these two guys and we decided to start a business to protect copyrights on the internet.

You met two unknown guys and decided to start?

M: This was 1998. E-businesses were picking up speed. They didn't have a business plan, had done no research and had only the business idea. They asked me to join them as a co-founder to try to raise capital and start the company. We started the company called ebrary in 1998. I raised our first $1 m. We then wrote the business plan, moved from the house where we were working to an office behind the train tracks, hired some engineers, built a prototype and started to talk to publishers as well as customers. Over the course of six years, after many different business models, various growth and downsizing phases, the internet bubble burst of 2001 and 5 rounds of investment in which we raised an additional $28 million in funding, we finally hit profitability. In 2011 our sales had hit almost $40 million and we exited the company.

TechKnowledge was based on my ebrary experience.

How did you start?

M: We went to Starbucks…

R: And wrote a business plan. We then used my brother's contacts in the industry to raise some 'smart money' and establish partnerships with some publishers. I then took a small office, a 10×10 in Knowledge Village, and started calling and visiting universities.

Anything interesting?

R: He told me that I could work for other publishers. Since he was my brother, he couldn't give me representation until I had credibility with other respected publishers.

M: Credibility is an important issue in the US. Rany had to show track record. I could then add ebrary to the business.

How did you create a product value proposition presentation?

R: When I first visited AUD, I didn't have business card. I met the librarian and pitched electronic databases. She listened to me and said, 'Young man. This is all very well. But come to me when you have a business card.'

How challenging was the original selling and pricing?

R: In 2004, libraries were starting to become digital. We came into the market when there was a major shift happening in the market. Our efforts focused on helping them understand the value proposition. This required education. The truth is that they taught me a lot too. It was not a straightforward supply-side approach, 'This is how it happens in the west.' A simple question, 'What are you doing in the electronic world?' would elicit information on the demands of the region.

This is complex B2B selling. How long does this take?

R: First deal for 15,000 e-books with AUD took about 6 months. Value of contract was $3500.

Did it become more predictable?

M: There are hiccups but the growth strategy is simple. We start with simple offerings of basic information needs to make a trusted connection with an organization. The connection is like a pipe. After the pipe is laid, it is easier to send more sophisticated information and other associated products/ service through the pipe.

Are the companies sticky?

R: After professionals start using information as part of their professional life, they cannot imagine life without information anymore.

When did recruitment begin?

R: In 2005 we hired our first chemist. In the first year, we were just three people. We became five-six people by 2007 and twelve people by 2008. Today we have almost sixty employees in offices in Dubai, Riyadh, Jordan, Cairo, Ankara and Istanbul. Recruitment of sector-specific staff is always a challenge. As a startup it is difficult to recruit from the oil and gas business where remunerations are high. Only thing we sell is our open culture of a startup. I have found that people are attracted to it.

M: Initially, they find it daunting. First impressions count. In the early days, when the recruitment was being done in a loosely furnished windowless dark office, potential employees could have wondered about the stability of the company and the employment.

Is the TechKnowledge business self-sustaining?

M: We have been profitable since year three. Every year we say this is the year to pull out dividends, but every year we find new opportunities and make the decision to reinvest for growth. We have over 1500 customers, six offices and over fifty employees across the region. We manage subscriptions for over 1500 library customers around the region.

Challenges as you grew?

M: Managing cash flow. We have never taken on any debt to fund our growth, so cash management was always a high priority.

Having done three businesses, does it become easier?

M: No, it doesn't become less tense or easier because you end up focusing on new things. Things still worry me and take all my attention, but I may have learnt to manage stress better.

How did the idea for Al Manhal come up?

M: We were educating our customers that the same print library budget could purchase nearly 100 times more electronic than hard copy titles. We discovered one segment of consumers slightly uncomfortable. Arabic students going to a library did not find any electronic material in Arabic. This triggered the need to create an e-publishing company in Arabic. We established Al Manhal in 2009. We raised seed capital of $3m. We didn't have to struggle with customer acquisition. We went from zero to ten customers immediately and staff strength of fifty.

Al Manhal is about product development – digitization of Arabic content?

M: Its social value proposition is also real. It is helping students learn in Arabic, removing the disadvantage of not knowing English and it is giving regional publishers a new lease of life, an opportunity of earning an income beyond printed books by digitizing the content. For new academic books it is easy. It can be done by creating publishing e-tools like Amazon. For older materials it is more like scanning, rewriting and indexing to enable search.

Was it easier starting Al Manhal?

M: I had imagined that since I had done it once in ebrary, I could do it again. I am an Arab-American. I have grown in an Arab household and spent time in the Middle East. Even I had a culture shock; I couldn't imagine how different it would be setting up a company. A part of Al Manhal development operations are in Jordan. We have a multi-cultural team in Dubai – Indian, Pakistani, Pilipino, Russian and Arabs. In Jordan all are Arabs with a similar work ethic. Once I had crossed the setting up phase, I encountered a widespread lack of respect for copyright laws. I tried to push the envelope and received a pushback from the industry. People were suggesting I digitize without formal agreements with copyright holders.

An unforeseen legal minefield?

M: In addition the companies I was engaging with, publishers as suppliers had a trading mindset. They had no interest in perpetual income streams. They wanted all payments upfront.

What did you do?

M: The model morphed. To convince the suppliers we started ebrary to protect copyright on the net. It was never my intention to be an eBook company. So I took ebrary's technology, licensed and Arabized it. It took longer and cost more than estimated.

What about the customer side acceptance?

M: Our buyers, the libraries, required convincing about a new purchase model that was subscription based. It was no longer about buying books. Buyers had to start looking at their customer engagement as a service transaction. They needed a business understanding of what was earlier envisaged as a cost. It was not about 'a' book but about diversity and specificity of content for each customer. They also needed to be educated to not just opt for the cheapest option.

When was the product ready?

M: Product was launched in July 2011. We were behind our target of customer acquisition and revenue by nearly 18 months. It took longer than expected for our database platform to fully support Arabic. The minimum criterion was to enable full-text searchability of all the documents. External reason was the Arab Spring. Our entire content base was put on hold.

Are you risking your business by focusing on one language – Arabic?

M: The Arab world has a challenge. English is the preferred language of the young. Courses taught in Arabic have lower enrolment rates. And there is negligible scientific research work appearing in Arabic. There is economic and linguistic stratification happening. The children of well-to-do Arabs learn English and are able to access a richer variety of books and material. The poor who learn in Arabic by default are excluded; they have less access to the universe of knowledge. Our intent is to even the playing field.

Competition?

M: Many competitors have emerged. They are focusing on quantity rather than quality and standards. As I mentioned earlier, it is easy to slap together a bunch of Arabic pdf files and sell them. It is much more difficult to negotiate copyright license agreements, digitize the content, create a full-text searchable platform that adheres to international library standards and integrates with library systems, develop a secure and transparent royalty management system, build a global distribution network to ensure sales and servicing of the content, etc.

Successes?

R: We started with one customer in 2011. In December 2012, Georgetown University in the United States subscribed to Al Manhal. Students in Georgetown University have access to content coming out of the Middle

East. Georgetown was our first customer outside the Middle East. We ended 2012 with over 80 customers in the region. All fifty universities in Saudi subscribed as well as all universities in Qatar. Most in the UAE, Jordan, Lebanon, Palestine. Many in Iraq, Libya, Tunisia, Yemen and Egypt. We currently have over 150 university customers across the world including such names as Oxford University, Yale University, Duke, Chapel Hill and University of California Berkeley.

Source of material relationships?

M: Over 300 publishers provided us information, books, journals, dissertations, etc. We have tie-ups with universities in the region to supply us with over 400 academic journals.

Are you profit making?

R: We are still in the investment phase.
M: Al Manhal will breakeven in 2015.

You have two products – databases and books?

M: We learned from experience. With ebrary, in hindsight, we focused on books too long. We were labeled as the 'book' guys when we attempted to branch out. At Al Manhal, we decided to work on all content types from day one. We launched e-Books in July 2011 and journals in July 2012. We have since added reference collections, dissertations, intelligence reports, conference proceedings, etc.

Pricing of Al Manhal?

M: We had to discount a little in the beginning to get things moving, but were pretty diligent about it. We need to price adequately in order to pay our Arabic publishers their due royalties.

Can't you create a B2C model?

M: We are on Amazon and are launching on iTunes and Google Play.

How have you changed after becoming entrepreneurs?

R: I definitely have more patience. I look at all issues from a fresh point of view. In the first five years there was very little personal life. We were doing everything. Then people joined, learned and started innovating themselves. My work changed. I learned to give people space, enable and then manage them.

M: Each startup evolved differently. TechKnowledge emerged from an idea. It started with one person. It was more personal. It now has over fifty people. It started from scratch. Al Manhal started differently. It had capital when we started. We sat in board meetings with both investors. We grew from no employees to thirty overnight. We now have more than sixty people. It is more structured. The challenges are different. TechKnowledge's challenges were how to get people to work together for the benefit of our publishers and customers. Al Manhal's challenges are how to keep producing more content to meet your publisher and customer expectations, without continuing to increase your overheads. So you have to take your entrepreneurial lessons differently, based on context. The challenges differ every time. In terms of overall learning, I am focusing on the fact that as a company or companies grow (with over hundred employees) a manager needs to spend his/her time continuously tracking and managing data according to KPIs and in turn set or reset direction in order to hit all targets. As opposed to the early days of being an entrepreneur which required you to actually get out there and do the actual work. The thing I miss most is customer interaction and relationships.

What worries you about the business?

R: Cash flow, customers not paying on time in some countries and some customers not honoring contracts.

Hardnosed Stance on Value Drivers

Entrepreneurs	Binod Shankar (B) and Mohit Malhotra (M)
Company and website	Genesis Institute/www.kaplangenesis.com (Genesis Institute was acquired by Kaplan in Feb 2017)
Company services	Provider of financial training programs
Year started	2008–9
Tips for entrepreneurs	• Passion makes the difference between make or break in an industry. • Be a full-time entrepreneur to build the business of your dreams. • Managing a business is different from knowing your job and doing it well. • Be prepared to feel lonely and uncertain.

How did Genesis start?

B: CFA Emirates is the local chapter of the CFA Institute. The global qualification rates of the CFA exam are low. In the ME region, they are even lower. CFA Emirates wanted to popularize the qualification by making the qualification accessible and increasing the pipeline of aspirants. A CFA aspirant can self-study and take exams to get the credential. CFA Emirates wanted to provide subsidized preparatory and training programs as an option to commercial training providers in the market. We started as volunteers sharing our knowledge with CFA aspirants. The participants gave us good feedback. We realized the need for the training programs (high) and the resources (high) we spent doing voluntary work. The value and effort justified charging money.

M: It happened more as a coincidence rather than an active approach to addressing a need-gap. It was a discussion, a spark and a decision. Initially we thought that we could voluntarily participate together in organizing courses which would help students. Our initial motivation was altruistic.

How did you start?

B: We realized the model is workable as a business after a number of participants had gone through the program by paying money. We were delivering better quality at a decent price. The latent demand became visible.

M: We needed key resources to implement the idea. We needed study material. We started talking to a company called Kaplan Financial, the market leader for CFA material. We needed a venue. We got a free deal with Canadian University of Dubai. We needed faculty. We sent an email to the CFA community across UAE seeking paid volunteers to participate in sharing knowledge to kick-start the courses. Lots of people volunteered.

At which stage in the business did you realize that this was now going to run as a business?

B: In the first year itself. That is why we quit our jobs. We had about a hundred customers. The student feedback was fantastic. They were doing better in their exams, crediting us with the outcomes and promising to come back for the next two levels. We could see that we were being ranked ahead of competition.

Initial pricing?

M: We did not research the quality and price of training in the market or what price we should charge. We were aware that the market price was AED 10K. We decided to price the training at AED 4K. There was not much of a thought process.

Value of Genesis?

M: The needs of the participants differ. Some participants have subtle pressure from their employers to do the CFA program. Acquisition of the credential entitles them to higher paying jobs and/or promotions. This has a viral effect. For others it is self-development. Private companies in the GCC are hesitant in investing in developing expatriate employees. Contractual nature of employment is a possible cause. They never know the longevity of the employee. Our customers are investing in their own development.

B: External training that is paid for imposes disciplined learning. Self-paced learning requires self-discipline; when I am learning on my own, I am often more casual about timing and achieving learning milestones. This was the unexpressed need we realized we could address. We also sensed that pricing was precluding people who wanted to acquire the qualification. We could lower the entry barrier.

Do clients understand that they can recover their investment in training?

B: We have seen an increasing inflow of fresh graduates from universities in Dubai. Most of them have grown up in Dubai. They have already done BA in Accounting or Finance or Banking. They are keen to work in Finance and CFA is a qualification for that preferred job. We also get participants who come from non-banking sectors who want to switch to finance and banking. An underlying desire of the participants is to move up vertically or laterally and keeping their jobs safe. For three levels of the CFA exam that requires around 3 to 4 years, a participant pays AED 35,000 to Genesis and another AED 5,000 to the CFA Institute. It's incredibly cheap compared to going to college full time.

How does the program work?

M: The nature of the program creates a need. CFA program consists of staggered exams called levels. Once a payment is made for a phased exam, the applicant receives books. The applicant has to master the material and take the exam. CFA is designed as a self-study course. The entry requirement is a graduate degree, a relatively low threshold. Many people apply, majority of who are working professionals. Their challenge is to manage their diverse commitments to allocate time for serious study. This is where a training institute comes in.

We have competition from organizations that provide 'study notes' as a substitute for intensive study. The notes are easy to understand and exam-centric. At the early stages of the CFA study, where one studies economics, basic finance and business courses, using study notes is an 'ok' idea. I used them too. As one graduates to higher levels, the utility of the study notes diminishes unless complemented with serious self-study. Here is where a classroom setting presented by practitioners helps. Participants learn from practitioners in a disciplined three-month program split into weekly sessions, held in the evenings to accommodate working professionals.

Have you consciously tried to create a slight differentiation between Genesis and others?

B: The USP is very clear; our entire faculty should be CFA Charterholders, which is easier said than done. To get a CFA Charterholder status is difficult to start with. There are so few of them out there. Then to get someone who is willing to teach is a challenge. There are a lot of CFA Charterholders who are very good at their jobs but are unable to simplify the concepts of CFA. We need credibility as well as expertise and we don't compromise. There have been several times in our journey over the last four years, we mulled over diluting standards to achieve growth and get faculty that is a CA or an MBA. We discuss and then don't compromise. Our classes are interactive. Faculty needs to bring real-world problems into the class to engage students. They better come prepared. They will be asked questions. They will be tested.

Where was the seed of entrepreneurship in you?

B: There was a push and a pull. My entrepreneurship journey was triggered by my personality. I am not the kind of person who likes a boss above me. I don't know how I have survived in a tightly controlled world of audit, consulting, and corporate life. I turned forty in 2009 and ruminated on how much there was left of life. For forty years I had been working to become a CFO and maybe a CEO. Not much to do after that. At that point of time I was doing that job purely for the money. It suddenly didn't make any sense whatsoever. It was like a revelation. The money was very good but everything about the job was completely dreadful. The pull factor was the freedom of running something you love to do because I have been teaching since 1997. The idea of teaching was very appealing. I thought I was very good at it. I thought: 'why not do something which you are good at and like and is also commercially viable?' We knew we could do better than other people in the market. And it was a commercial opportunity. Stepping out of a job was not much of a risk. I am single, with no family to support. A potential free fall environment wasn't a big deal. I could fall down and stand right up. Personal finance was the least of my priorities.

M: I was a part of the learning group at Deloitte. I used to train associates. When I am in a class I am a completely different person. I enjoy doing what I do. So I decided to put all my effort into Genesis.

The decision to enter into a partnership?

M: That was a coincidence. We asked a question about commercializing the voluntary training programs of CFA Emirates and who amongst the volunteers wanted to pitch in. Three of us raised our hands.

Investment in the business?

B: Around sixty thousand Dirhams to set up in TECOM.

Did you estimate a return required to maintain a quality of life?

B: We haven't reached where we left off four years ago. We sustain ourselves and don't assess it as an opportunity cost. We are focused on adding value to the business.

Your growth rate?

B: We started in July of 2008. Our first batch had eighteen students with one faculty. Our 2012 estimate for an exam coming up in December is 450 students across Dubai and Abu Dhabi and a teaching staff of about twelve, of which four are full-time instructors. We are two of the four.

Is your revenue per participant close to market?

B: Yes, probably even higher than market because now Genesis is synonymous with CFA.

You have increased your pricing from below market price to the market price.

B: Our price now reflects how we are positioning Genesis to the target group and their affordability. Our conversion rates are around ninety percent – who we meet and how many join.

Was access to customers an issue?

B: With our CFA Emirates involvement, no.

Staffing?

B: Retaining staff is not a challenge but getting quality staff is. We have struggled with this over the last four years.

How important is personal engagement with participants?

B: When students walk-in, I engage with them if nobody's around. I try to enquire where they heard about Genesis from. What did they hear about us? Why CFA and why us? I make customers feel we are like them. They give me information about competition, the market and about Genesis. All of which is invaluable.

Any surprises when you started, something not envisaged?

B: The trial was the test. There were no tense moments. We journeyed the same path as the participants.

What worries you about the business?

B: Growth and where will we get people to manage growth. It's not so much about customers but about people to fuel the growth.

Were there any personal challenges when you started this business?

B: I had a narrow remit in my last job as Director of Finance – do the assigned works, keep your boss happy and pray for a promotion every year.

Switching to entrepreneurship, I had to manage everything from HR to IT to marketing to sales and business development. This was a steep learning curve. I hadn't handled quite a few of those functions in my earlier jobs. I had to start from scratch. This required some relearning and for all those things to be implemented. My personality had to change. I was used to being an employee, listening to orders and executing them, making a few random suggestions along the way. Now the buck stopped with me and that was liberating. It was hugely satisfying and very challenging.

Challenges.

B: Our biggest cost element is staff. We do draw salaries but we don't draw market salaries. We don't draw what we used to get before we joined Genesis. That is a deliberate choice. We draw salaries to meet our living expenses. We don't take money (profits) out of the business. We plough it back to fuel growth.

When you started the business, did you have a formal agreement signed amongst the partners?

B: We had an agreement defining our responsibilities. When we were starting, we were unsure about what was going to happen and who was good at doing what. Over the last four years things have evolved into defined roles for each of us. Mohit handles IT, HR, operations and teaches as well. I handle sales, marketing, business development, faculty recruitment, training and I also teach. Our third partner is passive. His role is strategic. His contribution is invaluable.

Your guidance to an entrepreneur starting out.

B: Mohit and I love teaching. We have a passion to interact with students which is why our classes often go on till midnight. We have this desire to achieve something. I think if you have passion, it makes the difference between make or break in any industry. Whatever you do, you will encounter difficulties. You will find yourself alone. You will find issues confronting the company. But there has to be a reason why you are doing what you are doing. There has to be a single purpose, an objective to carry you forward. To be a successful entrepreneur you have to be a full-time entrepreneur. I was a part-time entrepreneur when I had a job and also taught. I didn't have the time for more than just a cursory look at things. There is a lot to be done apart from teaching if you want to grow the company. I had gone from being a Financial Analyst to Finance Manager to Director and CFO. I had to transition from a teacher to a business owner and then learn how to manage a business to make it the way I interpreted it to be.

New opportunities?

B: In the past we launched a few courses which we thought were good opportunities but for various reasons they didn't work. We tried to launch a course called FRM – Financial Risk Manager targeted at bankers, risk managers, etc. We also looked at Corporate Finance Qualification based on ICAW which is Chartered Accountants of England and Wales. Both FRM and CFQ have fantastic curriculums but this market is probably not ready for them.

No Fear of the Unknown

Entrepreneurs	Michael Trueschler (M) and Nicolas Bruylants (N)
Company and website	Citruss TV/www.citrusstv.com
Business	TV Home Shopping Network. Citruss designs, scripts and produces the promotions as well as sources and manages the supply chain of products from around the world to the doors of the customers.
Year established	2005
Tips for entrepreneurs	• Believe in the business and be 100% dedicated. • Engage with and understand customers, answer their needs and make them happy. • Try not to do it alone. Get a good partner you can trust. Sometimes you look at things as a dead end. New perspectives emerge when you have a discussion. • Don't think that because you have the idea you have to do everything yourself. Surround yourself with great people and empower them.

How did Citruss start?

M: I came to Dubai from Germany to start a business after my MBA. I had never been here before. Dubai was getting a lot of positive press coverage in Germany – about the infrastructure, economic dynamism and zero tax. TV shopping from home was a successful business in US, Europe and Asia. The Middle East did not have a TV network for shopping from home. So I said, 'Wow, let me tap the possibility here.' The idea was to develop TV shopping programs and broadcast them on different channels and share revenues.

I needed to go to work with existing companies and channels. I did not know anyone in Dubai. Using the internet I identified the big TV channels in this region. Taking initiative, I called the operators and asked to be connected to somebody in business development or marketing. Before coming from Germany I had fixed appointments with TV, call center and logistics companies.

I explained to them that home shopping did not exist here and I wanted to do it. They had the TV and the studio. They could do the presentation, something I didn't know how to do and couldn't do. I would do the back-office stuff – sourcing, selling, delivery and collection. I presented an investment proposal. They had to invest in the business. It would be a company we set up together. There was no discussion on shareholding.

Everyone I met was friendly. People were listening but nothing tangible came out of the discussions. I sensed a low appetite for risk or change. I realized that profit was not a motive for government TV channels.

After 3-4 months of running around, I had to adapt.

N: I met Michael while kite surfing on the beach and learnt about his TV shopping idea. I accompanied him on his meetings. People had a poor perception of TV shopping. They looked at our idea as an infomercial- TV programs made in US or Europe dubbed in Arabic for cheap products from China. The economy was booming in 2004. No TV channel wanted additional revenue from home shopping programs on their channels.

I suggested to Michael the possibility of creating a channel to broadcast the programs. We started looking into producing TV shopping programs and owning a TV channel. I helped Michael put together a business plan.

M: Everything was turning out different from the way anticipated. At the end of the day, I said let me go ahead because I didn't come to Dubai blue-eyed and dreaming.

Every channel said no and you decided to create a channel.

N: This was a big decision. Two factors helped. One, we didn't have much fear at that time. Fear comes when you have a family. And two, we didn't know. We didn't know the business we were getting into. Maybe if we knew how difficult it is, we would not have done it at that time.

How did the partnership happen?

N: I returned to Belgium after my work finished in Dubai. I had the business plan in my hands. I was happy in Belgium, but was missing Dubai. Dubai gives you a push to do things. Here, everything seems possible. Rules are strict in Europe. One has to do many things to be a broadcaster. Taxes are even more complex. I thought, 'I have this business plan. If I can raise finance from amongst the people I know who are venture capitalists, add my personal finances, maybe I can put together what is required to build this business.' I started meeting investors. In a month I had raised some money.

I called Michael and said, 'If you are still keen and you can bring a percentage of the required capital, I will come and bring the rest.' He readily agreed. I moved back to Dubai, and Citruss TV started.

How was the start?

M: We had no knowledge of the TV business when we started the business. We had to go on air in mid-April 2005 and had four-five months to fill 24 hours of programming every day. The task was daunting. We needed know-how and people with experience in this field. We did not realize the enormity of the challenge when we started. We didn't know how the business worked. If we knew the TV business and had established connections, we would not have done what we managed to do. Had we known what the business involves when we started, we would not have done it with the amount of capital we raised.

N: We had to do an incredible amount of learning. I knew nothing about products, promotions, programming and photography. We learned by trial and error. The channels were helpful. They were guiding us to access infrastructure – studio, cameras, directors and presenters – to implement the idea.

When did you know Citruss was working?

M: We had set up the complete infrastructure – products, warehouse, call center and TV programming, but people didn't start to order. Sales didn't start and grow as expected. People were not used to buying from TV.

N: We had not put in the equation that even if we had a successful plan to create viewership, customer trust takes time. We needed capital to pay our employees and for marketing, for the time it takes to create trust. This was the most stressful part.

M: The startup is stressful. We also had to get used to unforeseen things happening that had to be managed. The company running our call center became insolvent. They gave us a week's warning before closing. We would be dead with no one taking orders. Stress became more manageable in 2009 when we reached breakeven point and we finally could fund ourselves.

How did you decide which products to sell?

M: TV shopping works for products where product demonstration enables customer understanding and choice. A brick and mortar retailer cannot explain and demonstrate a kitchen appliance or a beauty product to all customers walking through a shop. Based on global experience, we started with cosmetics. We then added kitchenware and jewelry. We have now added electronics- laptops and computers. Kitchen and beauty are our main categories.

N: It sometimes happens by chance. I was sitting next to a Lebanese lady at a dinner in the Belgian Embassy. We got talking about what we were starting. She told me, 'You should sell whitening products. Europeans and Lebanese like to look tanned. Here they want to be fair.' We found a high-quality whitening product from Spain and sold it very successfully. Today, product selection is structured. To sell a coffee machine, we search for the best coffee machine. We select five, test them and put our guarantee stamp on it. Then we present coffee machines to our viewers. In TV shopping, I can test products. After deciding on an item, we do a program, put it on TV and get a direct response. We gauge the uncertainty and can tweak our product, presentation, and/or message to answer all customer questions.

Citruss is full of surprises. We have dud products and great surprises too. We had a big hit in a 'joint cream.' I had joint problem in my knee, imported a joint cream from Belgium, used it for two weeks and got rid of the pain. We had a customer from the US who had a stiff shoulder. I gave him the product and he gained movement of his shoulder. He was effusive about the product. I decided to sell the product. I would never have thought and expected to sell cream for joints on TV.

How challenging was the product sourcing?

M: We first tried to get everything on consignment. Only one in ten suppliers would agree. We started the business getting the goods on consignment, paying only for what we sold. This approach narrowed down the possibility of attracting suppliers.

N: The supply side is the difficult part for any business- how does one find a unique product that the customer wants? We also want it at the best price and good payment conditions. Even now, every contract is a challenge. It was more difficult when we started. We didn't have the sales numbers to justify requests. Getting brands to trust us was tough. Now when we open negotiations, we have success stories to narrate.

M: Suppliers now want to work with us. We have been in business for 8 years and are the biggest players.

You don't know Arabic. How do you create programs?

N: People wonder how we know what is happening on TV because we broadcast in Arabic. I first make sure that the team understands our idea. We make a storyboard of the message. The team brings their cultural experience and it is translated into Arabic. We then test it to see whether people understand what we want to say. It took a long time for the team to learn what was in our mind and for us to learn the cultural differences. It is a lot of trial and error. TV shopping has an advantage. We have a direct response to what we are doing. We listen to the phone calls and understand what the customer is thinking. This helps us develop. We go back to producers and presenters, and recalibrate our message; what was good, what people liked and what needs to change.

What about logistics, the other backbone of your business?

M: We started with Al Futtaim and moved to Aramex in four months. We needed to manage the last mile- deliveries and payment. Deliveries require speed and accuracy, which require easily understood address systems. These are non-existent. The delivery system had to be capable of receiving cash on delivery. People don't use credit cards to buy on TV.

How did you price products?

M: We have a pricing structure and strategy – introductory price for a majority of products in the first month we show a product. The final price is 10–20% higher than the introductory price. After that there is no change except the specials that we run e.g. during the Ramadan when we have bundled offers with gifts. We don't like giving discounts.

N: We have a basket size of US $150 compared to $60 in Europe. This is a very high basket size. We discovered a low sensitivity to price in the region. Pricing is benchmarked with products in the market.

Potential of Citruss?

M: In early 2010 we integrated TV and e-commerce through the website. We are seeing more customers getting used to buying through the TV and online. Electronic retailing is important and home shopping is part of it. Our advantage is that we can show a video of the product unlike a static presentation on a website.

HR challenges?

M: We have sixty employees. Recruiting and getting the right skill-set has been a challenge. We were not familiar with the names of the universities. If I saw a name on a CV I couldn't connect it with anything I knew. I use a more direct approach. I look for logical thinkers. If I give a person a task, his way of thinking should be practical as well as intelligent and he must show enthusiasm for the job. We had to get used to a work ethic different from that in Europe. Cultural differences are real. In trying to balance work and family life, I sense people here give a greater emphasis to family life.

What worries you about the business?

M: Political instability of the region. Europe and the US have economic uncertainty and political stability. Some MENA countries targeted by Citruss have political and economic uncertainty.

N: I did not know that as a CEO and co-owner of a business I will never stop thinking about it. I find it difficult to get away from work. Wherever I am, I always want to know whether we have the new product launched, how we did today, what is the feedback, did we get a ready feedback from customers who received goods, did they post the review and so on. I am interested in the business all the time, not only because I am in a business that I have learned to love.

How have you changed as a person while implementing the business?

M: I have had to adapt to the mentality of people. We took a conscious decision to adapt to the local culture by doing local content. To do this I had to work with a lot of Arabs to understand them and the culture. I have learnt that I can't expect German precision at work; I can't get things done in time and in the detail that I want the first time round. It was important to learn to be more relaxed. There were many problems we have had to solve and there will be more to come. But you have to give it time and deal with problems one by one. Don't stress yourself too much and make sure you also have a private life. So as a person I am surely more laid-back than I used to be.

N: When I started the company I had no real experience of managing people. This is what I do most of the time. We have great people in key roles in the company and I spend an awful lot of time making sure we manage them right. I did not have the faintest notion about this when I started. I thought it would be my job to decide, to let people know what to do. This is totally wrong. I have changed completely now.

The Social Attribute of Sports

Entrepreneurs	Davindar Rao[3], Ravi Bhusari and Brian Sigafoos
Company and website	DUPLAYS/www.duplays.com
Company services	Social networking platform established on sports
Year established	2007
Tips for entrepreneurs	• Sell, sell, sell. Selling is the most valuable skill for a startup because everything you do in business is to sell.

How did DUPLAYS happen?

I studied science in Toronto en route to medical school. Eight years of studying medicine looked forbidding so I did an MBA. I then worked in Johnson and Johnson in sales for six years and really enjoyed work.

And then I pivoted.

I was watching Oprah interviewing an heiress of the J&J family. Oprah asked her, 'What is the most difficult thing you think about every day.' She replied, 'What shoes I am going to wear?' My mind switched off; I couldn't imagine working for someone to decide which shoes she wanted to wear. I resigned, got a seven-month severance package and decided to travel till the money ran out. I saw a video of Dubai, came here for two weeks, moved to Nepal and then Tibet. I was at the Beijing airport on the way to Toronto when I decided to return to Dubai. I had no idea what I was going to do. I took a room in Jumeirah and started applying for jobs. I reconnected with Ravi, whom I had met at a party. I wanted to meet people, outside the social scene, to play sports. This is how DUPLAYS started; twenty people started meeting to play. Slowly more people started joining us. In September 2007 I talked to Ravi and said, 'Maybe there is a business here. I don't need a lot of money to survive. I need my rent of 5000 Dirhams a month. You keep working. Let me test this.' I took my first salary from DUPLAYS about 2 years ago.

---

3 Interview with Davindar

There were three drivers that created the business. One, I was a consumer; I played sports four nights a week and was paying somebody else to do what I now do as a business. Two, Ravi and I are avid sportsmen. We play all sports. So when we wanted to organize a game we understood what we were doing. Three, we were doing what we love.

When did you know that sports networking could become a business?

Our start was low-key. We attracted customers by making and displaying posters at different Spinneys. For the venues, we made presentations to owners of facilities. We first organized a game of football in October-November 2007 at the Metropolitan Hotel, then added Touch Rugby and Basketball. The idea had unanticipated traction. There was a demand for our services. People were paying to network around sports and we were getting different sports facilities to use. DUPLAYS was in startup phase for 18 months.

When did you first price your service?

We charged a participation fee of 20 Dirhams almost straight away. Our initial price was instinctive. We said, 'let us see if people are willing to pay for our service. We can then figure out the business.' We quickly realized the 'true' cost of running the business. Our pricing was based only on the cost of equipment and consumables; Ravi and I were not accounting for our time.

Any surprises during implementing?

We thought we understood sports. I didn't realize the detail and discipline that business needed. Our initial costing was out of whack. We didn't budget for office costs. We were working at 'The Shelter' and in coffee shops. We didn't realize that business involves many indirect expenses. We now know that the true cost of an employee to a company is 25% higher than the salary because of additional costs, such as health insurance.

Who helped you start?

We connected with Jimmy, who runs a large family business in Dubai. He made entrepreneurship and business real for us. We stayed in his place for two months. It was 24 × 7 mentorship. I realized the difference between connecting with entrepreneurs managing their own businesses and professionals who work. In Toronto I rarely met entrepreneurs in my social circle. Dubai is different. We meet more entrepreneurs than professionals.

How has DUPLAYS evolved?

We started with a few users. We then offered services we thought everybody wanted. Two-thirds of the customers didn't want 'our' services. We went back to the drawing board to identify and deliver new services for people who didn't want what we did. Some customers wanted to search and book sports facilities for their kids e.g., a swimming lesson in a pool. We discovered hotels and schools with unutilized facilities and built the bridge connecting need with supply. Our business is evolving as a platform website, like Airbnb. Airbnb is a community marketplace for people to list, discover and book accommodation whereas DUPLAYS will become a platform to connect users with sports facilities. The site is becoming more sophisticated with the ability to book and manage facilities. We have met Dubai Municipality. They realize the economic value of having an organized system to give users the ability to book a tennis court or an open field at a nominal fee. A corporate market segment has emerged and become a large part of the business. Brands come to us and say, 'Organize a sports event for our customer demographic.' Companies ask us to organize off-site events for team building. We have learnt the psychological underpinnings of the games. This business will develop.

Number of employees?

We have sixteen employees. Sixty part-time employees work as referees and administrators. Web development is outsourced to Egypt.

Important milestones of DUPLAYS journey?

We realized that business is more than just latent customer needs; we had to do different things to reach and convert customers. The second realization was the need to hire people to grow the business; delegating tasks would allow us to work on bigger things. Brian joining us was an important milestone. He is technical as well as analytical in his thinking and impacted everything in the business. He brought in structure. Ravi and I are MBAs; if we wanted to do something, we just went ahead. Brian is a detail person. He brought metrics into our thinking. He made us realize that some things work and others don't.

When did DUPLAYS become a company?

About three years ago. We needed capital to hire people to grow. We started looking at our numbers, trying to figure out how to evolve the business, how to make it investible, how to pitch, and we began meeting investors. Investment was a self-test; if somebody would invest then we must be a business. Fadi Ghandour invested in us two and a half years ago. We have raised two rounds of capital.

Have you organized work amongst the three partners?

We complement each other based on our skill sets. I focus on events because it is a big chunk of our revenue. Ravi works closely with investors. Brian leads the technical web development team. Brian is always thinking ahead. I think of the now. And Ravi thinks of what is best.

How do you manage customer satisfaction in a service business?

We started this recently. We are about to raise a second round of funding. Our investors told us that we needed to become organized in getting feedback and reporting what was happening in the business. We mobilized the entire office to call customers and solicit feedback.

Staffing challenges?

Startups require long working hours. We look for staff that is unencumbered and ready to invest time. We initially recruited staff with full compensation packages, including housing. It didn't work. Financial security did not result in intensity and productivity. This business is about people. We have to have people who understand sports, are passionate about sport and play sports. We can't give a manual and say do this. I fret daily that trained and experienced staff will leave. We invest time in people. They learn a new business. And then they leave. Knowledge goes out of the door and we have to start again. We have not been good at creating an incentive scheme. We give incentives but they are not directly tied to performance.

Do you now manage DUPLAYS with targets and metrics?

Yes, but it works backwards. We decided to give incentives so we had to establish performance measures.

What keeps you worried about the business?

I worry about payroll every day, about having cash to pay salaries every month.
   We diluted a minority stake in two funding rounds. We had a business that 'worked.' We had to stabilize and grow the business by launching the website in other markets. Most web business models are about connecting people. We raised money for staffing to build the web platform. We first decided to outsource the development. Outsourcing has the challenges of timely execution of evolving ideas and building of in-house knowledge. We now have a three-person full-time technical team – one developer, one designer and another lead person. And it is still not enough. I didn't realize it would cost us so much. Web team is a cost center. They don't make money. We didn't realize how long it takes to get things done.

How much have you changed as a person?

I am happier. No one could get me to open up my laptop at 11 pm. I do it now. I need to learn how to manage and prioritize my time. I need to work on bigger things because we have good people in the company. At a work level, I need to understand franchising. Growth of DUPLAYS will come from franchising of a service business.

Are you still a startup?

We are a startup because we are not yet fully organized. Our challenge is to self-assess whether we are spending time on the right opportunities. There are aspects of the business that we didn't know when we started and now are potential avenues of growth. For example, we get emails from talented county players from Africa who need an avenue to showcase their skills. We can build a website platform to make them visible to clubs. Our business can grow in many ways.

How has DUPLAYS grown?

First event had twenty players. Revenue was AED 400. We now have 40,000 members. Our annual revenue is 20,000 times that of the first event. We are reinvesting all profits.

How much did you invest in DUPLAYS?

Ravi and I invested $30,000 each, plus lost salaries for two years. We started with an informational website. We didn't need upfront capital. We were neither building anything nor trading in products. We launched activities when we saw demand. The risk of loss, of a bad decision, was negligible.

Guidance for a new entrepreneur?

Selling is the most valuable skill because everything you do in business is sell.

What makes Derv an entrepreneur?

I don't know. I don't think analysis because I have a different outlook on things. My impatience may have something to do with it. Everybody has ideas. We often discuss ideas with friends. Discussions invariably focus on risks and why the idea won't work. I take a view, implement it and see what happens. In 2004 I was in Aceh, the epicenter of the Tsunami. I survived even though I was ten kilometers off the coast. I decided that day if I want to do something I will go ahead and do it.

Any tense moments?

I am a frugal person. My only monetary motivation was to live in a 'nice' place. I didn't make any money for nearly two and a half years. A year ago I went to visit my parents. Dad asked me, 'What are you doing?' I replied, 'I am organizing sports.' My dad just turned around and walked away. I began to wonder if I was doing the right thing. My dad came back with my mom and said, 'We got you educated. You did your MBA. And you are organizing sports?' I said, 'Yes.' They then asked me if I was 'surviving.' I said, 'Yes, I am making enough to live. I am not making money.' They asked me, 'How are you managing in Dubai? It is so expensive. Are you eating into your savings?' They breathed a sigh of relief when I told them that my savings were intact. And then they came to Dubai. They were much more relaxed when they saw my work and my life. They saw me doing what I love doing.

A Modern Twist to Cultural Inheritance

Entrepreneur	Fathiya Ahmed Osman
Company and website	Heritage for Henna/www.heritageforhenna.com
Company services	Repositioning Henna for tourists
Year started	2003
Tips for entrepreneurs	• You are alone when you start the business. Be prepared to be lonely. • Be realistic. Businesses start small. Plans show 1+1=10. Don't start believing that 1+1=10 will happen because it is a plan. It takes time. • Focus, focus, focus. • Be brave. Don't give up.

Why Henna as a business?

Henna as a cosmetic has existed in the region- from Rome to Arabia to India-as a part of our culture. A Henna night for the bride is a social tradition. Slowly the application of Henna became restricted to homes and beauty/specialized salons and to people who knew about it. I sensed that this was limiting. I wanted to take Henna to people who do not normally experience it and give them an opportunity to see, apply and experience it.

Why Henna and nothing else?

I felt that every other business needed money and education.

What was your friends' reaction to HH?

Everyone told me that it will not work.

What inspired you to start a business?

As I look back, my troubles motivated me. I had to take the responsibility of my three kids. This was a moment I felt very alone. And I didn't have any resources and or any unique skills. Survival and responsibility required me to earn money quickly. Before my personal turning point I wanted to start a salon.

But had not given it much thought. The intention began to take shape when I had to take responsibility for the family. Suddenly opening a salon required lots of money and was a risky choice; there were hundreds of salons. This is when I narrowed down the idea to Henna. For 2 months I was roaming around, literally walking around, searching for ways to do this business. The idea never left me; it was always in my thoughts. In my mind I was imagining how the operation would look.

Next?

Even for an Emirati, Dubai, a city with dynamism, gives an opportunity to dream big. I used to visit Dubai every six months. Each time I saw new roads and buildings. Dubai Development and Investment Authority had just been launched. I called up the office of HE Mr. Mohamed Al Gergawi. They wanted details of what I wanted to do. I never expected a call back. But they called back and said they were soon going to launch an SME initiative. I should await its launch in the newspaper. I saw a photo of Sheikh Mohamed in the newspaper, launching Mohamed Bin Rashid Establishment (MBRE) of Young Business Leaders. I approached MBRE and told them I wanted to do Henna as a business. The customer service person looked at me. He didn't want to say no, I think because I had my children with me. It was too small they said. I think they didn't want to hurt me. They finally asked me to make a business plan. I didn't want to give up. I had spent two months in reaching the establishment. I spent another three-months trying to convince them. I borrowed some money to make a business plan. It was very hard for me to make a plan. At that time I believed I needed a business plan to make my dream into a reality. I then realized I cannot wait for someone to do something for me. If someone else does it then it is not real. Whatever people told me about my idea, it was not close to what I had in my mind. Not even 1%. Everyone's intention was good. They told me that the business would work if I started in a particular way. They told me what a good business plan should contain.

After this experience I looked within to guide myself. The real business, I started alone.

When I approached MBRE with the plan, they again said no. They were looking for a business plan where 1+1=10. They wanted me to show 10. When outside people evaluate your business they want it to be 10. They will not accept a small business even if it has potential. Real businesses start small. In a 1+1=10 plan, nothing is real.

First breakthrough?

I finally started the business as a trial. I wanted to put up a traditional tent for Henna in the lobby of a hotel. A manager of Jumeirah Beach Hotel liked the idea. He was willing to try it till we could come up with a different idea. I borrowed the money for the tent. I had no employees. I was living in Sharjah. I used to change three buses to reach the Jumeirah Hotel.

When did you know it would become a business?

In the first hour of startup. Even when I was doing the setup, I had a lurking fear, 'This is traditional Henna. Will customers come?' Once the tent opened I found that I had surplus cash every day in the evening. Other than the income, I engaged with customers. I sensed what they were feeling and what they wanted. There were occasions when customers would queue up awaiting their turn. I recollect that the first day it was AED 300, second day AED 700, third day AED 1000 and fourth day AED 2000. When I saw the business improving on a daily basis I guessed that I could make my dream into a reality. The first tent in Jumeriah Beach Hotel was 10 years ago during Ramadan. At the end of Ramadan I had some money left over after taking care of the initial investment for the tent. The money was just sufficient for my household expenses. I believed that Henna could be a business. I wanted to grow and I had nothing. I still needed money for my family. I was still uncertain. But honestly I had no other options. I couldn't take up a job. I had dropped out of college after 2 years. My dream and what we were seeing happen in Dubai were still driving me.

Did you come back to MBRE?

I came back later. I had no option but to knock on doors to allow me to put up a Henna tent. I got nearly five new locations – one mall and four hotels. It is then that I contacted Abdul Baset, CEO of MBRE. I showed him what I had done and the opportunity for more locations. And then he put the entire organization behind me.

How did you convince him?

I showed him numbers. The numbers were real. I didn't have to convince him. I think he knew that if he rejected the business, the startup would collapse. He supported me even though as a policy they were looking for new innovative ideas. It took them a while to appreciate that it could be an old idea done in a different way.

How are you different as a person after you started a business?

I have had big shocks in my life. And I have responsibilities. Nothing else. I said to myself at each stage of my work, 'No, I will never give up or sit down.' There is God and He will help me.' I have always prayed to him, 'You know everything. Help me.' And until today He has supported me, at every moment.

How are you different from your friends?

I am more serious. People sometimes are not. And I work harder. Even today, I am working very hard. I don't take it easy. I have learnt to manage a business. I have learnt the art of working with different nationalities. This experience is very important and valuable. Even if you put me in a new environment and ask me to create a business, I think I can do it. I am focused. I had nothing when I started. Therefore I think I can do it again. An employee has everything that an entrepreneur has – money, house, clothes, etc. But an entrepreneur starts with nothing and creates everything.

How did you learn to price?

When I started I was charging AED 50–100. Pricing was influenced by our locations. Hotels helped us price. In a hotel, customers on holiday were ok with AED 300–400. We have customers who spend AED 3,000.

How long did it take you to learn 'business'?

I learnt how to manage money when MBRE gave me funds. I had AED 250,000 and I did not yet know how to build the business. I just had the idea and the desire. I was not smart. I started aggressively acquiring locations. I learnt how to negotiate rents, getting staff, training them, doing contracts, etc. In the past ten years I have opened and closed locations. If a location doesn't work, we close it immediately.

Other developments you have done?

We cater to foreign customers and have tried to internationalize Henna designs. Six to seven times in a month, customers bring designs and ask our artists to reproduce them. We now have an in-house designer. We have added two-three additional colors to Henna.

When did you start taking a salary from the business?

The business is profitable. I just draw the money for my expenses. That's the reason I started the business. Everything that is earned is invested for growth.

How many employees?

Nearly sixty-five. Training staff is a challenge. Everyone knows application of Henna. Customer service and retail standards need improvement. I have been desirous of starting a Henna training school.

Other challenges?

Managing multiple locations and franchising. I manage the locations myself and my experience with franchising has not been good. Henna is a cash business. In a service business like Henna, if the staff doesn't create a bill we can lose the money. What if a franchisee doesn't show sales? And most of the value is in the location and staff. If I don't control both, how will we make money? Franchising in Kuwait failed. We started. The shop made money. The partner then decided to operate the business without us; they changed the name and continued the business. I lost my staff and with them, the business knowledge.

Starting a Business Is like Pushing a Wheel till the Wheel Picks up Momentum of Its Own

Entrepreneur	Gilbert Ashram
Company and website	INCON Infrastructure Contracting LLC/ www.incon.ae
Company services	Contracting
Year started	2008
Tips for entrepreneurs	• Do what you are good at. And what you are passionate about. • Business is not the idea but the execution. • Learn. Try everything. Never stop trying. • Mistakes will happen. Build on mistakes.

What is INCON?

INCON is a contracting company that plans and builds infrastructure. We have the capability of managing the infrastructure that we plan and build. INCON currently focuses on three sectors – Electrical, Mechanical and Telecom. As an example, we plan, procure, supply, build and manage 33 KVA electricity distribution infrastructures. In the telecom industry we have executed contracts to connect remote areas with fiber optic cables. INCON is also an approved mechanical contractor for infrastructure for the industrial sector.

Where did the idea of INCON emerge?

I started my career with Consolidated Contractors Company (CCC) and gained experience in doing infrastructure work. I realized that large projects were broken into smaller contracts by main contractors. The main contractors focused on executing the most important elements of contract and outsourced the others. Infrastructure projects were usually outsourced to specialized subcontractors. As I gained experience an opportunity presented itself in 2008 to provide services to the contractor executing the Dubai Metro. We developed the business on top of this prestigious work; after which we became approved as a contractor for DU, Etisalat and so forth.

Where was the seed of entrepreneurship in you?

I suspect it was dormant. Twice in my work career I managed to increase the size and scale of the business I was assigned responsibility for. I began to think that if I could do it twice then I could do it for myself. I also got the confidence based on the diversity and quality of work experiences, in both site and project management. With CCC I used to be assigned a site where I managed people to implement projects. I used to wonder, 'If this was work then I could do it for myself.' CCC took me to the first turning point. After CCC I worked for a trading company managing suppliers. I worked in remote project sites e.g., Ruwais. It took me 6 months to understand how trading works in a city. I felt like a villager coming to a city and discovering new things. The GM of the company was a shrewd business person. He inspired me to learn the commercial aspects of business. I learnt the business that underpins work. Those two years were a second turning point. I went back to a construction firm, worked directly with the owner and expanded the contracting division from a handful of persons to a few hundred. This tempted me to be on my own, work a business as per my own plan.

Explain?

As an employee I was often required to work as per the ideas and plans of others. I wanted to implement my own ideas, build a business according to my plan. I guess, by expressing my creativity.

After starting INCON, how did you go about pitching for business?

I leveraged my network. I had to create a jobs list. I used my network to get jobs and again used my network to do the job because I did not have resources. I had relationships with people with whom I had worked for many years. Some were prepared to support me with small and risk-free trial projects. Risk here refers to the personal and professional risk they took supporting an untested newbie. They promised to give me bigger projects if I delivered on smaller projects. I was looking for such opportunities. My plan was to deliver the projects using resources by affiliating with bigger partners. But the plan worked differently. As soon as I got the first job, we immediately got our resources and started making money. We started with the company that did the Dubai Metro. DU, Etisalat, the Army and the Municipality followed.

Example?

The first job was a very small job – AED 75K. I was told 'Gilbert, you do this one. We may require more work after a year.' When we did that in good time, we were given another one, valued at AED 1m. The first job was as a subcontractor to the main contractor. Within 3 or 4 months of the first job we began taking jobs directly, establishing INCON as an independent contractor.

Contracting requires capital – requirement in terms of performance bonds, bid bonds, advances to subcontractors, etc. How did you manage this?

I injected capital and managed the cash flow. We had the support of the client who knew that we were a new company. Similarly the suppliers were a part of the network and were willing to give us credit facilities. Things fell into place the proper way from the beginning. I can modestly say that the business got built around my personal credibility.

How did the family respond to you becoming an entrepreneur?

They believed in me and supported me. They did not doubt me. It was a new company but we had a plan. We were not chasing an idea, incurring expenses and waiting for customers to buy and then pay. They knew I had developed businesses. They also knew that businesses take time to become financially sound. I don't want to make it sound logical and give a feeling that there was no risk involved. Starting was a big risk. My GM joined me because he trusted me.

When did you start increasing headcount?

We started with twenty people. In the first phase we hired smaller numbers, giving sub-contracts to others. We started adding people when we got approved by DU. We are now around 150 in UAE.

Has the nature of your business changed with growth?

INCON has always been in the turnkey infrastructure business. We have been adding new teams that support the main business doing related work, servicing all the requirements in-house as opposed to outsourcing. We are also serving new markets. We intend to do MEP works for commercial and residential projects. This is very different from industrial projects, our original market, requiring lots of resources-planning, staff (engineers, draftsman and coordinators) and procurement.

Has this evolution been driven by the customer asking INCON to do additional work, is the customer helping you grow the business?

We have grown with the support of our customers. This happened with the Metro. It is happening now with the army, DU and others. We did an infrastructure job for DU in the Dubai region. They extended it to Abu Dhabi.

How is INCON growing?

We have diversified our activities and market segments. We have grown geographically, first to Abu Dhabi and now Doha. As we are growing, our client base is expanding. Once in a new region like Abu Dhabi, we search for sectors where we think we can add value e.g., we are exploring options in the Oil and Gas sector. In Doha we are venturing into commercial and residential work.

Challenges of the past seven years?

Financial challenges are the most difficult to manage. We have to execute and collect. But before that we must have the facilities to start the projects on schedule. Since we are a small company, every delay hurts. Sometimes resulting cash flows make it difficult to start another project. We have to grow because we are a small company and many members of the crew have joined us from large companies to grow.

Size of current contracts?

4 to 5 m each.

How do you balance your time – identifying new opportunities versus execution of the contracts?

I focus more on business development now. We have managers dedicated to every geography managing project execution. Managing cash flow takes a good part of my attention at this stage as I am developing Abu Dhabi, Doha and Dubai.

Why do clients work with INCON?

We are an execution company. But we don't just execute. We have the know-how to improve designs given to us by clients as we execute. Sometimes when we reach a remote site the design given by the client is unworkable. We then provide them better solutions. Our relationship with the clients is such that we give feedback, brainstorm and sometimes even argue with them trying to convince them of our ideas. This approach of partnering clients has paid us dividends in more contracts.

Any special way you have organized?

To be a quick execution company I have had to delegate certain authority to my managers to allow them latitude and authority in decision making. They can react to emergencies to meet urgent client requirements. We learnt the need for this early in our work when we faced challenges with clients like the

Army, Metro or DU. Working in this manner gives us credibility with clients. Any company can provide contracting but there are certain values that will differentiate companies from others.

You sound relaxed about INCON.

I took my last real holiday 10 years ago. I do take off for a week but when I am away, the mind drifts back after 24 hours. It is always working. Not that anything urgent requires my attention. But I just want to be in the middle of the action.

Does anything stress you about the business?

Now it is positive stress. I want to be better at what we do. I am not worried about failure. I am impatient to see where we will be after 10 years. I discount work-related stress. It is a part of the day-to-day problems of contracting. It was not always like this. In the beginning adequacy of financial resources was a challenge and stressful. Things have improved and I can feel the wheel turning. I have realized that a businessman has to keep the wheel turning until one feels the wheel turning on its own.

Challenges to growth?

Recruiting right talent. This is a continuous process. We have made errors but corrected them quickly. If we had the right talent the company would pick a momentum of growth on its own. And after we get the right people, giving them a good vision of INCON is important. I will give you the positive example of Doha, of what a good team can do. We created a team whose first contract was AED 6 m. They are now negotiating an AED 20 m contract. I go to Doha every two months. And the revenue is double that of Dubai.

Did you give discounts to win contracts?

Yes, in the beginning. I was taking time to understand how pricing was going to work for a new business and developing ideas of penetrating the market. Penetration required discounting.

And now?

I am winning contracts based on service proposition. My pricing has become better.

How long did it take you to understand the cost structure of your company?

It took us the first eighteen months because we were growing quickly and needed time to stabilize, to consolidate.

Have you changed as a person in your entrepreneurial journey?

I look at things differently. I am more tolerant about challenges and mistakes. I made mistakes on my entrepreneurial journey. I sometimes feel I take a 'bigger' and 'different' perspective of issues facing the company than others.

When did you start drawing a salary from the business?

I took a salary after two years of starting up. We were growing and I was re-injecting every penny into the business. We are still growing in Qatar and I am still reinvesting. Our revenues dropped during the recession because we work with the governments and they had bigger challenges. This is when diversification to Abu Dhabi and Qatar happened.

Series of Experiments

Entrepreneur	Suhail Bin Ahmed
Company and website	Happy Yummy/www.happyummy.com
Business	Kiosk retailing
Year established	2003
Tips for entrepreneurs	• Decide, roll up your sleeves and execute.
• My startup was a series of experiments.
• Learn the business by doing. I was observant and inquisitive. I learnt from customers and suppliers what I needed to know about running my business.
• Minimize startup costs and pay attention to cash flow. I used every Dirham on growth.

How did Happy Yummy start?

Starting a business was a financial aspiration. I am from a humble family. I was also motivated by a desire to show that an Emirati could start and run a business. From childhood I had seen people starting businesses and reflectively wondered why business owners were invariably expatriates. In 2003 I got a chance to sell ice cream in a supermarket using 1.5 m wide counters. I took the risk when I got the opportunity. I had no business experience. I knew nothing about sourcing products, selling, marketing and managing employees. To start the business I had to manage self-doubt. I took the plunge knowing that many expatriates who started businesses were like me; they were neither from rich families nor had business experience.

How did Happy Yummy begin?

The startup was slow and sequential. I first negotiated rent. Not to carry a burden of fixed rent, I requested the supermarket to charge me a percentage of sales. They surprisingly agreed. I then got a business license. To keep costs low I searched for carpenters in Dubai and Sharjah. A carpenter made a counter for AED 2,000. I personally sold ice cream in the supermarket to learn details of the business. Having learnt to sell to consumers, I could train new salespersons as the business grew. I needed to differentiate my product from others in the market.

Were there any missteps?
No. The startup was a series of experiments. I was learning how to do the job.

How did you convince organizations to work with you?
I keep a positive outlook on things. I think transparency and openness has worked with overseas suppliers. I target a company to work with. If they decline, I search for others doing similar things. I don't give up easily.

With how much money did you start the business?
I started the business by taking a personal loan of AED 70,000.

How did Happy Yummy grow?
I started with two locations, one each in Dubai and Abu Dhabi. Growth started in Abu Dhabi. I was offered two additional locations in Abu Dhabi a month after starting up. I had to solve supply and distribution challenges. I took a small 3 m × 4 m shop and installed three freezers. Ice cream was delivered and stored in the shop itself. I delivered ice cream from this shop to other locations using my car. I quickly realized that I didn't have free time to grow the business. I was still working and taking hours off from my job to give to the business. This was not a good idea. I resigned. I was single with no encumbrances. I dedicated all my time to the business.

How did you know you were doing the right things?
I was operating thirteen locations by 2004. I saw an advertisement for the Sheikh Mohammed Bin Rashid Establishment for Young Business Leader awards. I applied and was interviewed. I had to explain the profitability of the business. My accounts were poorly maintained. Intuitively I believed I was making money. I had finished my startup money by the time the 7th kiosk opened. I was depositing the sales into a bank account which had surplus cash after paying for purchases and expenses. For me increasing surplus cash was profit. Hence I had continued opening additional locations.

I got the award! I couldn't believe it. The business was my life. I was working 24 × 7. The award was an affirmation of my work. I was on the correct path. The award removed a burden of risks from my shoulders. My family saw me in the paper. They too believed in me.

When did you draw a salary from the business?

I didn't draw a salary till the opening of the thirteenth location. I was conserving cash. I used to collect the sales revenue and promptly deposit it in the bank. I was worried. What if I needed additional money for the business? No bank would give me a loan. I didn't have a job. And I was new to business. One of my sales staff with administrative experience helped me keep track of sales at the different locations. I debited my business expenses for petrol and food and drew AED 150 per day as personal expense. Apprehension made me save money. But I had self-belief. I believed in growing. On the positive side, I wanted to expand quickly. I first started taking salary as a percentage of sales. This became unwieldy as the business grew. I now have a fixed salary. I am also very careful about using company cash as my personal money.

When did Happy Yummy become a business?

2008. I think of the present office as a milestone. For four years I operated from many locations; sometimes from small shops or temporary offices. I was continuously shifting. In the initial years I did everything myself. I learnt business. I grew the business. It reached a stage where it needed organization. The physical office helped me get organized. I could no longer be everywhere. I learnt to manage the business from a distance. I can give examples. Retail business is people dependent. I discovered pilferage in some locations. I brought in managers and supervisors to control the locations. Recruitment, training and management of counter staff are all properly organized. I installed cameras to monitor locations. I started controlling costs. We now have vehicles for delivery. I installed GPS tracking to manage fuel costs.

What challenges did you face in people management?

I have created a team spirit in the company. It is participative. When selecting a new product to sell, I ask all team members to assess and comment. I am naïve but when I work with or recruit people I start from a position of trust. I have been cheated many times but have never initiated legal proceedings.

How do you evaluate new product ideas?

I learn everything from the market. I search for competitors, selling same or similar products. Then I assess product salability. Food and beverage market has lots of products. Opportunity is large but I can't start anything. The local market has changed in the past 15 years. I'll give you the example of how I started the corn business immediately after starting the ice-cream business in 2003.

I was always searching for new locations for the ice-cream kiosks. I used to visit colleges and schools. They were reluctant to have ice-cream kiosks. This induced search for a second product. I went to every exhibition, not necessarily related to food, in the World Trade Centers in Dubai and Abu Dhabi, in search of ideas. I saw a company selling sweet corn. The idea seemed good for kiosk retailing. Corn was not available from local suppliers. I needed a supplier. I networked with Dubai Municipality Food Inspection Department to locate the source of corn. I was unsuccessful. A web search located a farm in Malaysia. I took a flight and landed up at the farm without an appointment. They were surprised to see an Arab reaching the farm. I introduced myself. We clicked. They were prepared to sell to me and I started bringing in small quantities of corn. The locations, hesitant to allow ice-cream retail in a kiosk, now had a choice, and the corn business started to grow. Today I am more careful. Capital-rich business competitors exist. They can invest and patiently wait for profits. I need to carefully understand competition, costs, selling price and risks.

How many products do you test before selection?

I am in a position to experiment with new ideas. If they work I will continue or else back away.

How do you manage the risk of a wrong location?

I have 37 locations. A kiosk-based business is easy to startup. It has low costs of entry compared to fixed format retailing. I work with the mall owners to select locations. I give them the list of products that I retail. They select the products; sometimes all, sometimes a few. It is also easy for me to exit a location; exit barriers (costs) are low because I recover the entire kiosk. We recently closed seven locations. I take chances with locations. It is easy for me leave if the location is not working or if the rent goes up.

Tell me about yourself.

I was in the army for 3–4 years. Then I managed my father's small tire shop. He had problems with his partners, and the shop closed. I always worked in private companies.

What prepared you for entrepreneurship?

I don't know but I can share some personal traits. I am inquisitive and hardworking. I saw people starting businesses in Dubai. I realized I was no different; if they could, so could I. I wanted to do something different. I am observant. I am always searching for what to do, whether in a mall or an overseas trip. I am very active. I cannot imagine sitting in a coffee shop for 5–6 hours. My business meetings last an hour. After that they are unproductive. I am a restless person. I am always thinking, searching for ways to grow and improve. I like to meet other businessmen. I learn from them. One never knows where ideas come from. And I like to execute. I learn by doing.

When you started, did you think the business would get big?

I never thought about the size and details of the business – number of employees, branches, locations, organization and control. The business grew naturally. I implemented the business and opportunities came my way. Even now I am sometimes asked to reassess my decisions e.g., paying a high rent for an office. My decisions and reactions to emerging situations are spontaneous.

Where do you see the business in 2–3 years?

Happy Yummy is now a 10 million business and we have over 50 employees. I tried geographic expansion three years ago. I opened a branch in Qatar. Within three-months I was offered fourteen locations. I invested AED 950,000. I did it alone, without a partner or a franchise. I wanted to try the business myself. I wanted to understand the management challenges of geographic expansion. I chose Qatar because it is nearby. I tried and lost. I closed the company. The employees let me down in Qatar. I learnt the importance of people. I needed to have given importance to hiring before growing. I realized the costs of managing business in another country. I will now franchise for growth. Franchisees know their territory and have networks in place. I am developing a franchising plan. I am always searching for new products. I make careful investments. I don't want to start new businesses and take risks. I am focused on improving the profitability of the business through cost control.

What is the most important worry you have now?

My biggest tension is the expense on rent. Malls are very inflexible. We have no capacity to negotiate. A high rent has a direct impact on selling prices. Higher prices impact customers and the image of Dubai.

A Mix of Boldness and Being Conservative

Entrepreneur	Ishwar Jodha
Company and website	Triple Crown Shipping and Logistics/ www.tcsldubai.com
Company services	Freight forwarding
Tips for entrepreneurs	• Focus on the consistency of revenue. • Budget adequate working capital during startup. • Quickly establish corporate governance.

Where did you get the idea of 3C?

I started my career in shipping in 1977 and did it for 20 years in Dubai. That is all I knew and this was the business I could start.

Your knowledge of the domain enabled you to start the company. But what unique value proposition did you envisage to serve?

There are numerous freight forwarders in the market. I worked with many of them. There was no 'product' gap in the market. The gap existed in the service provided and experience of customers. I experienced the gap first hand. I leveraged my experience with APL. APL focused on quality, trained staff in delivering a quality experience and used IT effectively. I realized that if I used the practices I learned in APL I could have an edge in the market.

Was market entry easy?

When I entered, the market was highly fragmented. There were many large and numerous small freight forwarders. I needed to compete with the big guys but the real opportunity was in the market space occupied by the smaller players. That is where I could provide service and win business.

If I am an importer of goods, what would be the specific edge?

I thought of some of the things before starting but I learned most of the things after entering the business. When I started the business, I was a novice despite my years in shipping. It was like getting into the deep end of the pool and learning how to swim. We have developed responsiveness to the needs of customers. This has become the culture of the organization. We are also able to track shipments and provide real-time information access to customers via a website. This is today an industry standard. The difference of TCSL is that when you call, a person talks to you. We provide a human touch. I worry for how long we will be able to sustain this as organization grows.

What prompted you to take the plunge, to take a risk?

In 20 years I had become the Managing Director. Senior positions come with the need to take transfers. I did move out but the desire of coming back to Dubai was real. A friend who is into freight forwarding convinced me to enter the business. His assurance was the tipping point. It became a perfect opportunity to also test the latent urge that every corporate executive has of trying something on their own.

What was the family dialogue like?

I started the business when I was fifty. Most of my family obligations were over. My wife was more matter-of-fact. She said, do it if you feel like doing it. Though I feel she was a bit concerned. Not only did the business start with my end of service benefits but I also had to sell some property to keep the businesses going in the first three years.

Did customers sense the difference in TCSL service?

I like to believe this. A lot of customers have stayed with us from the day we started. I have also lost customers. There are occasions where I let go of new customers or jobs that would require the commitment of extra resources.

I am an intermediary between shippers and lines; often my service quality is dependent and confused with the carrier's service level. If the carrier messes up there is very little we can do to change the situation.

In terms of pricing, is TCSL at the market level?

We are at the market level. I have not discounted the prices to get business.

You were running a corporate outfit with salespeople. When you started you needed to get back to selling. How did you do it as a person?

One has to decide to do it. It is not a time to think. It is the time to get on with it.

How did you develop the business model of your business?

I was fortunate. I started with some business. I did not have to wait for six months for my first business. I had a contract before I had an office. The revenue stream helped me sustain the business and build my confidence that the business would work.

Has the business growth been as planned?

The business growth reflects my conservative attitude. I have grown steadily.

Why did you feel that starting the business was like being pushed in the deep end of the pool?

I was venturing into the unknown. There was tremendous uncertainty. If someone came to me for advice today to start a freight forwarding company, I would advise him to start with a couple of long-term contracts in place. I was surviving month to month. I was visiting customers who were giving me contracts but they were short-term, usually with a six-month horizon. There was an uncertainty about predictable revenue. I was unsure whether I would be able to meet my costs next month. This is why I had to sell my assets to build the business. I estimated my fixed costs and went to banks that declined my request for a loan. Imagine my situation. I did not have a long-term contract. I did not have deep networks in the shipping business. In my MNC experience we had offices everywhere. I did not know where to go or whom to contact if I had cargo coming out of China. I got an email out of the blue requesting me to join a shipping network. Nobody in the local market told me about the network. I decided to join a 'network.' It was like a jackpot. I took a chance, more out of a necessity. I think I took the step because to do business I needed to travel to many locations. There were costs involved. In a network I could engage with agents across the world. The network started generating business. Today I don't spend too much time in customer acquisition, for which I have a team. I focus on nurturing the networks.

What unique steps you took stand out?

My first focus was on managing the cash flow. I did what I had practiced as a manager. My second work practice was tracking month on month performance. I ensured that our performance was measured against a budgeted number. When the team looks at a number they know whether they are ok and are able to focus on what we need to look at.

Did you create a compensation structure?

I did not give a performance bonus for achieving a target. I showed them where the company was, the growth plan and the budget. Budget was higher than the easily achievable. The team was eligible for exceeding the budget.

When did you draw a salary better than your last job?

Not for the first eight years. I am there now. But importantly my company value and worth is what is encouraging.

Are you still worried about the momentum of growth of the business?

I am still a little tense; positively tense. I am more confident now that we are working with agents and regular enquiries are flowing in. I am not developing the business entirely alone. Customers also want to work with us. This is comforting. I face the uncertainties of a small business. The team doesn't have any fat. I have a person doing a job. If he or she goes on leave or is unwell, pressure builds up. Large organizations have specialized staff. A customer service person may only be serving customers. So I multi-task my team members by cross-training them. They back up for each other.

When you started did you need to unlearn your professional experience?

As a professional I was used to a certain lifestyles. I told myself that it didn't exist anymore. The first step was to curtail myself and not the organization. I learnt to do cost cutting myself before doing it on the organization. I have sustained this restraint through the startup and growth phases. I am today at a stage where I can afford to loosen up a bit. This has now become our culture. I have given salary increments to the staff. But did not take any. These are small signals to the team. As MD of APL I was an avid golfer. As an entrepreneur my mind was occupied 24×7 with the business. I was always worried about how the business would work or thinking what had to be done next. I stopped playing golf. My daughter was a budding golfer and I wanted to send her to golf school but at that stage it was too expensive. This was a big personal sacrifice. I did not take a holiday for the first three years.

Any slip-ups while building the business?

I tried to keep a watchful eye on everything while starting the business. However errors did happen. Attention to detail is an important requirement in shipping. One of my team members authorized a delivery of shipment in India without the collection of freight. That is a total no-no as far as shipments are concerned. I was not in the office as I was on an overseas trip. The customer had been with us for three years. He was not in Dubai and requested for release of goods confirming his return the next day. The customer got his goods and didn't live up to his commitments. He also had an expired trade license. We had no recourse. I had to visit Mumbai searching for him, trying to file a case in alien jurisdiction. This episode in hindsight made me realize the importance of corporate governance. Today 3C is a Dubai SME 100 company.

Learning?

Taking/checking a trade license of a business is now an integral part of the process. We run the risk of dealing with businesses, giving credit, where the owners can just skip the country and fly away. For a small set up, this is a big deal. I have to pay much more importance to detail in my business compared to what I was used to in APL where every detail was embedded in operating systems. In my company I was building bottom-up. I am always alert and worried if we have checked everything.

Growth plans?

Growth plans are a function of opportunity and costs. Geographic growth is a good idea based on markets where we do good business. In 2008 I did think of warehousing and distribution. We are currently outsourcing warehousing. And it is expensive. So it was a make or buy option. Now with the boom back in Dubai getting a warehouse is expensive.

What worries you about TCSL?

Succession planning. My son and daughter are in totally different careers from freight forwarding. There is always the uncertainty of a small business. We have not reached a stage where nothing will happen.

How have you changed as a person in the last 7 years?

I have become a lot more conservative than I ever was in expenditures and controls. I have experienced uncertainties and want to be very cautious. I have had to dig deep to make ends meet. I have seen difficult times. I feel that to overcome challenges one needs savings and surplus.

In APL I was a part of a corporate culture taking large capital decisions. To decide I had to manage getting lots of approvals. As an entrepreneur, I decide. I take smaller steps but a lot quicker.

A Good Way to Start a Business May Not Be the Best Way to Run the Business

Entrepreneur	Hydros Jassem
Company and website	Fragrance Delivery Technology/ http://www.oxygenpowered.com
Company business	Manufacture of fuel cell based fragrance dispensers
Year established	2005
Tips for entrepreneurs	<ul><li>Believe in yourself.</li><li>Self-assess and leverage your strengths.</li><li>Get people with domain expertise.</li><li>Be smart to hire people who are smarter than you are.</li><li>Delegate and empower your staff to make their own decisions. Even if they make mistakes.</li><li>Be ready to adapt. Have a plan A, Plan B, plan C, and plan D.</li><li>Don't be scared to fail. Success will come to you if you are willing to work hard through a series of failures.</li><li>Starting a business is easy, making it successful requires perseverance and hard work.</li></ul>

Where was seed of entrepreneurship in you?

My first business was a video library in India which I started when I was eighteen. My sister bought a video player for us in Mysore. We had a video player but no videos to watch. I looked around and saw there were 10–15 families with the same problem. I looked at this as an opportunity to go to Bangalore to visit my friends and bring back videos to watch. After seeing the videos I started lending them to others on a daily basis. And soon this became a business when my dad and a friend gave me some money to start a shop. We repaid the money in a few years.

Did it grow?

It was huge success and still exists, though I don't own it anymore. I then started a flower shop which I quickly shut down. I was unable to maintain customer commitments because of the unpredictable supply of flowers. I then started an advertising agency with a friend of mine and later a company to export condoms and disposable syringes from Indian manufacturers.

Reaction of the family?

My parents were in Dubai. I had not told them about my business adventures. They believed I was continuing my studies. My dad did indirectly give me Rs. 40,000 as my first investment for the business, which was a lot less than my college fees.

How did it all unwind?

When you are young, you don't think about cash flows. We were at an age where our needs were small and we were seeing a lot of money flowing in and out. At that moment you don't realize the importance of cash flow and make careless mistakes. I had to close down all the businesses when I landed in debt. I came to Dubai to look for a job in 1992, nine years after I started my first business, to repay my debts.

What happened in Dubai?

I worked in sales for a couple of companies. I finally got an offer to manage a new agency for a distribution company, Gulfax, selling Colgate-Palmolive branded institutional cleaning products. I didn't know anything about cleaning products. I learnt the business by going out, cleaning toilets/washrooms and experiencing the product. Within 2 years we, my wife and I, worked and cleared all our debts. In 1996, the itch to do business restarted. Two things conspired. A college friend of mine was keen to come to Dubai and start a trading business. And on my travels in the region I used to get enquiries about the supply of diverse products from Dubai. I was now cautious. My business partner and I each put in 16,000 Dirhams. I sold my Toyota Corolla whereas he had landed from India and put in his life savings. The business startup costs were covered from the start. Our first order was a container of biscuits, chocolates and diapers from Dubai to Seychelles. The business developed based on the knowledge of timber that my partner possessed. I started meeting timber suppliers in South Africa and US and tying up supply partnerships. My partner focused on selling.

Next?

The turning point came in 1998, Colgate-Palmolive sold the major chunk of their institutional products division. I declined an offer to work in Europe, instead established a cleaning products distribution and service company in Mumbai, India while working for Gulfax. The Indian company imported all products from the Dubai Company. It was a cost-plus model. A time came when this relationship was uncomfortable; I had to spend more time to develop my business. And we separated.

Where did air fresheners come from?

Technical Concepts (TC), an international company in hygiene solutions, including air fresheners. After my departure from Gulfax they offered me a job to manage their regional business. I declined, offering them an option of appointing us as the master distributor and to develop the business. We exchanged business plans, won the agency to manage the TC business in the Middle East, Africa and South Asia and have since grown the business to a leadership position. We understood the business, the economics and the value proposition for a distributor and so it was easy to set up distribution in the region. Meanwhile in our Indian company 80% of the business was coming from air fresheners whereas only 20% of our effort was going into managing the company. In two years our focus shifted entirely to air fresheners. Our Indian company now has a distribution network of over 50 distributors. Four years ago we also started a very successful service company that provides hygiene products for washrooms in India, with sixteen branches and 200 employees

How much capital did you put in your business?

Not much. It was an agency business. It required capital only for traveling.

The leap from indenting to manufacturing?

The regional MD of Technical Concepts (TC) approached markets differently. The traditional logic says – build market, get volumes and set up manufacturing. TC senses the market potential and begins with manufacturing even if the current market volumes are low. I never agreed with them but in hindsight it was the best decision. I was then responsible for setting up manufacturing facilities for their products in India, South Africa and Saudi Arabia.

Why do you think it makes sense?

For example, South Africa is a big market but a far-away market. To get goods it takes six weeks. The Rand is a very volatile currency. An importer is unable to predict his costs and this jeopardizes the entire business. The distributor, as a provider of hygiene services, enters into annual price contracts with customers for a fixed price where he installs an air freshener unit and supplies refill air freshener cartridges every month for 12 months. When the product price goes up because of Rand fluctuation, he substitutes the imported cartridge with a cheaper local poor quality product. Local manufacturing enables predictable pricing, speeds up time to market and upgrades market. Manufacturing is challenging but not complicated with a good strategic plan. It requires engaging a reliable contract manufacturer, developing an agreement, sharing the formulae and monitoring quality. The more experience I got in manufacturing, the more I realized its potential and understood how it impacted competition. I also sensed the size of the hygiene and air freshener industry. The business was akin to a razor and blade business model. Once a fragrance dispenser is installed, 12-month cartridge replenishment follows. Around this time I realized the market worldwide was looking for greener products that were not the routine aerosol refills with propellants. Customers were willing to pay a premium for a continuous fragrance system over a metered spray system that gave a fragrance only for a few minutes after it sprayed. I came across a technology that was being used in the pharmaceutical industry using pure oxygen to deliver drugs to humans and animals. I spoke to the scientist who had the patents and came to an arrangement that he would develop a product for air fresheners.

Did you want to put up a factory?

No. My original idea was not to establish a factory. Once the fuel cell based oxygen generator was ready we could have contract manufacturing in Taiwan to assemble the dispenser. We wanted to license the technology. We would develop new products and market them worldwide. We could share the royalty with the technology developer who manufactured the generator. The economics looked good. This is how it started. I thought I didn't need much money when I started.

And then?

Suddenly the technology developer changed his approach. He wanted to sell the technology and not work on royalty. He promised to transfer a portion of the IP that we could use to develop products for our application and markets. My first reaction was a no. I just couldn't afford the investment.

You now carried the entire risk.

I thought we can make the generator and contract manufacture the components.

And then reality hits you when you start. To buy and own technology one needs capital. To raise capital one needs a 100% ownership company with share certificates. Such a company has to be in the Free zone. In the Free zone, the smallest place you get is 600 sq. m. One doesn't need such large spaces at the early stage of business development. As a startup you want to do the components in the most economic location. I wanted to do the tooling in Taiwan, plastic component manufacturing in India and assembly in Dubai. We discovered this was not a good economic idea, time-wise and control-wise, in the product development phase. This forced me to establish the manufacturing in Dubai. I was here; I could take quick decisions, adapt, manage and get it right.

At which stage did you have the confidence that the investment was going to work?

After two years and investing $4 m I wasn't sure what was going to happen. This was the most uncertain period in my last 15–20 years. I had 'put' money in the scientist. He had given proof of concept that the idea will work. I had sent an engineer to get trained. He came back, worked with us for over a year, declared that he could not make it work and quit. Till then I believed that if there was specialized expertise in the team, I should not get involved. I, therefore, did not go for training, even though others cautioned me. In hindsight I should have. A part of me still tells me it is not the right way to work. The entrepreneur in me tells me it is good to know everything. But what may be a good way to start a business may not be the way to run the business.

When the engineer quit you were still developing the product. You say that you wish you had gone and engaged in product development.

No. My first choice would have been to get a better person. Even the second engineer didn't work out. So I picked up the pieces, went and learnt the technology from the scientist myself. In retrospect, I realize it was the best thing to have happened, since I got that technical information transferred in a proper manner.

Did the scientist make a prototype and prove it?

The science behind it was known. It was being used in the pharmaceutical industry. He had to adapt it for a particular use. The challenge was to convert it into an air freshener at a low cost. He made a prototype that works. Our job in Dubai was to use the prototype and establish a manufacturing line for mass production, so that it produces the right quality and a cost economic product.

When we started I did not know what product development involved. I thought it just involved replication. How difficult could that be? I didn't know I would be working on multiple fronts – R&D, timely production, product quality, sales and marketing. I now know how difficult it is to get a new technology product launched. Now we have developed the product. It is working and has been accepted by the market. Now we have to scale up. Today we are selling our product in twelve countries worldwide including the Middle East, South Africa, Australia, China and India. We are getting ready to launch our products in the USA and Europe. Our product was shortlisted for the innovation award at the industry show in Amsterdam and Chicago.

How much money have you put into business?

$8 m. I never thought I would invest more than a million dollars. I had no experience in running a large business, preparing proper cash flow projections and seeing as well as assessing risks. I had set up so many small businesses and went through my share of successes and failures that I thought I could do it. A friend of mine looked at my business and remarked, 'It is a great technology but do you know how much risk is involved in this?' This remark made us rework our approach. I had never looked at it from the risk point of view. The second phase of the product development started from that one statement.

Explain?

I will be technical. The oxygen generator is a part of the refill. It has over 13 different components and each component has to be 0.001 mm accurate. If one component is defective, the refill wouldn't work. Only when the oxygen generator is activated, will the refill get used. This implied that you could never guarantee the working of the refill until it works. One can't test a refill and stop the oxygen generator. This is when I shifted gears. We had to guarantee every dispenser and every refill. We separated everything we were doing into modules and reduced risk.

Challenges of manufacturing in Dubai?

We do manufacturing and assembly. The challenge is sourcing components and sub-assemblies. We can't go to local companies with designs and drawings and ask them to make things for us. So we end up going to India, Taiwan, China, US and Europe. We face a similar situation for the supply of components. If I need a standard tube I may not get it off-the-shelf. It is easier to call Mumbai and get it shipped by air or order it from the USA and get it couriered. Also when we go overseas Dubai is known as a trading center not as a manufacturing hub. It takes time to establish credibility with suppliers of manufactured components.

Customer challenges?

Product performance was the key to acceptance. I was in distribution so I knew that customers were looking for better products.

Did you also change the pricing model?

Yes. With time the model flipped. In our earlier concept, the oxygen generator was integral to the refill. Then, because of the risks involved, we put the fuel cell and the oxygen generator in the dispenser. Now the dispenser became a one-time cost and the refill an affordable recurring cost.

Was the approach accidental?

It was not deliberate. I expected the modified concept to come after we had exploited the market on the new fuel cell oxygen generator idea. When the original idea was not going to work, we had to immediately bring the alternative idea to the fore. I would tell every entrepreneur to have a plan A, plan B, plan C and a plan D. If one doesn't work, be ready with an alternative plan.

Has your trading network helped?

Relationships help in opening doors and fast-tracking product evaluation, not selling. Sometimes relationships are a problem when people ask for sweetheart deals.

Most important worry?

Cash flow and capital. I don't want to discount the product to get volumes. Now I have orders and need capital. I can now sit with investors and promise them a return. It is now a question of pricing the shares, not the product. Two years ago the risk was whether the product would work and if the market would accept our product. That is no longer the issue. I am not going to lose the $8 m investment.

Today the product is accepted, and orders are flowing in. We need the capital to keep pace with our growth. The challenge is finding working capital financing. Banks fund companies which have sales for 3 years and a good balance sheet. The sales cannot be sustained without a good working capital funding. So it is a Catch 22 situation. However, we are confident we have a great product, a great team and a great attitude. We are confident to raise the capital shortly. After all, the exhilaration of running a business is meeting the challenges and rising to the occasion. This is the entrepreneur's elixir!

How have you changed as a person?

I have learnt a lot more than what I knew before. I do regret not completing my studies. A lot of things I am learning now, I may have learnt earlier.

Business Is Not About Training but About How to Make It Happen

Entrepreneur	Jolly Thomas
Company and website	Eduscope International/www.eduscope.me
Company business	Specialized training institute for healthcare professionals
Year established	2008
Tips for entrepreneurs	• There are occasions when you will experience being in the middle of the sea, alone, lost without a raft or even a lifeboat. • You've got to learn to live and manage by your wits alone.

How did you start?

We are a specialized healthcare training and development company. We serve the needs of continuous professional development of healthcare professionals-doctors, nurses and technicians. I started the company focused on the training needs of the nursing profession.

If I'm a doctor what would trainings offered by Eduscope give me?

Healthcare system is getting more complex every day. New technologies and developments are becoming mainstream. Professionals who take care of our health need to keep themselves updated with new developments. This is now mandatory. The Health Authority has made it mandatory for healthcare professionals. Licenses to practice medicine are normally renewed every two years. The Health Authority made a certain number of credit hours of training equivalency as a requirement to renew licenses. This is where we come in. We train health professionals and they get the credit hours required.

What inspired you to leave a profession and become a businesswoman?

Inspiration and coincidence. I am a qualified nurse. Nursing is my passion. A person inspired me. She, a teacher, started a school with an idea, passion and drive. She did this despite personal challenges. I was a nurse working in the military hospital in Sharjah. I used to see nurses unable to use their knowledge in their practice. I noticed differences in their dealings with patients; they were not always following procedures that were required and prescribed. I was always committed to my professional development. I used to pay from my pocket to attend courses and trainings to remain up-to-date. I thought there must be others like me willing to pay for their professional development. This perception of need evoked a desire to resign and start Eduscope in 2008. Dubai Healthcare City was a coincidence. I helped a friend conduct seminars to recruit nurses for the US. She established a professional training company. I took over the license when she wanted to close her business.

Where did you get the motivation to do business?

I have been acquainted with people who have started businesses. They all had courage to start. Many succeeded, some failed. I reflected on why they succeeded. The successful entrepreneurs lived their business; they focused, giving one-pointed attention on the business and were motivated with a desire to succeed. I was motivated by them. I compared myself with them. I was similar in some ways and dissimilar in others; stronger in some traits and weaker in others. I was thinking and discussing this for two years with my family. I have a housemaid, 65 years old, who brought me up from childhood. She is like family. She was the one who said 'go for it.' My husband instilled the confidence in me that I could do it. Everybody was ready to support me. Even my superiors in the army, hesitant in letting me go, offered a fallback if I wanted to return. By that time my motivation had crossed a limit, a threshold and I just wanted to start with full risk. It was then easy to start.

You had no personal fears?

Initially no, I was very ignorant.

What happened?

I plunged into a lot of things. I was willing to do anything. Doing business was not easy. I was innocent of how business worked. I started dealing with friends. Some of them took advantage of my poor business understanding at that moment. I had a network of relationships in Dubai. I made introductions to solicit business for others that resulted in contracts. I was then forgotten. I did not understand money in business when I started. I did not understand that business is about doing 'cold' transactions. And that while doing business people focus on transactions and often do not value relationships. Relationships were valuable to me when I started. I have changed. I have learnt to document all work-related relationships.

How did the business start?

Very slowly. Professional development training was a new business for Dubai. We had to work with many government departments to make them aware of the need for continuing training of healthcare professionals and the value of our service proposition- trainings in Dubai. It took a while but we succeeded. Professional development became mandatory in 2010–11.

You started the company in 2008.

We organized seminars and trainings within organizations between 2008 and 10.

Who did the training?

I did the training in the early days. We engaged experts for programs I couldn't do.

Did participants acquire credit? And did the participants pay for knowledge?

Yes. We certified the credits. The certificate was based on the number of hours spent in the class. The certificate said 'ABC participated in a learning seminar conducted by Eduscope and delivered by XYZ who is a respected person in the field, profession, or specialization.'

Did you know how to price trainings? And manage the costs to deliver?

I didn't have a clue. We used a thumb rule; we priced 20–30% above cost. I don't know whether what we did was right or wrong. In subsequent years we tested the price. We raised prices and saw our results dip.

Did you go to organizations and offer services like training and seminars? What kind of reception did you get?

I visited organizations but the reception we got was very cold. Most people were disinterested. They had no need for training. It wasn't mandatory then. And if they wanted to pay, their willingness to pay wouldn't cover our costs. The Health Authority of Abu Dhabi supported and guided us on how to go about getting business. They were our first client. They gave us accreditation and directed us to organizations that needed our services, what was needed and how to go about working with them.

How did you select which courses to start?

We started with courses based on my nursing experience. I collected evaluations and feedback as we implemented the program. Many of my initial customers, nearly 60%, were self-paying. Others got support from their employers. I learnt that the real market need is for professional self-development. Few organizations invest money in development of their people so a lot of people invest from their own pockets develop themselves. And they are careful and judicious in where they go for training based on quality and accreditation. This has changed because of the mandatory requirement by the Health Authority. Now we are unable to identify where they are coming from and their motivation. I have some participants who have attended 100 hours of training when the law requires only 20 hours.

Do you make more money in the business compared to your salary when you left the army?

The business paid me a salary higher than my last salary in the army three years after I started the business.

Have you changed as a person?

I have become a tougher person. People used to fool me. I used to do a lot of free work. I am more careful now. I am more commercial. I calculate a lot. Sometimes even in my dreams. It wasn't like this before. I sit in a lot of meetings. I get preoccupied with work so I need to keep some time to reflect on what I am doing. I can't just flow with the current.

Any surprises? Things that happened differently from what you were expecting.

I was surprised at the behaviors of customers. As I engaged with organizations I would sense they wanted to do programs with me based on what they were saying in meetings. Then they would make a U-turn. They would give weak reasons for declining our proposals e.g., the terms offered by us. I learnt to manage disappointments after engaging with organizations and spending lots of effort and time.

Have you learnt to identify who are good potential customers? And others with whom you don't need to spend too much time?

I can figure this out.

Was anything easier?

When I started I had not thought of the number of years required to create a business. I didn't think in those terms. I thought we are going to start and it would begin working. I had not thought about how slowly it would start to work; it would take long to convince everyone of what we were doing and make them pay for it.

When did you realize that business would not be automatic? Give me an example of how you began to control the business.

I realized late in the second year that the business doesn't work because I am there and I created a business. In the beginning of the second year I was still thinking of just going with the flow and waiting patiently for the business to gain momentum. Then I changed. I started to drive the business in a different way; in my way.

You started making more choices.

In the first two years I learnt what to market and to whom to market. Starting a business is tense and stressful. I am now able to manage situations that make me anxious. To be frank even now I have more occasions when I am stressed. When I do a training program I am tense till the training finishes. When we get experts from overseas I am tense until they arrive and start the training. I have had occasions when they decided not to come at the last minute. I am tense because unforeseen things have an uncanny knack of happening. A new training commences as soon as another one finishes. As the strain of a training finishes, the next one begins evoking uncertainty. Most moments are tense.

How much did you invest?

We put in money in stages. Around AED 800K. I did not draw salary for the first three years. I don't draw a fixed salary even today.

Developments?

In the first year we organized only one training program- Continuous Medical Education Training for Accreditation. We are now investing in more specialized training programs e.g., training provided by the American Heart Association. This will enable participants to get specializations in Dubai. We are also getting approvals from the National Board of Health and Safety from the United States as a training facility. They have inspected us. I am waiting for their course details and faculty. We developed some new curriculums to help nurses become specialized; we worked towards differentiating nurses working in schools and hospitals. This has been our biggest achievement. Until now a nurse got a license that enabled her to work in all locations where nursing services are needed. I presented to the Health Authority a curriculum for nurses working with children in schools based on the additional skills needed for taking care of children. To demonstrate the need I did research in schools and worked closely with the Health Authority to make special training certification as a part of the licensing process. We then trained school nurses in schools of Abu Dhabi in what we call 'School Nurse Refresher Course.'

You're now in the situation where you're able to identify needs, work with the authorities, create a curriculum, deliver it and even help them certify it.

Yes. We are trying to develop a program for nurses working in prisons. I prefer to work with an organization and take care of all their needs. We have also trained doctors, nurses and technicians working in the Abu Dhabi police force. We went to their work environment to understand what they do, sat with an educator to make the curriculum and then presented it to them. I am yet to learn how to work with many organizations to create a policy.

How many persons do you train every year?

Approximately 500.

Your biggest challenge in achieving growth?

To reach key decision makers and make them realize the importance of training.

Is Jolly today more of a saleswoman?

I had to learn the art of selling. I may not do clinical nursing but I do a lot of reading and research. I also need to keep in tune with what is happening in the country.

What worries you about the business?

The daily uncertainties of business and opportunities that arise that we never thought would come our way. Once we started business this has been happening continuously. We got an opportunity to work with the Clinton Foundation to prepare a 'School Health Index,' followed by execution of the plan to help improve the ranking of schools. All such opportunities are examples of potential inherent in the business that we never visualized when we started. But it is not the kind of opportunity that is ready for execution. Once we work on an opportunity, disappointments also arise as we work to realize the opportunity. I am challenged because I often wonder why other people don't see it the way we see it, a high-impact or result opportunity. The 'School Health Index' is one such case.

Was there a time when you wanted to give up the business?

No. Never.

What did you unlearn when you started this business?

I am a quality-obsessed person and this doesn't always work. The world doesn't pay for the quality. You have to throw away your ideals and get ready to be flexible. It is wrong in the heart but right in the head. I try to always sell to the customer what I think he wants. But I have to give him what he wants. That makes me uncomfortable when I know it is a compromise. If I am providing training services I want to provide the best trainer. But the best trainer is not affordable by the client. I have to settle for a more viable alternative versus the best alternative.

Guidance you would give to an entrepreneur?

You have to be ready to see yourself in the middle of the sea without a raft or a lifeboat. You've got to learn to live and manage by your wits. Entrepreneurship will bring you to a place where you will feel you are alone and lost. You will have to manage with only your own strengths. Businesses don't get built on their own. Entrepreneurs build businesses. You need the right kind of people on the boat with you.

You had challenges?

People are assets when they share a vision. If they have different agendas it is tough. Recruiting the right person takes time. It really takes time. You have to have with you the right person who understands what exactly you want to do and how you want to do it. Business is not about training but about how to make it happen.

Differentiating a Trading Business

Entrepreneur	Kamran Torjani
Company and website	Atlas Safety Products/www.atlas-uae.com
Business	Trading industrial safety products
Year started	1996
Tips for entrepreneurs	• Know what you want to do and stay the course. • Don't start if you don't know what you want to do. • Be persistent to grow.

How did you get into business?

My route into business was not straight even though the seeds of my business are from my family. After graduation I worked for four years before joining the family business of safety equipment in Iran. Marriage brought me to Dubai. I started work as a sales engineer, a job in which I excelled. After two years of being an employee I realized I needed to be on my own. Searching for business ideas I reconnected with family back home, asking them what they needed from Dubai. They gave me their requirements and I established myself as a supplier of safety equipment.

Was it so simple?

My first company was a one-man show. I was selling whatever people wanted. Atlas started in 1996 after I became a distributor of two large companies- Aearo and Ansell. From 1998 the business steadily expanded as I added products and services. Today Atlas is an umbrella company. We manufacture safety signs, custom-made uniforms and chemicals that are consumed by the textile industry.

From being a salesperson to a businessman?

Being in business was triggered by my being a salesman. I realized if I could be the best salesperson in a company as an employee then I could start a company of my own. Initially things didn't work as I thought they would. Business wasn't that great. At a low emotional point, a desire to be successful motivated me and kept me going. I had also told my family that I will make ASP the best safety company in the UAE. I had no choice but to find a way to be successful.

How?

I did what I had done as an employee. As an employee I often worked twenty-four hours. I used to be relentless. I started using mobile phones to connect with customers. In 1993 only pagers were popular. I fixed a computer and fax machine at home. I used to wake up at 2:30 am to send faxes. And then call principals to confirm deliveries. My suppliers liked my persistence. I had done this for a job. I now had to do this for myself. Responsibility and persistence lead to success. I use this as an example to motivate my team.

How difficult was it to convince companies to work with you?

This was challenging. I had two ideas when I started; either buy locally and sell or become a distributor. Companies that buy locally and sell make lesser margins but can grow rapidly. The purchase prices made this option unworkable. Selling prices needed to be competitive. The idea was risky from the rate of growth perspective. What if I didn't grow? I shifted focus on companies that didn't have exclusive distributors or were not in the region. I searched, found some companies, started discussions and negotiations. The introduction and dialogue were easier with companies not present. I had to convince them about the potential of the region, my vision for my business and the seriousness of my interest. Aearo was the first partner. I started business with them with a purchase of US $20K. This became $2 m when 3M acquired Aearo 12 years later.

How did you develop a trading business and make a principal reliant on you?

I learnt by observing others. I had to be different. Everyone focused on products. But no one was developing staff to deliver service and results. I focused on creating a good team to delivers customer results. I demonstrated to brand owners that I was investing in developing a team through training. I ensured that the team, and through them the customer understood the complete value proposition of the product and brand. I safeguarded the product and brand value in the market. For this, price management was important. I also focused on developing knowledge of the staff of our customers. Companies have different safety cultures. Some, like oil and gas, are diligent. Others, in logistics, are somewhat lax. Knowledge sharing with customers helped us establish high standards in our customers.

Is trading about business or relationship with brand owners/partners?

Companies like you for the business you bring. After Aearo was acquired, their VP came personally to the region to present my credentials to 3M. It wasn't easy even after that. 3M doesn't work with exclusive distributors. Our competitors were able to access products that were exclusive to us before the acquisition. This became an opportunity for us. We worked harder to stay ahead. And we got access to new products of 3M. Our sales volumes grew.

Was getting staff a challenge?

Distributorship requires three things. One, having brands to distribute, two, keeping inventory and three, the most important asset are the people. I have spent and lost a lot of money to understand this. Finding the right people is the challenge of every manager. I had a lot of difficulty in finding the right people. After 15 years, I believe have the right team.

Is retaining staff an issue too?

People always leave if they don't fit. I don't try to be what I am not to retain people. I am a tough manager, strict and give space to people to transform and deliver. I accept and admit my mistakes. I am also happy to learn from the staff.

How important was pricing when you started?

It has become more important now. I started as an exclusive distributor and could price products higher based on market conditions. I maintained prices in the market on behalf of my brand principals. Today every distributor can get the brand and products. This makes pricing an art. Today pricing is a function of stock availability. Customers don't wait to acquire products from a supplier. They shop around. Hence predicting purchases, keeping inventory and providing service have become more important. I handle more than 1000 SKUs. As a one-stop-shop, product variety is a value we bring to customers and brand owners. Customers get everything at one place. Brand owners know we are specialists and attract more customers. Pricing a product is different from pricing a complete package with services.

When did you start to draw a salary from the business?

It took me six years to draw a regular salary. For six years the company was only paying my expenses. I didn't consider taking a salary as something important. The company became strong enough to pay my real salary after six years from the start date. I ensured that the staff and suppliers got priority in the initial years.

Any other challenges?

Contract law is very challenging. One can't do much if somebody doesn't want to pay. How good is a post-dated check that can't be cashed? I have had bad experiences, both while selling and buying. A customer, manufacturing oil rigs, announced bankruptcy. A supplier sent us the wrong goods. We returned the products and got no money back. These problems have helped me grow. I am establishing systems (ISO 9001) to safeguard against such risks.

What prompted you to start the factory?

We had achieved a big market share trading some products. We had technical people in the team to sell. They had been working on the products. Analysis showed the breakeven point of establishing a factory was low.

Mechanical engineer making chemicals?

We started from logistics. Volumes went up and after years it became manufacturing. It is a small plant with few machines for blending, mixing and packaging. It can be easily controlled. We were already selling the product. We just had to make it. We did all the small things – make samples, request tests, get feedback and make adjustments. The plant still took a year to stabilize.

Gut Feeling Is Good but Finance Is Better

Entrepreneur	Kanwar Marwah
Company and website	Subway and Curries and Grills/ www.curriesandgrills.com
Business	Food & Beverage
Year started	2008
Tips for entrepreneurs	• Learn finance. • Convert every business decision to a finance or productivity decision, not a cost decision. • Manage stress, don't let it overwhelm you.

What is your business?

Food and beverage focused on quick service restaurants. I started with a Subway franchise back in 2008. I was new to the business world. Subway, having a well-established franchise module, was easy to learn and start. Setting it up gave me an insight into running a business in Dubai. This required dealing with local authorities and knowing the law of the land. I learnt about Rules & Regulations, Laws, Procedures of the labor law, the immigration law and Dubai Municipality do's and don'ts.

Where were the roots of becoming an entrepreneur?

Every hotelier, or most of whom I know, is always thinking of starting something of their own; a latent urge to bring out their creativity. I have been an hotelier all through and I too had a desire to create and grow an idea from the beginning. I graduated from the Institute of Hotel Management & Catering Technology in 1996. I have since worked with Sheraton, TAJ-Singapore Airport Terminal Services Catering, Taj International Hotels and Dubai International Exhibition & Convention Centre. I was waiting for the right time and opportunity. Once Subway happened, I realized I could do it. And the idea grew roots.

You have lived in many countries? Why Dubai?

I worked with Dubai International Exhibition & Convention Centre for a while. That gave me valuable insight into the nature of Dubai's growth. A Cityscape exhibition will show you what Dubai will be 10–15 years later. This was 2008. I realized it was the right time to start. I could be a part of the growth. I needed to start with selling a 'few' sandwiches to become a part of 'rapid' growth. Dubai is a constantly growing city. Cities like London and Delhi also grow but at slower rates. Dubai provided an excellent environment for entrepreneurs to develop their ideas and grow the business in the country and globally. Dubai offers an infrastructure where you find it very easy to open a company, recruit people, set up the business and market the business to create a word-of-mouth publicity. The barrier to entry is a lot easier in this part of the world because physical infrastructure and business foundation are very well laid down in place. The economy is also a rich one. This also helps a lot.

What prompted you to take a risk?

It started in 2007. I was thirty-two and working. I was married. I felt I could do more in terms of my time and my skills. I wanted to realize my true potential and always felt the joy of setting up a brand really overtakes everything else. The urge to do my own thing surfaced after I stabilized my first restaurant. I told my wife I want to do business. She was initially surprised. She asked me if I was sure I wanted to start because of the risk involved. Did I really want to rock the boat? We reflected together. Our lifestyle was comfortable. We were young. The real question I was asking myself was- Where does one go from here and what is one's true calling? It took me almost four to five months to complete the feasibility study. We then spoke about it, discussed feasibilities, risks and assessed fall backs if the business didn't work. She is a hotelier and was understanding as well as supportive.

And then the choice, either take a franchise or do your thing?

Yes. I wanted the first restaurant to be a franchise. The know-how would become a guide for us. I knew a franchise would cost more. I was going to rely on personal loans knowing that business loans for startups were not easy. We put all our savings and gratuity into the business. We took full risk. We limited our lifestyle to see what will happen.

You walked into Subway and wanted a franchise.

The first thing they said, 'Who are you? Why should we trust you?' I had to convince them I had food experience, was committed and would run the restaurant. I was an individual and not a company. I knew that if the business didn't work, my credibility would be at stake. They asked me to come back with a location for the first store.

How long did it take to convince them to trust you?

It took a while. They asked me many questions – why I wanted to do business, had I assessed the risks, what if it didn't work, etc., questions that we had discussed as a family. They wanted to be sure I had the capital to initiate the business and understood the risks involved.

Why Subway and not another company?

Subway is the number one franchise in the category of food retail. It's a successful brand and they franchise their business to individuals. I was confident they would guide me. As a startup I needed that kind of support. Fresh sandwiches are like staple food. The base business would work if I could find a location.

You wanted the franchise to learn how to run a business?

Not really. I needed an insight into food retail in this part of the world. Franchise was for ease of operation. I could operate the store. I had worked for a company, never managed it. Management of the business requires other skills like finance, procurement of diverse goods from different suppliers, developing relationships, credit terms, etc. With these things taken care of, business is a plug-n-play.

Did you learn what you wanted?

Yes I did and a lot more too. From managing the cash flow to credit limits, from shelf life to best before dates, etc. I implemented the business from the frontline to the office. I worked the weekends on the counter making sandwiches as a sandwich artist. I passed the mandatory online exams as I worked my way up and ensured I understood the business 360 degrees.

You gained customer insights.

Yes. I engaged with customers. I understood their behaviors, likes and dislikes and how it varied based on their nationality. I learnt how a big brand details every small thing at the point of sale that engages customers e.g., having the menus in English and Arabic. Living in Dubai one may not notice the need for dual language signs. But cultural adaptation is required to connect with customers emotionally.

Why diversify from Subway?

It never could have stopped at just a Subway. I am an hotelier who needed to do more within the industry, serve and bring something new for the consumers. This pushed me to create my own food concept. Connecting to my roots and bringing the taste of India to the consumer was an easy and natural choice. I had accumulated over 16 years of F&B experience with the Taj Group inside and outside India. I came up with the name 'Curries and Grills.' We wanted a generic name that was easy for consumers to understand. Indian food is synonymous with curries. Indian cuisine is also known for cooking in clay ovens i.e., tandoor. I believed customers would connect with a tandoor as a grill and curries as Indian.

Were you going to do something different?

I had to adapt Indian food for a quick service dining concept. For example, it is a challenge to serve authentic Biryanis in a QSR and reach the quality expectation of a fine dining restaurant in a QSR setting. Customers are in a hurry. The preparation and service is rushed. This was the thinking that went into the concept. And this was the challenge. And then the detailing of a food business – processes for maintaining consistency of the food, taste, the look and feel of the restaurant, kitchen design, staffing and their uniforms, logo, etc. I hold the concept very close my heart.

What did you learn from Subway that you are using in Curries and Grills?

The important need of engaging with customers, even standing outside a restaurant and reaching out to customers walking past the restaurant. I learnt that this customer engagement registers our brands name/cuisine in undecided minds. One may not convert the customer but they remember that a restaurant exists. This is important in a food court environment where customers have diverse choices. We do the same now for Curries and Grills. I learnt the importance of measuring food wastage as a way of managing restaurant costs. If we slice a tomato, the trimmings are weighed before disposal. The weight of trimmings multiplied by the price of tomatoes becomes the weekly wastage. The wastage percentage is then benchmarked against how the same store performed the previous year. I learnt to do the same for all productivity and cost measures. These weekly comparisons enable continuous improvement of business. I manage costs and store productivity weekly. Hotels, where I had gained experience, have higher gross margins and work on monthly food cost percentages. In retail I do this weekly. This means effectively I have 52 opportunities to review and control costs. Subway instilled in me the importance of staff training and regular follow up training. I had to undergo 15 days of training when I first became a franchisee. I would have been unable to become franchisee if I had not passed that training. I enforce the same discipline in my business.

What is the meaning of 'passing' in a franchisee setting?

I passed the training examination as I scored over 80% in a practical and theoretical examination. I was on the Subway store shop floor for seven days making sandwiches, serving customers and handling cash. Seven days of classroom training followed. I am proud to say I was the topper of my batch.

When did you overcome the uncertainty of profit- the fear of starting up?

We were financially comfortable in six months of starting up. Our feasibility study had worked. In the last quarter of 2008 the global crisis impacted the region. This got me worried. We had loans to repay. I had done the cash flows for the business and the family. I did not draw salary from the business. I used to keep it aside. The accumulation of salary became the capital for starting my own concept a few years later. The loans been paid. I also started drawing a salary after the third year.

Any unforeseen surprises when you started?

I learnt that when you hire a staff, you typically invest close to Dirhams 9,000 per staff. To hire five people I need to inject capital of Dirhams 45,000. I had not envisaged this. I had no guidance when I started. I was in a hurry to start. Capital had been committed to the business. I was going from one government office to another, standing in a queue, getting approvals. We didn't know what kind of contracts to use to hire the staff. Dubai has two types of contracts- limited or unlimited. We didn't think this through. This became important when trained staff wanted to leave in the middle of their contract.

How soon after starting Subway did the idea of Curries and Grills take shape?

In 2009, after Subway had been operating for 5 months. I had time to reflect on what I could have done better in setting up Subway and got a grip on what managing a business was like. Starting the first business was an enjoyable experience. I wanted to experience the startup feeling again. During the construction of the restaurant I used to leave the site at 2 am and return at 5 am. The diversity of challenges- setting up the drainage, sewage, exhaust, meeting the government norms, coordination with different agencies, etc.- that I faced and solved made the startup process very interesting and engaging. Once Subway was working I had time on my hands. I started to work on growth. The choice of Subway or another concept was important.

You went to your family and told them they aren't going to see money for a little while longer?

Yes. Absolutely! I discussed the decision of creating our own concept with my wife. If we had to do it we had to be patient. We had to give up on our vacations and cut corners on personal expenses. Restaurant business is capital intensive and has longer payback. It was challenging and tricky. I started the business in a challenging location. The size of the area was bigger than what I had envisaged and foot traffic was lower. Yet it is the birth place of Curries and Grills.

What prompted you to focus on Indian cuisine?

When I thought of my own concept, I could only think of Indian and Chinese cuisine. I don't have knowledge of Arabian cuisine. I could not compete with established Indian concepts as they had an advantage of having better locations. I needed to look for a new location where the established players were not present.

How did you tweak the technology, translate and develop recipes for an Indian QSR concept? Was it is easy to develop a menu?

We had to start from the basics. I had my chef with me six months prior to the starting date. It took us six months to develop recipes, identify sources of good raw materials, etc. I realized every small thing made a difference to the outcome. As an example we couldn't use Syrian onions. Or garlic from China. They didn't produce the right taste for the Indian palate. This is what back to basics means in the food business. Starting the business from scratch was a great feeling. The creation of recipes was a 'fun' hurdle. This required detailing of recipes, the way of cooking and the garnish. Each dish had to taste the same no matter which chef was preparing it. Consistency of Kadak Chai was of great significance, especially being in an office tower with a lot of Emirati staff. I also learnt to deal with price fluctuations of raw materials. With a lot of raw materials being imported we had to deal with taste variance and still produce a standard product.

Where were you doing this?

My chef and I used to meet at coffee shops, in malls, trying food from different Indian restaurants to identify the salient features. We used to brainstorm what we could learn and what we must not do. The second startup was a homegrown concept. I couldn't leave anything to chance. I couldn't let any issue escape my engagement. Subway was an execution story. This was developing a concept from scratch.

Where did you try out the innovations?

All creative work was done in the kitchen of my apartment. We conceptualized the menu, the cooking process and raw material quantities in a domestic kitchen. We couldn't complete the entire development. We couldn't replicate a clay oven in a domestic kitchen. The clay oven was planned to be the centerpiece of the restaurant. It took us a month to stabilize recipes after we started. We had to use a gas oven. We had to standardize each variety of bread and each grilled meat recipe. They had to be made to a standard. It was not a case of just adding variety and getting anyone to cook.

Your first location was Business Village? Why BV?

BV was a very great location. I still think it is from a location point of view, not necessarily from the operation point of view. It is in the heart of Dubai. BV is close to City Center and Clock Tower, which for any city essentially means the heart of the city. It is the big building that has over 300 offices. If an average office has five people, the potential BV market was close to 1,000–1,500. This was the calculation for the first venture.

But it didn't work.

Every challenge has learning. We established the brand there. We got to develop our own systems in terms of portion sizes, look and feel, taste, etc. We also understood the market: how easy and difficult it is. We always thought the location would work because of the catchment. We attempted deliveries. We distributed 25,000 menus in the vicinity and understood how people respond to marketing and promotional activities. I gained insight into what the actual market is, compared to what you think of it.

Your business is highly competitive. Customers have multiple choices. Why would they try a new eating place? What consumer insights did you get?

I think our concept stands out by its very nature. But at the end of the day this is a generous market. It allows everyone to enter the business. However, more importantly, there is a fight for quality. The consumer in Dubai is a consumer that seeks quality. And I think when we compare ourselves to quality service providers, I think there is an opportunity for us to share the market and coexist in a healthy manner. It was a challenge for me to get footfall in the evening in an office tower. To attract customers we participated in the Good Living Vouchers of Gulf News. We found customers coming to the location. On seeing the food court environment they told us they had expected a sit-down restaurant. What they found was not what they expected. We were a QSR and not a restaurant to celebrate occasions. This led us to go to them. We created a database with birthdays and anniversaries. We developed a catering menu and started marketing. In a short duration of time we started to receive two or three catering contracts a week. This worked for us as we had negligible footfall on weekends. And that's when customers wanted us to cater food.

How did you set prices other than the portions and costing in the supplies? Did you have an understanding of what was the right price of the products or what an average customer would pay for a meal in a QSR or was it trial and error?

Our spending six months in the market helped a lot. We tasted and assessed prices of all direct competitors. We did customer trials with friends and family. Friends always give guarded replies. Family is more direct and critical.

Learning from the home delivery business?

I learnt the importance of logistics. I also learnt the customer's need for urgency of delivery. There were occasions when I hopped into my car and delivered. I did this because the bike delivery boy had set off in the opposite direction.

And then you took a decision that the location was not working and relocated.

I was unable to meet my cash flow commitments. The trajectory of business growth was challenging. Very few people got to know of us. Being on the first floor with no road level exposure was problematic. The location was not helping brand exposure and development. I reflected whether we were heading in the right direction. The answer was a no. We realized branching out will help us grow, increase our presence and more importantly, divide costs. We now were armed with a better profile and a running restaurant.

Was it easy to get the location in Outlet mall?

We had applied for various locations around town. We were confident of our concept and food and that we understood how to run a business. Once I got a call from a mall, I took along all the relevant documents and invited them to our restaurant. We had been operating the first store for 2 years and the Curries & Grills trade license was over a year old. This was a turning point. I think my professional background helped. I promised to meet their standards if they gave me a chance. I confirmed to give them checks for the rent (as guarantee) and sign the contract on their terms.

Did you run out of money?

In the initial phase, yes, I was hand to mouth. I had to raise another loan as setting up a restaurant involves lots of expense.

What other learning, other than the customer?

I learnt about the efficiency I could gain in the purchases. We were initially dealing with numerous suppliers. They would deliver food and raw materials at the restaurant. We realized the prices were high. We started getting our hands dirty after the business was operating for a month. I started visiting the fruit and vegetable market. This was a learning experience for the entire team. I returned at midnight on the first day we visited. We had to bargain for everything. Till then we used to send a fax and get everything at our doorstep. We realized the margins in the supply chain when we visited the market. We learnt how the market functions, how to bargain, when to walk away, etc.

What worries you about the business today?

We have been in the market for over eight years now. The challenge of operating a Food & Beverage operation is always on the higher side. Global events like swine flu in Brazil or onion price rise in India, all affect our business. I have learnt to take most startup challenges in my stride. I keep on working to solve the challenges. I ensure that we have alternative options to implement.

Was there any time you wanted to give up the business?

Yes. We had been open for three-months and our revenue was in three digits. It was a challenging time for me and the team. We had a seven-member team. All of them had given up their careers to join my company. There was no way I was going to let any of them down. We persevered, kept the brand alive and today people know us in Dubai. Our customers come back to dine with us, we get repeat orders for catering.

Have you changed as a person after you started your business?

Yes. I think before I act. Earlier I used to do and discover. I was a more 'easy going' person. Now I evaluate things. If a staff tries to talk to me when I am in the middle of something, I request them to come back later. Because I really want to listen to them, not just hear them. I pay more attention to things. I try to understand and then give my response. I have become a lot more patient. I am less impulsive.

What is an important thing that you have learned starting the business?

I learnt finance. This is an advice I would give to an entrepreneur. Today I am able to convert every business decision into a financial decision. Gut feeling is good but finance is better. And I have learnt to take stress well. It is a part of everyday life of a startup. I have asked my staff to keep me updated with all the good and bad issues. I have to learn how to tackle all uncertain and unforeseen events. One has to have the confidence that you can manage or tackle everything. And not let the stress overwhelm you.

What next?

I cannot sit still. I dream like a seven-year-old. So it's in my nature to be overworked, to have sleepless nights. Now having a successful sandwich shop, a Curries & Grills place serving everything from Biryani and Naan to Tandoori chicken and Grilled Fish, I have often thought about the next variety of cuisine I could try; something that fits in between heavy meals. I thought of introducing Momos to the market. Momo is Tibetan steamed dumpling and is eaten in Nepal and Tibet. This came naturally to me as I am half Nepalese. My mother used to give me a hot steaming Momo in my childhood days whenever I was craved a small snack. I have started a small café called 'It's Momo'. I am glad to see my chefs being able to replicate the authentic taste. We now have two branches of It's Momo. I have also started a Food & Beverage consultancy to help and guide entrepreneurs and businessmen who are new to the food business.

Passion Is the Substance of an Entrepreneur

Entrepreneurs	Stephane Jacques and Pornthep Booncham
Company and website	Lemongrass/www.lemongrassrestaurants.com and www.livingbrandsintl.com
Business	Thai restaurants
Year started	2002
Tips for entrepreneurs	• Look at the risks. Be prepared to mitigate risks. • Once you decide to start, proceed with speed. • Once you start, no looking back.

Describe Lemongrass.

Lemongrass is an authentic Thai eatery concept created in Dubai that offers four-star full casual dining restaurant services. The dishes are prepared by Thai chefs and presented in a modern Asian environment. We celebrated our thirteen anniversary recently.

How did you become an entrepreneur?

I have been a resident of Dubai for over twenty years. My partner, Pornthep Booncham, who is Thai, has lived here for twenty-two years. We met while working in Emirates. I had been flying for 22 years, 13 of those in Emirates as a Captain. Flying gave us chance to discover the world. I got an opportunity to visit numerous cities, discover many new ideas, learnt how different ideas have been executed and see how they are working. We noticed a gap. The market was divided into two clusters. There were many low-end restaurants where tasty food was served in very basic settings. And there were five-star properties that offered a limited and often less tasty cuisine in feature-intensive and full-service settings. There was nothing in the middle. This triggered our imagination, gave us the initial motivation to fill the niche, and entrepreneurship kicked in. Dubai is a growth city. Everyone is always thinking of new business ideas. It was the same for us. We were searching for the right cuisine. I made frequent trips to Thailand and fell in love with the country, its people, with its food and culture. It was then easy to think about setting up a Thai food concept. Thai food would work. Thai food had not yet been very present in the Dubai Market. One of the very first was a small eatery in Karama: Thai Terrace. And then there were high-end restaurants (e.g., Blue Elephant, Sukhothai) but no mid-market players. We felt we could promote Thai cuisine in the most appropriate manner within this mid-range restaurant niche.

How sure were you of the opportunity? What was the urge to experiment?

Nobody who starts a business is sure. Success lies in a person's ability to trust his gut. Trust his vision. And the rest is hard work to make things happen. One doesn't have full control on the end result of the effort. There is an element of chance. Passion, for what we do and the industry we are in, is a large contributory factor for our success.

Flying to business, how was the shift?

It was very difficult in the beginning. The challenge was internal. I grew up in Luxemburg. My dad set up his own business. I grew up in and around the business. I was working in the business while studying. By taking up a job and being an employee, I was like the black sheep in the family. But for me flying was a dream. I am glad I did it. I was on top.

Entrepreneurship bug kicked in when I shifted to Dubai and started analyzing the market and its opportunities. It is great to have an idea, desire and vision but one needs the tools to realize the vision. One also needs to calculate, assess and accept the risks of setting up a business. You need to be reassured about what you are embarking upon. At that point you are accepting risk. When I started I was unaware of what was ahead of me. I had a feeling, a perception of what to look for. It was very difficult because we did not get any kind of support from the country. When I am talking about the country it is not just the government, it is basically the system and network of organizations that support startup entrepreneurs.

Exemplify?

You talk to a new commercial property and say, 'I have a great concept.' And they ask you, 'Do you have something established? Do you have any other business? Who is your sponsor?' Ask them at that moment for the commercial terms of the lease, the answer is, 'Not interested. Thanks. All the best.' It took us 6 to 8 months to find a location. Embarking on a new business requires all stakeholders – entrepreneur, landlords, suppliers, financial institutions and employees – to take a commercial risk. Should enabling entrepreneurship require a facilitating support system that speeds business startup without eliminating risk? Time is a big cost in business and we did consume a lot of it just ticking off all the boxes of the administrative process.

Flying to business, what enabled you?

In the aviation industry, as a pilot, you don't really need to have an education degree or diploma. I graduated through a flying school and had a license granted by the Ministry of Transportation. My real business education was my father's business. In addition to the sheer pleasure of flying, it is also about managing a sophisticated machine, a team of people and emergent situations. Aviation has no grey areas. Everything is either A or B. Target is to reach A. If anything goes wrong you have to have a plan B. We are trained for plan B. In the pilot's chair you are a prepared person and you learn how to handle the responsibilities you bear.

You started with a lot of 'greys'?

Everything is in the mind. Life has far too many facets. If a person knows all that lies ahead, it wouldn't be life. At my age I have experienced many situations. I have concluded that there is no need to dwell on experiences gone by. I have to be confident I handled the situation to the best of my knowledge and ability. I keep the experience in my mental database to manage similar situations that may arise in the future. When I started I had no idea about the difficulties I would face while setting up the business. All I had with me was my logical way of thinking, my vision and drive to make it happen. This has been the key to our business success.

Another important factor. To operate a business, one needs some drivers and some passengers. Passengers conform; they do what drivers ask them to do. In aviation, while flying, giving a command is necessary and comes with position. Ability to command is acquired through demonstration of good decision making and a lot of practical training. Even if my experience as a commander helped me a lot in my commercial activities, I sometimes feel I am not an established businessman. I often reflect on whether I am taking a right decision. I have been blessed with good friends involved in businesses. They have always given me honest feedback and shared their experience when I was faced with difficult issues or decisions to take.

Pilots handle uncertain situations. Your ability to handle stress and ambiguity is high.

Flying isn't so complicated; after a while you fly a plane like you drive a car. Nevertheless, aviation is a thorough industry; it requires anticipation and concentration. I managed both activities for a period of 4 years after I started.

I was flying and had started a business. To give my business the right attention and work on its development, it was imperative for me to switch. I quit the airline in 2006.

Why?

I was not cooking, serving or cashiering. I am not a restaurateur myself. I am an entrepreneur and have chosen the field of food. Nevertheless I have been in the restaurant right from the very beginning. It was necessary for me to experience all aspects of the business and get direct feedback from the customers about what is right and wrong and how to make it better. I needed to be with the team. I did this with a pure desire to know whether or not I was on the right track.

Thai food was a strategic choice. Did you map the market or was it instinctive?

Instinct played a role. As a European I wanted initially to bring European cuisine. Study suggested that if I did that it would either be a coffee shop, of which there were many, or a set up that was very expensive. Europeans also like to have a glass of wine with their meal. Replicating this is complicated. The choice became obvious after a while. I was fascinated with and enjoyed the flavors of Thai cuisine. Thai cuisine is a delicate combination of flavors. For me, to then look for a gap in the market and define the opportunity, was easier.

How did you prepare yourself?

I learnt how to cook Thai cuisine. Once my business partner and I developed a shared interest in business, he helped me discover Thailand. I visited remote villages. A curiosity to learn was evoked with an interest in doing business. And I started to understand how to do it, what would work in Dubai, where to buy ingredients, etc.

Our motto when we started/conceptualized Lemongrass was to serve good and affordable Thai food in a contemporary setting. Thailand is very traditional. Restaurants mimic traditions in their décor to appear authentic. This often appears tacky. We decided to make a statement by being minimalist in colors, lights, materials and atmospherics. When you enter Lemongrass you recognize it as a Thai restaurant by the artifacts but we are far away from a traditional Thai place.

You focus on lighting and colors. Where did it come from?

This was an interest I always had. As a kid I dreamed about flying but always had an interest in architecture and interior design. As a kid I always used to occupy my time drawing and sketching floor plans. I am by nature a creative person.

Where did you get the time to start since you were doing two things concurrently?

We travel a lot as pilots. I also managed time off in between flights. I used this opportunity to set up the business.

Did you make an estimate of the investment?

It is very difficult to list all the specifics and convert your thinking of a new business into financials numbers. Many things went missing in the first project.

When you start you quickly realize the attention to detail that is required. We even had to discuss and debate the size of the tables. We can maximize space but need to give comfort. We made mockups on the floor. We designed space that would be a big part of the customer experience, including plates, lighting, linen, cutlery, etc. The concept was not a challenge. It was a passion. One thinks about it all the time. It is not difficult, after a while the behavior becomes natural. I value a lot of input from friends and from the industry. They helped a lot. What was burdensome and time-consuming was the administrative work- getting trade license, getting visas, getting food department approvals, etc. It took three-months. But was good experience in how to navigate government departments.

Did you test the location?

That is not the way it happens. We started thinking about a location where one would get foot traffic. The reality is that in the beginning a lot of potential locations that you feel might open based on your idea, presentations and commitment, are not the doors that will open. One then goes to secondary locations to find space that is available, not necessarily the one that you want or feel is right. It took us 5 to 6 months to finalize the location.

Was this choice in hindsight a better choice? Low cost to develop and test the business?

Yes, it proved to be a very good decision. Thinking of it today it was a chance we took; the initial investment was reasonable and the rental value was affordable. We were not located within a prominent area. Yet we were blessed by surrounding offices and a lot of residents. Investment cost is obviously a big issue for any new entrepreneur. And having cash flow right from the beginning has been a key element. We are in an industry where we collect cash at the time of delivery. Imagine other industries where 30–60–90 day credit is the norm.

A key element to fully appreciate is the rental value. Rent increases the risk and weakens the cash flow promptly if the business does not pick up fast enough. I was very worried when I signed our first lease. Two prior businesses located there had failed. Nevertheless the area had potential and we were setting a true concept. We knew we had to rapidly start to serve office goers during the day and residents at night. Our Emirates connection allowed us to tap into that market too. For the first 5 to 6 months we had 70% customers from Emirates and 30% walk-in. Today we get 20% customers from Emirates and 80% are walk-ins. The brand has been established.

Initial capital?

We set up our first branch near Lamcy Plaza with a little less than AED 800K. We had projected AED 600K but there is always some X factor to account for. We returned our investment in just 14 months.

How much adaptation of the menu did you do after startup?

We started humble. We got educated and have evolved the business. The brand has evolved. The menu didn't need to change as such; neither did the interior. But we needed to adapt and rethink the structure of our small organization. We wanted to quickly establish how to make our venture function as a real business. We started like a family restaurant. Very quickly we realized it wasn't the way forward. We needed a management structure, various in-charge positions. We needed to provide responsibilities and have team members who could assign responsibilities in our absence. This development happened naturally as we got busier.

Did you always want to grow?

I loved to fly but I was clear I would not be flying till my retirement. The job has odd timings. Furthermore the nature of flying today is quite monotonous thanks to advanced technology. Nevertheless a pilot has to remain alert. Imagine flying from Dubai to Hong Kong for eight hours. Nothing much happens yet it is challenging to retain focus and attention.

I always look for new challenges. It was easy to look at business as a growth opportunity. Even if I did not imagine the business would be where it is today, I had a latent plan. It had to start when it did and it had to grow.

It took 4 years to switch?

I was balancing my dream with my responsibilities. I couldn't put my family at financial risk. Flying has risks too. Pilots are medically tested every six months with potential risk of being grounded. I needed reassurance that the family would be stable. In four years I knew the business was working; the ROI was well achieved, and continuing flying would have limited the business growth opportunities. It was a good time to switch.

When you started the business did the family see this as a hobby or a full-time profession?

The decision to start business was made as a team. I got the support of my family. They understood the way I function and where my desires were.

When did you decide to convert a family run business into an organization?

We started the operation of our Oud Metha branch in November 2002. In a matter of 12 months it was clear to us that we were holding a concept with great growth prospect. We only needed to play our cards well. The structure we wanted to establish became clear in my mind in early 2004. The only things that rendered our development a bit slower was the lack of personal funds.

In Europe I would have most probably taken loans to grow the business. Interest is tax-deductible. In UAE taking loans is a real expense. It is a burden as it increases responsibility to manage banks. I didn't want that problem. So we did grow at our own rhythm and not any faster than what we could. We are reinvesting in the business regularly. I am proud of where I have brought the concept. Since 4 years, Lemongrass brand is managed by a full-fledged franchisor structure. We have a corporate office within the DMCC legal framework. This was another important step in our development. The structure offers us new opportunities. In 2015 we launched a new Brand: Asian5.

Which year did the other shops start?

We opened the Ibn Battuta Mall food court version in April 2005. Our casual dining version didn't fit in shopping malls. However it was important for the brand exposure to become a part of the Dubai Malls development. We had to tweak the original concept to create Lemongrass Express. We don't have adequate space within the food court area to establish a full-fledged store. We, therefore, can't serve the same food menu and give the same level of customer service in the two formats. Lemongrass Express and Lemongrass are two different Thai food concepts.

How did you go about creating the food court model? Any learning?

We hired a consultant when we started working on the food court model. We started with a blank sheet; the concept was started from scratch. A lot was finally done internally. Serving Thai food in a food court is complicated. The visual element of food is a major element in a food court environment; ready to consume food has to be displayed. For consumers deciding what to eat, freshness of displayed food is an important decision criterion. The food court customer who buys a burger is not our customer. Lemongrass Express is the destination for a customer who wants to see food being made. We therefore chose to work with an open kitchen and make use of woks to display the food within our Bain Marie. We had to engineer everything. Noodles, for example, can't be kept in a Bain Marie. Similarly, other dishes have to move fast in order to retain their freshness. We had to think, learn, innovate and develop. Meeting Municipality norms was another matter. It took a while to create the concept but this is the creative element of entrepreneurship. Creativity happens under pressure. We have to learn to find solutions. The adrenaline kicks in.

Is the Food Court customer able to discern the delicate flavors?

We are proud of being a Thai operator serving authentic flavors and ingredients. In Lemongrass we are committed to serving quality.

Upon reflection I think it would have been more appropriate to differentiate the two concepts in a better way. Customers have been confused at times. They have higher expectations from Lemongrass Express appreciating what Lemongrass Thai Restaurant is known for. The two concepts and their environments are completely different. As such both the concepts should not even be compared. It has been our strategy to further develop the casual dining version.

Did you change as a person while developing the business?

I changed because of the situations I faced while implementing the business. I took bad decisions and suffered mentally. But I learned that it is part of the growth process. All the happenings around me influenced me. I manage my emotions better today. What does change when you enter the business life is your ability to detach from the business when you take a vacation, for example. I rarely take off more than 8 or 10 days in a row. WhatsApp, emails and phone calls always reach me.

Is the franchisee outlet making money?

Well I don't know their accounts; I can't tell you but I have an understanding of what they can achieve. We have good partners who are helping us grow the network. Together we opened eight outlets. More are on the way. Both partners are involved with other food brands in their portfolios. The franchisee's success lies in the selection of the location. We worked out the concept and provide guidance as well as standards to that need to be followed to ensure a successful operation. Given our brand, the footfall and a manageable rental value, the business will rock!

Is getting staff easy?

Staffing will always be a challenge in any business. Opening an authentic Thai food venue increases the complication. You have to get Thai nationals, which is kind of difficult. Thailand is not a country where people naturally look abroad for job opportunities. What made it a little easier is the fact that my business partner is Thai. We are recognized as a "Thai company" in the minds of our recruits. We employ Thai nationals in senior management positions which render communications easier within the organization. Retaining Thai employees is another challenge. Many of them get homesick. We have to be innovative to retain them. We needed to go beyond the salary guidelines of the government. Accommodation is a real issue. Bringing them to a country where they have never come before and have no relatives in, means that the company needs to accommodate them. We like to provide a good standard of accommodation. However, the staff is not well perceived by the market in general and by the government in particular. Rules and regulations are very strict and at times inappropriate. Eviction is always a risk that lurks somewhere on the horizon. And labor camps are not always suitable for hospitality employees. The country forces us to handle difficult situations. Payments of labor guarantee are another financial commitment. Roughly AED 6,500 is required for each employee. Once employed, a company doesn't like to lose the employee. Nevertheless, occasionally something happens that creates additional financial losses. The whole concept of sponsorship is challenging. The company is always liable for their employees but isn't always supported by the authorities in discharging the responsibilities. I have lots of respect for Dubai and for the Ruler's vision. However, considering the importance of the SME sector in the country's economy, I still believe that a lot should be done to unleash entrepreneurial potential.

Has positioning of Lemongrass in terms of pricing changed?

Our quality, price and ambience are steady.

What worries you about Lemongrass?

I might not have worries for Lemongrass. I am more worried about how business will develop within the UAE considering the saturation of food outlets which have mushroomed over the last 4 years. The retail developers keep developing new projects where a large percentage of retail space is targeting the food industry. Plus the very high rental values are impacting our profit margins. We are unable to raise the casual dining prices per head. And if we cannot raise prices for consumers we have no option but to absorb the costs.

Do you earn the salary that you left in Emirates?

I left Emirates once my business and income were stable. Today I earn more. Many colleagues were aghast when I quit. Today the same people admire me.

Advise to a new entrepreneur.

Look at the risks. Be prepared to mitigate risks. Once you reach a tipping point, decide to proceed based on your own perception of an idea and/or based on research. You should proceed with speed. Once you start there should be no looking back.

You said you want to learn to become a CEO.

Title does not mean a lot to me. I need to do the job I need to do, even if I end up doing it myself. I appreciate the concept of the 'team' over titles and the ability to create and foster a certain kind of organization. Passion is the real substance of an entrepreneur. I also think that all of us entrepreneurs have a little part of us that is crazy. If we don't have a little bit of craziness we may not be able to take risks, and if there is no risk-taking, there is no entrepreneur.

You mentioned to me in the beginning that you knew only 10% of what you were going to do when you started. The rest of it you developed and learned along the way.

It has been an amazing journey. I am very happy with the way it has turned out. I still have concerns. I realize that it is all about perpetual efforts. You never achieve everything. There are still milestones to achieve. I don't like the glamour attached to a position. I get embarrassed when I am introduced as the Lemongrass CEO. You have to make an effort to remain grounded. I have been fortunate to succeed in building the business. And yet I don't know what lies beyond. I like to retain my values and keep my perspective. At the end of the day the most challenging task is for each and every one of us to educate others to prepare a life for themselves, see the future and gift them an opportunity to adapt and grow.

When you started where did you source raw materials to give the customer an authentic Thai culinary experience?

Fourteen years ago we used to get original Thai ingredients in Dubai. Traveling the world and to Thailand, often I was able to bring back ingredients that were difficult to find or to get fresh from our local market.

Today we have quite a few suppliers who import fresh goods from Thailand on a weekly basis. The supply chain has changed a lot.

How easy was negotiating supply contracts with suppliers?

Negotiations are always as good as what two parties like to agree on. To be healthy it has be a win-win situation to both. Obviously negotiations get easier as volume of purchase grows. The most important thing to me nevertheless will always remain the trust one can build with his suppliers. I like business ethics and always honor my dues on time even if we are keen to obtain good credit terms.

How did franchising change the way you think and work?

Franchising our concept has forced us to think in a more structured manner, to ensure that we understand and implement all possible features of the business in a systematic way. We have to be even more innovative as we are not only handling our own units; we need to appreciate the needs and constraints of our partner units. It is very interesting and keeps us all on our toes.

Any developments?

LivingBrands today is an F&B specialist; we operate, franchise and further develop new food concepts. Our latest brand is Asian5. It is successful and we have a large expansion plan in mind for which we are welcoming a private equity investor. New brands in the field of Fast Casual Dining are in our drawers.

Evolve Technology, a company we established to support our network of franchisees with their restaurant IT requirement is further developing and extending their service to a large portfolio of SMEs, mainly within the F&B sectors. We have been appreciated for our office networking solutions within the medical, real estate and even hoteliering fields. It evolved out of our own needs to control costs and manage operations by connecting our brand stores and accessing information in real time. The solutions in the market were expensive and designed for bigger companies. Today Evolve Technologies has commercialized an affordable ERP solution offering response to all the needs of the F&B SMEs. We are now looking at being known for our professionalism in the field of access control and security.

Naiveté, Luck and Focus: Nothing in the Business Was Easy

Entrepreneurs	Suzi Croft (S) and Manar Al Jayouchi (M)
Company and website	Appetite (www.appetite.ae) and 1762 (www.1762.ae)
Product	Packaged sandwiches and salads, a gourmet deli
Year established	2005
Tips for entrepreneurs	• Keep going. Just don't give up, no matter how tough it gets. • Focus and be true to your vision. • Be flexible. Listen to people who know. Learn and adapt where necessary and grow. • Project cost will be a multiple of your estimates after factoring the unforeseen. • Learn to manage the unexpected. • If it was easy, everyone would do it!

How did Appetite start?

M: Starting a business was not on the agenda. Things conspired. I was made redundant in 2003. A friend asked me, 'What are you planning to do now that you've been without a job for a while?' I replied, 'We can do something in food, maybe a Bagel house. It may be a good idea because it is unique.' He spontaneously replied, 'Let's do it.' We had AED 150K saved up. My friend invested another AED 150K. The deal was simple. We had to do it. The plan was for Suzi and me to manage the business, and he would be a silent partner. However, after research, we discovered that bagels were not feasible, so we decided to do a sandwich business and supply to stores like ENOC (the gas station stores). We set up a catering company and that was the start of Appetite.

S: I love cooking, trying new recipes and food. In 2005 we sensed a gap in the market for good high-quality sandwiches. At the time, sandwiches at gas stations and supermarkets tasted alike; one couldn't tell if the paste was tuna, chicken or cheese. Whereas every street corner in London has great sandwich deli shops.

Did you think you could make a business out of sandwiches?

S: Yes, but we were very naïve. We put everything into the business. I gave up my job two months before we started. We had a six-month-old baby. We didn't have a car and hadn't sorted out our finances. Everything looked very uncertain that first year.

Why naïve and not confident?

M: I think it was super naïve. We had no safety net. Once we paid the first rent check we needed to make it happen. Our entire confidence was in the image of a sandwich in Suzi's mind and Excel projections. Business looks easy with Excel and forecasts. Projections of a new business are expectations, not what will or does happen. The reality was very different. We started with a capital of 300K Dirhams. We estimated setting up the kitchen with 180K Dirhams and still have 120K Dirhams to work for 3–4 months. We finished the project at 260K Dirhams. We thought 40K will last for 3 months. It finished in three days. We were very tight on money for the entire first year. Our partner put in an additional 70K Dirhams.

Where did you get the knowledge to design the kitchen?

M: I read, networked with people and incrementally acquired knowledge. I met a designer who agreed to make a layout and get the kitchen HACCP certified. He charged us 6000 Dirhams, serious money for a startup.

How did you decide the products to make?

S: Salads and Sandwiches were the main focus. I used to work in London for many years and I wanted to recreate all my favorites that were not available in Dubai. We did a lot of testing with friends!

M: We decided to create products for a person on the run-a business person or an executive. We have over 300 different products, but our customer focus is the same. We picked a customer segment, focused on them and have not shifted.

Did the products change, from as planned before start and as accepted by the market?

S: There were a lot of lower quality products in the market. We were not going to compete in that space and always knew we wanted to produce high-quality gourmet sandwiches and salads. An interesting conversation happened after startup. A caller said, 'I love your product, and need 2000 sandwiches every day.' He continued, 'They have to be cheaper. I want to pay 2 Dirhams.' I responded 'They are priced at 10–12 Dirhams. I can't do it. My packaging and bread cost is more than that.' He persisted, 'Then use different bread, packaging and filling.' I told the caller, 'Then you are not going to get the sandwich you tasted.' We have been asked to do many things along the way and have always declined when it did not match our vision. We are doing what we specialize in, and are going to stick to this standard and quality.

Did you plan before you started?

M: We had a general idea of what to expect.

S: Nothing was straightforward. No one supports you when you start up. You have no standing in the market. You need small quantities, not bulk. No one wants to give you credit. No one even delivers to you. I used to drive to suppliers to pick supplies. Now the suppliers chase us for business, but it took a long time to get there!

M: Logistics were a nightmare. We couldn't afford to buy a van. We thought, 'We can rent a van. How difficult can that be?' It was very difficult. Finding a driver was a nightmare. Juggling cash flow was another constant challenge. We prioritized paying salaries and suppliers. Suzi and I did not draw a salary from the business because there was nothing to draw.

S: I started taking a minimal salary after one year. We still haven't reached the salary we made as professionals.[4]

Startup challenges?

M: Once at 6 am I discovered that the delivery van had sunk into the ground. We needed a crane to get the van working. We had two delivery cars. Market demand required the cars to work 17 hours a day. And one day the two cars had crashed into each other at a red light. For a startup, unexpected events can be disorienting. One feels vulnerable because there are no extra resources to handle these situations.

S: The startup stretched us. We were keeping 14–15 hour days. We had to complement each other. This continued for 3–5 yrs. We worked Fridays. I took a Friday holiday after one year. Manar took a Friday off after three years.

---

4 2013

Something easier than you expected?

S: Our growth has surprised me. I, with a salesperson, started making sales call to offices. We knocked on doors, showed and sampled our products, passed our little menu and asked them to call us with orders. People started recommending us to their friends. Soon we needed a second salesperson and this snowballed. We had twenty-five salespersons within a year. We have grown entirely on word-of-mouth recommendations. We never budgeted for marketing, advertising and promotions. Maybe it is a testament to the product. Nothing else in the business was easy. We have managed the challenges because customer acceptance happened in a natural way, giving us a lot of confidence.

How did the business develop?

M: Spinneys and Carrefour initially rejected us because of the price. ENOC liked our sandwich quality. The commercial aspect of the deal was a losing proposition. We decided to go ahead. We did well with them in terms of volume and distribution. We did not have money to promote our products but there was no better promotion than to be visible at forty gas stations. We are now in Spinneys.

Was there a time when you felt it was not going to work?

M: I have felt it every day, for the past eight years. We worked through the uncertainty.

S: Manar kept me going. There have been many occasions, while facing challenges, when I have reflected on whether "it" is worth it. It has taken a lot of commitment in hours, blood, sweat and tears to continue. I could have easily given up in the first two years.

How did your pricing develop?

S: We are not always good at knowing our food costs. I approach food development from the idea of what we want to create, not the bottom line. We make the product and ask people what they would pay for it. We assess and price it.

Key milestones?

S: Moving from Qusais to Al Quoz was a big step. Our growth had stalled. We couldn't supply customers. We diluted 20% of the company to build our current facility in Al Quoz.

Next 3–4 years?

M: Three years ago our net margin was small, just 3–4%. All the money was being reinvested. This was draining us. We had to make our margin more sensible. We decided to go into our own retail. We came up with a new concept '1762' – a deli serving sandwiches and salads.

S: 1762 is what we do but in a deli environment. I came across recipes and developed ideas of doing them in a deli shop. Opportunities need careful assessment. When a company reaches a certain size, you can go off on a tangent. We got it right with 1762 deli!

M: 1762 has started well. We break even. 1762 started on leap of faith. But we had to take a few steps to jump further. Again luck was on our side. DIFC was the perfect location for the idea but they don't accept anyone walking in. We decided to establish a location to showcase the idea in Jebel Ali. We finished the design and a friend coaxed us to visit DIFC. I printed a few color sheets, combined them and did the presentation. They sensed our commitment gave us a location.

How have you changed as persons in eight years?

S: I think reality hit us when we started Appetite. I have toughened up. I am passionate about the business and love my work but it has been a struggle. I am a little tired, and a bit worn out. Then again, I tell myself, it is not like we just did Appetite. We did that and then we did 1762.

M: But as persons behind the business, we are more humble because we understand things are not as they seem. As entrepreneurs we are never away from the business. Our mind is always working on business in the background. We are observing and learning. 1762 is an example of that. We developed the idea by looking around the world. We looked at 20–30 different outlets in terms of design and food. We saw different things, learnt and created the concept.

S: It is always ideas, ideas and ideas.

Where was the seed of entrepreneurship in you?

S: People talk about ideas they want to do. But not many people implement their ideas. Implementation is triggered by the need to do it.

M: Let us call it the X factor. It lies dormant. The X factor was evoked when I lost my job. Some people cave in, others put up a defense mechanism and some just confront and manage it. I wanted to do something. Not working was not an option once we started. I think the need to do something was much stronger.

Has your management style evolved?

M: We have learnt that choosing and managing people committed and passionate about what you are doing is very hard. This is the biggest challenge we have ever faced. We were particular that we will not run 1762 the way we run Appetite. We had to have to have a proper team; specialists doing what they are good at. An entrepreneur needs to a hire a committed team and create an environment for the commitment to be expressed. If you don't get this right, it will be challenging to succeed.

Do you think you will have regular hours and a GM running the business?

S: That will be nice. I don't think that will work, realistically. I don't want to do these hours forever. It is going to get better. It has become better and the salary is getting better. We are getting there. It has taken a long time. I think we have gone on with it for so long but I am always saying that the type of person we want in 1762 is someone who can do what matters for us and allows us to concentrate more on the new business instead of being so hands-on day-to-day. We would like to sit back, reflect a little and grow the business by concentrating on "angles" that we really need to. We are getting to a stage where we can do that. I wouldn't necessarily say we will sit back and take it easy.

M: We are very passionate about Appetite. I still cannot see how we can convert this passion into a corporate entity. Once we become corporate, we take a lot of passion out and bring in procedures and compromises. Appetite is about food and food is about passion, it is not about industrialization. We do have a big production line. We consider it almost an industry, but still control the ingredients and quality and this is the way we want to do it. We do it manually and it is handmade, with a lot of love. But can this be transferred to commercial setup? We are still artisans even though the volume is quite high. I think this is the challenge Suzi and I will face because we cannot continue this way. We are still young; we have many years to do different things. But we cannot do 12 hours a day, 7 days a week. We are trying to find a happy balance.

Architects of Information

Entrepreneur	Mark Hirst
Company and website	Blue Beetle/www.bluebeetle.ae
Product	Website design and digital marketing
Year established	2004
Tips for entrepreneurs	• Once you decide go for it, execute. • When challenged, don't fret. Focus on solutions. Define small problems and solve them a step at a time.

What is the business of Blue Beetle?

We are a website design and digital communication company that specializes in the creation of online business solutions that are simple, intuitive and functional. We are 'digital information architects'.

How did Blue Beetle start?

The "push" into entrepreneurship happened after an unpleasant job experience in Dubai. The seeds of entrepreneurship were latent in me. I always wanted to work for myself. I recall two influences- a vivid childhood memory of my dad telling me, 'You'll never make any money unless you work for yourself,' and my love for web design.

I didn't feel like I was an entrepreneur when I decided to give business a shot. I had noticed a gap. Basic web design is easy. There were a lot of companies doing ordinary websites. I didn't see many high-quality websites. I realized companies were not taking advantage of the potential of websites and digital communication. I came from an industrial design background. I was not an IT person who wanted to do websites. I set out to design good websites and harness the potential of IT. I knew that to do a website that serves a strategic purpose requires a diversity of skills, experience, knowledge and hard work.

I started from a cubicle in the business center in Dubai Media City. I initially did everything, from coding to designing. Slowly the assignments started to become more complex. I am not a programmer, so the first person I hired was a programmer; Blue Beetle had become a two-man company. About four years ago I decided to take business seriously and establish Blue Beetle as a more solid company. By then we had gained a reputation in the market for our work. Some of the assignments we got required additional resources and skillsets. I got an office in Dubai Studio City. Over the last four years we have grown steadily and had to move again. At the end of last year we moved into an even bigger office in JLT.

Was customer acquisition easy?

Customer acquisition was easier when I started. I did not make any cold calls. My first job was for Sharjah Airport Duty Free. It was a small job. I worked hard to impress the client. I think they were impressed, since they referred me on to other jobs.

How was your initial pricing?

When I started I was alone, flexible and willing to negotiate price. My overhead was low and I didn't need a great number of projects to keep me going. Today it is more structured because we need several projects a month to keep the business going.

Do clients give jobs to Mark the designer or to Blue Beetle the company?

For the first few years it was definitely me as I was always the one meeting them and doing the work. They were hiring me, even though I branded the company as Blue Beetle from day one. People knew me as Blue Beetle.

Have you ever walked away from a client?

Yes, we have walked away. We have learnt to say no. I have learnt to recognize clients we should not work with. There are some clients who we have mutual respect for and there are some we have had bad experiences with. Being able to recognize that before you get too far down the line is good.

Is a client who will make you compromise on your creativity not a good client?

Yes. If a client is too cost driven and expects the work to be delivered in an unreasonable time frame, we know we will not be able to deliver quality and we generally take a decision to bow out.

Important learning while developing Blue Beetle?

I learned to develop long-term relationships with clients. We had two clients from the early days and did a lot of recurring work for them. We worked hard to impress them each time we worked with them. We realized companies always have work that needs to be done and building ongoing relationships is important for our business. I also realized the importance of credibility. What set us apart was a simple thing; we did what we said we would do.

How did you go about building the company Blue Beetle?

In the beginning I was deeply involved in the production of all the websites. I recognized that even though I was good at what I did, and was getting clients, there were better people out there who were more specialized than I was. My second employee was a designer. I passed on all design work to him and moved onto the business side of things while still doing some front-end development. I maintained my responsibility for the front-end work until I hired a person who was better than me. My aim was to completely remove myself from production. This is where I am today. I've even gone as far as removing myself from business development. I am now involved in business strategy and organization systemization.

If I was joining you three years ago, how would you sell your company to me?

I would be completely honest and explain the situation. And then I would ask you if you are willing to jump into the deep end with me. This is what I did with my second team member. He came from a big agency background. He had to believe in my dream and trust me. I explained to him why it was a good time to join; he could grow from the start, be involved in a company focused on quality and have an opportunity to affect the direction of the company.

Has creating a compensation package to attract talent been an issue?

Recruitment has been a steep learning curve. Mistakes have been made. To attract good people the company needs to be of a certain size and caliber. This is a chicken and egg problem; you need good people to do good work and they attract other good people. It is risky to take on more overheads. Ninety percent of our overhead is salary. I do it incrementally.

What is the future growth trajectory of Blue Beetle?

The short-term strategy is to get Blue Beetle to a point where we have enough people to be able to do the work we want to do, of a quality and standard we want to deliver. Right now we are at a challenging point- we are too small, we need more work but we are very busy, so we need more people. But we need the work before we can hire people. The aim right now is to get to the stage where we are the right size. We're now in a space that will allow us to grow.

Do you worry if you will be able to pay the salaries?

It is a worry. In this business growth is difficult to project. Sometimes there have been 2–3 months without additional business. I begin thinking, 'Oh! My word,' and suddenly a customer who was sitting on a proposal for 3 months comes back saying, 'We are ready to move forward.' And we find ourselves very busy. I have come to terms with the fluctuating up and down nature of the business now. Now I don't worry when it is quiet. I used to worry. I know something will come through. It always does.

What is your investment in Blue Beetle?

The starting capital requirement for the trade license was Dirhams 50,000. That is all that I had. Four years ago when I decided to take the plunge, scale up and grow, I actually had a million Dirhams saved in the company account after three years of operation.

Have you changed as a person on this entrepreneurial journey?

I wouldn't say I have changed in personality, but I have learnt and developed a lot. I was a web designer who was suddenly in charge of a company and people. I was unconsciously making a transition from a technical "doer" to a managerial entrepreneurial position. Business was not my background. I never thought I would start doing this kind of a thing. I do miss designing and coding, and yet I couldn't go back. This is what I want to do now. It was a lot for me to learn and do and to let go of what I was doing before. I still have a lot to learn. I am by no means a great manager or entrepreneur yet. I know a lot more now than I did four years ago. I am learning all the time- how to hire people, what to look for, what not to do, how not to react right away and how to take a breather in a situation. The most important learning has been to focus on solutions and not worry about what is going to happen. One can worry as much as one wants, but that is not going to change anything. It is better to focus on solutions and as long as one does it on a daily basis and works hard, it is a good place to be.

What is an important piece of advice you would give to an entrepreneur?

Go for it.

Were you sure from the first day that the business would work?

I have to admit I was pretty sure. Even if it does fail, you keep on going. You learn from what happens and push on. There is no real failure unless, of course, you give up.

This thinking – "Don't keep thinking about what ifs. Go for it. Define small problems and keep solving them one step at a time." Has this been your mantra?

This is something relatively new. I am a workaholic, I worry too much and it stresses me out. I am beginning to realize there is no point in doing that. You have to have faith and believe in yourself. Rather than putting energy into worrying, it is better to focus on solutions.

What worries you about business?

Whether we will get enough work and getting it done to the highest standard.

Do you see a change in your business model going forward?

There are things, in terms of what we deliver, that we need to improve. A project lifecycle has three stages – beginning, middle and end. The middle of the project, design and development, we do very well. We need to improve the beginning and the end. The beginning is about strategy – determining business objectives, identifying what the client is trying to achieve, the research that goes into analyzing competitors, current website and so on. We are putting more focus on this. The end of the project is about maintenance and evolution of the website. There are business opportunities here as well. We are working to a point where after delivering the website, we have an ongoing relationship with the client to support and develop their website as their business grows and evolves.

Getting the Right Bite

Entrepreneurs	Ibrahim Mohammed Abdullah and Mohamed Akbari
Company and website	Naturalway Sweets/www.naturalwaysnacks.com
Business	Manufacturing energy, nutrition and cereal bars
Year started	2009
Tips for entrepreneurs	• Don't just decide, start and go. Make a plan – what you will do and what it will cost. • Self-belief is critical. Be flexible and focused. Stay focused on your goal. Adapt the way you execute. • Establish distribution, how you will reach customers. Otherwise nothing will work. • Things take time to happen. Learn to manage extreme uncertainty. Self-assess your stress-taking ability before you start.

Why Naturalway?

We started when we noticed two things. One, all healthy or nutrition nut-based products in the supermarkets were imported, priced high and didn't taste fresh. Two, we, in MENA countries, have lots of nut and date based local products available in souks. The question was, could we create products and sell them through organized retail? We decided to create nutritious products based on traditional recipes using 100% natural ingredients.

Why manufacture products? Why not trade?

The idea of doing a packaged food business came from my earlier work as an agent distributing branded chocolates. As an agent I was squeezed between the Principal and the distributor. So a thought came to my mind – why not become a Principal by creating something? Naturalway is not my first business. I have dabbled in eyewear retail and real estate business. Before that I was part of a family fashion business. I even studied fashion technology but dropped out because I did not like it. I just liked the creative part of the fashion business, where you create something- a dress out of fabric. I now believe that every creative process is almost the same thing. In Naturalway we create bars out of ingredients. In hindsight the tuition for the fashion course isn't going to waste; I am creating something out of scratch. Making the product has not been easy. Rather it has been positively difficult. We are only now, after 6 years, starting to be successful. Our products that are gluten-free, low cholesterol and natural sugar-based are starting to move. We use fruit sugars so we are not sugar-free.

How did you start?

Deciding to make a nutritious and gluten-free product was the easy part. I had no clue on how to start the business. It took me over 6 months of research, self-study and learning to convert the idea into a business proposition. I went to Cavalier in Belgium. Their staff gave me ideas. I visited a friend who has a factory making nutritious products. I visited another factory to understand how to put a food plant together. I worked in product R&D with a chef who knew how to cook/prepare the products.

Why would someone share knowledge?

They were willing to sell their ideas and their knowledge to me, not share. We paid a fee. Then we met a person in Lebanon running his family sweet shop. All the knowledge about making products was in his brain. He had no scientific knowledge. His business had shut down. Fortuitously we were looking for someone at the same time. I needed a person and he needed to survive.

How did you develop the products?

We started by copying existing products in the market. We saw what our competitors were doing, analyzed their products and put the same concept together with different ingredients.

Why not create your own recipes?

Creating products is a long process. I was a startup. Time and money are always short. I had to balance the pressure of "getting to the market" quickly to generate revenue and spend time "developing perfect products." To develop a gluten-free product we prepared over 650 bars. Each bar had to be tested for coloring, appearance, texture, taste and nutrition values. And then testing for shelf life test required us to wait for over 6 months. We finally zeroed in on two bars. These are undergoing customer testing. I have also learnt not to rely on my judgment alone for product selection. We test the product taste with customers. Nutrition testing requires the product to be sent to a European lab for testing. The entire process takes approximately 9 months and there are no guarantees that the product will work. Product development takes time and money. I think we spent around 200K Dirhams developing our initial product range.

When did you get a "feel" that it was going to work?

I recollect two events. One, when we realized we could make the product, and two, our meeting with the owner of the company that distributes the product. We had a group of people try the product every day for a month to test the consistency of taste. And we tested the consistency of nutrition values of the product over a month. The distributor meeting was more crucial. A new business can create a product but the most important thing is getting it to the customer; on the shelf where customers make a choice. It doesn't work if you have the best product in the world but there is no way of putting it in the market.

During product development did you focus on production cost?

I focused on the cost right through the development. It had to be below a target amount. I had started with a belief that imported product was expensive. I was targeting to sell Naturalway product at half the imported product price. This was essential to creating our space in the market. When we first approached Carrefour, the manager asked us a simple question, 'Why should I keep your product on the shelf?' I replied, 'Freshness, quality and price.' He seemed convinced when I told him the target shelf price. He replied, 'Not everyone can buy an eight Dirham bar every morning. Three Dirhams is a different deal altogether. Many can afford it.' I learnt that we were a local unknown brand. Price difference at retail would create a reason for customers to try our product, to give us a chance.

Did you achieve the target price envisaged?

No. We planned on selling it for 2.5 Dirham. It sells for 3.5 Dirham. Luckily overall prices have gone up and we are still nearly 50% less than competition.

From selling price to cost – how did you understand costs of distribution?

My earlier experience in distribution helped. When we started we had no idea of the production cost. So we didn't work from the factory to the shelf, rather from the shelf to the factory. We knew that the product on the shelf should be 50% below the competitor's price. We also knew the supermarket and distributor margins. So we could put a number on the ex-factory price.

Did you estimate money required to start?

We actually estimated the money we had and put all that in the business. No estimate worked. The uncertainty associated with shortage of money doesn't go away. But neither does effort. I just keep at it.

When was the first time you saw the product on a shelf?

In 2009 we started with selling three items through ENOC. I cannot express my feelings when I saw the product on the shelf. I asked the sales staff, 'What do they think about the product?' Some liked the product but disliked the design of the packaging. I then realized that presentation matters. We went back to the drawing board, reworked the packaging, added three more SKUs, created a complete "look" and went back into the market.

How challenging was locating a distributor?

It wasn't straightforward and easy. I started the business by meeting a lot of distributors. All distributors, except our eventual distributor, told me I was biting more than what I could chew, and they didn't believe what I was trying to do could be done. Such meetings were disappointing and discouraging. Our first distributor taught us that a distributor has to first believe in the business, and then make effort by "pushing" a product till the market starts "pulling" the product. This requires a capacity to do point-of-sale activities. Aal Mir is our second distributor. They believed in the potential of the nutrition product category, the gap and the Naturalway products.

You staff strength?

We have twenty-five full-time and fourteen part-time. It is challenging to recruit domestically. It is very difficult to find someone with product development experience.

What worries you about the business?

Naturalway is growing but not stable. We have lots of uncertainties. Everything worries me about the business. I haven't slept much in the past seven-months. To manage very high level of stress I have to do what I do, except I have to do it better. We have managed to establish the infrastructure for the business. Now we are focused on increasing sales through POS marketing and competition. As a small company I can't do everything at the same time. I can't delegate to a member in my team because we are a small team. I have to do everything myself.

How do you manage uncertainty and stress?

When confronting a challenging business problem I start with a self-belief that hard work or application will be able to solve the problem. Everything has solutions, is doable, if you are able to apply your mind to it.

Was there a time you wanted to give up?

Yes. The trigger for the thinking was financial. Not the hard work, not the stress.

Do you draw a salary from the business?

Salary was supposed to come, but we are still on survival mode. I just draw some expenses. No salary.

How have you changed as a person doing Naturalway?

I have become responsible. All businesses I started were easy to start and close. Naturalway is a huge commitment. Not just for the people who have invested and the staff. Aal Mir has commitments to the market. Supermarkets have committed space. People are used to seeing the product. We have commitments to the banks. If anyone doesn't see the product, it makes a huge difference. This is commitment. This is the difference.

Printing Success

Entrepreneur	Mohammad Al Hashimi
Company and website	Emirates Trans Graphics/www.etguae.com
Business	Regional distributor of printing machinery and consumables
Year established	2005
Tips for entrepreneurs	• Start a business in the industry you know; not a product you like. • Identify the value that you add. Think hard and you will discover ways to improve and innovate. • Network, network, network for growth. • Challenges will arise for a new business. Learn not worry. Manage them by working on them along the way.

How did ETG start?

The seeds of ETG lie in my father's business. He distributed printing machines in the region. I absorbed the knowledge of the industry from the family business. In 2005 I started to feel the need for my own company. I used to get a lot of respect from employees, suppliers and clients working with my father. But I felt constrained. I felt I was not in control of what I was doing. My ideas and decisions were often questioned. I wanted to take decisions and test the workability of my decisions. I did not like waiting for other people to take decisions that I had to implement. I did not like being watched over by others. Initially I was hesitant but then I took the plunge. I didn't know what business to start. I thought of starting a printing factory since I sold machines to printing companies. I hesitated. Printing was like "manufacturing" whereas my experience was in trading. A few equipment suppliers called me when I left my father's business. They wanted me to be their agent. I didn't even have an office. A European company reposed confidence in me. They gave me open credit. Their trust was invaluable for me to begin. I started small. I was cautioned about competition. Friends wondered how I would grow. I had accepted a challenge. I decided to grow in a controlled way, not taking big risks.

Did you ever want the security of a Government position?

I worked in Emirate Airlines after University and realized I couldn't work as an employee. I felt suffocated in the office. My thinking was different. The way I approached problems was different. I used to meet entrepreneurs. They used to tell me, 'The mindset of a government employee is different from the thinking of the private sector.'

How were you sure you had knowledge to start a business?

I started in my father's business, in the warehouse. As a warehouse executive I learned about materials and logistics. I then graduated to understanding spare parts followed by sales, accounts and general management. When I look back I started at the bottom of the organization. To learn it is necessary to start at the bottom, near the frontline. Learning doesn't start from the top. One has to keep opinion of oneself, ego, aside and start learning from scratch. I learnt the importance of respecting the ideas of each person. One cannot create a business alone. An entrepreneur needs everybody, from a junior employee to a senior manager. Feedback and information from a storekeeper can sometimes save a lot of money. I always kept my mind open and receptive to ideas, information and learning.

What was your father's reaction when you started?

He supported and blessed me. ETG is an independent business. We are competitors. We also collaborate on turnkey projects. I have increased the geography of the business- in the Emirates, GCC as well as parts of Africa and have become known in the industry. I carry the name of my father 'Hashimi.' I grew his legacy- 'Hashimi' as a trademark, linked to printing. Now he is proud of me.

How different was it starting a business as an Emirati?

I was challenged when I started. I was competing against my father's company, a very big company in the ME. I was married and had family responsibility. And I was starting a company. I had social pressures as an Emirati; I had to maintain my social standing. All this pressurized me to succeed. When I look back, ETG is the achievement of my family and with my family.

Did the family invest in ETG?

I never asked my family for capital. I invested AED 300,000 and started the business with my partner. Our revenues today are AED 40 million.

How did you acquire customers?

One thing I did well when working with my father was being good with customers. When I left I had built strong relationships. Customers started calling me, they wanted to support me. Customers not only called but started buying from me, whatever machines I had. Suddenly I had agencies, equipment and buyers. It just worked. Building relationships is the value I had earned from many years of work. Even now I help customers beyond the sales transaction. A salesperson is also problem solver. Opportunities arise to build strong relationships when solving problems. For example, I once supplied a second machine to a customer when the first one I had sold him broke down and production was affected.

How did you learn selling?

I used to open the "door" and lead the sales team when targeting important customers and government entities. Customers used to be surprised when they saw an Emirati, who had product knowledge, making a sales call. I used this opening to build personal connections with customers and understand their needs. I have followed this approach of personally reaching out to customers and suppliers to understand their needs to build the business. Initially I depended on my technical team for normal sales calls. I learnt the hard way that personal selling is not enough to close the deal. I had salespersons who spent a lot of time engaging with customers and then lost opportunities to competition. I realized the importance of selling skills and being quick on one's feet to sense opportunity and close deals. I have a sense of urgency. Time is my most important resource. When I close deals I don't think I can wait till tomorrow. I am also flexible. A customer may not have money for a down payment to buy a printing machine. I don't give up. I ask the customer for alternative assets, like motor cars, that I can take as a down payment. A problem in the market is that people have printing jobs on hand but no capital to implement them.

How did you go about pricing?

When I started I wanted to open the market and sell machines at cost. I was learning how to price and made mistakes. In hindsight it worked; the early customers are loyal and have done a lot of business with me.

How did you grow?

We grew in two ways. Digitization of printing was happening. To sell we needed to educate customers about technologies and printing options. And to buy machines customers needed finance. I needed to arrange finance for my customers to grow. In selling machinery, we sell products and finance customers. We cannot ask customers for cash. To grow ETG I had to find ways of financing customers. I started selling the products at cost by financing the buyer. I was cautioned about my sales approach. But I sold lot of machines.

Where did you get money to finance customers?

I have followed a path of finalizing the contract by financing the customer myself. I take the advance payment, sign a 24-month repayment schedule and then search for a bank or finance company to finance the contract, either the customer or ETG. My competitors take the longer route of working with banks and customers to make sales. I am more persistent. I believe that if I wait for the customer to think, I will lose him. My customers prefer working with me because it is easier to postpone a check with me. They know I will help them. The bank will not.

But customer finance is a difficult business?

When I calculate a 24-month credit term, I build a profit rate in the pricing because I know the customer, his business and risk. We know the region better than European suppliers so we know which buyer could be given credit. I had to learn to manage business risk. Some customers will default. I am not worried because I retain the right to pick up the machine in the event of default without paying back the monies collected. I can always sell the second-hand machine because I have maintained it and I know its quality. This happened during the crisis. I sold a machine to a customer in Sharjah on credit. He went bankrupt and absconded. His company was sealed. He repaid us half the contract amount. I contacted the owner, asked for his help in recovering the machine. He helped us get the machine back. We organized a buyer for the machine and profitably resold the used machine.

How do you manage people in business?

I started ETG with three staff. We are now twenty. I have created teams of four, one of whom is a team leader. They are all free to connect with me anytime. The team leader monitors the performance of the team and engages with me for critical decisions. I developed commission system from the start of the company. The sales and engineering staff make commission. And when the engineers are free, they go on sales calls. I realized early that engineers are critical to the sales function. They go to install new machines as well as to maintain installations and play a critical role of guiding customers and recommending purchase of new machines.

Where do you get business ideas?

I normally don't sit in the office, unless there is a meeting. I move about meeting customers, suppliers and visiting exhibitions. This is how I get ideas for business.

What is your most important challenge in business today?

As a business owner, every day is a challenge- to take a new agency, sell a product and give finance. The business is on my mind at all times. I sometimes wake up during the night and find ways to close a deal. I relax only when I identify a business challenge or weakness of a customer and develop a solution. When I started, we faced challenges as a new company. I learnt not worry about them, to manage and work on them along the way.

When did you draw your first salary from the business?

After four months of startup. I took a salary from the capital I put in and the sales. I could do this because I closed a lot of deals when I started. I actually did my first sale of AED 2.8 m before I started the office. The customer was from China. He opened an L/C with a 24-month payment.

What advice would you give to a new entrepreneur?

A person should start a business in the field that he knows. The business need not be identical. It needs to be done in an original way. Don't do a business because you are interested in a product. See what you bring to the business to add value. Start a business in the industry you know and improve it; if you can think deeply, you will find ideas to improve/change and become successful. An entrepreneur should have confidence in himself and ideas will come from within. An entrepreneur should also develop contacts. This helps in business growth.

What are your challenges in ETG?

I sell in many countries. Being in Dubai, I have learnt to engage with different nationalities. It is necessary in business to understand different cultures and be accommodating of the different ways of doing business. Similarly I buy from many countries. Again I need to engage with different persons and cultures. Finance is constraining the growth of ETG. If I have an enquiry from outside the geography and seek facilities from the bank, they hesitate. I have given cross-border credit. I gave credit in Yemen when the crisis started. My brother warned me. He said, 'You are crazy giving credit in Yemen.' I said, 'No, I am not worried. I am a salesman and know when and whom to sell to.' I gave credit to a customer in Saudi. I cannot accept checks because ETG doesn't have an office in Saudi. I get regular checks. I don't deal with names. I deal with people. I think I know how to gauge people – whether they will pay or not. If I get a poor feeling, I don't give credit.

We Shut Our Business. the Tough Choices of Entrepreneurship

Entrepreneurs	Mohammad (M) and Peyman Parham Al Awadi (P)
Company and website	Wild Peeta/www.wildpeeta.com
Business	Gourmet shawarma café
Year established	2009
Tips for entrepreneurs	• Be prepared to work 24 × 7 for at least 3 years. • Too much startup capital is a problem. • Be patient. Business needs 5–6 years to develop. • Know what you are good at. You don't build a business by doing everything. Don't reinvent. Use specialized complementary resources. It is cost-effective. • Fast pivot – if something doesn't work, try something new.

How did Wild Peeta start?

M: We saw an opportunity for reinventing the shawarma; the sauces, way of grilling the meats and the bread. And make it more nutritious. We experimented with the idea for ten years in our kitchen. We didn't have the capital. We wanted to use our savings, not ask the family for money.

What in your education and work experience prepared you for business?

M: We were exposed to different cultures from a very young age. Between us we speak five languages – French, Hindi, Arabic, English and Farsi. We studied in the US, came back, worked with our father in his business and learnt from his style of working. We saw business as very personal. It is about goodwill. You build relationships. This, I think, was a foundation for entrepreneurship. When we started working we wondered whether we were good enough for a multinational company. Many doors were shut on us when we reached out and asked for jobs. All we heard was, 'I am sorry. We are not hiring Emiratis.' We were persistent. Peyman joined Master Foods and I joined Philips. Later I moved to BAT and Peyman to Pepsi. The MNC work experience sharpened our functional skills. It helped us benchmark our capabilities with people from around the world giving us the confidence that "we too could do it." It was during that time we started thinking of Wild Peeta. In hindsight starting a business was not a deliberate move. We went where our fate took us. We got offered a job. We took it. We got an opportunity to start our own business and we did that.

You had no knowledge of the food business. Did you hesitate when starting WP?

M: On the contrary, we were excited. This was an opportunity, a journey of sorts. We tried to prepare for the "adventure."

What surprised you when you started the business?

M: I think ignorance is bliss. We didn't have the faintest idea how challenging it was going to be to open a small café in Dubai. We thought we were ready when we started. We were trained by the best MNC companies in the world. We had managed multi-million dollar budgets. So we thought we could open a store. But it was the most challenging work that we had done. It was tedious, difficult, bureaucratic and time-consuming to open the first outlet. We did not get a fix on tackling the networked procedures of different government departments. We rented an outlet in DHCC. Converting it for use as a restaurant was a nightmare. To install the infrastructure required paperwork and procedures that took ten months and added pre-operating costs. We thought we knew how to start. We actually didn't know the execution details. It was a steep, long and expensive learning curve.

You also changed your concept of doing Teppanyaki cooking.

M: We learnt that a new business concept evolves through trial and error. What looked conceptually beautiful in the business plan didn't work in reality. The Teppanyaki was an interesting idea. We were to cut the meat off the skewer, put it on a Teppanyaki griddle, add sauce and theatrics, put in a sandwich and serve. The process was unnecessary. It was taking too long. And customers didn't care how we prepared the meats. We confronted cross-contamination of sauces, something not envisaged earlier. The fad was just too expensive. We looked at our competitors, saw what worked for them and adapted.

Did customers understand a gourmet shawarma?

M: Gourmet shawarma is not a market segment. We only have two segments-cheap and expensive shawarma. We were trying to establish that we are gourmet shawarma but we are not expensive shawarma. When we started, we couldn't sell our shawarma at a price of 25-30 Dirhams. We had to lower our prices, restart at a price point similar to Subway and gradually increase price.

Would you have taken a person knowledgeable in the food business as part of your team?

M: We would not open a restaurant without a full-time partner, who owns a stake in the business and has operational experience related to the business.

Was it easy to connect with suppliers?

M: The first challenge was finding the suppliers. Then we ended up buying products that were much more expensive than planned. We were a small new business, our purchase volumes were low and no supplier wanted to work with us. Vegetable suppliers told us they will not deliver. We sent a person to buy and pickup goods paying cash. Customized packaging has been a challenge. Prices are high and this distorts margins. Our bread today is the best it has ever been but it still is not the bread we want. Our meat is good but it is still not exactly what we want. We have had to compromise in producing the shawarma we had planned.

Did you try too much innovation too quickly?

M: We started with a broad view of our core products. We thought we should make everything with something special from WP. In addition to Teppanyaki, we erred in buying a bread making oven. We wanted to make our own bread and realized it was a business in itself. In hindsight we rationalize this by saying we wanted to try a lot of products to see what happens. We should have started small, with a few products, established the product and the process, and then added products.

How would you start the same business with the knowledge you possess today?

M: Very differently. We were green when we started. We invested too much money in equipment we didn't need. Our project management would be a lot better. We wouldn't open so many outlets at this early stage of our business. We have gone through three outlets. Our first outlet in DHCC shut down because of flooding. MAF were kind enough to give us space in Diera City Center. We discovered that a food court customer is not our customer. The World Trade Center outlet was unviable, being a seasonal outlet. We would not start the business with AED 1.3 m. We could start the business with 70–100K for a 600 sq. ft. outlet. We wouldn't custom build anything. We would do a low-cost build. Try it for several weeks and if it works, go to next step. We would stay in a location for at least three years, doing all the experimentation to tweak the process, menu, costing and supply chain.

Getting too much money was a bad idea?

M: Access to large capital early is a problem. If we have money we stop thinking deeply about decisions and use money to solve problems that can be solved differently and at a lower cost.

Was it a right decision to resign your job to start the business?

M: Yes. Startups evolve. They can't be explained by writing. Every day brings new challenges that require adaptation. And only the idea creator can do it. It was important to lead from the front. I was in the café every day. The staff saw me take orders, make shawarma, serve customers, manage the stock, etc.

What worked in your social media strategy and what didn't?

M: Social media helped get us to where we are. We used social media to access resources and get customer feedback. Social media gave us a potential customer base who wanted to try our product before we started, and they did. But we had to be accessible, otherwise customers have alternatives.

Was HR an issue?

M: We couldn't recruit people from within the UAE. We started by paying a little more than the market. We had attrition before we identified good staff. Even sacking staff was a challenge. Our challenge was in teaching staff to make a shawarma. Our overall HR experience has been time-consuming and expensive. The existing visa and employment system is very anti startups and small business.

How have you changed as persons?

M: We have constantly evolved. Sometimes it feels like endless changes. The real challenge was different. In an MNC they give you specific jobs, responsibilities and roles. You are within a box – finance or sales or marketing. When you start your own business you need to do everything- marketing, finance, how to hire, how to train, how to fix a Wi-Fi router, how to make shawarma, cook a sauce, clean the floor properly and so many different things. We have become confident as persons. I think we are the happiest we have ever been. We feel our lives have been enriched. Entrepreneurship has given meaning to what we are doing. We are doing something we love, that we believe in. We have our challenges, but we will get around them.

Advice to an entrepreneur starting out?

M: Entrepreneurship is a long journey with a lot of ups and downs. What will keep you going is your enthusiasm and intense commitment. Do something you are passionate about. The reality is that nothing is easy. It takes times and effort to establish a successful business. Success doesn't come knocking. What outsiders don't see is the hard work successful entrepreneurs put in. They don't sleep. Don't go on vacation. They don't rest for a second, business is always on their minds. Perseverance is the input.

Time, Tenacity and Trust – Building Blocks of a Trading Company

Entrepreneur	Mohamed Sharif
Company and website	Dimara International/www.dimara.ae
Business	Manufacture and supply of guest amenities and supplies to hotels and airlines
Year established	2005
Tips for entrepreneurs	• Business starts with a promise, people believing your words. You tell people what you are doing, and do it. Money is earned after trust is secured. • Be determined. Believe that you can create your business. A new business undergoes many changes during startup. • Time is the precious commodity to make the business successful. Business is a 24 × 7 commitment. Forget personal time.

How did Dimara start?

Watching my country grow and prosper, I wanted to start a business that paralleled the growth and success of the tourism sector of the economy. I looked for products to serve the hospitality industry, where I could add value. I found a niche of hotel amenities where the trade was leaving a "space" for innovation and creativity led growth; they were the little things that always make a difference in the hotel experience. Inspiration came from hoteliers who believed that local companies could not provide them products of similar or better standards than companies from the US, UK, France or Germany. We have proven them wrong.

How did this happen?

I had two things when I started Dimara. I had sensed an opportunity in the hospitality business. And had passion as well as commitment to serve customers to my utmost professional capacity. Many companies were trading.

I was determined we will not supply to the hospitality industry blindly, trading boxes in and out, but would add value based on developing a deeper knowledge and understanding of customers. This became my business focus and purpose. To achieve this we have steadily worked to acquire innovative products and brands, customize solutions for customers and provide exceptional service. We didn't achieve this overnight. It has been a challenging journey.

How did you enter the market?

The first six months were tough. It was not easy to win the trust of buyers in the hotel industry. They were more comfortable working with Europeans. I was an Emirati and wanted to sell products to hotels! Clients would look at me and wonder whether I knew anything about what I was selling. Fortunately, I was blessed with a strong team that, through dedication and persistence, helped me prove that we could surpass the standards set by European companies.

Is being an Emirati businessman a challenge?

Initially, yes. People have developed biases which are difficult to change. They think Emiratis do not pay attention to detail and are not hard working. I had to prove to my customers that I care about what I am selling, about my business and that I can meet their expectations.

How did you overcome this barrier?

I did not anticipate the extreme scrutiny of our buyers. The only thing that helped me overcome the hurdle of establishing our place in the market was persistence and not giving up. I did actual selling after gaining knowledge of the product. I worked with my manager to handle the uncertainty of customers. We divided the work amongst us. Sometimes she fronted with the customer, pushing the sale, and I supported her. At other places, I led the dialogue and she complemented me. On occasion we brought the sales managers of the foreign companies, our partners, to assist us. I found at times that customers preferred to work with foreigners, even if I have better product knowledge. I also discovered hidden costs involved in purchase. Buyers and suppliers had cozy arrangements. Buyers were uncertain about how to deal with an Emirati, worried about their invisible benefits. I learnt to rise above this and get business, setting an example in the industry for honest practices.

How did you win customers?

We developed a marketing plan based on target customers as well as market research and allocated a budget to accomplish goals set. To position ourselves as different from others and gain customers, we used cutthroat prices and easier payment terms. We took risks in the startup phase. We made some mistakes and learned from them. I made it a principle to live the belief that the customer is always right to satisfy customers in their transactions with Dimara. I think what helped Dimara was our decision to provide value-added services to our customers that our competitors did not have – an in-house design team, consultancy team that works closely with clients and production units to make and customize products.

You had to learn everything about the business.

I learned by doing, through trial and error. To a lay observer the products we sell are simple and uncomplicated. Initially even I was completely misled. Amenities are more than just a shampoo and soap. A science underlies the creation as well as production of products and the development programs that we implement for hotels. Business has two parts – the products and the business itself. We are engaged in design, details of product composition, selection of fragrances, packaging design and branding of products we sell. I visited factories to understand production and to position our products. I learned to choose business partners and make strategic alliances. I learnt how different costs make up the final price of the product – the cost of product, packaging and branding and price markups. To learn the "business of the products" took even more time. I had to manage the suppliers, consistently manage quality, talk to customers about the products and satisfy them. I recount an important step I took in the beginning that has helped the business. I appointed a person, whom I knew, to manage the operations of the company. And I focused on developing the market, making strategic alliances with well-known hotel chains.

Did suppliers trust you?

Trust is something that is earned; when any new business starts there is a doubt about its ability to pay. Factories would manufacture goods after we paid 50% of order value as an advance. The balance was paid when goods were ready for dispatch. Our order volumes are now much higher and we have earned some flexibility with suppliers; we don't have to make advance payments. However we still make payments before delivery.

In B2B selling payments are delayed.

I give credit to customers that are well known in the market and have an established relationship with us. Local customers delay payments, however eventually they do pay. My initial investment into the company was a few millions.

How has the business developed?

The business has evolved partially as planned and in unforeseen areas. We seized an unforeseen growth opportunity when we hired a tailor to make minor alterations to some of our products for a client. Today we run a complete tailoring and production unit. We found that we were able to reduce costs, provide better delivery times to our clients and have more flexibility with raw materials with our own production unit. The decision to start a linen manufacturing unit three years ago was again unforeseen. It was influenced by a delayed delivery issue with an overseas supplier and the urgency to fulfill our commitment with a client. We realized the economic value of local manufacturing. From that time onwards we strive to provide enhanced service to our clients by local manufacturing.

Learning from the business?

There is a big difference in being employed and running a business. The service industry has no fixed hours, and to meet customer needs we sometimes work on Fridays. We also arrange deliveries during Eid; our clients have high occupancy during the festival and we accommodate them. My family sometimes feels that if I was employed, I would have given them more time. One has to make choices, either you build a business or are employed all your life.

Is competition a worry in trading?

Trading is a competitive business. Getting in the mindset of your client is the key to being successful in trading. Some clients want superior products while others are interested in the price. I strive to have products that are unmatched in their quality. And when we couple that with high service standards, we set ourselves apart from the rest.

It Is Not like a Walk-in the Park

Entrepreneurs	Murshed Mohamed Ahmed and Mareyah Mohamed Ahmed
Company and website	Yebab/www.yebab.com
Business	Region's biggest online wedding directory
Year established	2008
Tips for entrepreneurs	• You really need to be passionate about what you will be doing. • Don't quit your job with just an idea. Start the business part-time. Test the potential and quit job if it holds back the business's growth. • Be determined to take action. You can never take it easy. The moment you stop, everything stops. Especially in the early days. • Don't spend a fil unless it is important and necessary, that is until cash flow becomes healthy and positive.

How did Yebab begin?

Wedding planning as a business idea came up in a conversation with friends in 2008. Wedding planners sit with a bride, understand her needs and organize the wedding. A good wedding planner needs to understand the psychology of women and know fashion as well as the market well. The planning of a wedding takes a lot of time. I reflected on doing the planning online. A website could collect and present a lot of information enabling a bride to self-plan her wedding. I first spoke to Mareyah, my sister, about a website with shops that could perform the role of a wedding planner. She said, 'Yes. It will work. People are always searching for good wedding planners. They are beginning to search online.'

How did Murshed understand the customer – the decision making of brides?

Mareyah joined me to co-found Yebab. She added the customer perspective – what brides look for, which shops they visit and their choice-making.

How did you start?

We prepared a low-cost simple website using open source programs. Our first site had four pages. We believed that customers would be "forgiving" of the design because we were going to give them unique information.

How did you go about detailing the website?

The website had to be out-of-the-ordinary to be noticed. We first identified the selection criteria for stores serving the wedding market. I shared product category and shop ideas with Mareyah. She would agree or disagree, and identify the information needed from the shop for listing. Take wedding venues, Dubai World Trade Center and Grand Hyatt are established locations. We had to attract them as category leaders to the portal. We then needed information a customer would use for choice-making. We discovered that customers need surprising details of products. Customers wanted to know about the proximity of the "Bride preparation room" to the venue. This is a room where a bride gets ready before entering the venue. We focused on every simple detail of every product and category. Nothing was unimportant when we went to the businesses we worked with. Mareyah and I went to shop meetings together. I presented the idea. She convinced the shop owner that we knew what we were doing. I was able to convince them from a business and technical point of view. She convinced them from the customer point of view. When I reflect, I believe sometimes her presence was enough.

Anything difference in your approach to business?

Other sites focused on increasing users. Logic was that the buyer pays e.g., charge 1% from a million users. Yebab developed differently. I "saw" money before creating a website and I changed my implementation strategy. I don't know why suppliers agreed to pay for the unknown.

How did you convince suppliers to partner Yebab?

It took effort and time. The conventional wisdom was to make Yebab an open free site; customers would benefit from increased supplier listings and listed businesses would see greater customer opportunities. I did not want to make Yebab a free listing site. I felt that controlled conservative growth was better than rapid growth. I knew businesses would be hesitant to pay for a new untested product. And if they agreed to pay, I was unaware of how much they would pay and how they would pay. Would it be an annual fee or a listing fee? I was a startup asking for money. I quickly realized the need for credibility.

I took a trade license from Mohammed Bin Rashid Establishment (SME). This empowered me to open doors. We collected business cards at the Bride Show 2008 to identify vendors. I was getting married so I went to them, both as a customer and as a supplier of services. I started with a shop famous for erecting wedding tents. I said to them, 'Our offer is simple. We will display your products and services for three-months. After that you will need to pay us. The website is simple. We will add pages as we develop.' Some shops didn't believe in the idea but played along. I guess they must have felt, 'Let us support them and see how it evolves.' Dubai World Trade Center was the first listing. We showed their page to a competitor. They felt, 'Yes, if they are on the site, we too should be there.'

When did you know that the site would become a business?
I knew the business would work when the first supplier paid. We thought of twenty categories to list. We needed shops in each category before we could announce Yebab. We established a deadline which was three-months away. We were working on the project in the afternoons because both of us had jobs. We had client meetings every day. We had a bank account so that we could tell people we are a real business. We picked momentum slowly. The website increased one page at a time. We built the site with about thirty shops and launched Yebab in October 2008. We did a press release. The website traffic immediately shot up. We had launched Yebab. We emailed all our vendor partners. We told them that their membership started on that day.

How did you establish price?
We had no idea how to price. It was a learning struggle. We started in a basic way. Big amounts of the wedding budget are spent on few categories like the wedding dress, jewelry and the venue. We put premium prices for these categories. We didn't want to use discounts to attract brides. We wanted brides to believe they were getting premium quality. Some wedding services are provided by freelancers. We kept those prices low. We decided to give three prices in every category, one higher and the other, lower. Only two of ten customers were choosing the expensive option. We were losing a majority of customers and the associated effort and time. We changed. We tried a promotional strategy; giving discount on all pages for a short time. This worked. More people signed in. We learnt to be flexible. Customers decide whether they want a higher price or a discount service. Customers saw the benefit and we have seen them renewing at higher prices. Convincing them took time and effort.

How has Yebab changed over the years?

Yebab has changed in all aspects – customer interface, business process, data mining and marketing. Yebab started as a content site. That continues; we add and filter the content. We are now focusing on Search Engine Optimization and ranking high on different search engines. Social media has created newer opportunities. Yebab now has user-generated content. I was apprehensive about user-generated content; worried about listing poor quality merchandize. I learnt; user-generated ratings give social communities the capacity to self-manage the listings. The nature of customer interface and user experience is evolving. Visitors use pictures to absorb information. We use high-quality pictures to generate user-generated content. We have a feature like Pinterest. Users visit stores and create albums by collating photographs. Other visitors can see the albums to get ideas. We are also able to track pages visited by site visitors, identify their interests and send weekly newsletters. Our marketing emphasis has shifted to online marketing through Facebook and Google. Earlier, marketing created awareness. Many knew Yebab as a name, as a logo, but did not visit the site. The branding was bigger than the profit. We started to move towards online marketing because traffic brings business.

How did you go about creating a team?

We are three partners- my sister, my wife and I. I started full time in November 2011. My sister formally joined in April 2012. I used to work four to five hours every day after work and full day on weekends before I joined full time. Learning to manage people is a continuous learning process. The first employee joined in 2009. She stayed for less than a month. Then we didn't hire anyone. We recently raised capital, took the new office and hired again; two people in sales to solicit accounts. They got very few accounts. I thought it was startup trouble. I pushed them to make deals. The next month their productivity increased five times. I learnt to pressurize people to get results. I put pressure on myself too. The company mood was not positive. This was a scary moment. I didn't know whether the market changed. I was not in touch with customers. I knew that if I went to the market I would get business. I also realized it was difficult to transfer sales experience from one field to another. We have a development team of eight people in Egypt.

Where do you see Yebab be in 2–3 years?

We have seen steady growth. Using VC language, we are looking to make it like a hockey stick. I see growth in two parts – revenue and traffic to the site. Traffic attracts businesses to list and advertising agencies to allocate budgets.

What worries you, keeps you awake about the business at night?

Growth. Revenue. Traffic. My focus is on traffic. If real traffic is there others will follow.

What part of your education prepared you for entrepreneurship?

I always had an interest in business. I was always trying new things. I implemented and tested ideas, waiting and watching if they attracted customers and picked momentum. I based all my college projects on computers. This helped me understand the use of computing power. I was always thinking about taking processes online; using internet as an opportunity. I started two sites as a hobby before I started Yebab. My first experiment with business was in 2004–05. I found an adapter to link computers through electricity wires. In those days wireless networking was poor. I had a website, which was a famous forum for computers. I uploaded the details and asked visitors to click if they wanted to connect computers through electricity wires. It worked. I continued to get calls even two years after the listing because the idea was exciting and people were curious.

What is unique in you that made you an entrepreneur?

I take action. I think, and if I am convinced, I act. I don't just talk. I am exceedingly focused. I block out distractions, other opportunities and business ideas, when I sit in front of the screen. Close friends see me now as more mature, more restrained and more controlled.

What is the guidance you will give to a new entrepreneur?

Do it if you are ready for it. It is not like a walk-in the park. Don't quit with just an idea. Start the business part-time. Test the potential and quit when the job holds back the growth of the business. Be determined to take action. When you have a job with a salary, you sometimes take it a little easy. You never slacken in your own business. You can never take it easy. The moment you stop, everything stops. We didn't take annual vacations for 3 years. Be careful and cautious. Don't spend a fil unless it is important and necessary. When we were raising capital, I asked the investors, 'We are willing to be funded by you, but we want to know the value of the investment, other than cash.'

With how much money did you start Yebab?

$2700 and lots of time.

It Is a Marathon, Not a Sprint

Entrepreneur	Omar Kassim
Company and website	JadoPado.com/www.jadopado.com
Year established	2011
Business	e-commerce portal
Tips for entrepreneurs	• Manage your cost structure. Carefully. • Really focus on how you treat your customers. Build your business around it. • Be agile. Unexpected things happen. Build capabilities to adapt quickly.

How did JadoPado emerge?

JadoPado was conceptualized while thinking about business ideas in the technology space. A thought recurred as to why no one had done a serious scalable e-commerce business based on a unique consumer experience for the region. We spent six months researching, designing and building the portal, and launched the initial version of the site in early 2011. One little advantage that we had over a typical startup was a corporate parent that had capital available and the willingness to allocate it to new businesses. We managed to find some great talent that turned into a great team. This allowed us to figure out whether the idea made sense. We started generating revenue pretty much from day one. From a family business perspective, we backed an idea to execute, learn and grow in the technology space. It was clear from the outset that the venture needed to have an identifiable revenue stream with a fairly clear path to profitability over a reasonable timeframe.

You sound very clinical – idea, resources, revenue, risk and time to develop. Was it a head or a heart issue?

It's always a bit of both. Technology is something I've been very passionate about from a young age. And while I've always wanted to and would love to be doing things in the hardware space, it was clear that we needed to start with something that was realistic, an entry point that could potentially lead to other opportunities in the future. It started with what at the time seemed to be a simple premise- why hasn't anyone done an Amazon in the Middle East. I didn't understand then, but I get it now. It's extremely challenging to build a business in a sector that is yet to define itself in the region. Exciting, but challenging.

Your journey of product development?

It was an organic journey of discovery over six months. We started off with a few concepts of the site and the initial user experience, hired a couple of engineers and started to build it out. The little details have always mattered and continue to shape our business today. Whether it be the size of a button, or how many fields we decided to put into the checkout process; anything you put in front of your customers matters. The JadoPado logo was inspired by the old Apple logo; a company I've been a fan of, well before they went mainstream. We spent a lot of time thinking through how we felt customers should experience JadoPado. It eventually boiled down to asking a simple question- how would we like to be treated? We built and continue to build on the basis of that question. It's worked quite nicely as a guiding principle. The policies that we put together, such as our returns policy, were almost an antithesis to what our competition in the retail space had in place at the time.

When you use "we" do you mean the family or Omar?

We means all of us; the family, the team and myself. The family has been an incredible catalyst in allowing JadoPado to happen, but JadoPado remains my responsibility to execute and deliver. In some cases a business is inspired and driven by an individual, but it always comes down to the team. You'd be nowhere without them. They're on the front lines, executing every single day.

How did you get into a consumer-facing business?

It was the nature of opportunity. As a family we'd never done a consumer-facing business previously. One of our first hires was a "community manager" of sorts, a role that eventually turned into a social media buzzword. We started building and engaging with potential customers through social media very early on, almost before we'd actually started building anything. It's a lot of pressure to perform when your business is available for anyone to look at and judge. A focus on the details pushes us to try to get as many things right as possible, and when we do get things wrong, apologize and correct them fast. Today's businesses are built in the public eye. Everything is visible and scrutinized since a lot of communication takes place publicly. Reputations take years to build and mere seconds to destroy. It forces you to ensure that you build the right experience and live true to your promise to your customers.

How do you manage this?

We spend a lot of time building and cultivating a community by having honest conversations with our customers, while trying out different tools to manage those conversations. For example, we use a tool that pulls information from different channels such as Twitter, Facebook, Live Chats and emails into a dashboard from where we try to manage conversations across multiple channels. Our responsiveness matters a lot. If a consumer has unfortunately had a negative experience and has decided to voice his or her feelings publicly or privately, then how quickly and effectively we deal with that issue is critical. Prevention is always better than cure. Rather than trying to solve the issue after it occurs we focus on trying to get the experience right the first time. We're always discussing under promising and over delivering. Never ever say something that you can't deliver on.

How did you pitch to the family?

It wasn't really a pitch. We put a financial model together, discussed the idea and decided to kick ahead. I was involved in running a part of the family's business out in the region when we started JadoPado. The initial capital was available and the idea seemed feasible so we decided to go out and do it.

E-commerce is a low margin business. How will you make money?

JadoPado is a category focused play in the electronics and IT space. Margins are definitely very tight. We've continued to focus on building a differentiated proposition. For example, we don't sell anything we don't have in stock to try to ensure that we deliver product as quickly as possible. Last summer, we launched JadoPado Shield, in partnership with Allianz Global Assistance; a combined accidental damage protection and warranty product. It is the first of its kind in the region. Buy a device from us and we'll cover you against accidental damage, liquid damage and cracked screens. For free. The industry is at a very nascent stage, we're very early in what should be a seven to ten-year journey. It's a marathon, not a sprint.

The strategies made the business investment heavy.

The decision to invest in inventory, a delivery fleet and warehousing was a deliberate attempt to execute a differentiated business model versus our competition at the time. How could we convince customers to buy online versus jumping in their car and driving out to the nearest mall? The idea was to build and deliver an instant gratification experience. We held inventory to be able to execute our same day delivery model. It remains difficult to get visibility in the supply chain in the region. Some vendors don't have systems in place, others who do either can't provide you visibility or don't want to. Holding inventory was an expensive, but necessary solution. We've continued to evolve our model and recently switched away from our own delivery fleet and moved over to a third-party only model. The delivery fleet served its purpose in getting the word out about the business and we eventually came to the realization that delivery is not our core proposition. We're an e-commerce business, and delivery in the region is a solved problem. We decided to continue to focus our efforts in building out JadoPado as a highly differentiated offering.

What thoughts went into designing the user experience?

We like asking lots of questions. Why is something this way? Could it happen another way? Do we really need that bit of extra information or could we do without it? The goal was and remains to give customers absolutely the best experience possible and more importantly getting out of the way when a customer has decided to make a purchase. Make it super easy. We're always re-designing and re-building. For example, we're about to launch our fourth major redesign to our checkout process.

How do you iterate the user experience? Could you give us an example?

Customers give us a lot of feedback whether it is over social media, email or over the phone. Very early on we had a lot of queries about when a particular product would be back in stock. So we decided to build something to automate the process. We mocked up a simple system to allow a customer to sign up for a back in stock alert. Hit a button on the product page, sign into your account and you're done. We'd then drop the customer an email as soon as that item is available again. Then we went out, built it and pushed it out. We used that bit of feedback to eventually build out other features such as price drop alerts and so on.

How did you go about doing the business? Did you make a decision to create a team?

I like to think that from a technology perspective I have a fair understanding of the infrastructure needed to run the business. We needed to access a strong marketing and design resource. We ended up poaching in-house. Karlo is now a co-founder and remains at JadoPado. We hired an internal engineering team. We decided not to outsource any component of the business. I've always felt that the more control you have, the easier it is to deliver on a great experience. It's somewhat easier early on, but becomes difficult to scale. When we've had to partner or bring in outside help, we've always pushed them to hopefully live by and aspire to our standards.

Inventory buying is an art. How do you decide what to buy and how much to buy?

It's challenging. Initially we focused on product that we knew would sell and kept one or two pieces of them in stock. As a long-term Apple enthusiast we started with their product range and took it from there. We hired externally to bring the necessary skill-set onboard. We got lucky and ended up with a small but highly skilled team who've had a mixture of large retail and wholesale product sale experiences. We spend time trying to understand and source products that are not available locally while combining it with selling products we're personally passionate about.

Has the business crossed the bridge of sustainability?

It is work in progress. We're pretty close. Hopefully.

Team size?

15 at the moment. This has grown and shrunk over time.

Any surprises when you started executing?

Fraud and the extent of it threw me initially. We were very disheartened when it happened the first time. We decided to explore the system and executed a couple of sting operations with the CID to catch some of the culprits. Their cybercrimes unit is absolutely fabulous. Those cases went to prosecution, allowing us to understand the effectiveness of the law. We took those experiences, went back to the drawing board and eventually ended up building a verification system for card usage on the site, complemented with other processes. You can't hit pause when something isn't going the way you want. We had to think on our feet and build a solution while allowing the business to continue to run.

Was anything easier than expected?

Not really. Entrepreneurship and businesses are like roller coasts. You have these incredible snapshot moments that make for great memories, while there are other moments where it feels murky and difficult to breathe. You struggle and push hard to come out on the other side. It's important to not give in. Ever.

Changes in the idea?

It's always evolving, but the central defining theme of building a great e-commerce experience hasn't changed.

What keeps you tense about the business?

Lots of things, but it usually boils down to being able to survive. Will we be able to crack the profitability barrier that our industry struggles with? And if we do so, can we turn JadoPado into a world-class organization? As with any business it is always a cost versus time tradeoff. Apply more capital and potentially shorten the timeframes but while risking the entire business. You need to arrive at the right balance. Entrepreneurship teaches much patience.

How much time have you given yourself?

3 years to get it right. We're almost getting to that point, and we're close to that "getting it right" moment.

Relationships with suppliers?

It was tough initially, but over time the support has been tremendous. Everyone sees e-commerce as a great opportunity but aren't quite sure when it'll be the next big thing. It'll sort of sneak up on you and be the next big thing before anyone realizes that it's already happened.

When you started were there any naysayers?

Lots of them. Fortunately, family money is patient capital.

Start the Business First and Then Make the Plan

Entrepreneur	Paul Joseph
Company and website	AAA Middle East/www.aaamiddleeast.com
Year established	2011
Business	AAA Roadside Assistance and vehicle logistics
Tips for entrepreneurs	• Go meet customers when you want to start a business.
	• Business starts in a different way from what is assumed – first the customer, then the price, then assessing the cost and then creating a business. Business plan comes last.
	• Sincerity and commitment to the business. Persevere and one day things will fall into place.

Describe your business.

I first experienced AAA (American Automobile Association) in Portland, Oregon. I am always on a lookout for innovative ideas. I keep them in mind, waiting to use them when the situation arises. Everyone I spoke to in Dubai confirmed the need for an AAA kind of service and that no one was offering it to them. Twenty years ago when I started AAA our services were unique in the region.

Asking people was enough to convince you?

I had friends in Canada. I asked them about AAA in Canada and learnt that CAA Canada was working. They emphasized the need of the services considering the extreme climate. Every person I met, I must have met over 200 people to discuss the concept, expressed the need of the service. But when I started the company and called them, they said they will use the services when they need it. They were not keen on paying upfront for a future need by taking membership. The feedback did not stop me. I was going ahead with the business. I had resigned from my job.

The model of pricing needed to change.

I tell budding entrepreneurs never ask friends about a business idea. They always say yes.

You started something that didn't exist.

The first three years required tremendous effort; it was a mammoth task to educate customers. We were the only company providing services. Customers couldn't compare us with anyone. If they faced a problem on the road, they parked on the side and waved to a passing car or taxi. Someone would stop and help. This was not a professional approach to the customer problem. Our understanding of the need and nature of service was correct but it took a lot of money and time to educate the customers.

AAA in the US has a variety of offerings. Which were the services you thought would work?

AAA members in the US get a variety of discounts. We were able to offer some similar features when we launched; we had signed many companies to offer discounts. In UAE the value of the discount is not perceived as a value because we have a lot of sales and promotions happening all the time. We also had situations where customers would want AAA discount on a discounted or bargained price. No one wants to read the fine print. This created problems for customers, partners and us. Over time loyalty programs have diminished in value. There are too many loyalty programs with complex benefits and discounts. We don't emphasize discounts as a value. AAA in the US is very good with roadmaps. Roadmap in this region was not a market. Lots of construction was going on and new deviations emerged frequently. Maps could not be updated frequently. We were unable to give updates to people traveling into the country. We also discovered that not too many people were traveling by road to other countries. Google maps and GPS tools for consumers didn't exist when we started. The next was auto insurance. This region is controlled by insurance brokers. To offer the service we needed an insurance broking license. I didn't want to enter a field that was specialized. I focused on providing roadside assistance. When we started there was not much recovery as a business. Recovery was a service provided by auto dealers. Today, with lots of recovery vehicles, recovery business doesn't appear novel. When we launched, roadside assistance was a great solace to customers, many of whom didn't know where the spare tire was, or the jack, or that they needed to change a hot tire which had been running on a highway in scorching mid-day heat of 50 degrees. The service was very helpful for families in case the mother was stranded with children. We were a toll-free number away.

How did you convince customers to pay?

I was under the impression that we can sell the service to individual customers one at a time through telephone sales. This did not work. I had to change my thinking. The customers were required to experience the service for free to enable them to realize the value. I approached some banks and insurance companies to give the service to their clients as a value-added service from their side. We created a trend in the banking industry and today almost all banks offer our services with their credit cards. About fifty percent of our customers get the services free from different channels, either when they buy a new car or when they renew the insurance or through banks. The service need always arises in an emergency when customers feel helpless. This made customers think about the service as insurance. The customers started to "get" the product, started using it and then understood the value of the product.

Any changes?

We made some innovations. Motorbikes are not used for service delivery in the US. We use motorbikes. All minor roadside issues e.g., a flat tire, a battery problem and even delivery of petrol can be resolved by a person on a motorbike. Recovery is required for a major breakdown or accident. Motorbikes reach customers faster enabling quicker and better service. We now operate retriever motorbikes that can pull a car from an accident site. This is a good tool to reduce traffic jams when an accident happens on a busy road.

You needed a tie-up with AAA.

They did not entertain us because our discussion was about ideas. AAA is over 100 years old. They have many terms and conditions for an association. I did not fit any existing category. I was required to establish a company, run it for some time, get a quality audit, after which I could seek their approval. However they were supportive. I think they respected my initiative and guided me on their approval criterion. I got AAA approval three years after I started. I had to set up systems and they had to evaluate us.

They are a nonprofit club. You are a company.

They have associations or partnerships with organizations like ours in all countries. They are organized as clubs through memberships. We cannot use their logo. They only give full affiliation to official organizations recognized and supported by local governments.

What were the thoughts that went through your mind when you decided to leave your job?

Transition was easy. I always thought about business since my childhood. I started a business when I was finishing my chartered accountancy articleship. I am from a part of the world that produces rubber and the region is dominated by rubber based industries. I started a factory producing tread rubber for retreading the tires. I had relatives in different parts of India. I manufactured products and my relatives did the selling. I soon had sales and distribution operations across many cities of India. I was young and reasonably successful. As the business grew in size it became eligible to pay excise duty. It then became very difficult to sell our product against large tire manufacturers. We were not competitive in price and were unable to survive. When I shut down the business I had four units in different parts of Kerala. One of my friends sold me the idea to try my luck in Dubai. I came here and worked as an accountant. I changed a few jobs, becoming a manager and finally landing up with a Fortune 500 company. I visited the US to attend a conference, where I got an opportunity to experience AAA.

You didn't see resigning as a challenge because you had set up a business before. What did the family say?

My wife said, 'Whatever is your decision, we will face together.' We had two small kids in school. Setting up a business is a big task and a very challenging decision. My friends asked me not to be foolish by resigning. According to them I should start the business while being employed. I was not going to do that. I had to be present full time in the business.

Why?

The first three years was tough. Setting up the business was a herculean task. I was a one-man show. I would spend nights doing printing and mailing of cards. Money was flowing out. Nothing was coming in. I still remember that period. Commitment enforced me to survive.

How much did you invest in the business?

When I started I had AED 200,000 in my bank. I borrowed some money from friends. I had two partners who invested half a million each.

They trusted you.

I knew them from before. The real story is that after ten years I lost the company and had to start afresh. The company I originally started was called Arabian Automobile Association. It was taken over by one of the partners. It exists but has not grown. New businesses exist because of the entrepreneur's personal drive, effort and understanding of customers. Not because the business idea is good, service is needed and customers beat a path to your door in droves. The business was small and I had a personal relationship with all my customers. I believe my customers supported me and the business after hearing my story.

Did you get your investment back?

I started again from zero. What I had was hands-on experience of running the business and relationship with customers as well as AAA. I built the business again from 2006 to 2016, brick by brick, making it bigger than in the previous 10 years.

As an entrepreneur there is learning in this experience.

When I lost everything I had the knowledge of the business, goodwill in the market and a network of relationships. Employees of the old company did not join me. I had already tested an idea with individual customers and B2B clients like insurance companies and banks. When I restarted, I started faster.

How did you develop pricing?

Pricing depends on the volume of the customers. I knew individuals were not my customers. I was making upfront investment in vehicles. I needed to assess the number of customers and the number of cars that would need my assistance. With ten years of experience we have a reasonable feel for the number of claims. Claims determine the need for support services. I took a drastic step of acquiring potential customers. I gave a huge discount to big companies who were going to give me 100,000 or 200,000 customers. It was nearly a tenth of my price for individual clients. This was an early major decision which I had to take. It helped because most companies signed with me. I was then the only offer in town.

Customer acquisition was important when you restarted?

Yes, but I did not reduce the price to get customers. I had decided early on that I would try to give high-quality service and experience. I think I am successful because people are able to experience the difference in service. I attempted to provide the best service from the first day, irrespective of the cost. We did not have enough equipment and manpower when we started. We were learning the business. I also went to deliver services. I experienced how to deliver service. This helped me develop the staffing patterns in the business. Delivering the service and engaging with clients is the best way to learn the business. Knowing the details is the best way to learn. I used to sit in the call center and attend the calls. I used to do night duty when we had shortage of staff. My commitment to the business enabled me do this. I do this even today.

What was the investment in the new business?

Two million Dirhams. The second time I knew exactly what had to be done – people, infrastructure and vehicles. I have eighty employees in UAE. We have a 500,000 plus membership base. Ninety percent of the insurance companies are covered.

How did a startup win the trust of the B2B client like an insurance company?

I told them to pay me after experiencing the service. I had the confidence in being able to deliver. I was confident that when we serve stranded customers, the experience will be able to distinguish us.

Were you prepared to put yourself on the line, without a company, without a system, by saying give me the order and I will deliver?

I recruited some European ladies to sell. They queried me on how I would deliver and keep my promise. I asked them to leave it to me. I would do the operations. They didn't believe in me and I let them go. I have had this confidence from a young age.

Where did you acquire customer centricity?

As a young person I always lent a helping hand to others. When I reflect on my past I believe I have some leadership skills. I am in the service industry because I thought I didn't know marketing and customer service. I have a grasp of facts and figures. When I got into the service business I realized that I can sell and serve.

Which was the first company that trusted you?

Oman Insurance Company. I had been rejected by three others before I got to Oman Insurance. I told one company to call my office and experience what I did by doing a mock trial.

How easy was it to open doors to the decision takers?

Mashreq Bank was a challenging client. It was very difficult for me to call and get an appointment. They questioned me about roadside assistance with a bank. I wanted to meet and explain, and everyone was busy. This is where the sales staff I hired played a role. They called and got an appointment. I presented the idea and the project picked up momentum.

When did you get your costing right and started investing in call centers, people and machines?

I reached breakeven in four years. Till that milestone I was doing whatever was possible. I may not have done everything very professionally. But I was doing things. I was focusing on the customer. I was committed to serve under all conditions. Even today I tell my staff to serve customers without being sensitive to cost. Now I can afford it.

When did you take your first holiday?

I have never taken a holiday after starting this company. Before starting AAA I had regular holidays every year.

Advise for new entrepreneurs.

My advice to new entrepreneurs is to work with sincerity and commitment, and this ride will take you anywhere you want. I have experienced challenging situations, without money, and succeeded. You never know when things will fall into place. The traditional way in which entrepreneurs are guided is different from what really happens. Most people are told to get an idea, prepare a plan, put money, set up an office, recruit people, do branding and then sell. But actually it all starts the other way around- first the customer, then the price, then assessing the cost, then creating a business and then the plan. Office and branding come later. We study and learn a lot of things in college but in the real world nothing is possible until we get a few basics right. Execution is the most important aspect. Go meet customers when you want to start a business.

You are a finance person and you are saying this?

I have seen a lot of people fail doing business the systematic way. They invest in manpower, a beautiful office and then sales don't pick up. My office was and is simple. I didn't want people to be in the office and relax. I wanted them to work in minimum comfort and spend the most time with customers. I did this but today our strength is our staff. I take care of them; have never defaulted on paying salaries and incentives on time, irrespective of the health of the business.

Anything stresses you about this business?

My business is easy to copy. Two of my employees started a similar business, mimicked the software that we use to manage the business and approached my customers by undercutting prices.

Any new developments?

I have used the same infrastructure to add services. We do all the services that owning a car requires. Those that need your time and are a hassle e.g., I undertake registering cars. It takes about half a day. We pick up the car, take it to the registration center, do the pollution check and process the documents. I also help customers in taking their vehicles for service. Otherwise they have to drop the car at the service point, take a taxi to work and then go back to pick up the vehicle. We also maintain cars when customers travel. In this offering we drop customers to the airport. I have developed a logistics division using the tools and equipment. I had spare time once the infrastructure was built. We are one of the best automobile logistics solution providers in the region. We do last mile logistics – bringing cars from the port to the yard, take them from the yard to the showrooms and then to customers. We have special carriers to carry eight cars. And then we have special flat-bed carriers to carry sports cars with low ground clearance. I started this business with the support of my partner, who is in the logistics business.

Developing a 'Fuzzy' Business like Consulting

Entrepreneur	Ramesh Mahalingam
Company and website	Ideal Management Consultants/ www.idealmc.com
Business	Management consulting
Year established	2010
Tips for entrepreneurs	• Customers have to first like what you are selling. • Sense what the client wants. • Be flexible. Adapt to customers' wants. Don't expect customers to change and buy what you are selling.

What does Ideal do?

Ideal is a consulting and advisory company. Dubai had a number of consulting firms which were off-shoots of auditing companies. Very few companies offered consulting and advisory services to the SME sector. I saw a niche, a boutique company focusing on the SME sector. I had to figure out how to put it together.

Where was entrepreneurship in you?

After becoming a Chartered Accountant I decided to work in diverse sectors with the objective of becoming self-employed. The timing of the journey was undefined. Whether I would be self-employed in the future was unknown. The seed of entrepreneurship, I suspect, was sown by my observation of my father. He worked for 38 years with one company. I sensed that his dedication and devotion, which meant a lot to him, were not valued. I did not want to depend on an employer for my career. I wanted to craft my career. My career progressed in a variety of roles in finance and accounting, in diverse firms, till I realized finance in the region was considered a cost center. I needed to be a profit-center to develop myself. I switched to banking. I worked my way up doing asset management. I then raised capital for a PPP infrastructure project.

My last job was as Chief Investments and Finance Officer of Gulf Finance before starting Ideal.

Your first assignment?

We got our first assignment from Landmark. It was an HR job. We had to do an HR Due Diligence after their acquisition of Fitness First. We had been writing proposals for ten months. We had a license but worked from home. We went slow on doing up the office.

When did you know the company had started?

From the very first assignment. I had an instinct that the business would work. Our clients liked what we did and referred us to others. The work helped us in getting other similar assignments. Even though I had done some jobs that I had been assigned by my network of friends, this was the first job we won by pitching and convincing a client that we could do something.

When did you need an additional person?

I did the first three assignments alone. My biggest concern was whether I would be able to hire my first employee.

Was it a cost issue?

Salary was not the issue. Starting cost was AED 100k, some space, license, visas and furniture. It is the cash flow. Salary is a sunk cost till you get your first check. Salary is also an investment. Consulting assignments pay a multiple of the investment.

Any surprises?

HR work was never on my opportunity radar. I was focused on finance and cost management. We have done numerous HR assignments.

Any challenges in recruiting?

We hired a person every month after our first job. We are now eleven. In consulting, every employee added is like a partner. Each one earns his or her salary. The mathematics of our business is simple. Everyone gets a base salary. The rest depends upon the assignments won, delivered and the amount of supervision required.

Have you been recruiting from the beginning?

Yes. I thought of this early on. After hiring the third person it became evident they were putting their best foot forward. I wanted to sustain that motivation.

I shared the idea with them. I told them, 'Let us grow together. You are as much a stakeholder in Ideal as I am.' This was developed and is now the employment tool to share with prospective employees. We have a two-tier incentive system, not an end of year bonus. Plus we fund our end of year bonus in a different bank account entirely. Everyone is sure that the firm is not using their money for operations.

Any tense moments?

Our tense moments are all around jobs that we have pitched for and when the client is close to decision making. It is a positive tension. I am also tense when I worry that clients may not pay for services. Only two invoices remain unpaid. One client wants to pay after positive outcomes based on our suggestions. The other one is just being unfriendly.

You are a little uncomfortable soliciting business. How did you overcome this?

I don't think I have overcome it. Neerja and I have never gone to anybody asking for business. We promote ourselves as a firm. We network and spread the word about our capabilities. We prefer using referrals: when somebody senior, who knows our professional capabilities, talks about us at an opportune time.

Is this your customer acquisition strategy?

This is my secondary strategy. Primary is word of mouth.

Why do clients choose you? Is it a balance of quality and price? Or they want a boutique company that is a specialist? Or they feel that big companies don't pay attention?

It is pretty much the latter more than the former. Initially clients were gingerly taking their first steps and chances with us.

How did you select this niche?

We started with small clients. Our eyes were on bigger clients. Smaller ones give us the net practice, preparing us for the medium and bigger clients. We had connections with bigger companies, but all of them wanted to try us in a typically low-risk work and see how we performed, before engaging us in strategic projects. That is still evolving.

Your customer focus changed?

I am surprised by the diversity of work. We targeted small companies but have ended up working with medium companies; individuals coming to us, wanting to sell or start a business. We have to structure a proposal and look for buyers. As an example, we even do bi-lingual training work like we do for Mashreq.

How did you evolve pricing for your services?

My first thought was to discount the big 4 by a certain percentage. But I found out that we had to have our own cost-based pricing strategy. We initially underpriced and over delivered. We did not make money with our first clients. Neither did we have any system to track time spent on doing assignments. But being an accountant and having done activity-based assignments for clients, this was easy to do. We have developed our own templates based on our salaries, overheads, what it costs us to spend an hour of each person's time and then a markup on that. And we use certain capacity utilization tools to factor idle time in between jobs to account for the slack.

What worries you today?

In this business you can't go and sell your services. And without doing that how will people find you? My Rolodex has 5000 people. But I cannot go and pitch. This is a challenge. Another challenge is to scale up our organization; finding the talent to keep up consistent level of work, quality and client engagement without needing me to be present in each interaction.

Would you walk away from a job or a company?

Yes. We had done that when we are not comfortable with the declared intent of the client.

How long does it take you to win a job?

Between 3 days and 7 months.

Have you changed as a person?

From being a functionary in a pigeon hole, from having to confine my thinking to my role, I now have a lot more latitude. I can now be innovative, try to do work that stands out. I have had to develop a team, entirely based on my own ideas and experiences that have germinated over years. I have learnt to be patient with people, clients particularly. They pay our bills. And learning the art of client conversion.

Did you have to unlearn something?

No rigidities, no patterns. If I have to meet a client at 11 at night, I have to do it.

Entrepreneurial Intelligence: Knowing When You Need a Team

Entrepreneurs	Saif Abdullah (S) and Omran Yousef (O)
Company and website	HiPHONE TELECOM/ www.HiPHONEtelecom.com
Business	Retailing telecom products and accessories
Year established	1994
Tips for entrepreneurs	• Be an understudy to an entrepreneur. See how he thinks and works. • Learn business by doing – hands-on. • Start small. No business remains small. Keep eyes open for opportunity. • Don't take risks. Execute carefully. Don't be in a hurry to grow fast. • What you do in a job (big company) may not work in your own business. • Don't ask people for business ideas. Do what you like or what you know and believe in. Don't decide to do a business because it looks rosy in a plan. • Be different even in small ways.

How did HiPHONE develop?

S: I got lucky with my first mall location in Ajman City Center. I learnt professional retailing – products, displays and customer service – by running a cart in a mall corridor. I learnt that you have to please mall landlords and meet their standards to get good locations.

Why lucky?

S: We got recognized early as a kiosk retailer.

How did you get into retailing phones and accessories?

S: I started a 500 sq. ft. shop, HiPHONE, with 25,000 Dirhams when I was 21 years. In those days phones were big and did not have covers. I started selling battery chargers, replacement batteries, antennas, etc. Phones used to cost 3000 Dirhams. I could not invest all my startup money in phones. I started by buying accessories in Dubai paying cash. Accessories used to sell very fast. Plus I needed to budget for shop decoration and trade license. I was working with the government and used to come to the shop in the mornings and evenings. I observed customers and learnt what to buy to sell.

You created a full shop?

S: The shop had a second floor for a repair technician. I couldn't find a technician to service mobiles. I didn't even know what I needed to look for in a technician. I had not studied technology. So I got a technician who had worked on radios. He and I both together learnt how to repair mobiles.

How did you price accessories?

S: Accessories have better margins. I looked at prices in the market. I wanted to give a discount. But then I started evaluating the products, based on material and finish, and charged different prices.

Did you make money from the first day?

S: Yes. But I recollect giving the first customer a free product.

O: Accessory business is risky. You have to rotate capital; purchase stock even though there is previous inventory.

Why did the desire to do business arise?

S: I used to accompany my father to his store. I used to read my books but observed him doing things. I recollect him counting money. I wanted to open a business and be like him. I imbibed business observing my father.

When did the market start to give you credit?

S: 2004. I don't like credit. I prefer paying cash. I prefer working within my limits. I hesitate taking risks beyond my financial capacity.

When did you start going outside the country to buy?

S: In 2012. I had no need to go abroad. I was predominantly doing retail. Our volumes were still small. Direct buying was not cost-effective.

O: We started doing wholesale after we created our own brand. We needed variety and smaller depth.

How did you convince MAF mall management to trust you with space? You were from the souk.

S: I started in the mall with a cart, not a kiosk.

O: The mall was not designed for carts in the walkway. The risk of the mall management for a cart in Ajman was low. The mall had low foot traffic. They created the idea of souks and bazars. We got lucky to get a space for a cart.

You experienced the mall customer?

O: In malls we get all types of customers from nationals to tourists. They all need one thing and that is quality and variety. Also in malls, you may have 4 to 5 customers at the same time. That made us put more staff in kiosks. We wanted to attend to everyone and please them with our service.

How important was your sitting in the shop for the growth of your business?

S: We still do that. If we don't know what the customer wants, how we can know what to buy.

O: Aggressive growth happened from 2009. We were a small accessory company that also sold mobile phones. The business was stable with positive cash flow. We were growing in a controlled way. Our sales were around 27 m Dirhams, from nine locations, with twenty-seven employees.

How did you learn to design kiosks?

O: Saif had knowledge of carpentry and construction. He built a kiosk to his design, evaluated it and changed it till it worked. He changed a lot of designs. He may not know how to make engineering drawings but had an intuitive feel of how customers would engage with products.

What was important for the growth of your business?

S: My first desire is to make the customer happy. A happy customer precedes the flow of money. I am always looking to do that little bit extra. If the customer wants a particular thing I am always looking to give him something nicer, a better quality product. Customers, when they see better and nicer things, tend to buy more. I also learn from customers who don't buy.

How do you track trends and customers who browse but not buy?

O: We have a reporting system where frontline employees give feedback on what customers ask for and trends. There is nothing like direct observation on the ground.

S: We go on daily branch visits. The staff knows that I have been a salesman and understand their challenges. This helps us align the working of the company to the goals of the company.

Why did you bring Omran in?

S: In 2009 I was very keen to grow rapidly. I saw increased opportunity and competition. I had grown with opportunity. I now needed a strategy and a team to execute it. I was sensitive to the fact that I could not do it alone. I needed new thinking.

How did that come about?

O: Saif asked me to think about joining him. We sat together for a few months for me to understand the business. I needed to understand how he had implemented the business, his strategies, strengths of the business and the opportunities. He had the need. He couldn't do it alone. One has to respect Saif for the judgment that he knew he needed a person. It was a challenge. What we are today is a joint effort. He is not an owner who sits at home. He is hands-on. He considers himself to be an employee.

How did you go about taking the company to a different level?

O: Saif asked me to get him five new locations at prime locations. The business model had been established for mall locations. I had seen Dubai growing for 12 years. We started tracking the launch of new malls. His second concern was margins. The business was not using any bank facilities and ploughing cash flows into the business. Since the cash flow was healthy it had worked. But the net numbers needed to be healthier. The third thing which happened was that he did not only shake hands, he hugged me and made me a partner. He aligned his focus and mine.

Challenges of execution?

O: We decided to begin direct purchases from abroad and launched our own brands "Maestro" and "iSAFE", creating an asset in the business. We learnt sourcing in baby steps. We brought different varieties in smaller quantities from different companies. We could not put all our eggs in one basket. We needed to hire more people- create an organization structure and delegate roles as well as responsibilities. We worked towards getting ISO certified to get our processes defined and working.

Challenges of store formats?

O: We need to differentiate between full line electronic retailers and HiPHONE. Customers need to recognize what we do well. Customers need to have a reason to visit us.

How did you convince suppliers to tie up with you? You were not electronic retailers.

O: It was the other way around. We had nineteen locations. Suppliers were keen on evaluating our potential for selling mobile phones, even willing to give us credit. I think word had started to get around that we were professionally organized. If someone does due diligence on our credit history, we have no bounced checks. Saif's conservatism paid off. In addition, companies that gave us products to sell discovered the sales we were generating. We got awards from distributors.

Skills to sell phones are different from accessories?

O: We do training for new and existing employees. Plus technologies and products are changing rapidly. Staff needs to be current, always. Today's customers are knowledgeable. We strive to ensure that staffs are never embarrassed in front of customers. Mobiles are high-value purchases. We need to sell, activate and troubleshoot.

How did you manage shrinkage?

O: We have to be extra careful in kiosks. We have a robust IT system. We do tracking from purchase, delivery to store, sales and inventory. Regular physical stock takes are a must. Since malls are open till late we have to do stock reviews well past midnight. And because days are long, each kiosk is managed by five people over the week.

What worries you about the business?

S: The size of the market is becoming bigger whereas the price and shelf life of mobile phones are coming down. They change frequently. I am unable to buy larger quantities and take a position on price.

O: I was worried when I wasn't selling brands. I focus on margins. And what competition is doing. There are many retailers selling similar products. I have to track market prices. A competitor was selling out and started selling at low margins. The company is getting bigger. We are opening outlets more rapidly than before. Saif and I are signing bigger checks. So when I sign I worry because we are not risk takers. We don't want to make a mistake.

Growth plans of HiPHONE?

O: We have undertaken some innovative actions. We have tied up with DU to create shop-in-shops in their stores to sell accessories. We are also working with them to become their retail franchisees. We are planning to expand geographically in the GCC to wholesale accessories. We will wholesale our own branded products.

I Knew Nothing About the Business. I Focused on Costs and Learnt Everything

Entrepreneurs	Salem Abdulla Majia Al Muhairi
Company and website	Abu Dhabi Pallet Industry/www.adpiuae.com
Year established	2000
Business	Manufacturing wooden pallets
Tips for entrepreneurs	• Start with self-belief and confidence. • Study and learn the industry. • Be on top of the business. See and experience things to learn. • Focus on the business and not on competitors. • Identify the money you need. It is never enough. Have a backup option for raising more money. • Take quick decisions. Time is money. Project costs increase very fast. • Create and manage business reputation. Honor commitments.

How did you get into business?

My father had a business of trading groceries. I realized that trading was a low margin business when I studied business in the US. As a part of my education program I visited manufacturing plants. I told my father that we needed to get into manufacturing. My father advised me to follow my calling. He didn't want to change. I had seen products coming on pallets to our warehouse and getting dispatched to customers. I asked my father if making pallets was a good business to start. My father asked me to study the business. An uncle of mine gave me catalogs to study and leads to companies. We got invitations to visit factories in different countries. I wanted to see machinery working before deciding on what to purchase. I visited Spain, saw the machinery and collected all the details to start a factory. The initial investment was too high. I declined the proposal. And then the supplier came to UAE.

So what happened?

I told him that whatever he wished to supply must be commercially viable. I didn't need a quote that is about technical features and price, for a big factory. He gave me a price. I bought two machines, recruited five employees and started the business with AED 500,000.

Your suppliers helped establish the business?

I was advised to start operations in phases. Instead of buying blocks of wood, I started with pre-cut sections. The extra cost was offset by reduced transportation cost, reduced processing wastage and quicker handling. We needed guidance in raw materials. A pallet looks simple but the nail has a special design. It goes in straight and then flares. Nails had to be specially made.

How did you recruit people when you started? No one knew how to use the machines.

I asked for advice from the suppliers. I thought we needed engineers. I was told to recruit carpenters who could read and write English.

Then?

Startup was not easy. The supplier found it challenging to train people to use the machines. I was like my employees. I knew nothing about the business. The supplier was worried. He told me that if he knew this, he would not have sold me the machines. He was scared that a poor factory would reflect badly on his business. The machine capacity was around 1000 pallets in 8 hours. The first day we barely had made 120 pallets. The score on the second day was 360 pallets. I was ready to give up. We had not produced enough pallets to load a full truck. One employee motivated me. He made me focus on delivery. We decided to work continuously till we achieved our delivery volume. The supplier visited us recently. He told me, 'You are a completely different man today. On the day of the installation, I was uncertain about how you will run the business. You were much stressed.'

How did you get your first order?

When we entered the market, a company in Jubail, Saudi Arabia, was a big supplier of pallets. We analyzed their costs. Their location had cost disadvantages for servicing UAE. Their prices were high for direct shipments to Abu Dhabi. To offset which they were shipping goods to Jebel Ali and then trucking pallets to Abu Dhabi. The logistics arrangement was complicated with multiple handling and extra freight time. The first contract taught us to look at costs and prices very carefully. We estimated our cost at AED 60 and I gave the first offer at AED 60. This was better than the Saudi supplier. The customer was purchasing pallets at AED 45. My competitor was bidding at AED 42 to keep new suppliers out. We were called for a meeting, informed that our prices were high and that we could collect the order at around AED 40. We double-checked our costs. We were making a contribution of AED 2 per pallet. Quantity was 10,000. We took the order at a low price as a promise of growth. For 2 years the prices remained low. No one was making money. It took time for everyone in the industry to realize the uselessness of low prices.

Did buyers give you a preference as a National supplier?

All government companies prefer manufacturers in the UAE. UAE already had four factories when we started. They were strong and large companies owned by local business groups. So no, we got no preference. Competition was strong and pricing was sharp.

How did you use the first contract? Learning how to price. Learning how to manage.

Bourouge is a good buyer. They don't put all their eggs into one basket. Every supplier got a part of the contract. Everyone expected me to close my factory. I was uncertain but confident. I was a small player. Having started the factory, paid the rent and recruited staff, I was determined to work quietly, focusing, understanding and managing my business and each tender. I learnt to track and manage costs. I needed to manage all my costs – raw material, transportation, maintenance and people – if I could make only AED 2 per pallet.

How do you decide bid prices?

I keep track of competitors by analyzing costs in detail. To quote for Saudi Arabia I did a detailed analysis of the landed cost of the pallet and then made an estimated cost-sheet of my competitors – their raw materials, manufacturing and logistics cost. This comparative analysis gives me the understanding to know the range of bid prices for various contracts.

Growth plans?

We started with a factory of 900 sq. mts. It is now 11,000 sq. mts. This year we are entering Saudi Arabia to serve Aramco. They have been evaluating us as a supplier. We are now recognized as a pallet manufacturer. We are not the biggest. I have learnt to compete with bigger and better competitors. Over time our performance has improved. Our prices have remained firm. We have decided to remain small. And not reduce price to win contracts. I believe that size should not be an issue for a startup if the entrepreneur focuses on his business instead of focusing on competitors. Many digressions come. My advice is to concentrate on your work and you will win.

Did you ever think why did I do this?

Many times. Pressure from friends is always there. My father gifted me a Mercedes when I finished college and got a job. The following year I started the factory and sold the Mercedes. A cousin of mine commented, 'Before you had money. Now where is your money?' I showed him the factory and said, 'That is my Mercedes.' The business was initially not making money. Dubai was booming. Many of my friends were in real estate. They used to tease me, 'We are making money. What are you making?' I used to reply, 'I am making a loss and building the business.' They used to retort, 'Stop making a loss. Sell the business.' I was determined to carry on. There are always stories of people having made three times or 100 times their investment. One has to be careful and remain focused.

Innovations in business?

To cut costs at every point of the supply chain we have designed transportation trailer trucks to increase (double) their carrying capacity.

Is it important to do everything with your own hands when you start a business?

I believe one has to see things with one's own eyes to learn and develop the business. If you are not on top of the business it will not develop. I still manage and focus on everything in the business. I meet customers. I identify and inspect wood suppliers. I manage the production. I work very closely with all my employees.

Your goals?

I want to be a leading pallet maker in UAE. I define leading as profitability and profile. Not size. In twelve years we have established the foundation. We now have to grow.

How have you changed as a person?

I am far more mature today. I do things carefully. I also take my chances. I will decline business if it is beyond my capacity.

◉ ◉ ◉

Entrepreneurship Is the Crafting of the Business, Not the Execution of a Plan

Entrepreneur	Sana Rifai
Company and website	Tintbox/www.tintbox.com
Year established	2008
Business	Boutique design studio focused graphic design
Tips for entrepreneurs	• Know the field you are getting into; not a 100% but 200%

What is Tintbox?

Tintbox is a design studio that offers graphic design and marketing solutions. We create personalized designs for corporate or personal gifts. For corporate clients we create a brand identity and develop promotional material using print or digital media. For individuals, we create memorable gifts for special occasions.

How has the journey been?

It has been a very difficult journey. We started in April 2008. The global crisis happened in winter. We started small. In that sense we were lucky. Our size helped manage the challenge. We had met a lot of clients before we set up the business but what they required to continue working with us was a trade license and a bank account. Initially the business was slow. I had my full-time job and that covered us for two years. Our business is about design, sourcing and printing. Having a network helped.

Where did the idea for Tintbox come from?

I am a graphic designer with a passion for making personalized things for special occasions; gifts that are personalized with names, messages and graphics. My husband wanted to start a business of corporate gift items, customized printing and marketing. Tintbox was set up to do this, combine my skill with his interest. Tintbox was a natural step. We were freelancing for a couple of years before Tintbox happened.

Explain freelancing.

Three years before Tintbox, I did graphic designs for him and his clients, and he did my printing and production.

You knew that there was a business in what you did?

We were busy with our freelance work. Customers paid us in cash after completing the job, when things were good. Then we had situations where customers couldn't pay us in cash. Cash on delivery is difficult when dealing with larger organizations because of their internal policies. This was when we felt the need for taking check payment. This required a trade license and a corporate bank account. Tintbox emerged from this technicality.

Your skills as a graphic designer are versatile; you could be employed, you could freelance, etc. Why start a business?

I wanted to do a lot more in my job than I was actually doing. I was working long hours. Freelancing was not enough. I felt it would make more sense to do my own work (business) because it would free my creativity and time. I was never just a graphic designer. The company I worked in was small. I learnt the business side of things by default. We were just three people. The company did events and branding. Both the owner and the salesperson used to spend time with clients and I was left to manage the office. I got involved in making pitches, proposals, quotations, invoicing and billing, which helped me understand the business of design. I realized the 'value' of the work I was doing.

There was one more trigger.

My education was in multimedia design which is design with time-based media and I was working in graphic design, which was for print. My degree is not in print but I love print. So that is what I decided to do when I graduated. One of our clients commented on my work. He told the business owner, 'She is a good graphic designer. She should be your lead salesperson because she loves what she does and it shows.'

So here I was, a designer who loves her work, feels for the business as her own, getting recognized by customers and knows the business numbers. This is when everything started to change for me.

Is there business in the family?

My mom is a dental surgeon who had her own private clinic and my father was a banker.

What was the family's response to your entering business?

It was a bigger issue when I told them I wanted to study design. My mom had discovered along with me that she too had some artistic inclinations that she never knew existed. In our family and in our society children are expected to study to become engineers, doctors or businessmen. No one took me seriously when I started to study design. They thought it was a hobby, even though we worked hard, often without sleep. So when I thought of setting up Tintbox, it became sign of measurable progress, at least for me. It just made natural sense.

Is your husband working full-time in business?

He has been remotely committed to the business lately, because he is working full time in a completely different field now, and travel takes up a large part of his time.

Did you get any help when you started in terms of finance and other resources?

Absolutely nothing. We did everything ourselves. My husband had experience in the market. And he knew the suppliers of machines and consumables. He knew where to go to get the work done. Financially, we worked with the money we had saved up and set aside a monthly budget from our salaries from our other jobs at the time to cover monthly costs until we started making enough as a company to run itself.

How important for the business was it for both you and your husband to do parallel work while the business was taking root?

Extremely important. As a couple we worked very well together. He couldn't do certain things without me and I couldn't do some things without him. To complete a job, design studios will design, often they won't print. A gift supplier will supply gifts and possibly print but they will not develop the design. In Tintbox we were bringing multiple skills and capabilities together. We felt that we were bringing some value to clients. Tintbox resolves all these coordination issues and adds a bonus of an in-house creative team that can come up with ideas for completely unique gifts. We don't just take readymade items off a shelf and print your logo on it.

Do you go meet clients to sell?

You will find me with clients when there is more design involved in delivering the overall service.

At what stage, before you left the job or after, did you start understanding what clients will pay for the service?

We started with underpricing. We started as freelancers; as freelancers, I believe our rates were very competitive. When one sets up a company, overheads come into play. By then we knew what our clients will pay for the services. We got them used to lower prices than what we needed after starting the company. We have strived to build a loyal client base. Many clients have worked with us for several years.

Initial traction was with existing customer from your network. When did you start soliciting business from new customers whom you didn't know before?

It was always 100% based on existing network. New clients also came through referrals from existing clients. We never had to go to the market ourselves, knocking on doors and selling our services. We just had to keep our network happy. It was natural growth.

When you started did you have a doubt that the business may not work? Were you sure it would take some shape?

We already had a business when we were spending money for the office, license and equipment. It was a question of how big can the business become. We were lucky. We set up the business because we had the demand for the service. We did face cyclical ups and downs. People stop giving gifts when markets are slow whereas year-end and festival gift giving increases.

How did you manage the downturn?

Whatever be the situation some of our services were required. Some companies called us to help them with staff uniforms. Others wanted business cards. We had to decide to do jobs which we may never have imagined. We had to keep the team small and adapt.

Any surprises that you had not envisaged?

I had to learn and understand new skills. Mahmoud was dealing with the production side of the work – screen printing, factories, quality control, etc. I used to do the design and hand it over to him. I had to learn lots of new small details when it came to producing the material that I designed.

Any challenges in costing and the pricing?

I think there is always a challenge of making sure your price is firm yet competitive. I am always thinking of reviewing my rates and how to make the rates make more sense to customers. I am in a state of constant adaptation. I had anticipated this.

Was anything easier than what you imagined?

I think I was confident when we started. My husband was my pillar of support. He is a street smart person. Whatever be the challenge he knows where to go and what to do. He figures it out. He is from the market. When I meet other startup entrepreneurs they are usually worried about this part, but we already knew this part of the industry really well because of past experience, in fact, it is all we knew.

Pluses and minuses of both husband and wife in business?

We complement each other; we can speak to each other about our projects. We get very little time off work and we do discuss work at home. We have to nudge ourselves not to but since he doesn't put in his hours in the office, we have that independent space that keeps things healthy and fresh.

Your investment in the business?

In the first year it was around 80,000 Dirhams that we put in to buy the machinery and equipment and the rent was about the same as well. From the second year it became self-sustaining.

How many 'existing' customers supported you when you wanted to start the business?

All customers were positive. They wanted us to get a license so that they could give us more work. They could support freelancers only to a degree.

Most important current challenge?

Collecting payments. We are not usually paid cash upfront for the work we do. And sometimes projects take months to complete. We just worked on designing and printing an internal HR policy handbook for a client. We did not pitch for the contract. The contract came to us 'naturally'; we were working for different departments of the same company. They asked for a price we were comfortable with. They didn't have to search for a new supplier. The implementation period was three-plus months. If projects are long duration we request for a 50% advance. Even the advance we receive after a few weeks or months of start. And the final payment is after 30 days of delivery. Our cash cycles are long, something we didn't envisage when we were freelancing.

How do you price?

We have developed a rate card for our services and products. Some clients work with us on a retainer basis. It works well for some kinds of work. Sometimes the time demands of a project are disproportionate to the retainer.

Most of the business we are doing, we are actually investing all our time, effort and cash up front.

Should you be pricing differently?

I am, today. Our rate card now factors this. When I started I didn't have a business education. I had taken a couple of courses. But there is more to learn when it comes to pricing and cash flow.

Are there any projects you decline?

Not really because most of our clients are returning clients; they give us multiple jobs. We have relationships with them. They often need small jobs to be done in a hurry. I oblige. I apologize only when I know that the scope of work is not within our capabilities.

How many new clients do you pitch to, seek in a month?

We don't knock on someone's door. We are at a point in our business where we are 'stable.' We have customers, a small team that is busy and we manage our price. From a volume of work and time we are at full capacity. The question is how to expand and in which direction to expand to cover new demands.

Are you now making an adequate salary from the business, which you were making when you resigned?

No. I am investing. I have invested in new staff. To cover my costs I am compromising. I am now able to take bigger projects so this is not worrying. There was a time I could do only a 1000 mugs for a client. Now I can manage a full campaign – mugs, badges, T-shirts, brochure, fliers, etc. I wouldn't have been able to take on a job like that if I didn't have a full design team and administrative staff to coordinate the project.

Is the business stable for you to get a return?

Stable, yes. But I do need to expand to do bigger jobs. In next six months, end of the year, I have to decide how to and where to expand. Do we do bigger jobs or should I expand design or printing? A design team has helped me take on bigger projects. We are able to finish jobs faster. Clients are able to give us additional jobs because our turnaround rate has improved.

Have you now established minimum size of clients in terms of revenue? To service a client well, what is the minimum size of business you need, without which you may be losing money?

I am working on that now. I know I have to assess profitability for each customer. I also need to focus more on the business side of things.

You may need to have a cost-sheet for each client and track estimate against actuals.

Every single job has a job order. That has the details of the job and the direct costs spent on the job. I factor the time cost and allocate fixed expenses to the job.

Was there a time when you wanted to give it up and get back to work?

There was a time when the work just became too much. I was working till 2–3 am. in the morning, trying to meet deadlines. And I thought, I need a full-time job, I can't keep doing this. An opportunity arose where a friend asked me to manage a project. I took on that responsibility even though I was extremely full with work and with no time to spare. I lowered my salary from the business and decided to hire my first graphic designer at that time and that is how I started to build my design team.

Have you changed as a person while doing the business?

Definitely. I have grown. I see things differently. I am more confident. I studied multimedia, started working in graphic design, shifted to managing or coordinating projects within the company and now am managing a company with a full-time staff. I have changed.

I was always a person who wanted to know everything. For starting and managing a company I knew I had to know every detail.

I attended the entrepreneurship program of Dubai Chamber. It gave me a lot of confidence since I already had a company. I wasn't very confident because a lot of what I was doing was based on intuition and not on an education in business, but this course made me realize that I was on the right track and gave me confidence in my abilities. I was in the right direction based on logical thinking.

How much of your business learning was trial and error?

Everything! Becoming an entrepreneur was a learning journey. I was lucky because I learnt to manage a business without it actually being my business.

I gave you the story of how I learnt the business of design in the three-member company. In the next company I joined, I was again entrusted with business development. The owner focused all his attention on growth and I learnt a lot. Then I set up a design studio with a friend. Here a large part of the decision making was with me. Only thing I didn't do was sign checks. I was there for three and half years, and I felt very confident.

Elaborate this comment, you see thing differently after being a business head.

You realize your priorities very quickly. In a full-time job, you get a salary at the end of the month whether or not you are working at your 100% level. As a freelancer, you put in 200% of your effort, if you don't put in the time, you won't get paid. However, in your own business, you need to put your staff as priority and make sure they get paid on time, no matter what happens, and that changes perspectives quite a bit, it is a huge responsibility. Thankfully, I have never been in a situation where I didn't pay my staff on time. My responsibilities now lie beyond my family.

Sana is a creative person and a businesswoman. Is there creative tension here? Do you have to balance or manage this?

I don't think there is any kind of struggle. It is natural. Before starting Tintbox, as graphic designer, I was a very 'logical' graphic designer. Some designers work to create things that look great. I maintain that everything can look great. It is not about being the next Picasso. It must work commercially. I must work within the guidelines of the brand. For me, design is very systematic. If you need to create a poster, there are two ways of thinking about it; we can have a poster that strikes you, catches your attention or there is a poster that sends the message. For me, it was always about how people read it. Does it make sense? Is it too busy? Can we have a graphic to soften the impact and get the message across? These are the two extremes and I am squarely on the business side. When I design the business side is operative. I keep the client's budget and how my work will be used in the future in mind.

Where do you think Tintbox will be in two or three years?

Really secure is where I would like it to be. I am being realistic. My team would have grown. I would like my walls to show illustrations of our creativity and passion for design. I would like people to recognize the name when we have a ten year party. In a shorter time frame of three years, we 'could' double in size.

As an entrepreneur do you always seek confirmation from somebody that you are right?

As a person, my character, I would say yes. And that's why my husband and I are a good team. We always discuss things. Seek approval from both sides. As an entrepreneur, probably yes, because I always feel I don't have business background. I always think, what if I am wrong. Do I go out and seek someone's feedback? Usually no, unless I am in a new situation and need to learn something.

What would be the guidance you would give to entrepreneurs starting out?

Sana: Know the field you are getting into; not a 100% but 200%. I see many people who want to set up a business yet are scared and hesitant. When I look back I had no fear of uncertainty. It happened naturally. It happened this way since we knew what we are getting into. My earlier employers, where I learnt business skills, did not have knowledge about the domain. They wanted to start an event management company and branding company. If you are going to open a café, you need to be able brew the coffee; you need to be able to do the things that make the business work. I recommend entrepreneurs to be hands-on when they start.

Current issues?

People want to start a business because they 'love' something; the business field. They don't know how to go about it. So they make a business plan and do it bit by bit. When I took the entrepreneurship course I was 'unaware' that I 'had' a business plan in my mind and was implementing it. As I was preparing the plan I was going over the numbers after I had set up the business. While preparing the plan I ended up rethinking how to grow the business. At the end of the program I had a business plan. Halfway, while doing it, I realized the importance of it. But the plan was based on a lot of assumptions and forecasts; it was not the way my business actually got implemented in reality. I do think there should be a different way of preparing business plans.

There was a lot of trial and error. When you start a business or a job you have an estimate of the cost. Then you assess the price as a multiple. In reality the price may be 10 to 50% different. The plus or minus may not be good enough for the business. This is a continuous struggle. As a designer, I struggle with a part of me who is a perfectionist. I am not comfortable with variances.

Entrepreneurship is the crafting of the business, not execution of a plan. Plans are too rigid. I'm not sure making a plan helps before actually setting up the business, other than using it as a roadmap. I try something. It doesn't work.

I change it. I don't want to get caught up in believing that my plan is right. Making a plan requires research whereas the market is constantly changing, so experience is a lot more valuable than a plan.

Is it a struggle, being rigid and nimble?

I am very, very adaptable. There is always something newer, exciting and interesting in my head. I can't do everything that comes in my head. I would love to do many things but often, I am afraid to. Some kind of research is definitely important.

As a designer I designed many logos based on research and understanding of the market. However you present a few to the client, what you think the client will like. You mold yourself to suit the client needs and expectations.

You are close to your customers. A lot of business is repeat business. Do you struggle to ask for a price?

That's why I set up the rate card.

The struggle is that clients may not appreciate the effort required to design something. I may do the graphic element as a visible part of my work. But I need to understand their vision, how they want the design to feel to their clients, the kind of campaigns they want to run, is the design intended to sell a product, what may happen after some time to the brand and many such questions.

Challenges?

Sana: Recruitment of staff. I had a designer who resigned two days ago. The search has started again. Because of the nature of work that we do and the salary that we are able to pay, we need to run through a lot of networks to recruit right. And my secretary just had a baby. This is the perpetual challenge of a startup.

I Love Startups

Entrepreneur	Shirin Abulrazak
Company and website	Sisters Beauty Lounge/ www.sistersbeautylounge.com
Business	Grooming business for ladies
Year started	2004
Tips for entrepreneurs	• Look after the staff so that they have no choice but to look after customers. • Recruit people better than yourself. • Be honest with staff and clients.

How did the business idea emerge?

Many years ago, I looked around and couldn't find the perfect salon, so I decided to build one. In 2004 I sensed a need-gap in the market. The grooming business was so 'old school.' Nothing had changed over time and across generations. A visit to a salon took hours. Busy working mothers needed a place to do grooming as fast as possible. I think what we did was we 'streamlined' it; reduced the time it took to do what is natural grooming. We innovated by creating a workstation to reduce by half what took three-four hours. A garage is a good metaphor; once a car is parked many mechanics can service the vehicle. Clients sit comfortably in our workstation and are served by multiple persons, providing services like hair work, manicures and pedicures.

Just speed?

We made a necessity into a speedy experience with more pampering. We called our business a 'beauty lounge.' We brought a host of grooming services to a single location, focused on high-quality service staff and gave the customer a relaxed spa-like experience. Our salon has the ambience of a Feng Shui compliant luxurious spa.

Speed and efficiency in an experience industry? Are they dichotomous?

No. Customer experience is key. We are focused on the customer. We had to be good at everything, all the services that are required for grooming. We had to excel in all facets of the beauty business under one roof.

Execution of the idea?

We needed highly qualified and talented staff for each grooming service to enable clients to experience perfect service and not think of going elsewhere. This thinking emerged from my experience as a customer. I used to listen to the woes of underpaid and overworked staff. I hate to say it but it was something akin to slavery. When we started staff were working 12 hours per day. They never saw daylight except on their holidays. I did something different. The mantra was I don't believe that the customer is king. This was contrary to what everyone was saying. I said that in my business the staff is king. We needed to train the staff. Make them grow as technicians. We need to compensate them with bonuses and incentives, giving them an opportunity to earn more than their salary. We needed to give them health insurance which was not mandatory in the beauty industry. We first paid our staff then paid our self. We needed to look after them so well that they had no choice but to look after our customers. This became our winning factor in the business.

Competition?

In one sense competition in 2004 was intense but most salons were 'old' school. Good salons were difficult to find. We came up with a unique beauty salon positioning. New formats like nail bars were emerging. The industry has since changed. Nail bars have expanded their offerings by adding hair and beauty treatments. Basically nail bars are no longer nail bars but now look like a copy of our lounges. This was something we predicted would happen 10 years ago.

Where was the first salon located?

We started from the village on Jumeirah Beach Road. We had plenty competition along this stretch. We had probably 100 salons in the neighborhood. People asked why we were opening at the village and that too another salon. We asked for their patience. We had ideas that we wanted to implement.

Why Jumeirah?

I thought Jumeirah was a great catch. There will be loads of women who will have an easy access to the salon from where they live or work. The Village Mall had basement parking. It was akin to a community center. This suited us because we wanted to provide a homely atmosphere, where customers would feel invited, come for an hour, be called by their names and leave.

How did you implement the difference that you wanted to create?

I wanted to offer a differentiated tangible experience to customers, something they would not get elsewhere. I had the design of the station in mind. This has now become our trademark in the business. The stations have electrical outlets which customers can use for their laptops and digital devices while being served. They can bring their babies in a pram. They are served coffee and cookies. There were some salons that used to charge a Dirham for a bottle of water. When I started we were not driven by money but a desire to succeed. I just wanted the place to be friendly on the basis of transparency, honesty and good service. To do this I needed time to get highly qualified staff and train them in our way of working. In 2004 Dubai didn't have mega malls. Mall of Emirates invited us to start there but we told them we had just set up and were not ready. We really didn't know what was going to happen. We didn't know that we would become big. We were thinking of only a salon where we were going to offer what others were not offering.

How did you implement the difference in salon ambience?

It all had to do with the design of space and nurturing the right employee mindset. I have a background in fashion and beauty, and I love beautiful things. I can look at a core and shell space that is dark and bounded by concrete blocks and visualize a light and beautiful space that is feminine and women-friendly. I have been a customer so I knew the things I wanted to feel and didn't want to see. I didn't want my staff whining away about their employment problems to clients. I wanted to relax and feel happy. I wanted to engage with happy staff in an ambience that was positive and cheerful. We had to design and engineer space to influence the mind of customers and staff. To influence the staff mindset we have to engage with staff at a human level, understand their needs and motivations of coming to work and live alone in the UAE leaving their families. I have to help them fulfill their needs e.g., help them build a home in their village that may just cost AED 30K.

How long did it take to open – from idea to start?

90 days. I had an interesting fit-out company managed by a talented Iranian who is more of a poet than an architect who was able to understand the brief.

Was staff recruitment an issue? Training them, changing their mindset?

We just didn't know where to start. I wasn't going to go out and head hunt. We started advertising a little bit by word of mouth. Some people came to us and we did a little bit of test, a trial. We were keen to identify if they were good, had potential and were capable of reaching the benchmark I had set. We were not in New York or Thailand or Paris. I had to create something for the Dubai mindset, for which there was no real standard. The Dubai customer needed to be told what the highest standard was. So instead of just giving customers what they want, we invent procedures and policies that the customer really should want. We developed our own etiquette of starting the procedure, doing the procedure and ending the procedure. We asked the staff to visualize themselves as a hostess. They were to greet the clients as guests. After completing the procedure you have to escort the guests to the threshold of the house. Attention to minor details was important.

Did you visualize the details of the customer journey by trial and error?

This was the easy part. As a customer myself I knew all the things I didn't want to see. Sisters Beauty Lounge was not only for me, but for my sisters, daughters, their friends, my 93-year-old mother, my 6-year-old granddaughter. Thus four generations of women in my family use the services of SBL. They are the perfect representation of the collective intelligence of SBL. They all knew what they wanted from the business. And I had experienced in the past that nothing had changed from the time I went with my mother for a haircut, to the time I was taking my own child for a haircut. I just needed to provide honest-to-goodness service and nothing would go wrong.

Did you discuss the positive and negative customer experience within the family?

We knew we were going to have teething troubles during startup. A few days before the formal opening I called the family to test run the salon to give us a report on their experience. I can't tell you how bad the report was. They identified all the issues; something wasn't done, something took too long, etc. They even benchmarked me against other salons. This test helped us correct the areas where we were bad. It was all about trying to get the staff to understand our point of view. They had legacy issues from the businesses they were coming from. The staff had to trust and believe us. The new staff had to get used to electrical equipment/gadgets they had never used before. We had to understand the staff mindset and learn how to change that.

How was your pricing?

Honestly, there wasn't a plan. I had a gut feeling. I just knew that it was a salon for the rest of my family, hence named 'Sisters' and if it is good enough for them then everyone else would come. We did some rough numbers based on the number of stations and number of therapists. We had designed the stations for multitasking, simultaneous hair care, manicure and pedicure; we believed that we could triple the performance of the salons. This wasn't a plan which was going to work. It was an expectation. We just said that it looks like it is going to triple. And it did.

How did you create an awareness of the lounge?

I did a lot of the PR work at that time so I created awareness with the editors of magazines. I invited them for free treatment. I invited them to a lunch, took them to the lounge and have a run of the place. I also used some unconventional methods. If somebody in the family was getting married I invited them to hold the bridal shower in the salon in the morning between 10 am and 12 noon. I knew that if the bride invited thirty friends, word would spread. We advertised a bit but gave up on that quickly. You could say I was driven more by intuition than reason.

Did you have adequate number of customers in the first year itself?

No. The first year was scary and very challenging. Today I understand that the first year of every business is a big challenge, no matter how well known the brand. In the beginning customers would walk-in, experience us and were more or less hooked. But it took nearly six months of steady growth for the numbers to reach a sustainable number. For a new branch we need a year to reach a stage where a customer has to wait for 2 weeks for an appointment.

Customer acquisition and loyalty are important measures for a startup. Do you track loyalty?

We track walk-in, new and returns. If the percentage of new and returning customers is within estimates then we are doing something right.

How do you manage operations?

We invested very early in software to manage salon operations. We track productivity measures like – customer visits, ticket size per customer, percentage of product sales and service sales – of each staff member daily, weekly and monthly.

How much time do you spend managing the business?

There is a funny story. Once I went to school to pick up my youngest daughter. Her teacher told me that my daughter had told her that her mother never works. Truth was I would go to work after dropping them in school and return home by picking them from school. I have made a promise to myself that I would never let my work interfere in normal family life. I was always there for my children. Even though I was not formally working from 9 am to 6 pm I have always been hands-on with everything. I didn't have an office in the first year and would sit in the salon or in a coffee shop.

When did the business get systemized so that Shirin could go on a holiday?
I went on a holiday for a month after the first year and nothing fell apart. This meant that that processes were in place from year one. I had key people in place, established and institutionalized all the procedures through handbooks and manuals that people could go to when they had doubts about what they should do.

How did you go about doing this?
It started with a three-page manual. Pages got added. I used to put up bulletins in the staff room identifying issues and solutions. We started with a Staff Handbook ready on day one. This has taken the shape of a formal document when we started franchising.

When did you open a second location?
We signed up with the Dubai Mall in 2005 after seeing the Emaar Mall model. The mall opened three years later just as the economic crisis began. Imagine my mental state. Here I was in a mall with 4000 sq. ft. of space and a million Dirham rent commitment, a 4 million Dirham fit-out fee and graduating from the Village Mall. I thought that million Dirhams is often a budget for a PR campaign of who you are and what you want to become. I want the business to become an advertisement by being in everyone's face in the most iconic mall in the world. Dubai mall has been the basis of our business growth, the absolute jewel in the crown. Dubai Mall made Abu Dhabi happen. It made Kazakhstan franchise happen and so much more.

Uncertainty about expansion?
It was a new business. I appear as an entrepreneur and my background is beauty that was inborn. I don't have professional training in beauty. We also never knew if what we had planned was going to work. And now a new location was being thrust upon us. We just needed time to get ourselves into the new business. And then go into expansion with confidence. We had just started the Dubai Mall location. The fact that my daughters joined the business meant there was an amazing growth. The branches that have emerged from the

original salon ten years ago are a direct result of this fresh young blood! With each new location, our portfolio becomes even more stunning with the ideas and changes influenced by them.

Where was the seed of business in Shirin?

I became an entrepreneur out of necessity, a sort of an accidental entrepreneur. The seed of business was in a little rebelliousness that I had towards what I consider constraints of 'old' school; I considered going to school and traditional university. Starting a business was a way of getting out of it. I knew what I wanted to create. I also knew what I wanted to become. Working for others was not an option. It would keep me out of the house. And it would also not give me an opportunity to do things that I wanted to be free to do. I wanted financial independence that would not interfere with my family and children. I come from a family of strong women personalities. My mother is well known, has been a civil servant and diplomat, and has written books. My sister is a well-known TV journalist. I wanted to be able to conform to all the cultural requirements and not be like my high flying mother and sister who were always jetting off to different places. I wanted to always be in the background.

Where did you get the idea for your first uniform business?

This happened by chance. My children were always considered best dressed in their school. The Principal motivated me to develop similar uniforms for all the other children. Some parents had queried the Principal about the source of the uniforms, keen to get similar uniforms. I used to design the uniforms, copying them from somewhere, and have them stitched. Working through the night I created a business plan for a uniform factory. I started from a derelict place in Rashidiya, belonging to my husband. The business became pretty big. We were doing uniforms for schools and institutions all over the GCC.

How did you learn to manage the business? Pricing and cash flows?

The hard way.

Did you exit the business?

I sold the business profitably. Two things had happened. My children had grown up and I decided to take some time off. The lack of creativity in the uniform business began to hit me. I began wanting change. The business had thirty-five employees and sales of over 4 m some 20 years ago.

Then?

I didn't wait long to dabble in a new business. I came across The Bombay Company on a trip to Boston. I decided to take a franchise. The furniture business was different but I had the confidence to manage it, execute it. I had to buy the franchise from a Kuwaiti company. The business started well but the parent company went bankrupt. I ran the business with sheer grit for five years.

How do you manage a large (250+ employees) HR based service business?

I think it has to do with the ethos of this company, and the ethos that has been understood and absorbed by all the staff. Retention is a good measure. I don't think the ethos today is what it was when we started. Then we were just an extended family. We knew all the people by their first names. I knew about their families, their motivations. I have followed a practice, since the days of the uniform business, of employing people better than myself. I have never recruited people who needed teaching by me. I have also learned to nudge, show happiness and displeasure, through more subtle signals, not raising my voice. The biggest fact is that there is no way I would have managed so many women under one roof without my youngest daughter, Sara, who plays a very active role in the day-to-day management.

Challenges in the immediate future?

Our latest children's concept Caboodle Pamper and Play (18 months old, with two branches in prime locations) has so much demand for franchising all over the GCC that we don't know what to do with it. Setting up a salon Academy.

Starting a Business Is like Swimming Against the Tide

Entrepreneurs	Shobha Moni (S) and R. S. Moni (M)
Company and website	Triad Software Services/www.triadme.com
Business	Software solutions and services
Year established	2005
Tips for entrepreneurs	• Don't do what you don't know. • Differentiate friendly encouragement from real business; contacts don't always become customers. • Get ready to multi-task and quickly learn new things. • An entrepreneur has to roll up his sleeves and do what has to be done. • Entrepreneurs have no alibis for non-performance. Can you handle acute responsibility? • Be agile and flexible. Know when to cut losses. • Entrepreneur needs to be gritty to stay the course.

How did Triad begin?

S: The idea emerged from our work. My work experience was in software sales. Moni worked in diverse businesses like manufacturing and trade-in finance and operations. He had experience in buying software. We collectively sensed the supply and the demand side gap. We had been 'tossing' around the idea of starting a business for some time before we started Triad. The opportunity came along when Moni was looking for a change.

M: Wanting to start a business versus identifying the business to start are two different things. We were salaried employees. Two uncertainties confronted us; the fear of survival without a paycheck and the risk of capital loss. We were professionally qualified people. As a CFO I was buying and implementing software solutions. I experienced IT buyers' pain; nobody was giving me what I wanted. The suppliers were pushing software products. Negligible solution consulting was available. This was the gap in the market. The region was growing and the gap was becoming wider. The size of the market was expanding as companies searched for solutions.

This sounds too logical?

S: When we started the business we had an approximate idea of the industry, business and customers. We truly discovered the business over the years. The business refined and crystallized as our understanding of the market matured. We understood our personal capabilities and we created capacity in Triad. Today I think we have a very strong understanding of it. I don't think we had this strength of opinion when we started.

Uncertainty when you left?

S: Definitely. When I got my first Triad card made nobody recognized the Triad logo. I recollect noticing that it didn't have a designation. All it said was Triad. People would ask me, 'So who is Triad?' And I would start explaining. One would occasionally wonder if the step had been right. We were figuring out who we were. Today I feel very proud when I talk about Triad, when people recognize the colors of Triad. It is truly gratifying. I feel very personally attached with every element of the business.

What does Triad do?

M: We advise mid-market customers on software solutions that are right for them. We started our practice by providing Sage ERP solutions.

S: When I joined Triad I focused on CRM. When an entrepreneur meets a client he has to prove himself anew. When I met my first CRM client I drew a diagram on a whiteboard and convinced the customer about the value proposition. I then built up resources to deliver the value proposition. Triad now has momentum and resources to offer ERP, CRM and HRMS solutions to customers in different industries to suit a range of budgets. We sell a service. The software product we propose and sell is complemented with our consulting capability, our real differentiating value proposition. From the customer point of view they are not searching for a product on a standalone basis. What they look for is a team that will understand their business needs and implement a solution. We offer technology solutions with a business focus for growing companies. When companies grow we help their systems evolve in-step with their business growth.

M: Our customers are companies who suddenly discover that the simple accounting solutions which had worked well in the past are no longer adequate for decision making and control. The trigger to evolve from a simple accounting system in a company is actually a search for a better way of working. It begins when the person running the company feels he is unable to manage the operations or get things done on time. He then starts looking for ERP and CRM. Usually the person sensing this need and wanting to drive it is the CEO or CFO. But he is running the company and is unable to spend time identifying what is required. We offer our services and say, 'We understand your pains as a CEO or CFO. We will be your consultants and do it for you.'

How did you choose the software to represent?

M: We decided to work with a global and recognized product. Since we were going to add value around the product we decided not to struggle with product development. I drew upon my past professional role to understand what customers would need and how they would evaluate products. As a CFO I had been evaluating multiple software products to buy. The ERP product from Sage met my criteria, had the flexibility of working in different operating environments and supported databases. We decided on Sage as the product to represent. We met the principal, introduced our credentials and asked for support. They agreed and we were in business. It was easier than I thought.

S: This was a pure business decision. Sage is a clear leader in the mid-market space and the mid-market was growing at a rapid rate in the Middle East. Although I had the experience with Tier 1 solutions like Oracle and SAP, we decided to start in the mid-market space. Mid-market also offered certain advantages – like a tighter scope, smaller project teams and speedier decision making – all of which lowered risks for a startup.

What do you think they saw in you?

M: They asked us, 'How do you plan to run this business?' I explained to them my business plan – how as a CA I could relate to the requirements of companies looking for solutions. And in a market thirsting for this approach, how I would be uniquely different.

S: Triad is now a Sage case study; a company started by a CA with no sales experience which then goes on to become one of their most successful partners.

Critical incidents of your startup journey?

M: Customer acceptance. We presented our ideas to different people when we started. Two things emerged. One, mere friendship does not lead to orders. Discussing an idea is different from asking a person to put money on the table. Two, learn to take advice from people who know and are adept at implementing businesses. Sage gave us guidance using best practices of their other distributor-partners. Experiment with new ideas once business is up and running.

Did you develop ways of acquiring customers?

M: This happened organically. We didn't think of a strategy initially but experimented and identified what worked for us. I had been cautioned by Sage that the sales cycle is long. My experience was pleasantly different. This happened because customers were looking for solutions. They found that a Chartered Accountant talking about an IT product made much more sense. We could talk to CEOs and CFOs of companies, articulate their pain and then offer real solutions.

S: We are different today; strategic and tactical. For example, we are actively leveraging our web presence. We use focused webinars and seminars to improve product awareness. We use Sage CRM to efficiently stay in touch with our prospects.

How much time did it take to get the first contract?

S: The first client we got was where one of our employees had a business relationship. The second client, we got through a phone call from a well-wisher.

M: The first thing we did when we started was to invest in a person who had experience with the product. I could spend time and learn the product. That wasn't an option. I couldn't be dividing my time facing the customer and learning the product. Revenue had to be generated quickly and time was a precious resource. We had our first revenue four months from the time we started.

How long before cash breakeven?

M: One and a half years. But after nine months in the market we knew the business would work; we had started collecting significant orders giving us the validation we needed that we were doing the right thing. It gave us the confidence to invest in people and to grow.

S: In 2006-7 Sage gave us two awards, one for ERP and the other for CRM, for increased orders from the Middle East. The award was a fantastic motivation but it also put a different kind of pressure on us as it had raised the bar we had set for ourselves.

How did you get the pricing right?

M: This was not an issue because Shobha was in the business of selling. She knew the prevalent pricing in the market.

S: We priced our offering competitive to the market. We were able to do this because the customer discerned value in us.

Where does that competence to customize the solutions lie? In both of you? Or have you put it into an organization process?

M: We believe quality and a commitment to support are important, especially when the requirements are not standard. We are a small cohesive team. Whenever we talk about customer requirements, problems and solutions, we come into a room, discuss and come up with a solution. So everyone internalizes the commitment to act as a problem solver. Our employee turnover is very low. This has also enabled creation of a strong team.

S: This process has enabled our ideals to percolate. We encourage team meetings to formulate solution. This has influenced the type of people we recruit. We look for the right attitude. Skill sets are easy to teach; we can help the staff get certified. We focus on how to create enabling conditions for each individual to think, develop and grow. We keep helping them, nudging them and supporting them.

Was recruitment a challenge?

S: Initially. People buy into you as a person. They don't join the organization. You have to sell your idea. They take a risk; what if it doesn't work? We hired people with potential but who didn't have a Sage certification and made them certified.

What worries you about the business?

M: Every day we think about how to make it better.

S: Are we doing it right? What are we getting right or wrong? Business has daily challenges e.g., projects not following the original timeline. We try to satisfy every customer. We try to see the customer's point of view and work on that. I don't think we will ever get a feeling that, 'Aha, we have done it.'

Were there moments when you wondered why you got into business?

S: Yes, indeed. In the initial days.

M: Triad got off to a good start. Market traction was there. Four years back when the crisis hit suddenly the revenue stopped. Customers didn't pay. Cash flow became a real issue. We had to take difficult decisions but managed to hold onto our key employees and customers.

Was anything easier than what you had envisioned?

S: Running your own business suddenly makes every moment productive. I work much harder as an entrepreneur but it doesn't feel like hard work.

M: Finding solutions for customers. The Sage ecosystem has many partner products. This helped us provide clear solutions even to some requirements specific to the Middle East.

Third Eye of Retail[5]

Entrepreneurs	Zayan Ghandour, Fatima Ghobash and Dina Saleh
Company and website	S*uce/www.shopatsauce.com
Business	Fashion retail
Year established	2004
Tips for entrepreneurs	• Foster team spirit in the company so people work together in your absence. • People first. Be kind in implementing HR policies. • Treat staff as partners and empower individuals so they are inspired by what they are achieving.

What is S*uce?

S*uce is an award-winning multi-brand fashion and lifestyle concept store. From the very first season at s*uce, the emphasis was always on providing customers with brands and styles that are not available anywhere else and the most inspiring retail experience. S*uce is a lifestyle; it is a way of life. We focus on everything from the product to the interior design, in-store music, the special exclusive scent, the voice of the brand and the way it communicates with its fans. It's a long-standing relationship. For the first season we bought 12 brands that already had a cult following internationally but nobody stocked in the region. Then we added fifty brands for the second season. Currently we present over 600 brands at a time per season across different categories like- ready to wear, fashion accessories, lifestyle items and sometimes even a small kids' collection. The categories keep on growing. The concept has taken a life of its own. Two creative buyers and I now attend all fashion trade shows and scour the internet looking for the next big thing, or as yet unheard of brands. Furthermore, we work closely with many designers, both locally and internationally, customizing special exclusive collections for s*uce.

---

5 Interview is with Zayan Ghandour

How did you know that what you were doing for yourself had a wider market?

There was a demand for cool, fun and interesting brands that was just not met in the market, so it was pretty obvious really. There is a sense of discovery in shopping, that all women enjoy. They love to find new things and secrets, and share them with their friends. Today we travel the globe, from London, Milan, Paris and New York to as far away as Japan, Brazil, Mexico and Turkey, to markets that we didn't even know existed, in search of that next big thing, or a new designer. Our job is to find these talented designers and offer them in our stores, where our customers can then discover them for themselves. S*uce is designed to deliver a new experience of discovery every day.

When did you say, let me make positive feedback a business?

We were all new in business. We had an intuition that we could all bring something to the mix. But it all happened very naturally and organically.

How?

We had decided to open the store. That summer Fatima secured our trade license and we were ready for business. We bought 12 brands for the first season and they sold out very quickly. One of those brands was Seven Jeans from New York, which is now 7 For All Mankind and is very famous. We brought brands from Australia, which at that time was not necessarily known for fashion. Introducing new and unknown brands with a high fashion sensibility became our DNA, our winning formula.

Growth too?

Our first location was a small space in The Village Mall in Jumeirah. The store had no electricity connection on the first day we opened so we had to close at 6 pm after sunset. We started with one salesperson. Our knowledge of the business, brands and operations all grew along with the business. Then in 2007 we got lucky, as our neighbor was leaving. So we doubled our floor size.

How important was The Village Mall shop for S*uce?

I always say that the Village Mall was our lucky location because that's where it all began. The store was like our office. We met with the designers there, and it is where we met our customers. Getting immediate feedback from customers and staff on what we were doing was important. It helped us tighten the way we worked and focus on getting the formula right for the customer.

Future development?

The s*uce brand has grown from where we started. We know our customers and strive to remain true to them while bearing in mind the evolving and growing tastes. We have focused on organic growth even though we have received many offers to franchise. Retail franchising requires a lot of attention to detail. My two partners have contributed greatly to operations and PR. Each partner has a personal touch and input to the business. We were not sure whether we were ready for growth and franchising. We prefer to keep tighter control of the brand.

When buying how did you know how much to spend on what?

When I started I trusted my eye as well as instinct and felt that we had enough customers who would relate to my aesthetic. I think this gift is embedded in the S*uce slogan – Love What You Love Without Hesitation. I believed that if you genuinely love something there will be someone, another person, who will share the same space with you. Our stores give the appearance of a playground. Every product comes with a fashion sensibility, an edge and an element of surprise. We don't buy hundreds of pieces. We buy selectively which makes it more challenging. But we end up with deliveries almost every day and every customer feels that they are buying an exclusive product.

How do you discover designers? Say, in Japan.

We make an itinerary to visit stores that even most Japanese may be unfamiliar with. To prepare the itinerary we go through every possible fashion publication from Japan. We look for what is new. What is small and not yet mainstream Japan. We go to the outskirts of cities finding brands and doing comparative shopping. Japanese brands usually don't get exported. Brands are also happy in their cocoon; they don't have to deal with a foreigner who doesn't speak their language. I have to reach them inside their 'content' cocoon. It sometimes takes one week to get an appointment but we are patient. We wait and persevere!

But selling a Japanese product in Dubai?

Yes, why not? If the product is strong, is merchandized well and sits comfortably within the s*uce product mix, it does very well. Who cares where it is from? Everything at s*uce is curated to fit within the s*uce world and when customers shop at s*uce, they are shopping for that aesthetic, whether the designer is from Japan, London or UAE.

You have found a designer who is prepared to sell to you after much cajoling at a certain price. Where do you get a feeling that the price that they are selling to you at and the price you will sell at will make a business?

There is always a customer for every product, a customer who finds value in the exclusivity and creativity of the piece. Design, production and shipping are expensive and need to be taken into account for the final price. We understand the struggle of independent up-and-coming designers. Catwalk designers struggle with high street brands because they knock off their designs three-months after the catwalk show. My goal is to find designers that the high street has not or cannot knock off. So it is always special, different and unique. This is our expertise.

Where was the seed of entrepreneurship in you?

I never knew I had it in me. I don't think one learns entrepreneurship. You have a certain instinct. A food retailer knows the palate he needs to satisfy in his restaurant. I know my customer. I know what to give her. I know what I love. I go after it and make sure I produce it. You spoke about forecasting trends. I think it is like a third eye kind of a moment. I have also learnt that if there is sincerity in whatever you are selling things will work. In S*uce we try to do things right and believe in transparency, you get what you see. We have ingrained this culture in S*uce.

Are you an accidental entrepreneur?

Absolutely. Luck has played as much an important role as hard work. I found the right partners at the right place at the right time!

Any challenges?

The biggest challenge is to win the confidence of landlords and secure locations when you are competing with large retail giants or international luxury brands. Yet what we offer is totally unique. We create new exciting concepts that inspire customers. Landlords love the ideas but still worry about how bankable they are. Dubai malls still hesitate when it comes to locally bred products and brands. I think that is changing and s*uce probably had a lot to do with changing those attitudes.

When did you decide to have a brand of your own?

The plan was always there but once again, I needed things to fall into place before I could put the idea to action. For the first four years I was the only buyer plus creative director. So Zayan the Label had to remain on the backburner. Starting your own brand is a huge challenge; after the initial inspiration design is all about having a great production team and facility. We needed someone to make it happen. We now have four people in the production team, a small workshop in Dubai and produce in China and Bali. We will soon have a standalone store.

Challenges of a changing business model?

We have traditionally bought a huge variety with small depth. But now that we are opening new stores and concepts, we are buying more. Organic development is what I love because it comes with a lot of spirit, love, hard work and long nights. I don't focus on any big specific goal to be achieved. We just do it whole-heartedly and see what happens.

How have you changed implementing S*uce?

I just grew a little older but the child in me keeps me creative. I retain the spirit of a young person with a drive to experiment and do things differently all the time.

Business Becomes a Business by Selling

Entrepreneur	Govinda Siddartha
Company and website	Audioviz/www.audiviz.com
Business	IT consulting and solutions
Year established	2002
Tips for entrepreneurs	• Due diligence and gut create a business. • A startup is about managing dynamic emerging situations that arise. If a startup has everything going according to plan then something is wrong! • Stress of the unknown about to happen is an entrepreneur's companion. It focuses the brain.

What is Audioviz?

We are an ICT technology consultancy and solution company. We provide advisory services to companies upgrading or building their technology platform. We focus on creating technology infrastructure and take care of all data, voice, telecommunications and entertainment needs. We do small and large projects. An SME's needs are basic. Whereas an ICT package for a 20-floor hotel is loaded with technologies because entertainment needs are built on a common data platform.

How are you different from so many companies?

Our engagement starts early. We first help clients identify their needs. Many clients need to visualize their current and future needs. We then design the network platform to optimize the costs based on client's size, sophistication and complexity. ICT is a very big space. Few companies play in the entire ICT domain on a large scale. Many companies focus on parts of ICT, some on data, some on voice, others on IT infrastructure, etc.

Did you always do this?

We started Audioviz focusing on the audiovisual needs of companies. We have grown incrementally by focusing on other related customer needs and developing the ability to serve those.

How did this happen?

Our current business model emerged from client requests. Audioviz was not an expert in telecommunications when we started. Clients told us, 'We want you to execute the whole ICT package. We know your specialization is AV. Can you manage IT as well? We want you to.' Customers wanted a contract with one service provider to make their management easier. We subcontracted with other companies skilled in different ICT domains, who worked with us to provide quality solutions. We were transparent with our customers. We had subcontractors sit with us in front of the customers. Customers saw that we were not just hiring people and doing the work. We were working with specialists. Customers were comfortable with us because they saw that we were managing their interests. Our consultancy service evolved from here. We work as consultants and execute a part of the job. We partner with subcontractors to deliver a complete project. We manage the project. Customers see us and hold us accountable.

Where did a market for ICT consultants emerge?

Today data, voice and entertainment are based on digital and wireless platforms. Service providers of different ICT services were specialized in narrow domains. They took time to evolve. Take infrastructure needs for a hotel: A 20-floor hotel may cost AED 200m. Hotel consultants can build a hotel. They needed experts to detail ICT infrastructure and evaluate vendors of hardware and other services.

How did you believe Audioviz could be a consultant?

A key requirement of a consultant is to pre-qualify companies who can bid for various jobs of a project. From the beginning Audioviz always wore a consultant's hat when we worked with customers. We made efforts to understand their needs, transparently show our skills and identify others suppliers needed to fulfill client requirements. We never charged for this work. I had noticed that 90% of the time we won the assignment when we engaged with a client in a consulting role. We also discovered that clients were expressing their needs and expectations from projects which enabled us to detail and price projects better.

Example?

In a project I could use an LG or a Bang Olufsen product. One is five times more expensive. Customers were able to tell us what they want. We allowed customers to decide. Customers understood that their interest was being taken care of. We were upfront in telling them, 'We have helped you define your needs for free. You have everything on the table. Give us a fair chance to bid for the job.' They already knew the cost I was going to bid.

Why did you do this?

We were entering an industry with entrenched big players. We had to be creative in enabling clients accept our proposals. We had to win their trust. The fast rate of technology change gave us an opening. Today bigger companies are following a consulting approach to sales. Customers don't just want technology. They want to know what technology can do and the budget. They want to pay for what they will use.

Do prospective customers precisely express their needs?

50–60% customers can do their need analysis. They can define what they want ICT to do functionally. Others need external help. All need assistance on benchmarking technology. Clients have seen or read about technology developments but need assistance in defining specifications. Very often we help clients achieve their goals by paying less. A company had estimated AED 30 m for a project. We showed them how to achieve their goal with AED 17m. 17 m was not guaranteed to us because we had to bid and win the contract. Clients are not used to vendors saving them money. Sometimes in technology specifications, consultants over specify to be safe. This is our opportunity. Supplying as per specifications is also a risky option. A client can say that they have a white elephant that is not being used. And that no supplier identified the issue.

Where did you get the idea for Audioviz?

I was running a company called the Delta Business Products. It was an IT peripherals and consumables distribution company. DBP moved boxes. We had many products, customers and invoices. We also sold projectors. I had started DBP in 1995. My background is in audiovisual projection system for meeting rooms. I started in UAE with 3M in 1991, where I acquired domain knowledge. I started DBP because I wanted to do more than trading. I couldn't risk just focusing on AV products.

How did you give up a multinational job and get into box moving?

In '95, 3M spun-off the division into a new company, Imation. I was given the option to move to the new company, a small company, with the same perks. Or continue in 3M as a small fish in a big pond. I could have changed divisions within 3M. I saw a need for a multi-brand distribution company, a single point source of all customer needs. In 1995 most brands appointed exclusive distributors. If an overseas customer wanted to buy ten different brands, they had to go to ten different companies, make ten payments, consolidate ten shipments, etc. It was a logistical nightmare. For a UAE customer this didn't matter. I had sensed this because my 3M customers from Africa struggled to find a company to consolidate their cargo. Plus they had the issue of fake products. They didn't know whom to trust, who was reliable. They told me, 'We can trust you. We will order. You buy locally, consolidate and ship.' We set up in Jebel Ali, taking stocks from different suppliers.

How much did you invest?

I had a partner from the US. He was a passive investor. We started with AED 700,000, my entire saving of 5 years. My wife said, 'You are crazy. If this doesn't work, we are back to square one.' I looked at it similarly. If it didn't work it would be like taking my first job in Dubai again!

How did you price?

Customers were willing to pay 2–3% higher premium for the convenience. Credit in the market was always an issue. I used to give credit to my known customers, my old distributors of 3M.

Customer acquisition was not an issue?

My 3M network helped.

Is Delta operational?

The company exists but is not operational. With Delta I had a small store in Bur Dubai market which was a retail reseller store. It was my eyes and ears in the market. In 2000 I had started supplying to Carrefour and Lulu. I sold the assets of Delta in 2009 when it had revenue of AED 160 m. About 30–40% was retail and balance through other retail channels. We had about 65–70 employees in Delta.

Was Delta a precursor to Audioviz?

In 2002 I realized that AV business is not about trading i.e., moving boxes. We needed to move up the value chain by providing solutions. I was looking for a knowledgeable person and found Manoj, who is my partner and GM. He used to come and sell his products to me. I shared my vision as well as plan and my idea of focusing on providing solutions. I had networks to source products and he knew technology. I asked him whether he was prepared to leave his employment and take a risk with a startup. He took the risk and we set up Audioviz Technology.

How did you realize the solutions opportunity?

In 2001 Dubai Internet City was announced. The biggest ICT contract was for Burj Al Arab. I saw the technological shift away from traditional AV, projector and tripod screens. It was not a Eureka moment. It was a feeling. Some companies had entered the field. Some computer companies were integrating IT solutions. No one specialized in AV solutions. We stayed away from IT. IT network integration was a regular business. Every company needs some networking, servers and PCs. Since every company was doing it I didn't focus on it. We focused on AV, aware that it was going to be a slow business that would develop and become sophisticated. I bet on the future and knew I was going to lose money for a while.

Why a new company?

I didn't want it to be run as part of Delta. I didn't want it to be camouflaged within overall operations so we wouldn't know what was happening. Initially it was totally funded and supported by Delta. For the first five years we lost money in Audioviz. We had a helpless situation. Even Manoj used to feel low saying, 'I don't know what else to do now.' I used to counsel him to stay the course and not worry about money. I knew that the entry barrier into the industry was high.

Why?

One cannot just walk-into a company or go to a consultant and say that we can do their AV or ICT package. Two pre-qualifications are required; one, by the consultant, and two, by the vendors. AV was different from IT trading. We could go to a company like HP, give a bank guarantee and become a distributor for a new country. AV was a different business. It was a project business. It required expertise, track record and qualification, akin to construction.

What's your background?

I'm a BSc and then did my management from Bangalore. My first job was selling cigarettes for Duncan Agro in India. After two years I switched to selling computers for Mafatlal. Manoj is a commerce graduate with an MBA. Both of us are non-technical. We are both in an industry that is based on technology and provision of service.

Did you doubt that customers would trust non-technical people?

That's exactly what happened. We had neither history nor technical know-how when we started. We knew the functionality of the product but we were unable to talk to customers as engineers. We struggled. We were not given any time by consultants. They would ask us, 'Why should we even meet with you? What is your credibility? What is your background? What is your history?'

How did you overcome this challenge?

Business becomes a business by selling. I am at heart a salesperson. I want to go out and meet customers. I told my team, let your card say 'Business Development Manager.' I will accompany you with a card titled 'Sales Representative.' You be quiet. I will do the selling. I overcame objections because I listened to their concerns and answered them on the spot.

Where was entrepreneurship in you?

There's not a single entrepreneur in our family. My father was very disappointed with sales as my career choice. He even told me that no one will marry me.

What was driving you when you invested AED 700,000 and risked everything?

I considered two things; losing AED 700,000 and a job with 3M. 3M is a great company. For an employee it is a professional opportunity. I was on a good salary in 1995. We were a family of two. I did not feel comfortable in the new company or in a new division in 3M. Over the years people had been asking me to join them to start a business. 3M was an attraction to not becoming an entrepreneur. When the split happened, the attraction of 3M evaporated. I reasoned what could be the worst thing that could happen if I started a business; a loss of AED 700K. I would start again at square one. I had the confidence that I could get another job. I am a salesperson at heart. I asked my wife only one thing, 'Look, the chance of losing AED 700K over three years is there. What does it mean to you?' I didn't want my marriage to be in trouble because of this. She replied, 'When we got married we didn't have what we have now. When we came to the Gulf we didn't have what we have. What are we worried about? So go for it.' In hindsight at that time it was a big risk, a gamble of sorts. At that time I didn't see it as a risk. I was focused on the opportunity. I was motivated by the excitement of starting my own business.

Audioviz struggled for five years. Was recruiting people a challenge?

As a small struggling company neither can we attract quality nor pay the price for quality. The only thing we could give them was a dream. 99% of the people don't buy that. We are now forty-two people. Our topline will cross AED 36 m next year.

How was your pricing to enter the market?

We had to discount. In a couple of projects we provided the free consulting. But when the bids reached the purchase manager we were 2–3% higher. We were forced to match the price.

What worries you about the business today?

As we grow our fixed costs rise. Our salaries are above industry average to attract talent. We have to manage productivity and costs. Sometimes I think we should think about compromising our philosophy of being multi-brand customer-centric. I could be a representative of a brand and get better terms. But then I will sell what I have and not necessarily what is best for a client. Our strategy is also our problem now. The dilemma is to stick to your philosophy or pay our bills. I personally am not chasing the bottom line all the time. Of course we need to make a profit. I tell Manoj that we must always exceed customer expectations. I want this to be the company DNA. An extra margin of profit at the expense of the customer will not impact my lifestyle but will impact the company.

How have you changed as a person after becoming an entrepreneur?

I've become a little bit less daring than I was before, you know. When you have nothing to lose you are more daring. When you have something to lose, you become less daring. I'm responsible for forty-two families. I have to keep the boat sailing. I also gave a stake to Manoj. He has worked with me to build the company.

Guidance to a new entrepreneur starting out?

Do what you are convinced about. Once you have done your due diligence and your gut says yes, just do it. After that, no backing out. Problems are guaranteed. After you start, I can tell you that everything that you thought will go well isn't going to go right. Not because the market is changing. A startup is all about managing variables that happen. If a startup has everything going according to plan then something is wrong! The model needs checking. Startup is about managing barriers and challenges. Unknown things will happen. A lot of people give up. When I started Delta every brand of distributor threatened to shut me down. I was told I couldn't sell multiple brands under one roof. I was told I couldn't sell in Dubai. I used to tell them that customers are free to choose. There's no such thing as your customer or my customer. Customers can buy from anybody. A customer can go to Grocery X and Grocery Y. Grocery X cannot tell Y that they cannot sell milk.

Did you have to manage any stress?

Stress is always there. We have to manage expectations of vendors, banks, staff and customers. Banks are fair weather friends. When it is raining they take the umbrella. In 2009, at the start of the economic crisis, Delta had revenue of AED 16 million. It needed bank finance to run. Overnight I was told that I could not discount a bill of the largest hypermarket chain! They reduced the limits overnight. No amount of pleading helps. A promise to revisit limits 3 months later is not a solution for a running business.

Be Prepared to Rough It Out

Entrepreneurs	Toufic Kreidieh (T) and Yasser Beydoun (Y)
Company and website	Brands for Less/www.brandsforless.org & www.brandsforless.ae
Business	Outlet retail
Year established	2000
Tips for entrepreneurs	• Be prepared to rough it out. Entrepreneurship is not easy. It is stressful. But it is fun. • Be honest. Honesty pays. • Don't be greedy. Business is built through partnerships. Don't ruthlessly negotiate with suppliers till it hurts them. Greed can destroy a business. • Compensate staff well. They stand long hours to serve customers.

Describe BFL.

T: We are retailers. We are a chain that operates outlet stores across the GCC and Middle East. Every retail company needs a few outlet stores. All our stores are outlet stores. We started the business in Beirut with the intention of offering branded products at affordable prices. We initially looked at Germany and USA as a source of brands and merchandize. We couldn't get brands to sell products to us. We targeted major department store chains that wanted to liquidate end-of-season leftover stock. We help retailers manage their end-of-season inventory, a problem of the industry.

How did you begin?

T: Yasser and I are school friends. We started the business in a small underground garage in Beirut. We started our first outlet in Dubai in 2000 after establishing two stores in Beirut. We relocated to set up our HQ in Dubai because of the business environment – facilities, customs duty laws, tax-free jurisdiction and government facilitation of business. Our business has grown. We own and operate forty stores in seven different countries, with headquarters in Jebel Ali.

How much did you invest to start the business?

T: We just knew that the Lebanese love brands; they know brands and are big spenders. We started with US$10–15,000. We had nothing in our pockets.

Y: Our initial earnings were small but whatever we made we put back into the business. We had no help from banks or anyone else.

What was your background in retail?

T: Both of us studied business. We took jobs for a limited time. Once we started the business it required all our attention. We had taken a decision to start while being employed.

How did you think of walking into a company and asking them for inventory?

T: I assumed they would love it. But for them to believe in our ability of buying quantities was the first challenge we faced. We started with one container. We sold it and showed them what we had done. We then moved to two containers and then three. I believe they were encouraged by our consistency, loyalty and intention of developing a business relationship.

Which was the first company you purchased from?

T: Different USA Department Stores. We were lucky that they had a program of selling residual inventory. We had to fill up an information form to help them profile us. We fit their profile and business started. Our second big hit was Tchibo from Germany in 2004.

How did you pay Suppliers?

T: Cash before delivery.

Did you select merchandize?

T: In our business you don't select. We buy container loads.

How were you confident that you will make money?

T: We are Lebanese. We value brands. We know that brands mean something to end consumers. There is a risk in everything. We also believe, believed then and now, that every item can be sold for a price. This is our motto. We keep reducing the price until a product is sold. Even if the price reaches one Dirham and the cost is higher, it doesn't matter.

Did any company reject you when you wanted to buy old inventory?

T: Yes. But we keep on trying to convince suppliers till today. Some companies, especially high-end brands, destroy their goods rather than sell old inventory at a discounted price through channels like ours. Today the price of a brand at retail is a function of the cost of production that includes brand building plus profit. For a high-end brand the cost of brand building is often many times higher than the cost of production. It is therefore better to destroy leftover merchandize.

What was the cost of the first container?

T: $10,000. Our entire savings.

Did you expect to make money?

T: We had a dream to make money. We had to experiment. We opened the store in the garage of the building where we lived. Lebanon is disorganized. We had no restrictions on using a garage. Our fixed cost was nothing. Initially we just hired one person. We were able to make 70% profit. We then knew we had a business. The margin was based on no salaries for us and no overheads. We used to do everything with our own hands. When we started in Dubai we leased a warehouse in Sharjah. Yasser and I followed the same approach when the first container arrived. We ourselves worked to sort goods in the warehouse with no air-conditioning.

The same cautious approach?

T: Yes. We used to transport the goods from the warehouse to the store in our personal cars. I recollect sweating in the warehouse with no staff, wondering whether the temperature was 50 degrees. We had to go through all the containers, separate and consolidate products, do pricing and packing for store. We then had to display products in the store, open the store and start the cash tills. We were running the store and working the warehouse. Warehouse work was done at night after store closure. Those were 24-hour shifts! It was difficult but it paid off.

When did you give up your job?

T: Before opening the second store. About one year after the garage store opened. We knew that the business would give us a salary. We had to take the plunge and risk it. We needed to concentrate on the business otherwise we wouldn't cover our daily expenses. We knew it would be tough. We also believed things will start getting better. We had also believed early on that our jobs were always going to be temporary.

Did the business evolve as planned?

T: Beirut has uncertainty. The whole country is political. The economy can tank with one bad news. But we are resilient. No matter what happens we keep on growing. Plus we can make money. This is why Dubai came up. We needed a place that is safe and has no government bureaucracy.

This is why Dubai?

T: There was another important perception. Lots of Lebanese were coming to Dubai. We were selling to them in Beirut. We knew we could sell to them. If Lebanese purchased, we could then sell to other Arabs. Today we are catering for all nationalities.

Y: One thing that motivated us, shifted the balance to move, was the issue of customs duties; overnight they increased in Lebanon from 5% to 35%. Plus the levy was going to be on the weight of goods rather than the invoice. We became insecure about our business. We needed a place with more predictable laws where we could build a future.

You never felt that bringing end-of-season merchandize to Dubai would be an issue?

Y: Till date it's not an issue.

What was the capital required to restart?

Y: We had $100,000 between us. The shop took $50,000 and the first container was $12,000.

Who ran Beirut as you restarted in Dubai?

T: Yasser stayed in Beirut. We split when we restarted to keep the business running.

How did you decide the first location?

T: In October 2000, Deira was the heart of Dubai. Plus it had a mix of all nationalities. We needed Arab customers to jump-start the business by being visible. We bumped into an 1800 sq. ft. empty store. We leased half of it. Our first store was a tiny store. It fit our budget. We found an apartment next to it to cut our transportation time and cost. This is how we used to think. Plus this size was all we could afford at that time.

How long did you take to establish the business?

T: Three solid years. We opened the second outlet in 2002 but the business started working in 2003. We had expected the same level of acceptance for the products like in Beirut but it took time. Customers were very different. Our growth depends on word of mouth. In Beirut if we opened a store in any neighborhood, and are giving a good deal, in six months the whole city will know about it. Dubai has many nationalities. Every community is like a closed circuit. Word of mouth spreads within communities, not across communities. Hence it takes time. It's unlike Beirut.

Were your margins comparable to Beirut?

T: Margins are comparable. Products are cheaper because of duties.

When did Yasser join you here?

T: I called him when we reached the fourth shop. I told him the business here was going to get bigger. Both of us used to do the buying.

Did you start getting credit?

T: We expanded suppliers but it was still cash. We were credible outlet operators. Brands used to call us to help liquidate stock.

How did you decide the store name 'Brands for Less'?

Y: It was a description of the business. When it started a lot of things didn't happen in a logical way. We are now thinking of branding. It didn't happen in this way. And most things didn't happen the way we thought they would.

T: The name just came up in a discussion. Our business is something to do with brands. They want brands established in their mind. So we put this in a commercial name. It is a very simple name. Easy to recall and describes what the store does; it sells brands at low prices.

When did you start organizing the company?

T: It happened in 2001-6. We creating an organization chart and started to create departments. The present warehouse is our 6th. We moved warehouses as we expanded. Even in the last move in Jebel Ali, as we moved from 2000 m^2 to 10,000 m^2, we were already planning another move. We have over 1200 staff including Lebanon.

How did you become an entrepreneur? Was it in the family?

T: It is not in the family. I think it is in the country.

How did your partnership with Tchibo come about?

T: Tchibo is a large retailer in Germany. We were initially liquidating their overstocks. The business became bigger and we became their only franchisee in the world. As the business started growing we looked at our contractual relationship. We had started with a supply contract, guaranteeing supplies for two years. It got extended for another three years. Then it became a franchise with unlimited automatic renewal. This was a major landmark for us. All the stores sell Tchibo products and we have standalone Tchibo stores in malls.

You sell a wide variety of products – clothes, appliances, etc. How have you organized for category management within Brands for Less?

T: Most of our business works on trial and error. We see a product and decide what price it may sell at. Because we believe that everything sells at a certain price we tag a price and get it to our stores. We display it and watch the volumes that are generated. It is then no different from any other retailer. We accumulate knowledge based on which products have been accepted at what price by the clients. Pricing is the heart of our business. We establish guidelines to be followed.

How are you different from a traditional retailer?

T: We have the ability to buy four containers of unseen merchandize and create a store. We didn't know this when we started. We learnt as we evolved.

Y: We didn't have retail background so maybe we could think differently. We learnt how to price and bring prices down. Aging is our important variable. We don't allow goods to age. We are doing nearly 1000 containers a year. We don't have aged inventory. We keep slashing prices till it gets sold unless it is defective.

What attracts customers to your stores?

T: Our stores have a surprise factor. We deliver products every day to the stores. Customers know that they will see something novel/new every day. Our pipeline is always fresh. Our daily supply chain and IT system are our strengths. Plus our ability to change prices frequently.

What concerns you about the business?

Y: Finding the right suppliers. We have to keep looking. We have to keep on moving. We cannot stand still. One thing which is very dangerous for our business is the greed of the landlord. Rates are always rising.

T: We have 1200 families that depend on us. Nothing uncertain should happen to hurt them. Other concerns are the regular worries of a retailer – our ability to give novelty to customers every day, cash management and security surveillance. We must endeavor to entertain customers every day.

Were you impacted by the economic crisis?

T: It was a golden age for us. Lots of quantities were available.

How have you changed as persons with the growth of the business?

T: We became financially more secure. Financial security has given Yasser and me an opportunity to help people. It gives us real satisfaction to help someone who is in real need. And you know you're able to do it.

What made you succeed as entrepreneurs?

T: I think our partnership, the trust that underlies the partnership.

How do you manage different points of view?

Y: We have disagreements.

T: One should bear in mind that not all decisions are going to succeed, be 100% effective. When 10 or 20% failures happen it is a failure. No finger pointing should happen. In business, decisions can be changed.

What caused you to grow?

T: We worked with our own hands and reinvested all our earnings. Only in 2013 we started drawing full salary from the business. And we believed in ourselves. I believe luck plays a part; it's when you get the right product at the right time in the right place at the right price. We took a decision to come to Dubai and restart the business. We took a risk and worked for another three or four years before the business became successful.

Y: We didn't buy new cars. We deprived ourselves of many things for the first five years as we were building the business. We didn't take vacations with our friends who were employed. Our first vacation was in 2005–6.

Message for entrepreneurs starting out.

T: Be prepared to rough it out. Entrepreneurship is not easy. It is stressful. But it is fun. Be honest. Honesty pays.

Y: Don't be greedy. Business is built through partnerships. Don't ruthlessly negotiate with suppliers till it hurts them. Compensate staff well. They stand long hours to serve customers. Greed can destroy a business.

Need to Be Tense All the Time

Entrepreneur	Mohamed Nasser
Company and website	WMS Metal Industries/www.wmsmi.com
Business	Fabrication and installation of general and stainless steel products
Year established	2007
Tips for entrepreneurs	• Plan business execution time. It always takes longer than what you think. • Probability of your forecast numbers matching the real numbers will be close to zero. Preparation enables you to manage the unforeseen. • Other people's advice/guidance will not be useful. Every entrepreneur's journey is unique.

Tell me about the company.

WMS, established in 2007, is a fabricator and installer of general and stainless steel products for building construction, oil and gas, manufacturing and waste management applications. We are four partners who went to college together. My partners invested the capital and I was the managing partner. The company got established in the first year with the support of the partners. Dubai was starting to boom. There were just 10–15 tall buildings. We managed to compete. The market was small. We became the leader for the kind of work we did. We managed to establish very good relations with two of the biggest construction companies in Abu Dhabi to get work. We targeted revenue of AED 10 m per year. This required us to manufacture additional products using steel for different parts of buildings, beyond which it is commonly used. As an example we looked at opportunities in making stainless steel handrails. We wanted to offer multiple services and solutions. In 2008–9 there was a serious hiccup in the construction sector. We managed the downturn by using the strategy we were thinking of; offering a wide spectrum of services using steel in construction. It was very tough and still is tough. In 2008–9 it was a question of survival. Yet we grew year over year. In 2010–11 the cycle changed. We regained the confidence to start thinking about the future, not dwelling on the challenges of the past. We needed to restart using the hard work already done. In 2011 we divided the company into two divisions – WMS Fabrications and WMS Green. WMS Fabrication is the construction arm which fabricates steel solutions for construction. It is our bread and butter. We also had realized the need to be innovative to create sustainable growth. Tall buildings have steel chutes to manage waste so we decided to focus on waste management engineering. We have since developed our own technology for recycling. We filed for a patent in the US for a green recycling technology.

What were the first thoughts when you got this option to start the business?

The seeds of entrepreneurship came from my grandfather. He used to go to school on a donkey and at the age of forty was arguably the richest man in Egypt. I was fortunate to live with him when I moved to Egypt for three years. They were the formative years of my life. He used to tell me there are two paths in life, the easy way and hard way. All you have to do is know the hard way and know that that is the right way. I was working in a very large construction company in the UAE and was doing very well. I was one of the youngest engineers to occupy the position. But it seemed easy. I thought I needed to something a little more difficult, to push the limits of my potential. I think my grandfather was a strong part of the trigger. I enjoy working in teams but also like to work by myself. I don't like to influence other people's visions and ideas. I prefer to have my own visions. I always saw two windows of opportunities to do my own thing. One, I could experiment when I did not have any personal commitments. If it worked I could go do an MBA and get a career. Two, delay the choice to after having a career and saving money for family security and business.

What did the family say when you wanted to be in business?

My parents were always supportive. I am a product of their upbringing. They advised me to take the GMAT exam. They said if you don't do well with the business you can do an MBA. So they were covering up for contingencies, they supported me financially and morally. I was twenty-six at that time.

WMS has investors. How did you evaluate the business opportunity for yourself?

It is not all about money. Shohaib and I have a lot of mutual respect for each other. When he thinks there is a little idea then it is usually a good idea. We looked upon WMS as a launch pad. If things went sour in construction, we could grow in other areas.

I am just looking at it from the point of view of evaluation. You have a relationship with a person who is putting in capital. They come up with the idea and you are the brain to execute it, realize it. How did you evaluate the choice? Was it a risk-free opportunity?

Absolutely not. Not at all. You do a business plan when you start. Create a financial model of the business. We had lots of data in our financial plan that may or may not be accurate. Then you do a risk analysis. Yet without my business partner's revenue support I do not think the company would have taken off. Even though SMEs have a lot of focus in the UAE, a legacy business like the construction company needed a track record. We were relatively fresh. Our CVs showed we were starting from scratch.

Did it ever cross your mind to outsource garbage chute production? Why make something as simple as a chute?

Big construction companies subcontract work where they don't have in-house expertise like elevators and mechanical works like chutes, etc. These need to be installed and somebody has to do it. At a macro level it is possible to create smaller subsidiary companies within a large umbrella organization, each doing some specialized work so that they minimize outsourcing. We are a standalone company and there is no obligation between us and our partner's father's company. They had previous experience in market and it was an undersupplied market. The market needed a quality provider of this solution.

You had a customer who gave you a price indication of what they were prepared to pay and you reverse engineered the product that became your business. Did it cross your mind after chutes, what next?

From day one, we have aligned the company to become a steel and stainless steel fabricator. We were aware that chutes were to be used to enter a tight market because a lot of companies do steel and stainless steel fabrication and margins are low. We needed a niche product to enter the market at a healthy margin. We could then use the margin to focus on other niche work. We were not going to be a garbage chute company, and we are not one now. It represents about 50 % of our earnings presently and we now offer a wide variety of products and services to a range of customers.

Did you get a feeling when you started WMS that the salary would be guaranteed by the business? Or you had to earn it?

I took only a skeleton salary as the manager partner, just enough to pay for my basic bills. My life would be built based on profits. We decided that the managing partner of a business needs to have performance-based compensation.

Where did you acquire the technical skills to manage the business because you came from the construction industry? You said this was new for you.

As an engineer you are pretty much aware of processes and procedures. We tied up with a UK firm for the technical expertise of chute manufacturing. Our engineers got trained in the UK and then we developed our own solutions and customizations. Acquiring expertise is easier at a technical level. Managing business is different. I was working in a construction company in the technical division. I was always interested in financial numbers. I got exposure to numbers for over a year. Then I wanted to study Business Management.

Learning?

More and more is needed as you grow. We have grown from an eight-person company in 2007 to over 200 people in 2012. I have learnt the meaning and value of delegation. There is no sense in my controlling the business. It is inappropriate to want to do everything because then the execution bandwidth is limited. I am married now, have a family and need to maintain a work-life balance. There is no sense in creating a procedural bottleneck because it satisfies some egotistical need to be the one party that authorizes everything. I have to invest in support systems through which our management team can carry the burden effectively, if not better than me. While building the company, the first two or three years, centralization is fine. One is building the company brick by brick, buying machinery and looking at every single expense, while seeking business, getting every project on board. Only up to a certain point responsibility and accountability can be on my shoulder. This is one of the best lessons I have learnt.

You are starting an enterprise. You have a customer. You have a technology from the UK. Your team strength is eight. You have to execute a project. Was it as simple as this?

Everything we did was a learning experience. My first team member and I, we often reminisce. We had no idea about anything. We didn't know certain procedures of steel fabrication. Today we can roll, bend, cut, weld and drill to make a garbage chute using a few processes. It is very simple. Our first project was a two-story building. I walked past the building recently. We were so proud of our work and the first AED 5000 advance payment, our own money. We learnt how to deal with our subcontractors and if we were at the bottom of the supplier value chain we learnt how to manage clients. We learnt how to manage our suppliers because suppliers have more power over you when starting up. We learnt payment terms, advances, supplies and documentation. We learnt how to manage sites. We also learnt that work happens on sites and payment comes from the HO. We learnt how to document discussions on site so as to avoid payment hassles. We can keep the project site manager happy by giving him material or doing work as instructed by him in good faith. But the HO may be unaware of the going on and no payment will be forthcoming. Knowledge of legal contracts, managing staff, control of man hours, tracking projects, etc. were all new to me. Over time I learnt how to deal with cost fluctuations. The price of stainless steel when we started January 2007 was around AED 12000 Dirhams per ton. In June the same year it became AED 18000. We had to learn managing raw material price fluctuations.

Did you have a situation where you went to somebody for a prequalification and they said, who are you?

In 2007 and 2008 it was more of the rule rather than the exception with both contractors and consultants. We were competing with two or three big players. We did one thing and discovered another. We invested in our corporate identity. We made sure that our prequalification document was like a technical study. We learnt the important role of the consultant in projects. Whenever we met the consultants before the submission of prequalification documents, we had a greater chance of being approved. Otherwise we were dismissed from the outset. Once not considered it is difficult to get back into reckoning. We were once executing a project that went through lots of problems before completion. My sales manager and I used to wait outside the consultant's office every day for a few hours and we couldn't get a meeting. That is not the case now.

What about suppliers? Did they say they won't give you credit because they don't know who you are?

This was the case for at least a year and a half. After which our bank was supportive and gave us free credit facilities. We had an OD line running.

You were using your own capital. How did you grapple with the cash flow of contracting?

There are few moments that are not tense. I was in Egypt this weekend. I left on Thursday came back Sunday night. I am concerned every waking hour. I am worried about expenses, safety of workers in work being done on tall buildings. We recently had workers on the 58th floor of a building. When I am around DIP and I see a fire, I double check on my business. Receivables are a regular concern. I can't delay staff and labor salaries by a few days. I worry and can't sleep at night. There is only one day every month when I feel relaxed, the day I pay out salaries. There are tensions all the time. It becomes a way of life. I now believe you need to be tense all the time. The tension doesn't end. It is the business owners' tension.

You carry the stress. How do you manage this stress?

I think this is something that you are willing to sign up for from the beginning. This is the tradeoff. You have to have your family and friends understand the pros and cons of the choice. If you want to be an entrepreneur, your own boss, these are the sacrifices you make. How do I manage it? At my personal coping level I think through sports and meditation. My wife is my pillar of support. I was worried about getting married because of the responsibilities. I am responsible for my employees and for my family as well. Having a supportive spouse sharing the worry of the team at home helps in coping. I don't take office worries home. In a nutshell, a supportive family helps manage the stress.

Did you tell if your wife what she is getting into?

I am as upfront about the business as I can be. This is our lifestyle. We are living in a high-risk sort of existence and she is aware of this from the beginning.

Innovations that you have done?

I have four thrust areas. We wish be known as an innovative company. We are working on an innovative recycling system that separates different types of waste. We are developing bins that can be used in public places effectively, economically and innovatively.

Business concerns?

We have done well as a company. It's always a worry because business performance may be fleeting. We want it done very well today. We don't want it undone tomorrow. So I don't reflect on successes. Success is in the past and the past is past. I look ahead. It is more appropriate to ask what is innovative in what we do and what is not. And we are not magicians. We make a lot of mistakes and we continue to make mistakes, doing things that are not a 100% in terms of the operations and procedures. We do this because of our limited capabilities and resources. I am fine to talk about innovations that we've done in the business. The success is the fruit of a lot of hard work and sacrifices from everybody. It's my good fortune to be surrounded by people who see the company as much as their own as mine. And are willing to make a lot of sacrifices to bring us where we are. As I look forward to become an innovation-based company, I also look backward at where we started.

How was your customer acquisition process? How are you more efficient today?

I learnt from the rejections. The biggest lesson I have learned in terms of customer acquisition is customer attention that becomes customer satisfaction. The market is small. Members of the construction team – project manager, site engineer, site manager and procurement manager – may be allocated to different projects or may join new companies. It is from the satisfaction of these four people that I may get four more projects. Nothing beats giving the client-focused attention, providing good quality and maintaining customer satisfaction. When it comes to doing extra work to achieve customer satisfaction, I don't mind incurring a loss. I know what I will lose today by executing well, I will recover tomorrow. I have to make sure that the companies we work with are credible companies and potentially repeatable clients. We also work in a spirit of partnership. So even during the recession, when money wasn't being paid to us, we knew that our money was guaranteed. And we are part of a process where we could sit down with management and accounting departments of our customers to work through the situations. In turn we did the same with our suppliers. We have established the reputation that our word is important, we are here for the long haul, not to make a quick buck.

Next key steps?

We are looking to hopefully raise some capital and bringing a strategic partner into the business. We are looking to create products for three different markets – waste separation, recycling benzene and oil and grease separators for commercial use. We want to move into oil and gas as a sector to reduce our dependency on construction.

When you first started pricing, did people say give us to price or did they say, we know what the cost of all this is; we will do a cost-plus model?

In construction nobody works with a cost-plus model. In UAE construction is a cost-plus model for large contractors working on large projects. We price based on our estimates of project cost and add a margin. Our buyers care about their cost not what the costs are.

Most important worry?

Cash flow.

How have you changed as a person?

I much more humble. When I was 26, I was very aggressive. I thought I was the smartest person in the world. I have become wiser with age. We went through very tough times and have come out. I am more philosophical. I want to do my best and then see if the market accepts it or not.

After how many years did you draw your first full salary?

I started drawing what I would earn in the construction business after three years of start.

Was there anything you have completely unlearned after you started the business?

Working as a contractor you get away with thinking that aggression and pushing suppliers is a way to move the business. It is not. You can get the job done without being tough on suppliers, contractors or the people. I now appreciate the value of being nice. I was a young person in a responsible position. I probably used aggression as a means of acquiring extra legitimacy; to pretend to be older than my real age. You don't get away with success if you are a bad person. One needs to be a nice person and respect everyone.

Guidance to a new entrepreneur?

Plan your business execution time well. It always takes longer than what you think. Study your business well. Think of what if scenarios. But remember that what you envisage may not happen. Preparation will make you ready to respond to changing situations. Any advice that somebody gives you, would probably not be applicable because everyone has their own journey. You will have your own unique journey. Any number of articles and books you read will not forecast the future. The probability of your forecast numbers matching the real numbers will be close to zero. But it's also very important to talk to people and theoretically study the business inside out.

◉ ◉ ◉

Belief Was in Me and the Bet Was on Me

Entrepreneur	Khalid Al Shami
Company and website	Al Shami Sugars/www.alshamisugar.ae
Business	Sugar tube packaging
Year established	1999
Tips for entrepreneurs	• You have to deep dive into everything when you are creating a business.
	• Business requires sustained effort. Once water starts to flow, nothing will stop it.
	• Learn when to say no and what not to do.

Describe your business.

I am in the packaged sugar business. When consumers use packaged sugar in a coffee shop they often use it without much thought. I package sugar (and sweeteners) in ready-to-use single-serve packets. Consumers are discerning. I work to make the consumer feel the difference. Every small detail – the paper, its quality as felt by touch, the printing based on the inks used, visual detail, sharpness, etc. – all make a difference. This requires investment to achieve the desired quality of detail. I realized quickly that our business was about the presentation and not the sugar; packaging versus product.

Are competing companies giving high-quality products in this market?

Not in Dubai. Difference is more discernible in other parts of the world. I positioned our products at the premium end by increasing the quality of product and packaging. I knew what I did not want to make. My business is about attention to detail and no detail escapes attention because every small detail can add or subtract value. This approach emerged from our engagement with consumers. When we sit with customers, they go into details of paper, printing and product cost. It was appropriate for a vendor to offer a variety of options of product, paper and printing for customers to choose from. I started offering better quality at a time where competitors were offering cheaper quality raw materials. It starts with packing high-quality sugar, since the packaging cost is greater than the cost of packed sugar. We became sensitive to the quality and cost of paper packaging. We also focused on quality of the master carton, its look and feel. I instinctively pitched higher because I wanted everyone to experience quality. In matters of taste and quality I was projecting my experience of quality on consumers. Packaged sachets, apart from the B2B consumer, are used by convenience. I was not competing with loose sugar. A customer cannot compare packed sachets with loose sugar.

You created a product of high quality.

Absolutely.

When you started and met suppliers of raw materials and packaging material, were they ready to work with you as a new company?

Yes. If there is will, you can. It wasn't straightforward. We needed money. Lots of capital. I still struggle with balancing the books. It takes time to start with new suppliers and consumers. I used to pay cash to suppliers when I started the business. Rather, I started our business totally in cash.

Total investment?

I started with AED 280K in 1999.

After creating a sample how did you convince customers that you could be a new supplier?

It was difficult for me to get them to accept new products of a higher quality. It was very easy for me to convince a purchaser to agree about quality. The difference in price per carton of sachets was just AED 4 or 5. But every purchaser wants to demonstrate that he is doing a good job, that he is getting a cheaper product. They would ask me for the cheapest price. I was trying to start a business in my way and my potential customers were thinking another way. I targeted 5-star hotels. I thought they would be less sensitive to price. I didn't target small customers.

Who was your first big client?

The client that started me on my business journey was a large hotel chain. They said they will use us after approvals. I gave them samples of sugar, paper, etc. They obtained approvals from London. From that day onwards we supply their many properties in the GCC.

How did you decide pricing?

When I started I could not decide price as a markup of my costs. Cost is a given. Then there was the market price of similar products. I could not raise my price above this even if I was launching a new product. But I could use market price as a basis of some innovation. Profit margins in the industry or business are often a given. We are all buying and selling something that anyone else can do. What can we make above the industry norm is usually the question. Plus I was under pressure to speed to market. I had to start business cash flow. So I consciously took a decision to work with a lower margin, giving customers higher quality at the best price.

Should we be transparent sharing costs and margins?

I was selling quality. For customers to benchmark me with others they needed to see how my cost was built, the impact of quality at each component of cost. Commercial buyers are very detailed. I wanted them to know that I was not making an unreasonable profit.

When did you believe that you would make the income that you were making before you started the business?

Today customers accept that the product is of a higher quality and are willing to pay a premium price. They know that quality comes at a price. My idea was to launch and get it accepted. I wanted customers to experience quality. I believed that once they know the real costs, being a B2B product, an adjustment in price was possible. It happened the way we predicted. Today when a five-star brand opens, they call us. Initial years were challenging. Patience is bearing fruit now. We are now getting results. We are known in the trade.

What did your family tell you when you wanted to leave your trucking business and get into this?

They were afraid. In the initial months I worked two jobs. I worked in the other company during the day and in the new business after work. It was hard. I used to leave home at 7 am and return at 10 pm. It wasn't easy. But the goal was my motivator. The work, the journey to my goal, became my way of relaxing. I was absorbed in my goal.

How did you convince 5-star customers about your product? You were new to the business yourself.

Quality proves itself. More discerning the customer, the easier it is to sell. Convincing them about managing quantities and deliveries on time was a different matter. They sent people to visit our factory. We had invested in equipment for packing before we got a contract. We could show them that we had the capacity. We started supplying smaller coffee shops to assess acceptance, iron out all issues, before we approached the big hotels. Plus this quick start approach brought in cash flow. When we started we recruited a good salesperson.

When did the business become profitable?

In about six months. First few months were very slow. Once we made a few sales, we started covering our expenses. That is the time I quit my job.

When did you start taking the full salary which you were drawing earlier?

After two years. I took my first holiday three years after starting the company.

Any important challenges and milestones?

Managing cash flow was a challenge and a learning experience. Every supplier gives hotels 90-day credit. We didn't have the working capital. This was the gap I had to bridge. So I decided not to take a salary. I wanted to ensure that the staff got their full salary. Getting good quality raw material was a challenge. This pushed me to start importing. And this enabled me to learn about different qualities and sources of sugar. We source our own sugar. This also made us better in predicting quantity of sugar to be purchased. We couldn't do this for four years after we started. Our sales quantities were not enough and our working capital was not enough. We did not put any more money in the business. It was a lot of sacrifice. My partner did not put pressure on me but being an owner I sometimes didn't take salary for three-months and then took the dues when cash was available.

When did you shift the production to a bigger location?

First time, four years after starting the business. We have since moved three times. We will now move again. We have now managed three key ideas – sourcing, cash flow and scale.

Did you ever think, what have I got myself into?

No. I was always having the hope, rather, belief. That is why I left my job to do free work. Even though the family was skeptical. When they look back they know that the decision was right. They didn't support my decision in the beginning. Even though they said yes, it was more to just play along.

Was starting up easier than you had imagined?

No. Nothing was easy at the beginning. It looks easy once the business is established and when customers call us.

When did you create the FMCG model breaking into Carrefour?

We launched the consumer pack in 1999. Initially we didn't carry the consumer packaging. We had a 3 Kg pack for coffee shops. We then tested smaller packs and now most supermarkets carry our products.

Which year did you shift to selling to consumers from businesses?

It was in 2005. This required a completely different method of selling. We had to do point-of-sale merchandising. We had to ensure goods were always available. I didn't have to learn anything new. I partnered with a company that was in this business. They had teams to manage this. This was the best way to move forward.

What is the next phase of growth?

We are getting buyers from different countries. We have appointed agents in some countries.

Was recruiting people a challenge?

In the beginning. We couldn't find readymade operators for the machines. We had to start with inexperienced operators. Then they brought others. We now have many machines and have recruited a person to train others.

Did you borrow money from banks?

We have created the company entirely from the income and efforts of the team. We have injected some capital at each stage of company growth based on need. It never happens as people think – money first and action later. The initial startup capital exists but subsequent injections were need driven. Belief was in me and the bet was on me.

What worries you about this business?

We know what we are doing. We are in the commodity business. Sometimes prices of sugar shoot up. Our clients now work closely with us. We quote them prices for many months ahead. Sometimes prices can rise. We have to be agile and look for new clients at new prices. We then balance the loss of one client with another. Sometimes clients can also lose on a contract. It is a game of relationships and of mutual accommodation. I just signed a contract for supplying sugar for seven to eight months. The client couldn't commit for one year. This is risky; I am buying today and fixing the price as of today. I could win or lose. There is always a threat of losing clients when the contract terms are finishing. Some clients say no and search for cheaper products. Others are more aware of commodity prices, trust us and agree. This is the most difficult challenge. Managing clients in volatile price markets is a skill of the company.

Managing contracts is the second big part of your business.

Our business is about relationship and partnership. We are always searching for companies to lock prices for 12 months. In front of the commodity price swings, we are helpless. But this is where work experience teaches us. Our major clients are hotels. When the economy slipped in 2008–9 they took a big hit. It took three years to recover. We could not sit back and see business fall by 50–60%. We immediately started pushing our agents and offering products to other countries. It worked. Market dropped 50% to 60% but our drop was limited to 33%. The idea is to never take it easy.

Have you changed as a person implementing the business?

Pressure from business situations has pushed me to change. When the market crashed in 2008–9 I was under great uncertainty. I was pressurizing the staff to complete jobs. I had to make them work beyond normal hours but was compensating them beyond what is required by law. I lost a bit of heart, my humaneness. To maintain things you have to let something go. Change helped me grow.

What guidance will you give a new entrepreneur?

Business requires sustained effort. Work with a clean heart. Make little profit but make it honestly and in the right way. Once water starts to run like a river nothing will stop it. We are committed to make good products. Occasions arose where people asked me to use cheaper raw materials of lower quality. I rejected the opportunity. It wasn't me. We didn't have to sell those products. I learned when to say no and what not to do. I have even rejected requests for cheaper quality cartons. Some people have come to me to break distribution-agent relationships offering me double the sales quantity. I don't switch relationships in a hurry.

Is it easy to do business without paying intermediaries?

I have faced similar situations. People may ask but we have the option to refuse. We give gifts for office parties or host a seminar for our partners but we don't pay purchasers.

Should an entrepreneur test his idea before giving up his job?

Only if he can. Two jobs are not to test the idea. It is more about the physical capacity to do two things.

Is there a strategy which you have used throughout?

I have always maintained a close relationship with customers. I address their complaints immediately. I work on the principle that the client is right, even if he is wrong. In our business it is ok to give a few cartons free as an offer. It is a practice in the trade. I use this practice to keep clients happy.

How important was personally selling when you started the business?

This was very important because I got immediate customer feedback. I needed to win their trust. This happens only when you meet them. They need to read you, your body language, etc., and develop trust in you. In addition I was in a position to discuss price. It did not have to wait for a later time.

You learned about sugar, you learnt about equipment, you learned paper and packaging, as you set up the business. Why? And is this what an entrepreneur should do?

You have to deep dive into everything when you are creating a business. Now the startup has become a business. Therefore you find me in the office. There was a time when I used to travel with the driver when he was delivering goods to understand how delivery was being done, was he late, how much time he was taking, was my driver smiling, was he tough, was he clean, how was he responding to questions, answering complaints, etc. And was there anything I could do to make it work better for the customer and the staff. I went deep into the process, understanding all the steps. If there was any product feedback or complaint, I could trace it to the source. For your business you have to be on top of your work. You have to manage everything and correct the errors as they arise.

Entrepreneurs are like you. They observe a lot, see opportunities and are willing to learn.

Nobody pushes them. They push themselves. I push myself, even though it costs money. If I move a little, my people will also stretch themselves. I can lead and drive the people or push them. I prefer to lead. I am always experimenting. I want some innovation always. Chemistry is the basis of sugar. I have learnt how sugars differ based on where they come from. Some sugars are good with coffee. However, if you put it in tea, its taste may not be good. I am testing sugar with Cardamom flavor. It is just an idea I got because I observe people. They have tea and coffee with Cardamom. I thought why not use sugar as a platform to experiment. I have tested this.

Discounting Is a Downward Spiral of a Business

Entrepreneur	Ibrahim bin Shaheen
Company and website	DGT/www.igt.ae
Business	Trading of foodstuff and other grocery products
Year established	2003
Tips for entrepreneurs	• Starting a business is about execution details. • Time is the most important resource. • Learn, build and delegate.

How did DGT start?

I started DGTs in 2003. There were a few learning steps on the journey to become the business that we are today. I started trading fresh vegetables in 2006. I have an IT background and I was trading in vegetables through hypermarkets!

How did you enter hypermarkets?

Hypermarkets have procedures for fresh fruits and vegetables. They invite tenders. Potential suppliers bid. This is followed by a due diligence. After which we negotiate terms, supplies are made and collection happens. I was collecting the products from farmers and delivering to hypermarkets before collecting cash. It was a little challenging. It entailed risk. I was paying upfront and collecting later, with the risk of loss in between. Fresh produce is perishable. Shelf life is short. Not to mention the existing incumbents who had experience in managing the supply chain. We were new players. The threat of competitors managing price to pressurize us with a perishable product was real. This is where I learnt never to be overcommitted to a particular business and way of thinking. If something is not working, it is better to change. Alternative solutions always exist. New opportunities arise based on changing consumer needs and market trends. Speed is of essence. We need to have our finger on the pulse of the market and move fast. If we try to establish a business after the trend has become visible to everyone, establishing a business will become difficult.

What did you learn from this?

For me, business is about finding a product and a business model that works. As I experiment, I make sure I am not overcommitted. I enter, test and grow, or exit. An entrepreneur has to move on. The growth of Dubai is similar. We had oil. We moved on. We built the infrastructure, the port. We then added tourism. And we are now building the service sector. We have to learn from the DNA of Dubai and keep on persevering.

Where was the entrepreneur in Ibrahim?

I was working in the military. But the need to do something was building up. I felt constrained. I knew I was capable of much more. My creative urge found an outlet in my taking courses, assembling computers, etc. I finally decided that I had to take the plunge. I use the example of a fish out of water. I had joined the military because of family reasons.

When you started were you worried that the business may not work?

I embarked on my entrepreneurial journey in 2000. My first business was an IT company that was customizing applications. In 2002 our work was recognized as the best technology being implemented for schools. We developed an application using IVR technology for parents to engage with the school and teachers, and track their child's progress. Parents could use a password to access all school services like timetable, attendance and their child's educational progress. The application was a real-time bridge between schools and parents.

Was the business successful?

Yes. And then competition started. We had started working with banks as well. We could work in any domain where IVR was the basis of customer relationship. The IT business is about applications. The business model is long gestation – pitching, winning, detailing of the scope, execution and deployment. Competition worried me. This was when I realized the need for a more stable and growing business. Food was a natural choice. The move did not faze me. I am a flexible person. I am willing to take up any challenge. Imagine shifting from IT that involves working with professionals, based on procedure and goals, to working with many farmers, working with each farmer one at a time, without a backup team, without a purchase order and advance payment!

How did the food business happen?

I walked the aisles of supermarkets to guess the market potential of different products and assess the weak penetration of suppliers in some categories. My friends from the industry confirmed my perceptions and potential. Fresh produce had a lot of suppliers and most of them were small.

You had to get suppliers and customers.

I went directly to farmers. It was strange for them to see an Emirati coming to the farm. Initially they were scared. But I was friendly with them. I was like a student. I needed to be humble and polite to get into this business. I took my time. Fresh agricultural produce comes from different countries in different seasons. I learnt how prices change through the seasons. I also learnt how spot prices change. I had to tender a price for a period of time. If I gave an incorrect price I would either make losses or lose the contract. I decided not to have any storage. I would buy and deliver produce the same day. I wanted to keep costs low by not adding overheads. Even two-hour storage is problematic.

You needed to understand cost of the business?

And the risks. The fresh produce business has a damage repair policy. This can be expensive. I focused on products where the shelf life was longer.

Were the cooperatives willing to talk to you?

Yes. There was price competition. But I was a startup with limited overheads. So I took a price, a low price, to compete. I came to DubaiSME in 2006, learnt about the GPP and with their support could enter and compete.

How did the herb business begin?

I was more organized. I invested first; bought 2 trucks, 2 vans and recruited drivers. The challenge of the herb business is the cash cycle. Farmers want cash at the farm gate before goods are shipped. Here again the role of the Government Procurement Program of DubaiSME was important. They helped the cooperatives to release payments within 15 days of supply.

I tried to add fruits to my product mix. I experimented and exited the fruits business. I tried to use the formula of minimizing cold storage costs. The risk was much higher in the in-store wastage. I quickly realized that the business requires a very strong management of the field sales force. I exited the fruits business in 6 months.

I decided to focus only on herbs. It had a shorter supply chain and a process that was managed daily. My confidence is reflected in the decision I took to acquire a farm. I am today able to supply fresh produce to cooperatives and restaurants. Quantities are smaller but prices are higher.

After about a year in the herbs business, I got into the meat business.

Again for the cooperatives?

No, for the butchers. This is also a risky business. The product value is higher so is the risk of delayed sale. Once a container reaches, it needs to be sold within 24 hours otherwise the shelf-life risk kicks in. Prices can fall by 15 to 20% in a day.

How did you enter into this business?

My brother was area manager for Emirates in Bangladesh. He got the reference of a modern slaughterhouse searching to enter the UAE market. I used the connection to develop the business by obtaining all domestic approvals. The challenge of the business is in sales to small butcher shops on credit. They may or may not exist in a few days. Market entry was a challenge. Getting hygiene approvals is easy. I had to compete with products from Australia, India and Pakistan. Bangladesh was a new source.

How did you jump start the meats business?

I started with one strong client. He had fifteen branches. I was just lucky to meet him. I targeted pre-selling goods before arrival so that my cost of cold storage would be minimal. I was also lucky that the products from Bangladesh were experienced as superior. I have used a strategy of building relationships with key clients. If you are my customer, please get used to having coffee with me often.

Did you enter with a discounted strategy?

As a new player in an established market and I have to be flexible. I offer special prices to only few clients. The growth of my businesses has been driven by this approach. I develop volume momentum at a slightly discounted price.

Any other issues?

To maintain capital commitments into the business at the planned growth rate. Planned growth was based on the supplier's willingness to deliver quantities. Shortage of supplies became a challenge as the business picked up momentum. Since infrastructure in Bangladesh is weak and supplies often get disrupted, I had to maintain a bigger inventory to service customers.

When did the water business begin?

This was also a chance happening. I prefer the taste of French spring water. I tried this Turkish water brand and found it good. I wrote to the principals seeking exclusivity for the GCC. Experience had taught me to seek exclusivity.

I had burned my fingers in the meat business from Bangladesh. I established the brand and a Saudi distributor used the supplier to his advantage. When I was starting out seeking GCC distribution rights was difficult; who would give rights to a startup. My friends cautioned me that local water had higher standards than global brands and were available at low prices. Many people had attempted distributing new international brands of water and had failed. I really liked the product and went ahead. I think I got the distributorship because I showed them the team that would implement the business. I was able to gain entry into hypermarkets. This was critical for success.

How did you enter hypermarket?

I had to convince them personally. Push hard. It didn't happen naturally. I had to use all my networks and powers of persuasion. Not only does the water business require selling skills but also investment in supply chain and warehousing. I had to set up the infrastructure of the company – physical and intellectual. I am still a little different from a FMCG company. I work from farm to store and from airport to butchers; all channels where the products are sold. Supermarkets and hypermarkets had to be convinced that I could deliver quantities on order. Only then they would register the products.

In your story I am seeing Ibrahim developing as an entrepreneur.

I was willing to learn. If I went to a farmer, I listened more than I spoke. When you start a business, you learn to sell, present yourself to a supplier, learn to buy and learn to sell to customers. And there can be no delegation. You have to be involved every hour, every day. Who has the 'key' is very important. I can't send a salesperson to register a product. For him to meet the right people could be challenging. We are a small company. To instill confidence in our customers, our teams in office and our suppliers, the presence of a CEO who takes decisions and makes commitments is crucial. Also salespersons can often give higher discounts to achieve sales targets. As a CEO I am able to engage in balanced negotiations. As an entrepreneur you learn to be firm. You cannot compromise too early. You need to be aware of where you are headed – the scale of the business you are looking at – and see each sale as a step in that direction.

How did you know how much water to order? You didn't have a back-to-back customer?

We did not set up a target for the first order. I decided to use some initial capital for the first buy based on my confidence. I did some rough math. I could sell six containers, my initial order, in fifteen branches. I had to be careful. I could not target more than fifteen branches. If I sold more than expected, I would be out of stock. I could not lose the trust of the customer. I needed to build loyalty. A customer can easily switch. I also had to win the confidence of the supermarket. I called the supplier for six containers. I got the seventh free. The free container was to support launch expenses.

Wasn't this risky?

It was a risk and a challenge. It was better than discounting the product. Discount would have meant lower margin and no profit. It would have sent the wrong signal to the customer, that I was willing to accept a lower margin. I just wanted a small share of a large market. I had learnt it in my earlier business of IT, which wasn't very successful. Discounting is a downward spiral of a business. I had also learnt that as an entrepreneur I needed to think through the consequences of every decision. In my agricultural business I had learnt to always give more to customers, not less; give 101 gram in a bundle of herbs, not 95 grams.

You advise an entrepreneur to be involved in detail?

An entrepreneur CEO needs to be focused on detail. I needed to know how much time it is taking my staff to convert large supplies of herbs into 100 gram bundles – the entire process of unpacking, cleaning, repacking and labeling. Time is my biggest resource. Even family comes second. As a CEO I may have lots of time to myself in the future. Not while starting up.

Are you different from the other entrepreneurs you see?

I am a transparent person. I have established a meat and water business. I discuss business with my friends. Two friends have also established a water business. Rather, I forced them to get into the water business. Why? Ideas are free to share. It is not my unique idea but an opportunity in the market. What is different is the quality of business execution.

Where do you see your business going? And challenges?

I think I can grow the business in a competitive market. It is bigger than what I expected. I do think I now need to have proper governance, a team, since I am taking lots of decisions.

How has Ibrahim changed after becoming an entrepreneur?

I have become more mature. I study and think before I decide. I don't take quick decisions. I am more confident. I don't waste time. Time is my most important resource. As a distributor I don't look for products and brands where I will have to invest for ten years before making a return.

Lessons for a new entrepreneur?

I am a person who set up businesses by studying, learning and implementing everything with my own hands. Even today, after the business has grown, I still work the same way. Starting a business is about execution details. Do everything when you start to learn and build and then delegate. I have also seen that this helps the staff respect you. They know that you have done it. They know that you will guide and develop them. They come to me because I have done what I am asking them to do.

I am always conscious that I am what I am because of the team. This guides how I manage the business. I have learnt how to create internal competitions to boost sales. I make the team focus on customers. I tell them that customers pay our bills and our salaries. Our focus has to be on better customer service.

My business is about managing people to deliver. My job is to touch their hearts. Give them a feeling. Make them feel like owners. Give them the confidence to believe they can do it.

What is the bonus system you follow to reward performance.

Bonus is based on performance plus a share in the profits.

Is your brain of the entrepreneur always working?

I always look for what customers are doing and wanting. In a supermarket I don't look at shelves. I look at what customers are putting into their trolleys. I advise entrepreneurs wanting to start the food business to forget the project and see what your family members are doing every day.

Building a Business On-the-Job

Entrepreneur	Meghna Kothari
Company and website	McCollins/www.mccollinsmedia.com
Business	Digital Media and PR company
Year established	2010
Tips for entrepreneurs	• Self-belief is an entrepreneur's strength. Believe in yourself. Believe that you can do it.

Describe McCollins?

We are a 'Digital Brand Activation' and Public Relations company.

Explain.

Activation of brands on the digital space is much more than 'being' on YouTube, Facebook, Twitter, etc. The digital ecosystem involves numerous platforms that need to be integrated to work together. Plus the platforms are continuously evolving. We manage everything about a brand when it is taken online; how it is activated, nurtured and evolves. We integrate digital and PR because offline and online work well together. Say we launch a product. The PR conference may have a digital platform like a Google Hangout. We then track responses and reactions in the digital space. We create apps, manage Facebook sites, create digital videos, do SEO work, etc. We manage the entire digital domain work.

Exemplify.

Fujifilm as a brand is perceived to be about films rolls even though they make a range of amateur and professional cameras. Fujifilm cameras appear retro and are advanced cameras with lens akin to Nikon. Canon and Nikon have higher brand equity in cameras compared to Fujifilm. Our challenge was to position Fujifilm against Canon and Nikon. To activate the brand we needed to get cameras in the hands of professionals who know photography, use different cameras and could rate and rank cameras. We first used digital influencers and gave them cameras to use. We created a BlogSpot, a video blog, Instagram diaries, YouTube videos and a lot of user-generated content online. We created positive sentiment for the brand so that viewers feel that the brand is inspirational; if a person sees Nayla Al Khaja (first female film producer of the UAE) use the brand, she feels like giving it a try too. We started workshops to inspire amateur photographers to talk about Fujifilm cameras. We conducted workshops by brand advocates in all photography clubs of UAE. Fujifilm sponsored them and some Fujifilm cameras were given away. We discovered that there is a difference between the mirrorless technologies that Fujifilm cameras use and the normal DSLR lenses. If we see a person roaming around with the chunky big camera, you intuitively feel that he knows photography and is proficient. But if you see a person walking around with the small Fujifilm camera, the feeling is the opposite; you feel that the output of this camera is not as good as the bulky camera. We help create authored articles to educate people about the difference between mirrorless and DSLR technology, evaluate the pros and cons to enable judicious choice. Fujifilm camera started to get talked about. We went through an entire gamut of activities – creating awareness, educating people about the camera, getting advocates' pitch and motivating people to consider adopting the camera. Digital activation requires creation of content to be used on digital and social media platforms. Creating content enables the use of the content for traditional PR activities as well.

Are brands digital ready?

Digital activation happens in the context of a brand strategy. We often need to participate in the creation of the brand strategy because business goals for the region require adaptation to regional nuances. We assist in identification of brand goals, measures of performance, challenges and execution strategies. Most clients want us to participate in the creation of a digital strategy. We hesitate in executing a strategy without participating in its creation. We need to take responsibility for results. As marketing has moved into digital space, all KPIs can be measured in real time. This also enables us to assess what we are doing and modify it to reach brand goals.

How did you start?

I started three years ago. Our family is in the garment trade and retail. I joined the family business after my education in the US. I was born in a retail environment, studied retail and then discovered that designing and creating collections was not my thing. I learned this whenever I was told to market the collections, I would have my own ways of going about it. I was not very aggressive in my ways of working. I had short internship stints with Al Tayer and Virgin. I also realized that working with companies was also not my thing. My dad triggered the idea of starting an agency realizing my interest in brands and branding. I started my marketing company with a small business plan I had.

What was that plan?

I learnt from my dad to work the business plan backwards! Set the goal first. Say I want to sell 100 skirts. To sell 100 skirts at a target price point, I need to source or make the skirts at a target cost. He works backwards to estimate the costs of everything that goes into the business. I am comfortable with numbers. I guess that is inherited. Mom and dad always discussed business with us from the time we were sixteen. Our opinion was asked for and we were made to feel important. The dialogue was absorbing even though often not fully understood.

How did you target prospects?

I was selective. I discovered four kinds of companies. There were companies always in the news. There were brands that were well known but never in the news. There were companies whose websites were neither easy to use nor understand. And we had companies with zero social media presence. My research enabled me to identify companies to pitch to and how. I knew how to demonstrate our skills. My team does the same thing today.

How did you break into the crowded market of agencies?

No one wanted to meet me because I was so young. I called several people introducing myself. I never got a response. I had zero experience and zero credentials. People are very polite in giving me a listening but the interest ebbed when they realized that I was talking about my first project. This forced me to rethink my approach. If no one wants to meet me I had to discover a creative way of opening the door, to get my idea across. This is when the idea of using a courier came about. The recipient would have to open an envelope delivered by a courier. So I created a presentation that focused on what I imagined would be a strategy for a client. I needed a few known names on my client list. For a paint company (Jotun) I conceptualized the idea of a coffee morning with potential clients. I asked for a meeting, got no response. So I did what I could, I couriered the presentation. The manager who received the presentation, called me and asked me to start Coffee Mornings. That was my first breakthrough.

Why a paint company! How would you add value to them?

I had seen an advert on TV of how a person painted a painting in five minutes. It appeared very cool. I thought we could have a 'coffee morning' where an artist can come and paint a canvas. The idea didn't appear boring.

Learning in that first event?

I learnt how to create and execute an event and measure its effectiveness. I gave a detailed budget, the list of people I was inviting, invitation designs and an idea of a shopping cart to enable purchase. The objective was to reach 25–30 women who would participate and receive free consultation about interiors of their homes. I had to figure out who would come for consultation about their homes. The initial participants were selected carefully. I needed participants who knew about interiors and would buy or recommend to others. I managed to get a group together and the company sold something. We then had eleven Coffee Mornings till it became a monthly calendar.

And then?

The second client was Gargash Enterprises via my website. They wanted me to do a press release. I did not have experience in PR then. I was worried what may happen if it didn't work. I quoted a low rate and took external help to do the job.

The work you did with Gargash was not your skill-set. You were acquiring experience. They didn't have a problem with that.

They knew we were a raw startup. It was not just price. I had the backing of the family investment. We were not going to go out of business. I needed to decide to invest and acquire talent for doing the job needed. I was never short of expertise. I was confident in delivering on commitments. I never felt that I was young or I didn't know how to go about it or how business actually happens. I am sure they never felt us lacking. They got what they wanted or asked for. Better than they expected, I suspect and always on time.

The strategy worked.

We have worked with Gargash managing all elements of their marketing mix - advertising, design, radio, ATL, BTL, events and public relations. I recently approached them and requested that our work be reduced. We wanted to focus on being a public relation and digital brand activation agency. We still manage their PR and social media.

When did you decide to focus?

I never planned to get into the digital domain and focus. It happened eight months ago. I got three or four inquiries regarding social media. I went for meetings. Social media is not something you learn. It is a mindset and you create the ability through immersion, by doing. So I went right ahead, created strategies, proposals and impact assessments. I now have four social media accounts. And then I decided to focus on this emerging field.

How do you convince clients, who themselves may be uncertain?

I am confident about our skills in the social media domain. We have been working and experimenting with clients for eighteen months. We know what works and what doesn't. I have a clear idea of how the domain is evolving. We have not established guidelines on how we should decide what we should do and how we decide to do it after what has been firmed up. The digital space is dynamic. Each case is unique. When we meet clients, we present our credentials and case studies. I have to help clients increase sales and brand awareness. I first focus on identifying execution challenges. If I can enable sales brand awareness will be achieved. I rarely go to a client with a proposal of using social media to radically change the business. I only need to focus on and alleviate pain points. I am conservative in my proposals even when I guess that the client will be willing to spend more to increase sales. I am keener on allocating funds to strategies that can be tested and shown to work. Increased budgets can always be allocated when the business starts to work. I also don't cut prices to enter a business.

How do you price? You were underpricing when you started.

Underpricing is the wrong word in the creative domain. I needed credentials and cash flow when I started. Entering a new domain required me to work with clients who could be good references. The first few clients were acquired through sharper pricing. I quickly evolved to industry levels of pricing.

Challenges you face in your business?

Challenges relate to presenting a portfolio of clients. New clients trust me after I show them work I have done for others. People trust bigger brands; decision making regarding digital agencies is simple, 'If 'xyz' selected them, they are good.'

Do clients ask you to show measures or performance before signing a contract?

This has begun to happen. We have accumulated data after we had worked with ten odd clients and have case studies to demonstrate our capabilities. I am able to show the measures of performance and ROI.

How do you define outcomes of your work?

The focus of our work is always lead generation. I cannot check whether a client sold 1000 cameras. But I can certainly measure leads – additional new potential customers. Conversion of leads is the work of sales. Our goal is to create tools to make leads happen. This happens through all the social media platforms. A lead happens when a call to action occurs. We are working with an automobile client. We recommended the creation of big social media buzz by giving away a car on Facebook. The deal was for customers to give their contacts, visit the showroom for a test drive and have an opportunity to enter a raffle to win a car. This is an example for dramatic call for action.

Is the digital domain competitive?

The market has lots of competitors. Each company approaches business opportunity in their unique way; a different formula seems to be working for each one. Large agencies also have digital divisions doing this work. They also outsource to specialized boutique firms who have demonstrated track record.

You got the feel for business from the family. You experimented till you found the domain you wanted to work in. Were you sure that the family would support you as you experimented?

I never felt that there is a lot of capital and I could patiently discover my calling. This was not the type of capital my father gave me. My dad is an astute businessman. He gave me capital to show what I could do with it. It wasn't a free ride. My self-esteem and capability were on the line. I knew that if I did something wrong he would be there for me. I started with AED 250K. This lasted for six-seven-months. The first year was tough. He topped it up with an additional AED 150K. I started drawing a small amount for myself after year one since I was living with the family.

At any moment did you think that it might not work?

I did, even though I was profitable after the second month. I had done a few trading deals supplying promotional products. Then the recession hit. And I was chasing Jotun and Gargash. The initial opportunities (gifts, events) were like experimentation. I did events not because I wanted to. I needed clients. I gave up after eight months; too much effort for a small return. Gift item deals were for survival.

How much help did you get from the family?

He was working closely with me in the first year. The last two years the business has been smoother. He does not interfere. We have an understanding of the target we want to reach. I feel the need to go back to him. He must be having dreams for me. I always want to make sure that I am fulfilling his dream.

Surprises executing the business?

When I started I never wanted to label our company as a young agency. A big mature agency would connote experience. Now I love to call McCollins a young agency. This is our USP. We are selling a young team with fresh ideas. What we thought would backfire is working for us.

Is recruitment easy?

My initial team was very inspirational and did innovative things. They may not have had the best background and experience. But they wanted to achieve success. They are still with me today. I now don't use CVs for recruitment. I see the personality and digital capability before I recruit.

What do you look for in a person?

I look for self-confident persons. We are in the business of selling ideas. We need to be good in communication and social intelligence; know when to be loud, when to be silent, when to speak, when to listen and when to be calm, always focused and determined. Creative writing and visual creativity are very important traits for people in the social media business.

How do you manage the evolving nature of social media?

We achieve this through teamwork. Everyone can come up with innovative ideas. All of us – creative director, business development manager, social media manager and PR manager – brainstorm. Plus there is nothing like testing an idea versus evaluating an idea in a meeting. The cost of testing ideas in the digital space is low. We like to work with clients on three-month rolling plans. We can create digital assets like apps, videos, etc. The plan renews itself based on the outcomes.

Do you compete for marketing budgets of traditional marketing channels?

All the time. We want to and we want our clients to integrate with conventional channels. Since most global brands have guidelines on branding, marketing, digital marketing, e-commerce and use of media and channels, we like to conform. We also suggest options that factor the different nature of the consumer in the region and the need for digital assets in local languages. A realization is fast setting in on integrating social media and digital connectivity in all stages of the consumer journey. It is normal for a customer to Google for product information. In the store the use of QR codes on products enables instantaneous access to information. For our automobile client we worked on enabling customer access English and Arabic videos, consumer reviews and request for an appointment with a salesperson. The engagement with the salesperson is at a very different qualitative level when the digital engagement is high. Integration of offline with online is real and has to be engineered.

Would you walk away from a client?

I would, today. I need the client to trust my team and me. It is challenging to work with clients who doubt the agency. I use the metaphor of a doctor who operates. You can't question the surgeon, lying on the operation table. Some clients want the agency to execute what they have decided without creative engagement with us. We can do this but then we should not be held accountable for the outcomes.

What would make you tense today?

If client objectives are not met. If sales don't increase. I put myself in the shoes of the client and see the bigger picture. I track their goals.

Do you sometimes pre-judge prospective clients? You assess that you will not get an order. Or you still go through the full process of preparing proposals?

I always go through the full process. Every potential client and account is important. I may lose a client today but one never knows when our paths will cross again.

What is your people management style?

We are hierarchy free. We are in the idea business. We are open to new ideas and testing them. To nurture cross-fertilization of ideas, each person has to present workshops on particular subjects to everyone. Every person gets to know everyone else. Plus people realize how others are looking at the same thing and have a different take on the situation. We do a lot of other things e.g., Halloween parties, baking cakes for others, etc. In doing such activities we are relating to each other, we are working in situations where hierarchy disappears and we begin to appreciate other team members as people and not just professionals. I want every member of my team to believe that working in McCollins is like working in their own launch pad. I have grown with the team. With us each member can realize his or her creative and professional dream. I am different from my father. He would be a misfit if he came here. I have the determination to grow.

What worries you about the business?

Technology. Social media channels and platforms emerge and evolve. What is a primary platform today may become secondary tomorrow. The customers are also experimenting and evolving. Flickr was good at one point of time and then it became secondary. Facebook is in. Will it be displaced? We've got to be ready. Pinterest and Instagram are the new channels that have emerged. Customers are digitally overloaded with a plethora of channels. I am always worried about how we will get the attention of consumers in an age of digital overload. We will need to adapt and change rapidly.

How have you changed as a person in the last three years?

I have become a lot more confident, lot more enterprising and feel that I have what it takes to make things happen. I develop ideas and plans and make them happen. I don't wait for things to happen. I drive my team and network to achieve goals. I have become a better judge of people; when I meet someone I am able to gauge if he is serious or wasting my time. As an entrepreneur time is the scarcest resource. I want to be able to invest time to realize an opportunity. I have also learnt to spend time in defining a vision for my accounts and define how it will be executed. I have started to have and/or create a vision for each of my team members. When I started I was so young that I did not know how to nurture a team member.

Advise to entrepreneurs?

Figure out how you are going to be different. Be passionate and believe in yourself. There will be occasions when you will feel that you took a wrong decision. You just need to believe that you can pull through.

How important was business flexibility to you?

I did not change the business structurally. The PR team exists. Social media is vertical. I kept the verticals distinct. There were no cross-functional roles. As I grew, my search was for something unique that I could do for customers that others may not be doing. It was not about selling a service cheaper than somebody else. I have created my own ways of going about things. I have not picked up any processes, systems, or experiences from anywhere. I have done many things in creating the business of which I neither had experience nor academic knowledge. I have built the business learning on the job. It was quite a challenge to create a culture of an organization. I am very proud about the culture that I have created. That is our USP or my USP. I have created a team.

What is unique about you?

I think it is a vision thing, a thought process. I am a very practical person. I can break down any opportunity into its essentials to gauge its feasibility. I take decisions quickly. Where others may hesitate, I will quickly decide and test. I try to recover my costs quickly. I think this trait comes from my family experiences. The focus is never on big numbers. It is on doing quickly and not losing much.

Be Paranoid

Entrepreneur	Paul Oliver
Company and website	Absolute Adventure/www.adventure.ae
Business	Adventure Tourism
Year established	2005
Tips for entrepreneurs	• Commit 7 × 24 × 365 hours for three years (if not more) to make the company a success.
• Too much capital is bad for business.
• Don't just do what you are able to do. Match or better the best in the industry.
• Keep learning.
• There are no silver bullets. Focus on simple things, simplify complex things and take small, low-risk decisions.
• You will make mistakes and errors of judgment. It is like an entrepreneurial law. Take a decision, execute and correct the mistake if it doesn't work.

Describe your business.

Absolute Adventure is an adventure tourism specialist. We take our clients on outdoor trips, to destinations within UAE and overseas, giving them an experience of a real adventure. We give our customers a true adventure experience with excursions that involve activities like – rock climbing, trekking, mountain biking and water sports. I set up Absolute Adventure seeing a demand for professionally run local and international adventures.

How did it begin?

I started up Absolute Adventure to serve a need for outbound adventure tourism, i.e., residents of the UAE looking for adventure trips overseas. The company was born in my experience as the co-founder of a local charity – Golf for Good. Golf for Good used to take donors on adventure treks around the world. Golf for Good used 'travel adventure experience' to raise money for the charity. The participants had to collect a minimum amount of money for the charity. The adventure trek was a reward, a motivation for raising money. A major part of the money raised went to the charity, after subtracting the cost of the trek. A lot of people who engaged with the Golf for Good charity wanted to do multiple treks but had difficulty raising the minimum required funds. They used to complain that there was no company in Dubai that could organize outdoor adventures. This revealed a market need. I had acquired various outdoor qualifications over time. I was a trained as a mountaineering leader, a rock climbing guide, etc. I had participated in numerous outdoor adventure journeys. I knew the need and the pain points of the participants. With this insight I decided to start a professional adventure travel company. First thing I did was to resign from the board of Golf for Good. I didn't want any conflict of interest.

Was it a smooth transition?

The first couple of years of a startup are always hard. You wake up to the reality of business and how difficult it can be. I quickly discovered that it is very difficult for a small business and a businessman working alone, to promote overseas adventure trips and earn a decent profit. Adventure tourism has a term called 'safety ratio.' There is a 'load' or a number of people (participants) that one person can handle (manage) on an outdoor trek. Adventure tourism entails a little physical risk for participants. If the safety ratio exceeds a set norm, adventure expedition becomes unsafe for participants. The threshold of safety ratio takes experience to ascertain. There is a small window of opportunity. The guide can't have too few customers and can't have too many. To reach potential consumers one has to get the message across to a profitable number of clients. This was hard. It takes a lot of money to market a business; reach potential consumers and convert them into clients.

I realized that to become a sustainable business I could not depend upon only the overseas adventure travel market. The overseas adventure travel consumers could only travel during holiday periods. The business needed consistent revenue through the year. This is when I thought about the possibility of adventure travel to proximate domestic locations. A domestic destination business would complement the overseas expedition business.

How did you execute this thought?

After a year I found a perfect little base on the east coast of UAE, a two-hour drive from Dubai in a town shared by Oman and UAE. It is a traditional design Omani homemade with stone. I met the owner of the house and signed a

10-year lease agreement. The house became the base of my domestic adventure tourism business. But I must admit that the thinking did not proceed in a logical way. I wasn't searching for a location. The decision was spontaneous. I wanted to move fast when I saw the house. I was worried that someone else may see it, see the potential and have the same idea. The rent was very reasonable. I thought that if I can't make a go at this with this rent, I must be doing something seriously wrong. I committed to the rent and the focus of the business changed.

Next steps?

I had to develop the site to become the base for local treks, hopeful that local adventure experiences would become a springboard for overseas trips; customers experiencing the local treks would consider overseas trips. I had to rethink the execution of my business. I had to think about staff, because I needed a person permanently based at the location. We needed to have the capacity to prepare food, not just for lunch and snacks for day-visitors but also for customers staying the night.

I then got my first employees, a mountain guide and a cook, who helped me grow the business. I had a small house in Dubai where I used to live. They shared rooms in the same house. We were four – two staff, the watchman and I. That is how the business started and started to grow. Six years later we have 23 employees. We have our office in Dubai Silicon Oasis. We have reasonable revenue.

How has the business developed?

I had to organize to do business for the week. We explored the opportunity of bringing school students on outdoor adventure camps. We had the experiential knowledge of adventure. We had assets in the form of a campsite near the original Omani house we rented. The campsite can accommodate 180 students. It is in a plantation. We have built rooms for boys and girls, a permanent kitchen, a *majlis* area and storage rooms for adventure gear. We have built facilities for conducting additional activities like team building games. This helped me create schools as a customer.

Three things seem to have fallen into place. The location is on the beach and is beautiful. We can reach mountains within a few minutes, where we have a world-class rock climbing site. As an adventure company we have mountains to climb, we have lovely water body trails and we have a beautiful beach for water sports. The location is within a 2-hour drive from Dubai. It is because of easy accessibility and diverse adventure opportunities that we have become popular.

How?

We work all days of the week. We have individuals and corporate groups on weekends. School groups come on weekdays. We also connect with east coast hotels and serve their guests. We work in partnership with travel organizations. We have a contract with Ryman adventures and they send groups each Tuesday and Thursday. We have also worked in partnership with Adventure HQ, the adventure gear store in UAE.

How do you reach customers?

We use social media. We have run competitions on Facebook every month and given free adventure trips to people. We are also involved in organizing and taking part in adventure competitions occasionally.

What about overseas adventure tourism development?

We continue to do overseas trips. The original seed of the business continues. We have organized overseas charity challenges. This season we organized a charity challenge for Golf for Good. We operated one for the Palestinian Children Relief Fund and another for a charity which provides laptops to poor children.

Overseas adventure tourism also developed naturally. Ramdeen is our first employee. He is a first-class mountain guide and will be leaving us by the end of the year. He has acquired land for a campsite in Nepal and will be setting up a climbing and trekking agency. We will be working together. We will now be able to send international expeditions to Nepal. We will be doing everything as per international standards of safety.

We are expanding internationally in association with existing companies or helping form companies where similar companies don't exist. The nature of our business requires us to have people on the ground take responsibility for clients with a similar mindset as ours. We had started trips to Maldives. After two trips the country had a spot of trouble and we are waiting for things to settle. We did invest in the equipment which is currently in storage.

Our work was featured in the National Geographic as a company that organizes trips to world heritage sites, exposing people to different parts of the world, history and culture.

What were you doing before you got involved with Golf for Good?

I came to Dubai in 1982. I have been here for more than 30 years. Our family business in the UK was the yacht business. My father was a yacht master and I was qualified as a competent crew member. He was the skipper of the boat and

I was a crew. We would take people over to France. In a way, I have always been involved in the outdoors.

Your background prepared you for the business.

By training I am a graphic designer. I worked in the printing industry after graduation. I came here shortly after graduation, looked for a job in that industry and couldn't find one that would provide a decent package. I worked for a publishing company for the first four years in Dubai. Then I started my own printing design business in the Trade Center. That was my main source of income. I started doing the overseas tourism business concurrently with my print business. As the tourism business started to pick up, I sold my stake in the print business in 2003.

What prepared you for the business?

I was going on adventure holidays during the time I was in the printing designing industry. I acquired qualifications and experience to offer adventure tourism experience to customers. During my involvement with Golf for Good, I had felt a need of acquiring professional qualifications. I was expected to lead groups on the trips. I had to ensure that the adventure trips and experiences were safe. Plus I needed qualified people on the ground in the countries we visited to ensure that we were not on our own. Every country doesn't have the same safety standards and infrastructure to respond to emergency situations. As an organizer of outdoor adventure trips I had to think through every detail. Plus it was necessary for me to be trained to an internationally accepted standard of mountaineering leadership. I could then look after people accompanying me, to an acceptable level of safety. I could then also make the claim about our standards on the ground because we had people on the ground with acceptable qualifications. This is how I learnt to professionally manage adventure groups.

Having experienced the business as a customer, I knew the gap in the market. I knew how many people went on adventure trips and how many others wanted to go on adventure trips. I am now doing what I am trained to do. This has made business so much easier. And when you love what you are doing, you want to be with people who love their job.

Golf for Good was registered as a charity or as an adventure business?

It is a charity, not for profit, registered with Dubai Humanitarian City. Many people were involved in starting it. I was one of them.

Paul, who loves the outdoors, has a print business which is paying his salary and he is involved in running a charity. He sees a gap in the market for adventure tourism. What was the nature of the thoughts you had at that time? Would this business pay?

Once I started Golf for Good in 2001, I really started to work 6 days a week. I'm the first one to admit, I neglected my printing business. It had been running it for so long that one gets used to complaints. There are processes to manage issues which arise. The reality is that it doesn't happen that way. Once you are not managing the business, things start to suffer and profit starts declining. I had to reflect on what I actually want to do. Did I want to stop my charity and adventure work and concentrate on my business? The business is what makes my money. Or did I want to make a break and do something that I really want to do? I wanted somebody to manage the business and incentivize him with a share of the business. I needed to take this call and carry on. So somebody was brought in and he was given a share of the business that would increase with the performance of the company.

You got a partner to run the business?

The deal was that he would become the majority owner of the company once performance targets were met. I would retain a stake in the business so that I would have some income that would help me as I established my adventure business. This seemed like a great deal except it didn't work out that way. The company lost a huge amount of money with me out of the business and with the new guy in. When I sold the business, I got very little out of it because it had been run down. It didn't give me enough cash to run a successful operation. So I started Absolute Adventures on a shoestring budget. A year later, when I reappraised my work, I had to shift focus towards the local adventure market which required investment in the camp and equipment like mountain bikes, climbing equipment, kayaks, etc. And the associated marketing to get the customers in.

How did you identify that there was a potential for adventure trips within the country or in neighboring countries?

It was very difficult to do market research on the potential of adventure tourism in the UAE. UAE is an outbound market. When no market exists, any research is speculative or imaginary. When no market exits, how can a business be created? Others had unsuccessfully attempted adventure tourism before. I also talked with people from Golf for Good. They had no problems in getting people to be a part of Golf for Good. They had more applicants than the opportunities available. I also knew people who would say that they would do these adventures here if they were commercially available. This was my study or my market research. I did some research in the worldwide adventure tourism market and discovered that it was one of the fastest growing segments of the tourism and travel industry. There was no reason for UAE to be different. That gave me the confidence about the potential for adventure tourism. I suspected that it would grow once options were available. I am narrating the thought process since no data was available for an industry that didn't exist here and I did not collect any. It was my gut feeling. Everyone was telling me about what happens in the rest of the world. So I said, let me take a gamble and get into that industry space.

You started on a gut feeling. How did you go about marketing the concept, getting people to understand the opportunity?

Initially through media by telling them stories about the business. I got some coverage in newspapers and magazines. I used my relationship with the media that had been developed while I was with Golf for Good. Media had helped Golf for Good in promoting trips. I didn't have a lot of money for traditional advertising, which I discovered is very expensive. When you are looking at getting 10–12 participants on a trip, you can't spend high amounts acquiring customers through traditional advertising. One had to be more creative and use word-of-mouth, posters in shopping malls and sports shops to get the message across to potential clients without spending a lot on marketing.

How long did it take for you to get your first group together?

We had a level of interest right from the start. We did trips to Kilimanjaro and the Everest base camp. We also went to Yemen. Yemen was a non-traditional destination and was popular for two years. Yemen was not being serviced by traditional tour companies. Before marketing Yemen we did checked the adventure (mountain trails) and cultural aspects by going to remote villages, sitting and having lunch with the local population. We created a unique experience and got very good feedback. We arranged for participants to stay in very traditional hotels, in guest houses, motels and inns in smaller towns.

With your experience, you didn't have to network to find out with whom to partner and where to stay.

I had visited some locations on numerous trips and had contacts on the ground. In other places I walked on the ground to assess with whom to work. I did try to promote Afghanistan. In 2005, I was approached by the US State Department which had a base in Kabul. They heard of us through a magazine. They contacted me on how we could try and bring tourism and tourism investments to Afghanistan. We saw a great potential for adventure tourism. I explored the country. I met ministers, businessmen and traveled all over Afghanistan. It is a beautiful country. Most of the people were extremely friendly. I also believe that it is a wonderful adventure destination. I tried to promote it. Afghanistan evoked a lot of interest. It was very difficult to get people to commit to making a trip. It is perceived as a dangerous place. Even though it didn't work out, it taught me an important lesson. To promote a business I need to go to an adventurous destination and create new adventures that have not been created before. I learnt how to develop unique products.

How much of the business is domestic vs. overseas now?

95% is domestic.

Were you marketing UAE as an adventure destination to the tourists coming in?

It was a part of the plan to bring overseas adventure tourists to UAE. However, once we focused on the local market it was pushed into the background. It is a small part of the business. We market it through partnerships with hotels that bring tourists and promote adventures as part of the package. We also partner with Arabian Adventures, who sell our brochures throughout cities worldwide. This is a better business model. We don't have to spend marketing money. We have to focus on serving customers here.

Any turning points after you started the business which changed the direction of business?

There are two big changes. One, I brought in my friend as a business partner and two, the focus shifted towards the domestic market with the creation of a base for adventures in UAE. We were still focused on the tourist market. Shifting to address the school trip market was the third big change.

What did you see that made you change?

Having a local adventure base was always part of the long-term plan; it was only when I saw the location that I believed it could be better than whatever I could ever have imagined. The logic was in the destination itself; the ability to offer culture, sports, mountains and the sea, all in one location. This has proven correct. Customers love being there. That you will find something as perfect this is not something you plan.

It just happened?

It was one of those lucky moments. And you shouldn't say it was lucky. It happened because I was assessing the potential of the region. I was fortunate to see the location at a time when I was actually talking to people about the potential for adventure tourism in that market.

When did the school opportunity happen?

Four years ago we noticed that we were busy on weekends. It wasn't easy to attract people during the week. We did have some business from hotels. To make the business grow we had to find a way of being busy on weekdays. Families and individuals were busy with work to come during the week. We evaluated the options for outdoor adventure trips for schools. We had to create programs for children. We also needed to identify special equipment, if any, and think through safety issues. A lot research was done. We connected with people who had experience working with children. We started in a small way by bringing a small group to the camp. The kids would camp in the quarters behind the house and the teachers stayed in the house. We took them for outdoor activities – water sports or trekking or climbing.

Duration?

They would normally come for a duration between one night and four nights. It was a residential program. We would have a camp. The children could build it. We did not use the house. The interest was great right from the start. We quickly found out that the schools needed a much bigger capacity. We were taking up to about forty kids. A lot of schools wanted to send 100 kids. We realized that we needed another location, close by, to increase capacity. So through my local Omani contact we located a new site that we developed. We have thermal cooling tents, a proper professional kitchen and have upgraded all of the services. In addition to the physical infrastructure, we had to provide all activities focused on the school audience.

You have three market segments.

We have consumers who travel overseas for adventure and consumers who travel within the UAE. The domestic consumers comprise two segments – school kids and traditional adventure tourism. The schools market is now our biggest segment. We are also a seasonal business. Our staff comes in September with the beginning of the school term. The first month focuses on training and getting systems organized. The season starts in October and ends in April.

We continue working in May, doing a few trips but it starts to get very hot outdoors. We close our domestic operations in June, July and August. Our focus shifts to overseas work. Kilimanjaro and Everest base camp are very good for summer trips.

Any challenges while executing your business?

There are always challenges in every business. I think entrepreneurs routinely underestimate how much capital is needed to start and keep the business going until the business becomes profitable. This was important for me. I was expecting to earn a lot more from my business than what I earned as a salary from my earlier business. That just didn't happen. I had started my business on a perception. When I wanted to expand I had no option but to bring in a partner. I had no funds that I could use. I believe that we have done a great thing, especially in the year of the crisis. We have never taken a bank loan. We have never borrowed money. Everything has been paid from the income of the business. The only investment is the investment of the two partners in the business. This has made us stronger. We could have made commitments and gone for outside assignments. But looking back, being conservative was one of our greater decisions. We took the decision to grow the business by reinvesting the profits we made. Entrepreneurs know how difficult it is to get finance from banks. The finance costs are never in single digits. So we didn't go seeking funds. We knew we would be turned down.

When did you take a salary from the business?

I am still waiting for that day. I do actually have a salary. What I do in reality is, I take the money I need out of the business so that salary is accounted for. The amount I draw is small because I want to keep money in the business. Often I take a few thousand dollars for food and living expenses as well as my credit card payments. I don't take anything else. This behavior is driven by my priorities at this time in my life. Not having a great amount of money is a problem because I sold my other business. I need to build the value of Absolute Adventure. It is my future. And I need to do it in the shortest possible time. I don't take money from the business. I want to keep it in the business and make a valuable company in the shortest possible time.

How much have you put into the business?

We, two partners, have invested AED 2.5m. It was invested in three rounds that coincide with the stages of business development. There was initial investment, then when we took the Arabic house and then again when we focused on the school market and needed equipment.

Was it challenging to partner with tourism companies or hotels?

I concentrated on delivering great quality of service from the start. I wanted customers to experience the difference and our attention to detail. This takes longer but creates loyalty and word-of-mouth advertisement; people start to approach you and want to work with you. This is what happened. Hotels, tour companies and tourism departments began to approach us, seeking ways to engage, aware of our difference and quality. Our service offering was premium high quality. They always need to confirm the reputation by personal experience. In countries like UK, USA and Australia governing bodies exist to standardize and control the adventure sports industry. They stipulate things like qualifications of instructors, years of experience and safety standards for all kinds of adventure sports and activities to ensure that participants and service providers engage appropriately and fairly. We are a young, small and new country where adventure sports are emerging and governing bodies don't exist. We decided to set our standards to meet the most stringent national standards. To achieve this we had to ensure that we were audited for processes and safety. We have been audited by Camps internationals. We are considered worthy to be licensed in many countries of the world. Even though there is no legal or statutory requirement in Dubai and compliance requires additional investment and operating costs to meet tougher standards, I believe it pays off by evoking confidence in the clients that they will be safe and secure.

Lessons for new entrepreneurs?

I encourage all budding entrepreneurs to not just do what you are able to do but match the best in the industry or even try to be better than the best. Such an approach is beneficial in the long run.

How did you price? Golf for Good was a charity. A charity requires a vendor to keep costs low. Now you are a vendor.

When I started my immediate goal was for people to use us, get a client list and grow the business. The choice of making a lower margin to get clients on price was challenging. When I started I wasn't working hard to make a profit. I just wanted to establish and grow the business. I felt that customers would come if they saw that I had good experience. I charged a lower margin because we wanted people to use us. I was hoping for the virtual cycle to kick in, have the initial customers help get newer customers at an increasing rate.

For overseas trips it was easier. I had to get the cost from the ground handler. And add a percentage to cover the cost of marketing, time and effort. For overseas trips we made a margin of 50% on cost. This is low considering it is a manpower intensive business. And to cover the fixed cost of rent and licensing one has to work long hours. Our business model for overseas travel has not changed much because it is just a one focus area. Overseas trips have a big HR development opportunity. The trips give instructors opportunities to travel and gain experience for their career development. It keeps them happy. And gives them and us some income. The overseas trips are scheduled during the summer. Any revenue and profit during the lean months are a bonus even though often we cut our pricing to the bone.

Pricing for the local trips was a different proposition. Customers had little to compare us with. We then benchmarked ourselves with desert safaris and other local trips, the alternate choice options. We had to assess what customers would pay for a quality half day experience. We set our prices seven years ago, when we started local trips. The prices are more or less the same. From a business perspective it is not about the cost but the quality of the experience. Our volume of business has grown. So even though we have a lot more local trips now because we have maintained prices at a competitive level, the profit has grown. I think we did quite a good job at setting the right pricing for local trips. One thing that we did adjust a bit is the minimum number of people on a trip. When we first started all the private trips had minimum two people. We changed this to a minimum of four. We were not making money serving two people.

What worries you about the business? What keeps you awake at night?

Nothing much. I am an eternal optimist. I am very excited about the future of the industry. We now have many competitors in the market. I am not the only good adventure company. Adventure HQ opening in Dubai indicates the emergence of adventure as a leisure activity. There are other good adventure companies, some of whom we have worked with. We don't see them as competitors but as peers with whom we need to work closely to establish standards and grow the industry. There are companies that bring in quality gear. This was rare when we started. With good equipment, we have knowledgeable staff. This is driving industry growth. And we are a part of that growth. I think all entrepreneurs have some worries or conflicts as business starts and grows, with changes in roles and responsibilities and people leaving. This is not specific to my company or industry. We are small and growing and are adaptable; we make real changes quickly. The sector is big. We have opened new segments and markets. Changes in government rules always concern me. A change may jeopardize the entire investment. These are the few things that I will always be concerned about. But in general terms, I am really optimistic.

How have you changed in the last 7 years?

I would like to think that I have become a better boss. I would like to think that I have always been a reasonable entrepreneur and that the companies I have started have all been new ideas. Even my print and design business wasn't a common business. It was very much sort of a fast print, focused on fast service and quality of service, rather than competing on price. I started in 1986 when the industry was evolving. I bought equipment that was new to the region and offered a service that was not available before. The same idea/perspective defines the charity and the adventure business. As I reflect on my career I'd like to think I am a perpetual learner. I am a better judge of people now. I am a better judge of the market and am able to adapt to it. As I grow my business, I want to be an eco-friendly business. After an outdoor trip, I would like to measure the environmental impact. To monitor and measure the environmental impact one needs employees who are trained to do this. Our size constrains us in establishing monitoring processes. We keep focusing on how to improve our level of service.

Is there anything you had to completely unlearn when you started doing this business?

When I was a participant in adventure tours I was an amateur and a volunteer. The learning curve was steep as a professional providing the services that I had earlier consumed. I had to look and learn from overseas companies and mimic what they were doing here. I learned quickly. I made mistakes and errors of judgment that didn't work. Every entrepreneur must learn this. It is like an entrepreneurial law. Take a decision, execute it and correct the mistake along the way. I think that's what makes a person an entrepreneur. If you worry about making mistakes in the first place then don't go to business, because you're going to make a lot of them, and you have learn to put them behind and move forward. And because I also know my strength, I keep learning.

Guidance for a new entrepreneur.

A common mistake entrepreneurs make is assuming that life is going to be easy because they're working for themselves. They think they've flexibility. They are dead wrong. If you are not prepared to commit 7X24X365 days without holidays to make the company a success, don't even think of starting. You have to commit a 100% and that can be for quite a long time. The first two years is a real struggle. Sometimes it can be longer depending on the economic environment. There is a steep learning curve and no personal life for two to three years, a period that can extend. Now I come to capital. People often say, 'I have capital to last me six months.' This isn't going to get you to establish a business. Businesses take longer to become cash self-sustaining. This is a bit like a double-edged sword. Too much capital makes decision making distorted. We have a tendency to throw money at a problem whereas innovation may have worked better. One works harder when cash is tight. You look at minimizing costs and maximizing outcomes which then becomes the basis of increasing profits later. Plus one learns to prioritize decisions. There are no speculative choices made. You know the intense feeling when you evaluate a choice. It is a bit like marketing. You don't know what works and what doesn't. I am now a great believer that stress is an important ingredient in entrepreneurial life. I work best under stress. I don't panic. I get focused. And when you're focused you really see issues and choices in their simplest granular form. There are no silver bullets so you focus on simple things, simplify complex things and take small, low-risk decisions. Focus on things to get done. Taking the metaphor of the building of the Burj Khalifa. One constructs the building a brick at a time. Only the paranoid survive.

Middle of the Whirlpool

Entrepreneur	Mini Joshi
Company and website	Good Platters Catering/Company has closed down
Company Services	Food catering company
Year started	2010
Tips for entrepreneurs	<ul><li>Don't become an entrepreneur unless you are physically fit.</li><li>Don't become an entrepreneur if you're emotional and get hurt easily because another person said something unacceptable.</li><li>Choose a partner, if at all you want to have partners, but neither from family nor from friends.</li><li>Partnerships need to be based on partnerships agreements that define roles, responsibilities, accountabilities and exit options.</li></ul>

Your business

We started a commercial kitchen catering to hotel staff. Hotels outsource food preparation for staff. It is a bother for them to manage two kitchens and cooking teams with a common hotel infrastructure. Two different mindsets are required; a hotel purchase department searches for high quality at a good price for hotel guests and average quality at a low price for catering. To save them the trouble of managing two kitchens, hotels prefer outsourcing.

How did it start?

I had spent 10 years working in hotels in Dubai. My work exposed me to all hotel functions. A colleague expressed a desire to start a business. I had had some accumulated savings. Another friend joined us to co-invest and take care of production. He had relocated to Canada and returned.

What happened during startup?

The startup was difficult. Staffing was difficult. When we had visa approvals, we didn't have funds and when we had funds, we couldn't get visa approvals. We did manage to get a few good contracts. We are proud of our arrangement with the largest Dubai bank. We are now running three canteens serving 800+ staff. We always felt the business was short of funds. I had arranged for business loans to manage the cash flows of the business prior to my exit.

Exit?

I left the business and came back.

Explain.

Our partnership went through many tumultuous changes.

The first turning point was when, as the business stabilized, the working partner's (C) family started coming to the office and managing finances. C managed the business jointly with S (investor), who was based in India. The involvement of the family members became challenging. I offered the other partners an opportunity to buy me out. They expressed their inability to do so. I expressed my inability to continue as a working partner in December 2011. I left the business and remained an investor, a non-working partner on the trade license. Our informal agreement was that the other partners would buy my share at the end of the following year.

The second turning point happened when I got a call from S in February 2012 asking me if I could find a buyer for the business. They had lost a few contracts which they couldn't replace soon enough. I looked into the accounts and discovered that my share of the business was shown as AED 150K whereas I had invested AED 400K. I was livid. I had been working on trust. The partners had been taking decisions, keeping me in the dark. I also discovered that they had been trying to sell the business without my knowledge. They had turned to me because of their inability to sell.

I brought a buyer willing to pay AED 2m. More discoveries happened in the due diligence; not a single supplier had been paid since December 2011. The total payables were around AED 1.8m. The company revenue during the same period was nearly AED 2.2m. We needed clean books to sell the business. The two partners were evasive.

And then the real crisis happened.

My name had been removed as a bank signatory when I left the business. However, my mobile phone number continued to appear in the bank records.

On the midnight of 8th May I got an SMS from the bank about a company debit card transaction at Dubai Duty Free.

I was not going to work every day so I was unaware that things had gone from bad to worse. When I came to the kitchen the following day I found the chef talking to the security to allow him to access the petty cash. I was informed that C had not come to the kitchen for 15 days. The staff had been told not to connect with him because he was in meetings. I told the staff that C had left the country. They didn't believe me. They even said he may have gone for medical treatment. I asked them to send a driver to his house. The driver came back saying that the company car was in the parking lot, the apartment was empty and the apartment building security informed them that a container with the belongings had been packed for shipping out of the country.

I immediately called our business sponsor. He too was shocked. I called S in India. He was unaware of C's whereabouts. This was strange. S asked me to urgently sell the company. And then C absconded with the company debit card. The SMS of a Duty Free Purchase was the only evidence of C's location at an exit point of the country. It was not difficult for me to piece together the trickery.

Then?

S stopped taking my calls. He wasn't coming back to the UAE.

The sponsor asked me whether I wanted to run the business. I said, 'Yes, I know the business. I know what is wrong with it. I exited the business because of differences.'

He asked me, 'How will you do it?'

I said, 'I don't know.'

I didn't have a plan. I had no idea of the immensity of the challenge. I was a shareholder. I had no banking rights. I was not a signatory for anything. I was the only owner still in the country. There was a kitchen. It had the possibility of generating revenue. The company's debt to the banks was AED 1.8m. My option was to take over the company with all its debt, take responsibility of the staff, all customers, suppliers and government issues. I had the responsibility of the livelihoods of twenty people who were all breadwinners of their families. And we owed money to suppliers whose sales managers would have been badly hurt. The bank debt was a smaller challenge.

I couldn't think at that moment.

I had two choices. One was to sit down, cry and allow the company to be shut down. Two, take up the challenge to run the company. If the company shut down, I would be jailed for 3–6 months. I could then come out and rebuild my life. I decided on taking up the challenge.

With the wisdom of hindsight, if I had known what I have since faced, I would have legally exited as a shareholder when I gave up working in the company.

We restarted the business with billings of AED 350,000. The revenue has since fallen further.

How did you manage the team when you restarted?

I got everyone together, explained the situation and we collectively took up the challenge. I did not comment on the negatives, like the absconding owners. I told them we had three running contracts. We would get more. But we needed to cooperate and work together to 'survive.' We became focused on survival. The team was willing to pitch in. I came to know that they were getting salaries a month late. I have been trying to improve this. Today salaries are paid by the 15th of the following month.

Learning on partnership?

Business partners need unemotional work-related transparency based on trust, without a hidden agenda. Partnerships need to be based on partnerships agreements that define roles, responsibilities, accountabilities and exit options.

How did you manage the relationships with stakeholders?

I explained the situation to everyone. I promised to buy the absconding partners' shares to keep the company alive. I promised phased repayments to suppliers. They had legal remedy to recover dues by proceeding to the civil court. The court would visit the company, shut it and seize the assets. And no one would get a Dirham. I promised to repay banks. They seemed comfortable in getting an assurance from me as long as I promised not to run away.

Was your trade license changed?

Not yet. My sponsor owns 51% and my share is 12.5%. The memorandum requires 75% shareholders to approve changes. The way to change this is to get other shareholders to give me a power of attorney. This is not possible since both have absconded. I can't sell the company because I have no rights to sell the company. There is no law that will allow a smooth transition after paying all payables.

On paper, I am managing and owning the business.

Did you want to become an entrepreneur?

It was an accident. I was working for a large local hotel company in Dubai. I started as a sales executive and became a Deputy GM. I am a sales and marketing person. A GM role was not my aptitude. I couldn't get around to managing engineering and the garden! When the recession happened, very challenging targets, of 100% occupancy, were set. On one hand I was terminating staff while on the other hand I was telling my people to get business. By then I was free of family financial commitments. I had ten years accumulated gratuity. S was my colleague. I knew him since 1998. He was an executive chef. Our families had become close even though today we can't speak to each other. He had been suggesting business opportunities for two years. At the spur of the moment I said ok. S knew food and I knew selling.

I was from this market whereas his food antecedents went back to 2001. He has a couple of restaurants in India. His coming to Dubai was motivated by the need for investments for his businesses. When I reflect on it, I realize that he actually 'used' me. He made me the face of the company because I was from this country.

I graduated in German literature and followed it up with a one-year diploma in hotel management. From 1988 to 1997 I worked in the front office of a hotel in India. I came to Dubai in 1999 and joined Metropolitan. S was always an entrepreneur. He always wanted to work for himself. I was always an employee. My father worked for a company till he retired. My family did not approve of me becoming an entrepreneur. The idea of a fixed income was ingrained in their minds.

Where did you actually make an error of judgment?

Getting C onboard. He was known to S. I misplaced trust in S's judgment.

Did you sign a partnership agreement before you started the business?

No. Even when C joined the business, there was no formal partnership. We had signed an agreement in India but that has no validity and value here. Our partnership was limited to just the shares and how we will conduct the business. Roles were defined. Decision making, responsibilities and accountabilities were not. I was to handle sales, marketing and government issues. C was to manage the kitchen and the relationship with the sponsor's office.

What advice would you give a new entrepreneur structuring a partnership?

Define the key decision-making role of all partners in the agreement. No partner should be given the rights to take unilateral decisions for issues like disengaging with other partners or selling the business. Standard Memorandum and Articles of Association, based on a trade license granted in Dubai, gives a partner with 24% share many rights. S and C had planned to sell the business and pocket the proceeds. When friends become business partners it is necessary to detail all decision-making processes. This avoids discomfort. Every partner should have access to the numbers, with a proper audit of accounts.

Your economic situation is uncertain. Where do you think your determination is coming from?

I have been tested many times. I strongly believe in myself. I am a very independent person. I don't like to fail. I will do anything without compromising my self-respect. I will go on. It's inbuilt in me. I am still in the middle of the whirlpool.

Do you see the light at the end of the tunnel?

I see light but then I always see light. I am made like that. I am only uncertain about how the laws will work to enable me.

You have faced huge surprises in the business world. Why do you think the suppliers trusted you?

I was honest with them. I did not hide things. And I did not lose my composure. Some of the small suppliers came to the office to fight. They had been led astray earlier. Trust levels were low, if not non-existent. I learnt not to allow my emotions and anger get the better of me. There were occasions when they would shout at me. I wanted to shout back that I too had lost a lot of my money. But I had to make them sit down, gain composure, focus on their debt and solutions. They needed to appreciate that I was helping them. They also had to realize that the company had no money. And I could not sign papers. This is where my salesmanship came in handy.

Are the suppliers and vendors comfortable?

The outstanding amounts to suppliers, what I consider 'loans', are getting paid.

What about the customers' side? Switching versus continuing? It was high risk for them.

The customers were a lesser challenge. They are happy as long as we continued to serve them. I often get complaints about service quality. That is rectified by additional staff. I signed a contract with a staff supply company. I have twenty-eight company staff and hired another thirty-five. Delivery trucks are another issue for timely deliveries. I have three rental trucks. I have not defaulted on these payments.

Bank loans?

I am nobody for the banks. My signature is not on the accounts. I can't issue any checks. I can't tell the banks the real situation.

Who is signing the checks?

I am running the business on cash. I withdraw AED 8000 every day and use that to pay my creditors. I directly deposit cash in their accounts.

When C ran away he used the company ATM card at Dubai Duty Free. S organized to have the card sent back to me. I use that to manage the company. Since S sent the card back, it convinced me that they were hand in glove in the decision to abscond. C did meet him in India after leaving Dubai.

How will you legally to resolve this?

I contacted S to amicably solve the problem. I wanted him to give me a power of attorney and transfer C's shares to me. I promised to run the business and pay (buy) them out or sell the business. I was working under the assumption that he did not want to be a part of the business. He was willing to do this with a payment of AED 50,000 per month for 12 months; this was his price to give a POA. He didn't seem to understand that he had a liability as a shareholder, not a receivable from the company. He thought I would buckle because I am stuck. My father passed away recently and I was unable to go for his funeral because I can't travel. One of the suppliers has put a travel ban on all the names on the trade license.

How did you learn finance?

The hard way. I still don't understand it well. I am taking help from an associate, who is like a coach. He is helping me with banks also.

Acquiring new customers?

Reaching customers has never been a challenge. People are comfortable with us. I am now managing parties ever so often. We use a number of online portals to reach diverse consumers.

Isn't home party catering a different business? It requires different skills.

It is similar to what we did the first time after graduation. We started and learnt. I still recollect the first party we did. The client made a list of things she wanted. And I had to look for suppliers. My background in hotels helped. I connected with the supplier network. Some of them helped me to get the right-priced suppliers. The network helped in another way. I needed to buy supplies for the kitchen. The company had not invested in the upkeep of materials.

You had to manage people.

I learnt how to manage people. In the kitchen it is all about collaboration. My initial role focused on resolving quarrels. I now have a person who manages the kitchen. When I look back, I am thankful for the hoteliering experience. I draw upon my learning from that phase of my life to manage current challenges.

Have you invested any money in the business after coming back?

No. Some of my initial investment was by taking a personal loan. And I did not draw a salary for a few months after we started. Now I draw a small amount to manage my living expenses.

How much time do you spend doing sales?

Right now I don't have much time. I usually take one or two appointments and go for meetings. Contracts take a while, a month in getting formalized. My focus is private parties. I have chosen that as a segment to go after. Decision making is easier. Payments can be in advance. Customer satisfaction is easier and direct. I visit clients. Word of mouth happens.

Who helps you price products and services?

The executive chef we have. Being from the industry, I have learnt the margin required. My hotel experience is also helping me. I add value in the negotiation. I have to assess the customer and quote a price to ensure that the target margin is achieved after negotiation.

What else is keeping you going?

My determination and energy level. I don't get tired. I work twelve hours every day.

What guidance would you give a new entrepreneur?

Don't get in unless you are physically fit. Don't get in if you're emotional and get hurt easily because another person said something unacceptable. Choose a partner, if at all you want to have partners, but neither from family nor from friends.

How do you manage stress?

I jog around 5 kilometers every day.

When did you make a business plan?

In September 2009 I started putting a business plan together. I went around the hotel talking to directors and senior managers of HR, procurement, vendors, etc. I was in the industry so everyone helped. We were going to build a catering kitchen. It was not going to be like a hotel kitchen.

How did you get your initial business?

I networked. Once the kitchen was established we got contracts from two hotels. I can still recollect the dates. The contract was to start in August. It got delayed. Luckily we did not get permission in August because of Ramadan. September 23rd was the final inspection. On September 24th we got the Civil Defense NOC. On 24th Dubai Investment Park gave us the initial approval to start. We started on September 25th. We had business from the first day. The staff was busy when we opened. They never waited for business to come in.

Would you like to sell the business or a part of it?

I don't want to sell any of it. This is my business. I have brought it up from AED 219,000 a month to AED 460,000 a month. I want an investor or investment. And if get a power of attorney I can top up the loan and start paying the suppliers. I can then get a General Manager reinforcing management.

Surprise Customers

Entrepreneurs	Boy (B) and Mike Adnani (M)
Company and website	Costra/www.costra.com
Company Services	Retail fixture manufacturing company
Year started	1993
Tips for entrepreneurs	• Make sure that when you start, you make a big first impression. Follow it up by meeting commitments and exceeding expectations. • Dream big to make it. It then happens.

What is Costra?

M: We are a fit-out company that builds furniture for retail environments. We also do office and hotel furniture. We can design, manufacture and execute. In that sense, we create retail environments. We started in 1993.

Why retail furniture?

M: Different ideas came together. Hong Kong was an example of a hub. Dubai was going to play a similar role in the Gulf. Retail, hotels and offices were going to grow. We were seeing where Dubai was going. We wanted to focus on an industry that would grow. We follow visions of other people. Best way to drive is to be behind a police car. The leader clears the way, we follow. We used to travel to exhibitions and trade shows. That inspired us. We used to shop and see how different retailing was in the west; the way things were presented, the store designs were very different. These visits and observations inspired us. We were looking for things we could bring to Dubai.

Everybody sees Sheikh Mohammed's vision, everybody sees retail and everybody sees growth. What was different for you? What was the first step?

M: We started as freelancers doing projects. A friend of mine worked with the British Bank of the Middle East. They needed office furniture. The reference led to our project execution. Once we did one bank, we looked at the needs of other banks. Union Bank was becoming Emirates Bank. The branches needed to be changed based on new guidelines. We made a presentation and won that job. This was followed by our winning work with Standard Chartered Bank. They were changing their brand image.

We realized something. When you interact and deal with people on day-to-day basis, they get to know you, like you for the hard work and start trusting you. Then when they need some work to be done, they take an extra step to support you.

Where did it all begin?

B: Baby steps of business started earlier. The inspiration came from shopping. Big brands in the world had started to notice Dubai and they used to showcase their products in Dubai for the Middle East. We first started a business of printing business and Eid cards. We then traded gift items. This was followed by contracts. Our first office, in 1994, was on Bank Street in Bur Dubai. We moved to a bigger location when we needed fabrication and manufacturing.

Which of you has a design background?

M: None. We learnt contracts by executing the jobs. Without knowing the business, you can't run the business.

When did you shift towards retail?

M: We moved into retail by first manufacturing point-of-sale fixtures. In the early years, for nearly seven to eight years, we were doing POS work for the likes of Nestle, British American Tobacco, Procter & Gamble and Unilever. We were doing soft and hard POP material.

How did you win business from these large MNCs? Did you walk-in and ask for opportunity? Why would they trust you? Did you win on price?

M: We have always been aggressive in getting jobs based on design, services and price.

B: I have always attempted to add value beyond what the client specifies. I will try to do things that the client may not have thought about. I also make sure that my services don't end after delivery. Try to do something extra after delivery. See whether what the client needed is serving their needs. My goal is to engage with a client and once engaged, to not let him go. We don't sell products.

What do you wish to achieve?

M: Deeply engage with the client so that they notice a difference when they meet others.

B: We go a step further before they commit. We present to them ideas and alternatives they may not have considered. We invest in the project in a way that they notice a difference.

An example?

B: One of our first projects was a POP for KitKat. The company was re-launching KitKat. We were to make 34–35 POP items. We invested time and money to make a presentation for the thirty-five items. We left them with no choice of either rethinking options or considering anyone else. We got the big break with KitKat.

M: We created a POP with a motion sensor and audio option. It had never been done before. If a person passed by the display a voice asked, 'Have a break. Have a KitKat chunky.' What we did was an expression of Boy's creativity. He thinks outside the box. His goal is to do something so that the client will ask themselves, 'Why do we need an agency anymore? Why can't I go directly to Costra?'

You don't just execute. You add value and change the decision-making process of the customer. Where do you get ideas?

B: By traveling and seeing things.

You have a very strong power of observation?

B: Yes.

M: I think it is also about our whole way of working. If you look around, you may never see an ambience like our office in other companies. (The Costra lobby is like a lobby of a small hotel with a Piano and a crooning vocalist.) We realized that while working we were experiencing work-related stress and tension. To calm ourselves we used to visit hotels and coffee shops. We decided to bring a hotel-like lobby and coffee shop to our office for all our team members.

Where did the growth come up? What was the need for growth?

B: From within. I wanted to get bigger and bigger. Without growth organizations can become bankrupt.

M: You don't grow for yourself. You also do it for your people- staff and colleagues. If there is no growth, they may not stay with you. The growth is for the organization and its people.

B: An entrepreneur lives for his people. People are his biggest asset. He has to be a people's person. I take care of my people. It's my passion. And the business keeps on expanding. Growth also comes about in another way. It is like Dubai. Dubai attracts a lot of people. People who visit Dubai become spokespersons for Dubai. In the same way I want customers to be attracted to Costra. I want to do those things so that I don't have to sell Costra. My existing customers have already done the selling for me. This is the way I have been growing. This is how it works here.

The next big milestone after Nestle?

M: We began working on retail fixtures for perfumes and cosmetics. We became one of the vendors to P&G prestige products – perfumes and cosmetics. We then got numerous contracts, like supplying furniture to GAP for their worldwide openings.

B: We started to supply Burberry for their stores in Europe. My effort is to establish 'Made in Dubai' as a mark of quality.

How do you win the trust of clients like Burberry?

B: Before they could commit to us, we had committed from our side. I assumed that they would come to visit us for a due diligence. In a traditional due diligence I could talk to them about our design team, machines and the jobs we have done. Or we could show them a mock-up store. I decided to do that. We surprise clients. They get surprised even if we show them a few completed items before a decision is made, as a presentation of our capabilities. This strategy has worked. We have no marketing. It is all word of mouth.

M: We are executing projects in Singapore, Malaysia, Georgia, Romania and Azerbaijan. We are now a trusted supplier to many global brands.

How do you manage Dubai's cost structure?

M: We now have manufacturing facilities in China, India, Saudi Arabia, Muscat and Istanbul. I look at the cost structure of my clients. I know I have to compete on price. The client specs in retail are detailed. Spreading factories has helped us to deliver faster and at efficient costs. I have to fit into the global growth plan of my partner. We have to meet their expectations of quality and turnaround. And then price.

New projects?

B: We've got a project for 500 stores in the telecom sector. We've been doing Zain telecom and STC Saudi Telecom Corporation. We must have, all in all, done over 1,000 stores in the telecom sector. I show a mock-up kiosk or a mini-store to every potential telecom client when they visit us.

What was your total investment when you started Costra?

B: Zero and hard work! I think we put in $10,000. We started with one small project for Standard Chartered Bank. They needed some promotional products from China. We needed the money to pay upfront. We managed to do a few more projects using local vendors.

What makes you tense about the business?

M: I am tense when I am not busy.

B: The most important challenge is we have to be smarter, active and quick. We have to move much faster now.

You don't see shortage of opportunity?

B: We don't see shortage of opportunity. In 2002-3 we started looking outside Dubai. Again influenced by where our partners were going. If a brand wanted to be in China we wanted to compete, if in Turkey we wanted a chance too, and so on. We've been lucky during the recession period.

M: Our main growth came during the recession because brands were looking for global growth. We continued to grow during 2009-10. We were one of the few companies that gave a bonus during those years.

Doesn't China challenge you? It's a different culture, a different environment?

M: We have Chinese members in our team.

Current issues?

B: We have tried to embed continuous improvement into the culture of the organization. Our last job should not be as good as the previous one. It has to be better every time. I focus on quality. Value for money is secondary. It's a question of winning every customer's trust. At Costra we can manage anyone's expectations in an effective way.

What advise will you give to a startup entrepreneur?

M: Dream big to make it. It then happens. We did one job very well, pleased the client beyond his expectations and the momentum picked up. We then managed to grow.

B: We make sure that for any business we start, we make a big first impression. Then follow it up by meeting commitments and exceeding expectations.

Summary

Appendix

Summary of the book

The following images and tables encapsulate the essence of the book that anyone at any age of any background can become an entrepreneur.

1. An Advertisement that Defines the Experiences of an Entrepreneur Journey[50]

> Day last. It was directed to Mr. Robert Harrison. No. 34 Baker st.
> EDWARD HUGHES, 41 Fish st.
>
> **MEN WANTED**
> for hazardous journey, small wages, bitter cold, long months of complete darkness, constant danger. Safe return doubtful, honor and recognition in event of success.
> Ernest Shackleton   4 Burlington st.
>
> MEN — Neat-appearing young men of pleasing personality, between ages of 21 to 40 to work at leathershop com-

It is not too late to seek a newer world

Ulysses by Alfred,
Lord Tennyson

2. Start at Any Age[51]

The following table plots age, entrepreneur and the companies they started.

Age	Entrepreneur	Business
30	Fusajiro Yamauchi	Nintendo
31	Werner von Siemens	Siemens
33	Jan Koum	WhatsApp
34	Evans Williams	Twitter
35	Jimmy Wales	Wikipedia
36	Reid Hoffman	Linkedin
37	Doris Fisher	Gap
38	Masaru Ibuka	Sony
39	Gordon Moore	Intel
40	Henry Ford	Ford
41	Asa Candler	Coca-Cola
42	Soichiro Honda	Honda
43	Henry Royce	Rolls Royce
44	Sam Walton	Walmart
45	Thomas Edison	General Electric
46	Jim Kimsey	AOL
47	James Sinegal	Costco
49	Adolf Dassler	Adidas
50	Harold Stanley	Morgan Stanley
51	Gordon Bowker	Starbucks
52	Ray Kroc	McDonald's
53	Yoshisuke Aikawa	Nissan
55	Arianna Huffington	Huffington Post
56	Ferdinand Porsche	Porsche
59	Kawasaki Shōzō	Kawasaki
60	Amadeo Giannini	Bank of America
61	Charles Flint	IBM
62	Col Harland Sanders	KFC

3. Every past Experience Contributes[52]

The following table plots age, entrepreneur and the companies they started. Entrepreneurs dropped out of college and took odd routes to entrepreneurship.

Age	Entrepreneur	Company
	Entrepreneurs who dropped out of college	
19	Michael Dell	Dell
19	Steve Jobs	Apple
19	Julian Assange	Wikileaks
20	Bill Gates	Microsoft
20	Evan Williams	Twitter
20	Mark Zuckerberg	Facebook
20	Larry Ellison	Oracle
21	Jan Koum	WhatsApp
21	Travis Kalanick	Uber
22	John Mackey	Whole Foods
	Indirect routes to entrepreneurship	
25	Mark Cuban	Dallas Mavericks owner. Until 25 bartender at his own bar
30	Pejman Nozad	Angel investor. Until 30s rug dealer
30	Sheldon Adelson	Founder Las Vegas Sands. Until 30s sold shampoo and windshield defroster
30	Manoj Bhargava	5-hour energy drink founder. Until 30s taxi driver and monk
30	Amancio Ortega	Zara founder. Until 30 shirt shop helper
45	Mar Kay Ash	Mar Kay founder. Until 45 sold books and home goods door-to-door
52	Ray Kroc	McDonald's founder. Until 52 sold paper cups and milkshake mixers

FLIP OVER

4. Money Is Not a Constraint to Start a Business. Examples of Companies and Their Startup Capital.[53]

The following table plots name of the company and their startup capital.

How much money companies were started with		
Company	Product/Industry	Money started with ($)
Hewlett Packard	Electronics	538
Threadless	Designer t-shirts	1000
Dell	Computers	1000
Spanx	Apparel	5000
American Apparel	Apparel	10000
Whole Foods	Grocery chain	45000
Under Armor	Sports goods and apparel	60000
GoPro	Advanced cameras	164000

5. What to Remember on the Entrepreneurial Journey[54]

Appendix 1
How Experienced Entrepreneurs Create

Sarasvathy[55] (2001) description, reproduced below, of how entrepreneurs create new businesses is a depiction of what I learnt from the interviews. I italicized a few words (in parenthesis) for emphasis.

Sarasvathy[56] (2001) writes that business goals emerge in the process of business creation. The start is frugal. The 'fuel' of new business is motivation and creative imagination of the entrepreneur. The mixing of ambition and ingenuity of the entrepreneur with his social capital creates the spark for a new business to begin.

> (*Entrepreneur*)…begins with a given *(and limited)* set of means and allows goals to emerge contingently over time from the…imagination(s) and diverse aspirations of the founders and the people they interact with.[57]

The three inputs into the creative method, derived from the entrepreneur, are – his expertise (skills and attitude), his knowledge and experience, and his social networks.

> …entrepreneurs begin with three categories of means: (1) Who they are – their traits, tastes and abilities; (2) What they know – their education, training, expertise, and experience; and, (3) Whom they know – their social and professional networks…[58]

Entrepreneurs have a bias for action. They make flexible plans. They don't take big risks. They start small. They test, see the results, and keep improvising. Decide and build in the moment. Entrepreneurial thinking is like critical thinking and learning by doing; each entrepreneurial action is an experiment, a test of a business hypothesis and results in learning.

> …they start very small with the means that are closest at hand, and move almost directly into action… Plans are made and unmade and revised and recast through action and interaction with others *(stakeholders)* on a daily basis *(very frequently)*.[59]

Entrepreneurs take decisions and actions in the context of his vision and business goals.

> …at any given moment, there is always a meaningful picture that keeps…a continuing journey…[60]

The outcomes of entrepreneurial actions converge over time. Some actions don't yield expected results. They are modified based on learning.

> ...Through their actions...the set of possible effects change and get reconfigured. Eventually, certain of the emerging effects coalesce into clearly achievable and desirable goals...[61]

Appendix 2 How Artists Work

Gompertz[62] (2015), in his book on how artists work, describes the working of a sculptor's mind. It reveals the cognitive dynamic that underpins each stroke of the chisel. The description mimics how entrepreneurs decide, act, reflect and revise their work.

Take the sculptor who carves away at a block of marble until a recognizable figure emerges. Each tiny incision made by the artist's chisel is a question being asked. What happens if I chip this bit off? Will it shape the torso in the way I want? And that leads to another question: did it work? The final form is the culmination of hundreds, if not thousands, of similar enquiries, followed by decisions, which often lead to more questions and revisions.

Gompertz[63] (2015) reveals the determination that drives the creation of art. Art gets created in recurring cycles. Artists take baby steps. They experiment, assess and rework until the art encapsulates their vision. This is what an entrepreneur does.

Persist with this cycle of doing – experimentation, assessment and correction; the chances are there will be a moment when it will all fall into place…

The emotional experiences of entrepreneurs and artists are similar when they are creating their works. Gompertz[64] (2015) identifies concurrent existence of despair and doggedness as integral to the process of creating art.

Sculptor carves a stone…a form is revealed… Each strike leads to the next. Creating…takes a while…wrong turns…getting lost…feeling …hopeless. The crucial thing is to keep going…tenacious executors.

Entrepreneurs and artists concurrently can make themselves look at the big picture and focus on minute details.

We're talking about a very specific mindset that is crucial when it comes to the act of creating. It is an attitude that can be encapsulated in a simple but demanding rule: always think both big picture and fine detail.[65]

The entrepreneurial and artistic processes are iterative; new businesses and works of art are created through repetitive iterations.

If they don't succeed, they don't try exactly the same thing again… Instead they think, evaluate, correct, modify and then try again. Entrepreneurship is an iterative process.[66]

The end of the entrepreneurial and artistic process can be very different from that initially envisaged.

'I begin with an idea and then it becomes something else.' Pablo Picasso.[67]

Appendix 3[68] Mindset and Mental Models

There are three triggers to this appendix. One, I identified the word 'mindset' being used in business conversations with an increasing frequency. Two, a business school professor[69] delivered an executive education program on inculcating an 'entrepreneurial' mindset to a large global company. Three, a personal disconnect with entrepreneurial mindset being defined as a way of 'seeing' opportunity, which is different from what I had sensed entrepreneurs doing, i.e., 'discovering' opportunity while 'crafting' a business.

To understand mindset, I examine how cognition happens.

What a person sees and thinks is a function of where he stands, how he frames what he is looking at and what he chooses to look. I use three images (Figure 3.1) to illustrate the idea. In the first image, a marooned person sees an approaching boat as a means to his rescue. On the other hand, the boatman of the approaching boat sees the island as a relief. The second illustration suggests how framing can alter perception and understanding. The third illustration suggests how attitudinal orientation can also alter perception. A glass tumbler can be seen as half empty or half full.

Figure 3.1. What a person sees is a function of his – position, framing and choice

Perspective...

A marooned person is seeing a boat that will take him to safety, a person in the boat is seeing the safety of an island after being left in a safety boat.[70]

An environment problem can be framed positively.[71]

A glass of water can be half empty or half full.

To elaborate the idea of mindsets and mental models in cognition, let us examine the Indian parable of the blind men and the elephant.

The story is about a group of blind men who have never come across an elephant before. They learn and conceptualize what the elephant is like by touching it. Each blind man feels a different part of the elephant's body, but only one part, such as the side or the tusk. They then describe the elephant based on their partial experience. The first person, whose hand landed on the trunk said, "This being is like a thick snake." For another one, whose hand reached its ear, it seemed like a kind of fan. Another person, whose hand was upon its leg said, "The elephant is like a tree-trunk." The blind man who climbed a ladder to touch the side said, "Elephant is a wall." Another one, who felt its tail, described it as a rope. The last man touched a tusk, stating the elephant is like a spear.

In the story, each person connects his partial experience of the elephant with his prior knowledge to figure out what an elephant is. Each person considers his understanding as the true version of reality.

Let us analyze and discover what transpires. Five things stand out. One, our experience of reality is based on direct personal experience. Two, our experience is partial. Three, to understand a new experience we correlate it with our prior experience. Four, we then understand it by explaining it. Five, two persons seeing and experiencing an object (or situation) can have different interpretations and understanding of the object (or situation).

Figure 3.2. Six blind men and the elephant [72]

Mental Models

A mental model is an image of the world that we carry in our heads. It influences how we look at the world – what we see and notice, what we hear and listen, how we think and interpret, how we decide what to do and how we behave.

This influence of mental models on perception is exemplified by the visit of American auto executives to Japan in the 70s. Americans traveled to discover why Japanese automakers were steadily gaining market and profit share in the automobile industry. Prior to the visit, US automakers had reasoned that the success might be attributed to their management, cheap labor and protected home markets. The US auto executives visited Japanese factories but were unimpressed. They felt that the manufacturing operations were all staged for their tour and they were not shown 'real' plants because of the absence of inventories. They were unable to understand that the Japanese auto companies were tightly integrated with component manufacturers and followed a just-in-time inventory flow model. Such a concept was alien to their mental models that were formed on how auto manufacturers worked in the US.

Figure 3.3. The auto executives' perception versus reality

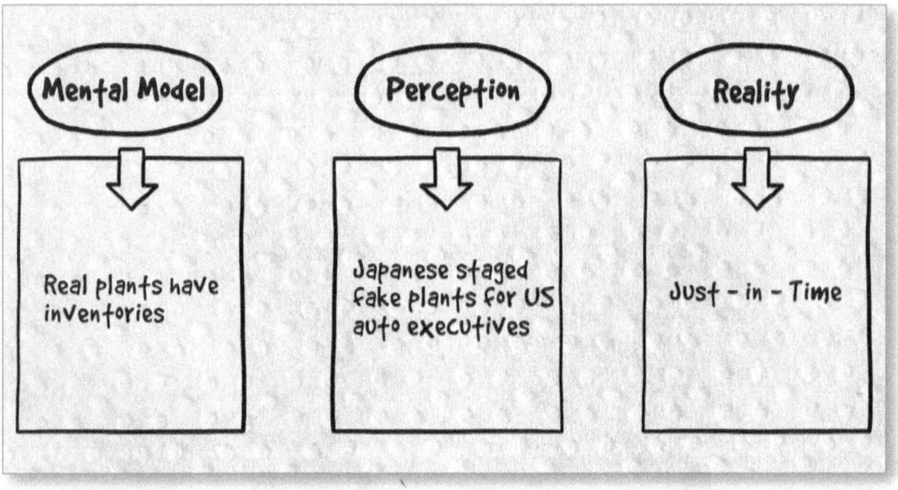

Mental Model	Perception	Reality
Real plants have inventories	Japanese staged fake plants for US auto executives	Just - in - Time

What Is a Mental Model?

A mental model is an internal representation of external reality (Figure 3.4 overleaf). Mental models consist of beliefs, ideas, images and descriptions that symbolize and exemplify how something works in the real world. The mental model depicts a connection amongst elements that constitute the mental model, indicative of a perceived cause and effect relationship. Figure 3.4 depicts the correlation of the mental model of photosynthesis – how plants convert solar energy, to the model of solar energy generation using solar cells.

Figure 3.4. Internal representation of external reality
Example of how photosynthesis of a plant is akin to photovoltaic electricity generation

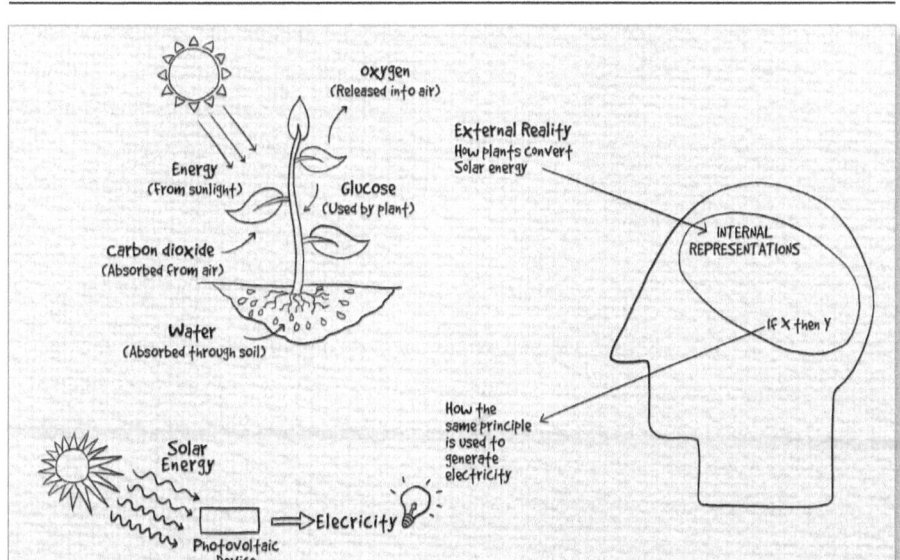

Mental models are like both a 'lens' and a 'toolbox' to see, understand and interpret a complex world (Figure 3.5). Mental models guide our actions, predisposing us to look and behave in certain ways by making us sensitive to how things work.

Figure 3.5. Mental Models [73]

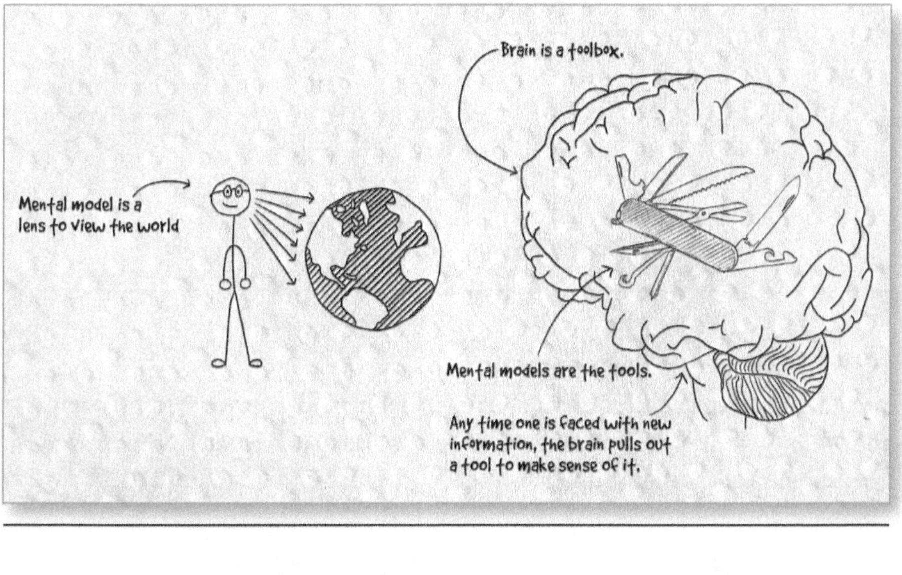

How Are Mental Models Formed?

The mind constructs mental models of reality that it uses as short hand or a rule to anticipate outcomes. A mental model becomes an explanation of how things work. If we see an event or action, X, causing an outcome, Y, it gets programmed in our minds as a mental model that X results in Y. We create mental models as a result of perception, imagination and knowledge.

Mental models are a subjective creation. Hence, the following influences shape our mental models:

1. Education
2. Training
3. Social influence in a person's personal and professional environment
4. Rewards and incentives. These rewards can be tangible, such as direct financial gain, or intangible, such as social approval
5. Personal successes and failures

Figure 3.6. How mental models form

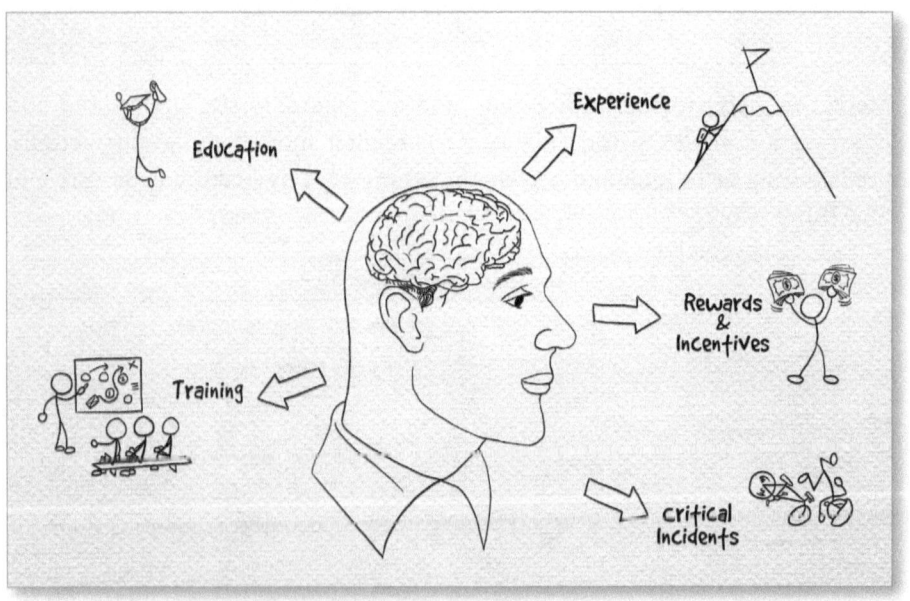

How Are Mental Models Useful?

Mental models are useful because they make life easier by providing cognitive shortcuts to understanding situations and taking decisions. Mental models help us edit the world around us so that we perceive the essentials and simplify complex situations.

Mindset and Mental Models [74]

Attitude is a synonym of mindset. The dictionary defines mindset as 'a frame of mind' and 'a way of thinking.' Mindset is the beliefs or ways of thinking that create an attitudinal disposition to behave in a certain way. Mindset has an influence on behavior. The following image (Figure 3.7a) depicts the diversity and the range of disposition that can be evoked when a person is confronted by a seemingly difficult task; the outlook varies on a spectrum from 'I will do it' on one end, to 'I won't do it' on the other. The disposition influences the type and the intensity of behavior to achieve results. The second image (Figure 3.7b) depicts a windy weather condition. One person, with her hair disheveled by the breeze, is distraught. The other, is joyous. The same context can create two different reactions and mindsets in two different people.

Figure 3.7. Spectrum of attitude when presented with a challenge that influences behavior

Figure 3.7a. Diversity of individual response

FLIP OVER

Figure 3.7b. Different responses in the same context

A mental model, on the other hand, is a working model of the world we carry in our heads that helps us understand what is happening and decide what to do. I highlight the difference using a sports analogy. A professional tennis player playing on court focuses and sees only the ball and not the opponent. His goal is to raise the quality of his game to play the ball racing towards him. His mental model is that winning happens when the quality of his personal game excels. The mindset is to excel in the quality of his game and not react to the opponent's game.

Mental Models of Individuals and Companies

Each individual has and uses his mental models. An organization is an agglomeration of individuals who work together to achieve a common goal. Organizations also have mental models. Visualize individuals embedded in organizations. Each individual has a mental model – a belief system, way of thinking, imagining and acting. Individuals acting as a cohort have organizational mental models, i.e., beliefs and values that are the basis of the collective, that the members of the group accept and embrace, and which guide their thoughts, words and deeds as members of the organization. Akin to organizational mental models, organizations as a collective have orientations or dispositions to deliver and achieve goals. CEOs imbue organizations with values and evoke determination in the participants to reach goals; organizations as a collective have organizational mindset.

Social Infrastructure of Mental Models

Mental models of an organization that are shared and accepted by members of the organization are built upon the social infrastructure of the company. Social infrastructure of a company is the collection of policies, procedures, organization structures, job roles, communication patterns, reward systems, etc., that support and enable the life in an organization. Managers and employees of an organization hold beliefs and expectations that are formed based on their daily experiences as members of the organization. The beliefs – mental models and attitudinal orientation – are collectively built into the company's social infrastructure. As employees interact, the beliefs coalesce together to create company-wide organization beliefs that reflect what they think their organization stands for, how they think it should function as a system and what are the goals to be achieved. These beliefs determine how the employees go about their daily work and business. These organization-wide beliefs take on a degree of 'firmness' that often makes it difficult for employees to think and do things in ways that may not align with the collective organizational mental models and mindset.

Mental Models and Business Decision Making

Mental models used in the context of business, encompass the beliefs that individuals hold about what drives success in their industry, which customers to serve, what those customers want, how to price, how to organize, which distribution channels to use, what the business drivers are, etc. Every industry and each company has a dominant logic (assumptions/belief system/mental model/business model) that 'governs' how each industry participant 'behaves.' The dominant logic is how things 'ought' to be done. This influences how key managers of the company work – what data and information they look for, what they perceive, how they interpret and decide (Figure 3.8).

FLIP OVER

Figure 3.8. Mental model of a company

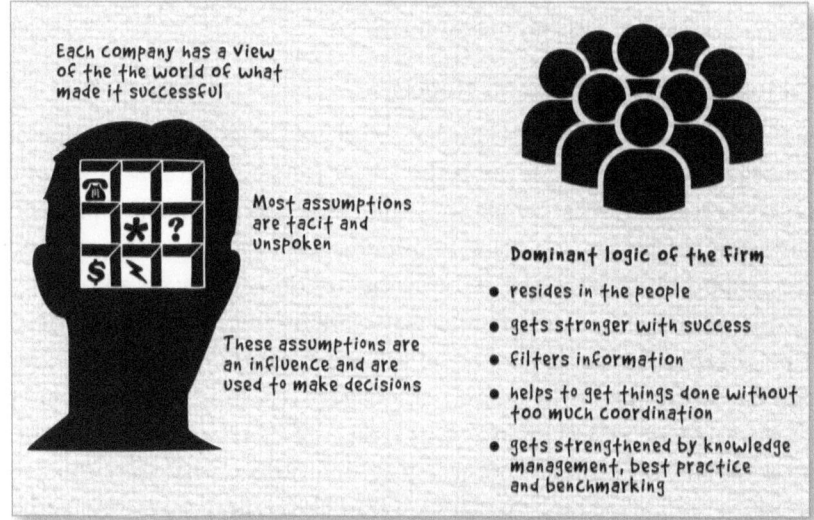

Many different mental models can coexist in the same industry. They define completely different competing strategies.[75] Contrast the customers of two grocery chains in Figure 3.9.

Figure 3.9. Coexisting contrasting mental models in the same industry

Whole Foods customer & Aldi customer

How organizational mental models influence behavior in organizations

A pyramid (Figure 3.10) is used to illustrate the compelling role of organizational mental models in shaping an organization.

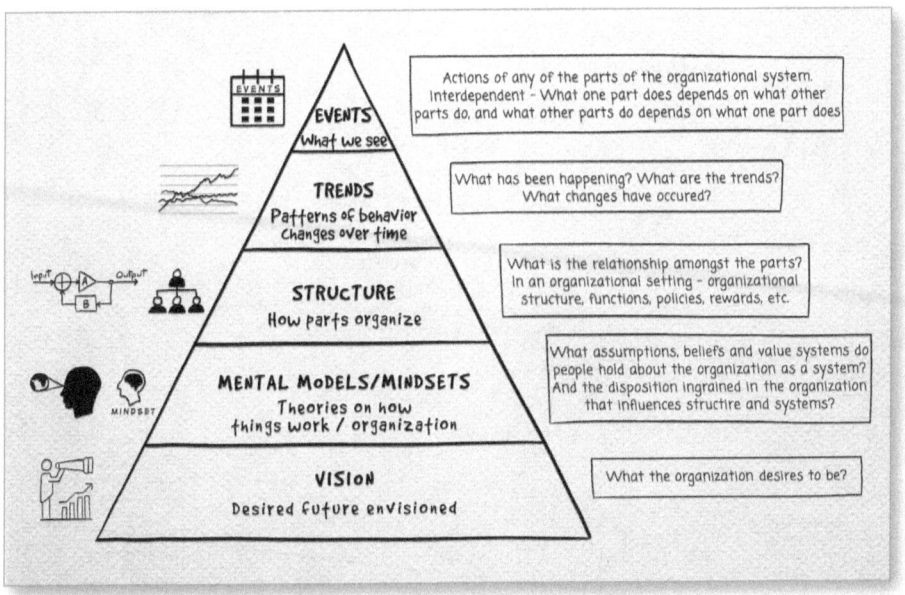

Figure 3.10. Influence of Mental Models on organization structure, performance trends and visible activities of the organization

At the base on the pyramid is the vision of the organization, i.e., what the organization desires to be or become.

The next level is the mental model/mindset of the organization. The mental model is shaped by and gives shape to the common assumptions, generalizations and images that influence how the institution understands the world, its place in it, and how it works to achieve its vision, mission and goals. Mindset is the attitudinal disposition of the organization to achieve its vision. Mental models and mindset are complementary and work in unison. Mental models are understood and accepted based on what has worked in the past. They create an orientation to make choices, decide and adopt prior behaviors. Mindset energizes the execution of choices made to achieve results.

The mental model is the dominant image which determines the structure of the system. Figure 3.11 depicts the mental model of Disney as sketched by Walt Disney in 1957 that influences the organization till today.

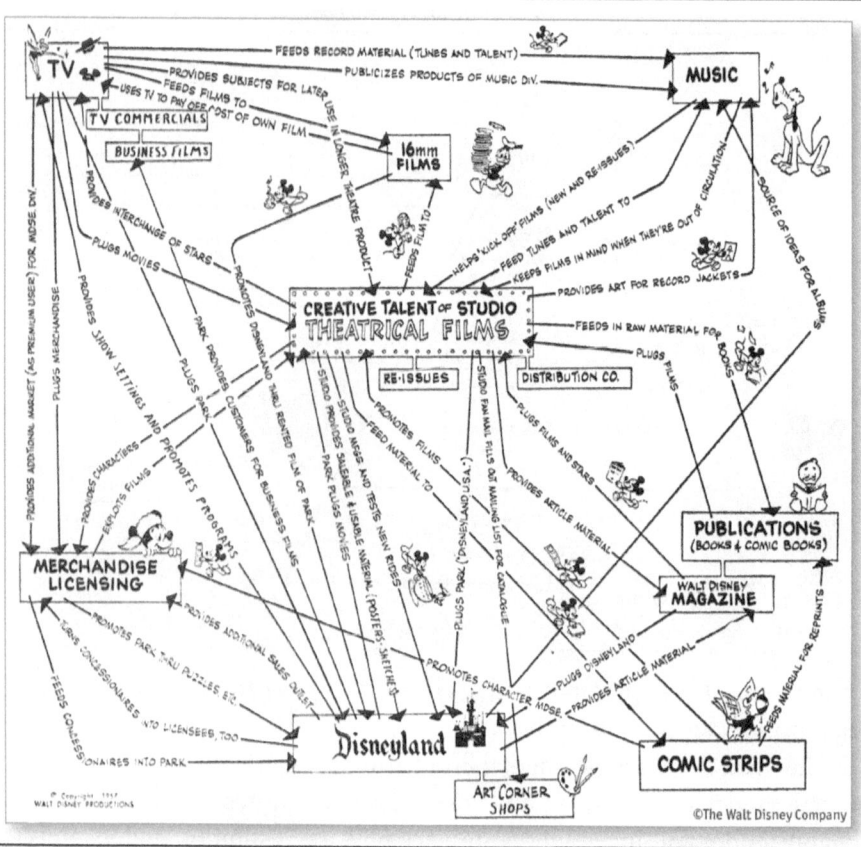

Figure 3.11. Mental Model of Disney sketched by Walt Disney in 1957 [76]

The structure is the mechanics of the system – relationship between its constituent parts. The structure gives systemic shape to the mental model that drives the system, i.e., how the organization is structured as a functioning system and how the constituent parts relate to each other. The structure of the system is determined essentially by the mental model of the organization. In an organization, structure is the hierarchical organization structure – how the functions are organized and who is whose boss. The real structure is how they interact to achieve the goals of the organization (Figure 3.12).

Figure 3.12. Structure of Disney – conventional and process (how it works)[77][78]

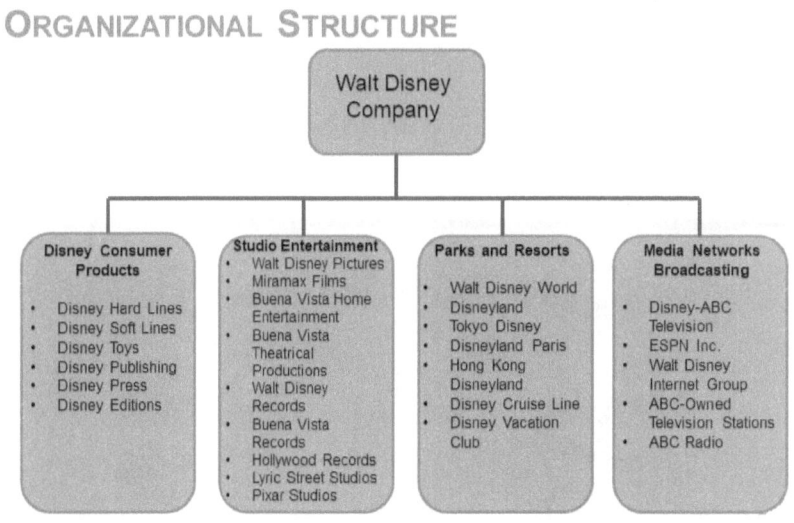

FLIP OVER

Figure 3.13. Structure of Disney – process (how it works)[79]
(Apologize for the clarity. Please refer web link for details)

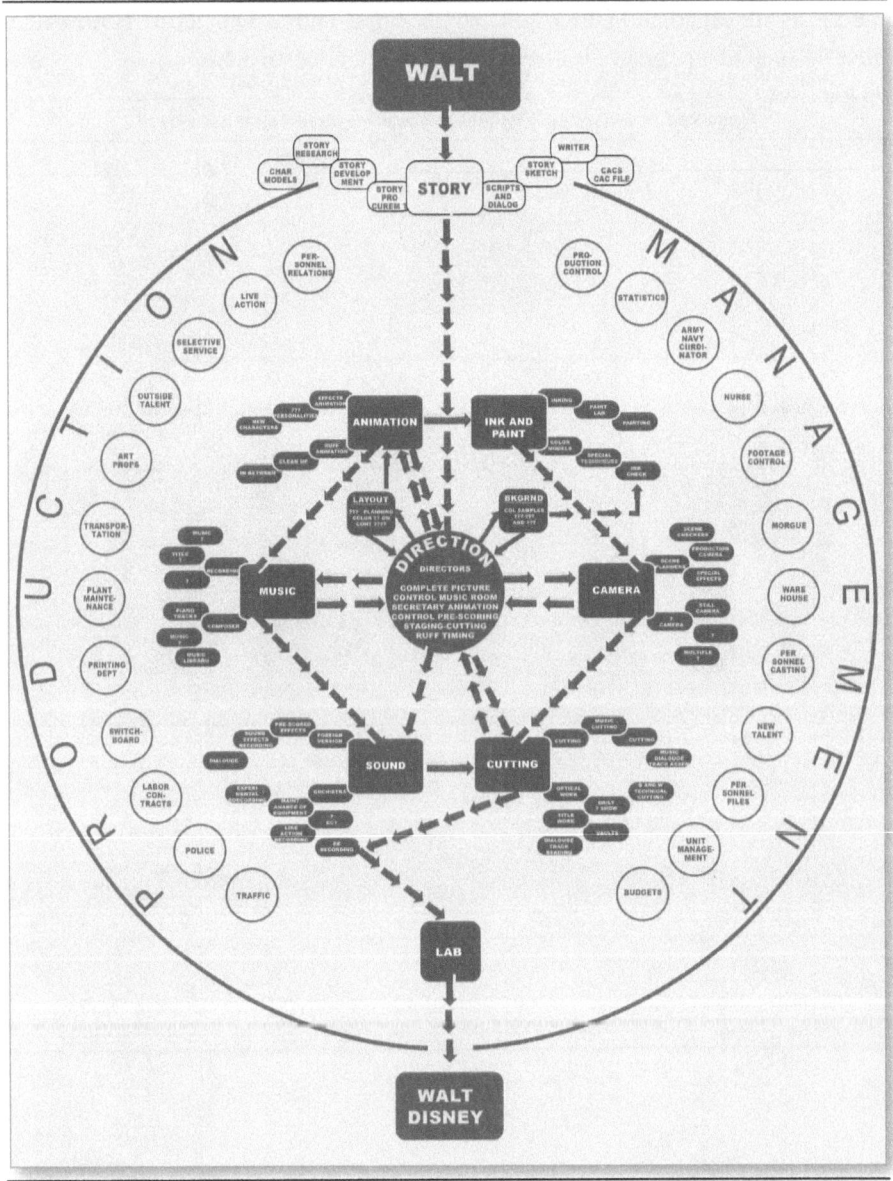

The trend of a system constitutes the actions that determine the current direction of the organization. Mental model is an idea. Structure is the organizational parts, the relationships, etc. Trend is the outcome of actions, i.e., the outcome of the actions in terms of results, their trends and recognizable patterns to discern actions to be taken in future. Figure 3.14 is the sales and stock performance of Disney over similar periods. The trend of sales and stock price are two inputs, amongst others, that influence decision making.

Figure 3.14. Trends of Disney performance – sales and stock performance [80]

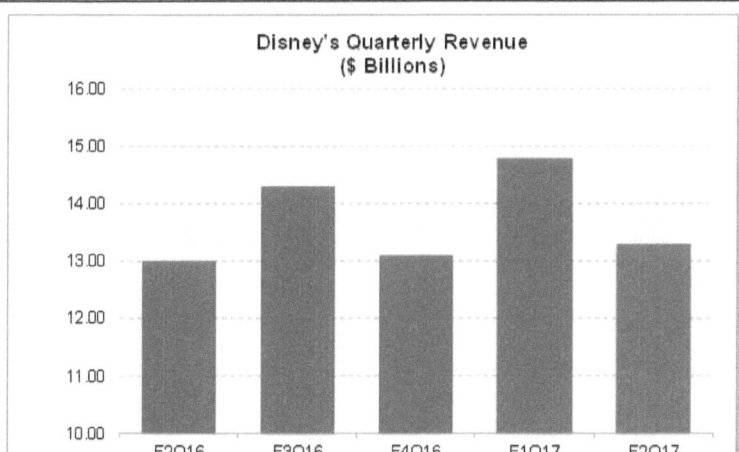

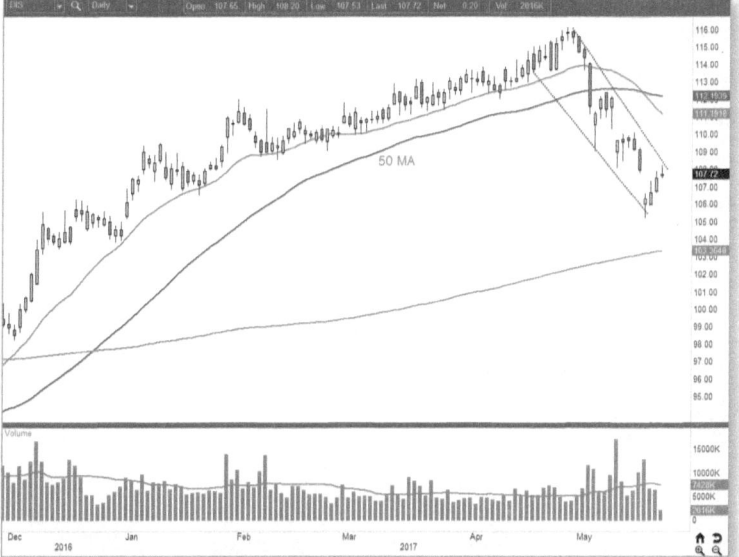

Events are the individual activities or actions of any part of the system. They are the visible actions that are repeated if the results and trends are positive. Table 3.1. is the timeline of Disney Studio movie releases. The events can be connected to future company performance. These in turn guide organization members to action.

Table 3.1. Disney release of films [81]

Title	US Release
McFarland, USA	20-Feb-15
Cinderella	13-Mar-15
Monkey Kingdom	17-Apr-15
Tomorrowland	22-May-15
Inside Out	19-Jun-15
The Good Dinosaur	25-Nov-15
The Finest Hours	29-Jan-16
Zootopia	04-Mar-16
The Jungle Book	15-Apr-16
Alice Through the Looking Glass	27-May-16
Finding Dory	17-Jun-16
The BFG	01-Jul-16
Pete's Dragon	12-Aug-16
Queen of Katwe	23-Sep-16
Moana	23-Nov-16
Beauty and the Beast	17-Mar-17
Born in China	21-Apr-17
Pirates of the Caribbean: Dead Men Tell No Tales	26-May-17
Cars 3	16-Jun-17
Coco	22-Nov-17

Tables

References

FLIP OVER

Application of the Idea

Table 3.2 tabulates four real-life examples of how mindsets and mental models influence behavior.

Table 3.2. How mental models and mindsets inform behavior

Examples	Sales	Product positioning	Pricing	Retail
Situation/ context	Achieving sales goals	Brand positioning of Tata Nano, the cheapest car in the world	In a weak consumer market can we change prices to increase demand? To maintain or change prices in an Airline business?	A digitally connected consumer and e-commerce
Belief/ Assumptions/ Mental Model	Staff is only motivated by money/If we give them juicy incentives, we will achieve sales goals	Huge market for customers graduating from two-wheelers to cars/Target a price of a car to make customer graduation easier.	Demand rises when prices fall/Shift focus from % margin to GM$	E-commerce, brick and mortar retail will complement. E-commerce business will be incremental to traditional retail. Drivers of traditional retail (merchandize, price, etc.) will also drive e-commerce.
Mindset	Incentive schemes alone can achieve sales goals/budgets	Price is key. Four wheels at a price.	Will more customers come to me when I discount prices? Price alone cannot achieve targets	Use same P&L metrics to manage e-commerce. Business model of e-commerce is same as traditional retail.
Trends	Budget numbers have not been achieved	Search for a new growth segment	Challenging market	Marginal reduction in foot traffic in brick and mortar retail because of e-commerce
Action/ behavior	Implement a sales incentive scheme with dramatic increase in incentives beyond targets	Manage product specifications i.e. features to achieve price.	Don't change prices to achieve higher gross margin value in a weak market	Manage an e-commerce team as a complement to brick and mortar retail.

Appendix 3 Mindset and Mental Models

Examples	Sales	Product positioning	Pricing	Retail
Unintended consequences	Successful in a strong economic scenario – increasing customer flows. Failure in a soft market. Singular focus on money as motivator ignores other self-esteem motivations of sales staff. In challenging sales environments if budgets are not managed, sales staff doesn't use creative skills to achieve numbers. If goals are challenging, sales staff stop chasing goals.	Customer did not want to be seen driving the 'cheapest' car in the world. Miscalculated the social esteem associated with car purchase. Technical compromises reduced the specs. Customer engagement during product creation?	GM$ strategy doesn't work when customer count cannot increase. Margin compromise is not supported by disproportionate increase in customers. If higher prices are sustained migration of customers to lower value offerings will happen. Loss of GM$ from lost customers is less than the loss of GM$ if discounting approach is followed. Gross margin value maintained at lower sales.	E-commerce, its metrics and business model is very different from traditional retail. Digital marketing is the foundation that drives e-commerce and retail. Marketing replaces rent as an operational cost. E-commerce hollows out traditional retail.

FLIP OVER

Summary

Table 3.3 is a summary of this appendix.

Table 3.3. Summary [82][83][84]

Item	Definition	Visual
How you see the situation	A way of looking or thinking about something. How an opportunity/issue is envisioned, defined and framed.	
Mental model **Or** **How things work**	Explanation of how something works in the world. It is a representation of the surrounding world, the relationships between its various parts and a person's intuitive perception of his or her own acts and their consequences.	
Mindset **Or** **Disposition, viewpoint and intention**	Self-confidence, way of thinking, attitude, outlook and behavior. Predisposition to think, believe and do things.	Chore or fun

Item	Definition	Visual
Trends	Patterns of behavior.	
How the situation is emerging	Changes over time.	
Behavior Or Execution	Plan and execution. Get things done.	

About the Author

Manoj Nakra - How did I get here?

Didn't have a clue what I wanted to do. Dabbled in everything – sports, theatre, and art. Drifted into engineering.

EDUCATION

Delhi Public School, Delhi, India, class of 72

Mechanical Engineering
Indian Institute of Technology, Delhi, India, class of 77

MBA
Indian Institute of Management, Bangalore, India, class of 84

Executive Doctorate of Management,
Weatherhead School of Management,
Case Western Reserve University, class of 2004

Went back to school 5 years after engineering graduation. Post-graduation had options to do PhD in US. Instead went to world of practice.

Returned to grad school 20 years after MBA and having 2 five year stints as CEO of 2 companies

WORK EXPERIENCE

1977-81
Assistant Engineer, Tata Consulting Engineers, Bangalore

Wandered into design engineering consulting. Didn't want to work in a factory or do an MBA. Sensed an ability to grasp large complex systems.

1984-89
Executive Asst. to the Chairman, Ballarpur Industries Ltd., Delhi.

Got a top down view of the 3rd largest Indian business group. Focused on business development and acquisitions.

1990-95
CEO, The Waterbase Ltd., Delhi.

At 33 became CEO of a startup Aquaculture Company. Did an IPO on Mumbai Stock exchange.

1996-2001
Dy CEO, Jashanmal National Co., Dubai.

Reached Dubai to head a $140m retail and distribution company. Learnt a new industry. Diversified and scaled a running business. Understood the importance of customer choice in making (or breaking) a business in a pennies industry.

2001-2005
Student and Adjunct Faculty, Weatherhead School of Business, Case Western Reserve University, Ohio

Back to graduate school to reinvent myself. Taught capstone strategy course. Learnt more than I taught.

2005- continuing
SmartGlobal FZCo, Dubai

Started an Executive Education company based on the reinvention I experienced when I returned to grad school

2005-2013
COO and Executive Director, DubaiSME, Dubai

Operated the Government of Dubai's entrepreneur development organization. Ran an incubator and funding program.

2006-2008
Just Chocolate Café, Bangalore, India

Experienced entrepreneurship to help entrepreneurs; established a Chocolate Café in Bangalore.

2013 – 2018
Chief Strategy Officer, Apparel Group, Dubai

Group is a 1250 store $1b franchisee-retailer. Focus strategy preparation & execution, platforms (IT and logistics) for scale-up and mindset change.

Other pursuits
- Advisory Board of online platforms invoicebazar.com (factoring) and Trunks Company (a luxury brand based in Jaipur)
- 'A 1000 days adventure,' a book on entrepreneurship.
- 'Sai Bhagvatham,' a book conceptualized on William James classic 'Varieties of Religious Experience.'
- Co-teach an Executive Education programs at Indian Institute of Management, Bangalore, on luxury and lifestyle brands
- Best Teacher award Weatherhead School of Management, Case Western Reserve Univ.
- Best All-round Student Indian Institute of Management Bangalore
- President of the Student Union Indian Institute of Management Bangalore
- Digital platforms for strategy execution, real-time research, and analytics based recruitment
- Creating an online startup ecosystem for incubation, acceleration, teaching entrepreneurship to K12 and college students and crowd funding.

References

1. I sensed the metaphor of film making and entrepreneurship while conducting the interviews. To confirm my intuition I interviewed two entrepreneurs who make films. The interviews don't feature in the book.
2. Source – http://artspla-site-austral.ac-reunion.fr/spip.php?article290
3. Appendix 1
4. Appendix 2
5. All articles at – http://gulfnews.com/search?action=search&submitted=true&sort=publisheddate_descending&freeText=manoj+nakra
6. These ideas are similar to ideas in Bhide, Amar. (2000). *The Origin and Evolution of New Business.* Oxford University Press, Madison Ave., New York.
7. Nucleation is a word borrowed from chemistry. It alludes to formation of new substances by mixing raw materials. Existing raw materials are stable substances. When mixed, atoms, the building blocks of substances, reconfigure to form new products. This process takes time. Nucleation determines how long an observer has to wait before a new stable substance appears.
8. Enabling, incubating and funding startups as Executive Director of Dubai SME.
9. In the period 1990–95 I had established a Greenfield startup in a corporate setting in India that was listed in the Mumbai Stock Exchange.
10. Inspired by https://www.pinterest.com/pin/83598136808605944/
11. Appendix 3
12. See Appendix – 1 for a simple explanation of mental models.
13. Adapted from source – https://strategyzer.com/canvas/business-model-canvas
14. Adapted from source – https://strategyzer.com/canvas/business-model-canvas
15. Questions that need validation in engagement with customers, suppliers and stakeholders are superimposed on a simplified business model canvas adapted from source – https://strategyzer.com/canvas/business-model-canvas
16. Source – https://www.apple.com/pr/library/2005/09/07Apple-Motorola-Cingular-Launch-Worlds-First-Mobile-Phone-with-iTunes.html
17. Source – http://www.applegazette.com/feature/6-things-apple-did-not-invent/
18. Source – http://www.businessinsider.in/The-10-Stupidest-Things-Ever-Said-By-Techs-Smartest-People/500-dollars-Fully-subsidized-With-a-plan-I-said-that-is-the-most-expensive-phone-in-the-world-And-it-doesnt-appeal-to-business-customers-because-it-doesnt-have-a-keyboard-Which-makes-it-**not**-a-very-good-email-machine-Steve-Ballmer-on-the-introduction-of-the-first-iPhone/slideshow/21167178.cms

19. Source – http://www.wsj.com/articles/apples-share-of-smartphone-industrys-profits-soars-to-92-1436727458
20. Hawthorne effect – Alteration of behavior by subjects of a study based on their awareness of being observed.
21. Source – https://www.strategyworks.co.za/2015/07/execute-strategy/
22. Steve Blank is a respected serial entrepreneur and teacher. Source – https://steveblank.com/
23. Blank, Steve. (2013). *Why the Lean Start-Up Changes Everything.* Harvard Business Review May 2013. Source – https://hbr.org/2013/05/why-the-lean-start-up-changes-everything
24. Blank, Steve. (2013). *Why the Lean Start-Up Changes Everything.* Harvard Business Review May 2013. Source – https://hbr.org/2013/05/why-the-lean-start-up-changes-everything
25. Blank, Steve. (2013). *Why the Lean Start-Up Changes Everything.* Harvard Business Review May 2013. Source – https://hbr.org/2013/05/why-the-lean-start-up-changes-everything
26. Blank, Steve. (2013). *Why the Lean Start-Up Changes Everything.* Harvard Business Review May 2013. Source – https://hbr.org/2013/05/why-the-lean-start-up-changes-everything
27. Blank, Steve. (2013). *Why the Lean Start-Up Changes Everything.* Harvard Business Review May 2013. Source – https://hbr.org/2013/05/why-the-lean-start-up-changes-everything
28. Source – https://en.wikipedia.org/wiki/Mental_model
29. Sources – https://en.wikipedia.org/wiki/John_Boyd_(military_strategist) and http://www.artofmanliness.com/2014/09/15/ooda-loop/
30. Source – https://en.wikipedia.org/wiki/John_Boyd_(military_strategist)
31. Source – http://www.artofmanliness.com/2014/09/15/ooda-loop/
32. Source – http://www.artofmanliness.com/2014/09/15/ooda-loop/
33. Source – http://www.martinries.com/article2007AG.htm and http://ineedartandcoffee.blogspot.ae/2013/01/the-light-bulb-is-sun-metamorphosis-of.html
34. Source Horowitz, Ben., (2014) *The Hard Thing About Hard Things.* HarperCollins Publishers, New York.
35. Source – http://lexicon.ft.com/Term?term=entrepreneurial-mindset
36. McGrath, Rita G., and MacMillan, Ian. (2000) *The Entrepreneurial Mindset.* Harvard Business School Press, Boston, Massachusetts.
37. McGrath, Rita G., and MacMillan, Ian. (2000) *The Entrepreneurial Mindset.* Harvard Business School Press, Boston, Massachusetts.

[38] Formica, Piero. (2015) *The Role of Creative Ignorance*. Palgrave MacMillan, New York.

[39] Formica, Piero. (2015) *The Role of Creative Ignorance*. Palgrave MacMillan, New York.

[40] Saras D. Sarasvathy, Causation and Effectuation: toward a theoretical shift from economic inevitability to entrepreneurial contingency, Academy of Management Review, 2001, Vol. 26, No. 2, 243–263

[41] Saras D. Sarasvathy, Causation and Effectuation: toward a theoretical shift from economic inevitability to entrepreneurial contingency, Academy of Management Review, 2001, Vol. 26, No. 2, 243–263

[42] Saras D. Sarasvathy, Causation and Effectuation: toward a theoretical shift from economic inevitability to entrepreneurial contingency, Academy of Management Review, 2001, Vol. 26, No. 2, 243–263

[43] Saras D. Sarasvathy, Associate Professor, The Darden Graduate School of Business Administration, University of Virginia, 2001, http://www.effectuation.org/paper/what-makes-entrepreneurs-entrepreneurial

[44] Saras D. Sarasvathy, Causation and Effectuation: toward a theoretical shift from economic inevitability to entrepreneurial contingency, Academy of Management Review, 2001, Vol. 26, No. 2, 243–263

[45] Dweck, Carol. (2006). *Mindset: The new Psychology of success*. Ballantine Books, New York.

[46] Entrepreneurs intellectual, social and financial capital

[47] Saras Sarasvathy interviewed over 30 highly successful entrepreneurs that had built companies with revenues from $200 million to $6 billion, and had each entrepreneur go through a 17 page problem set over two hours that involved describing how they would bring the same specific product to market. She was observing how these expert entrepreneurs think about starting a venture, and if there were any common threads among them.

[48] Saras Sarasvathy – Seasoned entrepreneurs tend to determine in advance what they are willing to lose, rather than calculating expected gains.

[49] Source – http://www.telegraph.co.uk/tennis/2017/01/29/roger-federer-vs-rafael-nadal-australian-open-final-live-score/

[50] Source – https://www.smithsonianmag.com/smart-news/shackleton-probably-never-took-out-an-ad-seeking-men-for-a-hazardous-journey-5552379/

[51] http://notes.fundersandfounders.com/post/79875850310/late-start-quarter-and-middle-life-crisis

[52] https://medium.com/visual-notes/lost-in-life-b7d2ca7d02f0 and https://blog.adioma.com/entrepreneurs-who-dropped-out-infographic/

[53] https://blog.adioma.com/enough-money-to-start-company-infographic/

54. http://notes.fundersandfounders.com/post/79982185553/howto-be-wise-entrepreneur
55. Saras D. Sarasvathy, Causation and Effectuation: toward a theoretical shift from economic inevitability to entrepreneurial contingency, Academy of Management Review, 2001, Vol. 26, No. 2, 243-263
56. Saras D. Sarasvathy, Causation and Effectuation: toward a theoretical shift from economic inevitability to entrepreneurial contingency, Academy of Management Review, 2001, Vol. 26, No. 2, 243-263
57. Saras D. Sarasvathy, Associate Professor, The Darden Graduate School of Business Administration, University of Virginia http://www.effectuation.org/paper/what-makes-entrepreneurs-entrepreneurial
58. Saras D. Sarasvathy, Associate Professor, The Darden Graduate School of Business Administration, University of Virginia http://www.effectuation.org/paper/what-makes-entrepreneurs-entrepreneurial
59. Saras D. Sarasvathy, Associate Professor, The Darden Graduate School of Business Administration, University of Virginia http://www.effectuation.org/paper/what-makes-entrepreneurs-entrepreneurial
60. Saras D. Sarasvathy, Associate Professor, The Darden Graduate School of Business Administration, University of Virginia http://www.effectuation.org/paper/what-makes-entrepreneurs-entrepreneurial
61. Saras D. Sarasvathy, Associate Professor, The Darden Graduate School of Business Administration, University of Virginia http://www.effectuation.org/paper/what-makes-entrepreneurs-entrepreneurial
62. Gompertz, Will. (2015). Think Like an Artist. Penguin Random House. UK. Pg. 43
63. Gompertz, Will. (2015). Think Like an Artist. Penguin Random House. UK. Pg. 43
64. Gompertz, Will. (2015). Think Like an Artist. Penguin Random House. UK. Pg 43
65. Gompertz, Will. (2015). Think Like an Artist. Penguin Random House. UK. Pg 116
66. Gompertz, Will. (2015). Think Like an Artist. Penguin Random House. UK. Pg 43
67. Source – http://www.goodreads.com/quotes/133519-i-begin-with-an-idea-and-then-it-becomes-something
68. Idea sourced from http://www.createadvantage.com/glossary/mental-model
69. Prof S Raghunath of Indian Institute of Management, Bangalore.
70. Source – https://hip-books.com/character-point-of-view/
71. Source – http://www.cartoonistgroup.com/subject/The-Environmental-Comics-and-Cartoons-by-Signe+Wilkinson%27s+Editorial+Cartoons.php
72. Source – https://caroline-smith.com/2016/07/14/truth-is-an-elephant-2/

[73] Images sourced from https://www.safaribooksonline.com/library/view/head-first-data/9780596806224/ch01.html

[74] (Hamel, 2002)

[75] Source – http://www.businessinsider.com/whole-foods-customers-vs-aldi-2015-5

[76] Source – https://medium.com/@cwodtke/five-models-for-making-sense-of-complex-systems-134be897b6b3

[77] Source – https://www.slideshare.net/callieunruh/strategic-management-walt-disney-case-study

[78] Source – http://www.atissuejournal.com/2009/08/07/walt-disney%E2%80%99s-creative-organization-chart/

[79] Source – https://www.hotfootdesign.co.uk/white-space/this-is-the-creative-flow-chat-walt-disney-gave-to-new-employees-in-1943/

[80] Source – http://investorplace.com/2017/05/walt-disney-co-dis-stock-has-lost-its-magic/#.WYVuBoiGNPY

[81] Source – http://disneyverse.altervista.org/il-calendario-e-le-trame-dei-film-disney-2015–2017/?doing_wp_cron=1501916533.5461220741271972656250

[82] Source – https://medium.com/@FarkleUp/once-you-see-it-you-cant-unsee-it-a12852a8f656

[83] Source – https://thevolatileguide.com/2016/09/27/64-human-maps/

[84] Source – http://www.watersfoundation.org/webed/habits/mentalmodels.htm

[85] Details about the author at – www.manojnakra.com

www.ingramcontent.com/pod-product-compliance
Lightning Source LLC
Chambersburg PA
CBHW031605210526
45464CB00004B/1433